BANKERS AND BOLSHEVIKS

To the Rye Free Reading Room

Bankers and Bolsheviks

INTERNATIONAL FINANCE AND
THE RUSSIAN REVOLUTION

HASSAN MALIK

[signature]
22/11/2018

PRINCETON UNIVERSITY PRESS

PRINCETON & OXFORD

Published by Princeton University Press
41 William Street, Princeton, New Jersey 08540
6 Oxford Street, Woodstock, Oxfordshire OX20 1TR

press.princeton.edu

Library of Congress Control Number: 2018937062
ISBN 978-0-691-17016-9

British Library Cataloging-in-Publication Data is available

Editorial: Joe Jackson and Samantha Nader
Production Editorial: Jenny Wolkowicki
Jacket art: 1) Champagne bottle: James / The Noun Project; 2) Top hat: Sherrinford,
FR / The Noun Project; 3) Gold bars: Artem Koryazin, RU / The Noun Project;
4) Factory: Icon Solid / The Noun Project
Production: Jacqueline Poirier
Publicity: Tayler Lord
Copyeditor: Joseph Dahm

This book has been composed in Arno Pro

Printed on acid-free paper. ∞

Printed in the United States of America

10 9 8 7 6 5 4 3 2 1

To my parents
and in memory of
Batool Ikram Ul Haque (1922–2011)

CONTENTS

Acknowledgments   xi

Note on Dates, Transliteration and Abbreviations   xvii

Introduction   1

  The Bolshevik Conception of International Finance   2

  International Finance and the Russian Revolution   3

  The Sociology of Revolution   5

  Financial Globalization and Russia   8

    Monetary Architecture and the Gold Standard   11

    Macroeconomic and Political Fundamentals   12

  Gatekeeper Finance and the Russian Revolution   16

1   Fault Lines: The Witte System and Missed Opportunities   19

  Pro: Witte the Revolutionary   20

  Contra: Witte the Revolutionary   22

  The Data: A Financial Revolution?   27

  The Evolution of the Witte System   34

  Good Tactics, Poor Strategy   37

  Conclusion   53

2   The Loan That Saved Russia? Reassessing the 5 Percent
Russian Government Loan of 1906   55

  *The Background to and Historiography
of the Loan That Saved Russia*   56

    The Financial Impact of War and Domestic Unrest, 1904–5   57

    "The Loan That Saved Russia"   58

  Starting the Negotiations   62

Domestic Opposition 66

The Impact of the Financial Manifesto 70

International Opposition 75

Conclusion 83

3 The Interrevolutionary Recovery and Rally 85

Economic Drivers of the Rally 87

Perceptions of a Revival in Agriculture 90

Bond Market Comeback:
The 1909 Conversion Loan 95

The Influence of Geopolitics on Capital Flows 96

Cartels and Distressed Opportunities:
Reassuring and Attracting Investors 99

Protecting Investors from the Slump through Market
Coordination 99

The Poliakov Affair 101

Competition as a Driver of Foreign Investment 106

An Increasingly Fragile System 112

Deepening the Financial Front: The Politics of Finance
and Social Implications of Foreign Investment 113

Financial and Operational Leverage 116

The Defense Stimulus 123

The Historical Significance of the Prewar
Crisis and the Haimson Debate 125

Conclusion 127

4 Investing in the Revolution 129

The Wartime Economic Crisis 130

Crisis? What Crisis? 133

Risk and Moral Hazard 141

Geopolitics 150

Buying the Revolution 152

The French Connection 157

Conclusion 160

5 Revolutionary Default   162

   The Politics of Default   163

      Ideological Drivers of Default   164

      Practical Political Considerations for Default   168

   The Economics of Default   169

      The Real Economy   171

      Financing the War   176

         Taxation   177

         Foreign Debt   178

         Domestic Bonds   180

         The Treasury Bill Market   182

         The Printing Press   184

      The Provisional Government as Catalyst of Economic Collapse   186

   Pulling the Trigger: The Decision to Default   186

   Investor Attitudes on the Eve of Default: This Time Was Different   194

      Ex-Ante: Discounting Signs and Talk of Default   194

      Ex-Post: Reactions to the Default   197

   Continuing the Financial Fight, 1918–22   204

   Conclusion: The Rationality of Revolutionary Default and Logic of Financial War   207

Conclusion   208

   Gatekeeper Finance and Global Capital Flows in a Russian Perspective   212

   The Personal Dimension   213

      Appendix: Rethinking Sovereign Default Rankings   217

      Notes   233

      Bibliography   275

      Index   285

ACKNOWLEDGMENTS

"IT IS MORE PLEASANT and useful to go through the 'experience of revolution' than to write about it," lamented Vladimir Lenin in *The State and Revolution*. Over the past ten years, those words have rung true on more than one occasion, and it is only with much help that I have seen this project through the difficult times. Niall Ferguson was the best advisor I ever could have wished for at Harvard, offering abundant and helpful critiques, guidance, and constant encouragement—all while giving me total intellectual freedom. Working with Niall broadened my horizons far beyond what I anticipated when starting graduate study, often from unexpected directions. Outside the classroom, Niall has been a true friend and mentor, encouraging me in a wide range of areas, and always taking a personal interest in me. Our seminars, dinners, and travels are some of the best memoires of graduate school. Terry Martin was equally generous as a mentor and friend, showing a concern not only for academic matters but also for my personal development. True to our shared Chicago roots, the training he offered was intense, and his standards, which sometimes seemed impossibly high, only improved me as a scholar. Chats with Terry often left my head hurting—in a good way. Charles Maier never failed to make me rethink my positions. I was often intimidated by his ability to ask the most penetrating, but always helpful, questions. His intellectual curiosity knows no bounds and is a quality I strive to emulate.

Academic supporters and friends outside my committee also contributed in a significant way to this project. Sugata Bose was a wonderful first supervisor in graduate school, when my interests were more focused on South Asia. Erez Manela made me think hard about what "international history" actually is, and encouraged my interdisciplinary instincts. Thomas Owen took a genuine interest in my work, critiquing chapters, suggesting sources, and sharing his prodigious knowledge of Russian economic history. In Russia, Vladimir Mau and Aleksandr Belykh were liberal with their hospitality, guidance, and encouragement. Jennifer Siegel gave me many useful tips from her own related research after our serendipitous meeting in Saint Petersburg. Mortiz Schularick graciously shared his work and thoughts on international capital flows. On the editorial front, Seth Ditchik first saw the potential in this book, and Joe

Jackson and his team at Princeton University Press helped bring it to fruition. I also thank the two anonymous reviewers for their thoughtful and helpful critiques and suggestions.

A number of institutions supported my research over the course of several years. At Harvard, the Weatherhead Center for International Affairs, Davis Center for Russian and Eurasian Studies, Charles Warren Center for American Studies, Center for European Studies, Graduate School of Arts and Sciences, Graduate Student Council, Department of History, and Hartley R. Rogers funded archival research and extended periods of writing. The Tobin Project, Institute for Humane Studies, and Krupp Foundation were generous sources of external funding. The Belfer Center for Science and International Affairs and the International Security Program at the Harvard Kennedy School supported a year of research in 2011–12 in the form of an Ernest May Fellowship in History and Policy. This research was supported by a grant from the Eurasia Program of the Social Science Research Council, with funds provided by the US Department of State under the Program for Research and Training on Eastern Europe and the Independent States of the Former Soviet Union (Title VIII). The Weatherhead Center's Graduate Student Associate program and Program on Global Society and Security provided funding and a stimulating interdisciplinary intellectual community in which to test ideas during months in Cambridge.

After Harvard, I was fortunate to spend three stimulating years in continental Europe revising my manuscript, conducting further research, and teaching. The European University Institute in San Domenico di Fiesole provided an idyllic environment in the foothills of Florence in which to rethink my ideas. Ramon Marimon and my colleagues in the Max Weber Programme for Postdoctoral Studies challenged me to think about interdisciplinary work in a deep sense. I was particularly fortunate to benefit from the mentorship, friendship, and hospitality of Youssef Cassis. Our bloc seminar on international financial history and discussions about European banking history over long lunches and dinners are among my fondest memories of Florence.

At the Institute for Advanced Study in Toulouse, I benefitted from a stimulating intellectual environment and tremendous support of both my fellow postdocs and the broader community of the Toulouse School of Economics. Paul Seabright was generous with his time, advice, and resources, and constantly encouraged my attempts to bridge economics and history. Mohammad Saleh motivated me to do the same through his own example. Ingela Alger and Jean Tirole actively fostered an atmosphere of openness and collaboration both within the seminar room and outside.

A range of archivists made the research effort infinitely easier and more pleasurable. In London, Melanie Aspey and her staff at the Rothschild Archive,

Moira Lovegrove and Clara Harrow at the Baring Archive, Julia Banks at the HSBC Group Archives, and Ben White at the Bank of England were all wonderful hosts and guides to the world of British banking. In Paris, I benefited from the hospitality and guidance of Xavier Breuil and his team at Société Générale, Anne Brunterc'h and her team at Crédit Agricole, and Roger Nougaret and his team at BNP Paribas. The staffs of the State Archive of the Russian Federation, Russian State Historical Archive, Russian State Economic Archive, and Russian State Archive of Social and Political History were also repeat hosts in Moscow and Saint Petersburg. In New York, Maria Molestina and her colleagues at the Morgan Library provided an ideal environment in which to delve deeper into Russian-American banking ties. Kerri-Anne Burke and Shira Bistricer at the Citigroup Archives facilitated access to a critically important document collection at a late stage. Claire-Amandine Soulié and Edwin Green generously shared their deep knowledge of banking history and banking archives.

A number of friends and colleagues in Cambridge made the research process enjoyable as well as interesting. Steve Bloomfield and the staff of the Weatherhead Center were liberal with their time and support. Mikhail Akulov, Matthew Corcoran, Stefan Link, Johan Matthew, Rainer Schultz, Heidi and Michael Tworek, and John Wong helped keep things from getting too serious. The crew at Greenmantle maintained my connection to the "real world." Ramnath Subbaraman and Şener Aktürk brought a Chicago flavor to my circle of friends in Cambridge. Aldo Musacchio was generous with his advice, encouragement, and friendship. Hannah Callaway and Brent Hobart made Paris much more fun. Tom Hooker took time off from his own work to carefully read and comment on an early full draft.

I also benefitted from the unfailing support of a large number of friends and mentors around the world outside Cambridge. Words cannot express my gratitude to Selim Akar and Wasef Mattar—for everything. Saif Siddiqui showed me how real friendship stands the tests of time and distance. Charles Chuman and Khalid Fakhro were the best of traveling companions. In Turkey, Hulusi Akar inspired and mentored me with talks about history and life, always encouraging me to take the road less traveled. Eren Merzeci and his family opened their homes to me during breaks in Istanbul. Giuseppe Scrufari Hedges was unstinting in providing his support and wonderful introductions to friends and places in Italy and beyond. Stefano Minoli ensured that Florence was not all books and seminars. Wahid Butt was a steadfast source of personal and professional encouragement.

In Moscow, Ruben Vardanyan and Gerrit Heynes took me on at Troika Dialog, where I was able to immerse myself in the Russian markets, and later encouraged my pursuit of graduate study. David Longmuir was a superb friend and mentor in the financial world. He helped shape my interests in financial history and bought a starving scholar many meals. Kingsmill Bond, Evgeny Gavrilenkov, Charles Howlett, Andrew Keeley, Oleg Maximov, Anton Stroutchenevski, and Igor Tishin provided much intellectual stimulation and camaraderie. Bruce Bower and Igor Sitnikov kept the Chicago fire alive in Moscow. Sergei Arkharov, David Amaryan, and Anna Lavrentieva were characteristically generous and helpful friends, always ready to go dancing till the sun came up. I am immensely indebted to Joe Ritchey, who took me under his wing from my first days in Moscow, mentoring me over the years, and reading multiple drafts of the material in this book. He has done far more than could be reasonably expected of any friend. Any mistakes that remain are my sole responsibility.

My own experience in the financial world sparked my interest in the topic at the center of this book, and friends and mentors in the present-day financial markets assisted me in writing the book through their thought-provoking questions and direct assistance in conducting research. Zdenek Turek provided perspective on Russian financial history and alerted me to a critical set of documents in the Citibank Archives. Eric Carlson, Steve Drobny, Bob Foresman, Keith Haydon, George Papamarkakis, Manny Roman, and John Paul Smith all encouraged my study of financial history and my attempts to leverage this historical perspective in today's markets. Tim Hayes has given me the freedom and encouragement to do the same. Farhan Sharaff has been a great teacher. I have learned much from him about markets and life. Hassan Ahmed was always ready with wisdom and encouragement through the tough times.

My family has been a limitless source of encouragement, support, and inspiration throughout. Zia and Shakeela Hassan were always welcoming and encouraging in Chicago. My aunt and uncle, Izaz and Irum Haque, and cousins, Sofia and Sabina, provided a second home in the Boston area and many sorely needed breaks from academic work. My uncle and intellectual role model, Nadeem Ul Haque, inspired me first to go to Chicago and then to pursue graduate study. My brothers, Zain and Faizan, showed endless patience with my intellectual pursuits, and made trips home a great deal of fun.

In the final stretch of preparing the manuscript, I was blessed to meet the woman I love. Hanieh has shown endless patience with multiple rounds of revisions and sunny days spent indoors poring over dry archival documents and spreadsheets. That this year marks not only our marriage but also the completion of the book will, I know, be a source of considerable relief to her. This book has become hers, too.

To my parents, I owe everything—without their sacrifices, encouragement, and unconditional love, I would be nothing. I can only hope that they do not regret the unintended consequences of all those trips to the Museo Nacional de Antropología in Mexico City so many years ago. Finally, it is my great regret that my maternal grandmother, Batool Ikram Ul Haque, did not live to see this book. I will always cherish the memories of the many summers I spent with her, especially those of our long chats about history on lazy afternoons on the verandah in Lahore. It is to her memory, and to my parents, that I dedicate this work with much love.

London
March 2018

NOTE ON DATES, TRANSLITERATION AND ABBREVIATIONS

UNTIL THE BOLSHEVIK CALENDAR reforms of 1918, Russia used the Julian calendar, which before 28 February 1900 was 12 days behind the Gregorian calendar used by most other countries in the world; after that date the number of days separating the two calendars increased to 13. Russia's conversion to the Gregorian calendar took place when the Bolsheviks decreed that 31 January 1918 would be followed by 14 February 1918. Unless otherwise noted, all dates in the text correspond to the Gregorian calendar in international use today. In referring to well-known historical events, standard conventions are maintained. Thus, the term "October Revolution" refers to events that took place in November according to the Gregorian calendar.

Russian words are transliterated in accordance with a simplified version of the Library of Congress system. An exception is made for those words or names with a commonly accepted English transliteration, such as Троцкий, transliterated as "Trotsky" rather than "Trotskii."

Abbreviations

BAR	Baring Archive
BNP	BNP Paribas Archive
BUP	Banque de l'Union Parisienne
CAEF	Centre des Archives Économiques et Financières
Citi	Citibank Archive
CLCA	Crédit Lyonnais–Crédit Agricole Archive
CPC	Correspondance Politique et Commerciale
FO	British Foreign Office
GARF	State Archive of the Russian Federation
HSBC	HSBC Group Archives
ISDA	International Swaps and Derivatives Association
MAE	Archive du Ministère des Affaires Étrangères
ML	Morgan Library

NA	British National Archives
NSR	Nouvelle Série–Russie
RAL	Rothschild Archive, London
RGIA	Russian State Historical Archive
SGA	Société Générale Archive

BANKERS AND BOLSHEVIKS

Introduction

My Aunt Léonie had bequeathed to me, together with all sorts of other things . . . almost all her unsettled estate. . . . My father, who was trustee of this estate until I came of age . . . consulted M. de Norpois with regard to several of the investments. He recommended certain stocks bearing a low rate of interest, which he considered particularly sound, notably English consols and Russian four per cents. "With absolutely first class securities such as those," said M. de Norpois, "even if your income from them is nothing very great, you may be certain of never losing any of your capital."

—MARCEL PROUST, *REMEMBRANCE OF THINGS PAST*[1]

THE 1918 BOLSHEVIK REPUDIATION of debts contracted by the Tsarist and Provisional governments—the largest default in history—punctuated the end of an era during which Russia had become the leading net international debtor in the world.[2] The French writer Marcel Proust's addiction to financial speculation was prodigious; at various points his portfolio consisted of positions in securities from a diversity of places, including Mexico, Egypt, and Russia, as well as in volatile commodity markets—often with disastrous results.[3] Proust's reference to Russian bonds in his *Remembrance of Things Past*—published after the Bolshevik default—underscores his own notoriously unpredictable personal finances, and the default's deep impact on French society. Although he sold a significant holding in a Russian iron ore mine at a profit nine months before the February Revolution, others in Proust's social circle were less fortunate.[4] The last years of his life saw the French author supporting friends left destitute from the loss of their life savings in Russia; indeed, the scene where he shows M. de Norpois pushing Russian bonds as a safe investment mirrors the experience of at least one couple Proust was supporting at the time.[5]

1

The Russian default of 1918 is more than a footnote in French cultural history. It is at once central to modern financial history and to the history of the Russian Revolution. The players in the drama included the financiers who poured money into Russia through the ebbs and flows of industrial booms, wars and revolutions, the bureaucrats and politicians in both Russia and the West who sought to exploit and control these flows, as well as—of course— the revolutionaries who, seeking to transform Russia and the world, triggered the largest default in history and one of the greatest hyperinflations of the twentieth century. Yet, remarkably, these events remain understudied.

This account of the Russian investment boom and bust of the late nineteenth and early twentieth centuries is based on, among other things, financial and economic data, as well as the correspondence, reports, and other documents in government and private banking archives in Moscow, Saint Petersburg, Paris, London, and New York. It is relevant to an extensive academic literature that stretches across the disciplines of history, economics, and political science. The secondary literature cited here relates to the Russian Revolution, banking and business history, the historical sociology of revolutions, and international capital flows. Given the crucial importance of the last of these, the story is international, touching on aspects of the histories of Russia, France, Germany, Britain, the United States, China, and Japan, among others.

The Bolshevik Conception of International Finance

Imperialism, the Highest Stage of Capitalism (1917), written in early 1916, and published in mid-1917, was Vladimir Lenin's last major work before the October Revolution of 1917, during which the Bolsheviks took power.[6] In the work, Lenin critiqued capitalism as he saw it operating globally and in Russia, focusing on the growing power of banks at the dawn of the twentieth century.[7] Lenin's critique drew extensively on the contemporaneous work of English economist J. A. Hobson and Austrian Marxist and future German minister of finance Rudolf Hilferding and their respective works, *Imperialism: A Study* (1902) and *Finance Capital* (1910).[8]

Lenin's *Imperialism* distills key points of the Bolshevik view of international finance in the Russian context. First, Lenin saw the growth of banks and the growing concentration of the financial industry as increasing their power within the broader economy.[9] Specifically, he seized on how increasingly powerful banks displaced the stock market—indeed, market forces more generally. In the process, masses of individual investors acting through the stock market ceased to be the primary drivers of capital flows, with a small number of powerful banks and bankers instead becoming the chief drivers of markets. While bourses remained, then, their function fundamentally changed, from an arena in which capital allocation decisions were really made to a channel through which major banks expressed and implemented their decisions.[10]

Second, Lenin saw both what he called finance capital and the associated rentier state as pernicious. Such disdain is evident in his discussion of the subjugation of industry to finance, of the informational asymmetries banks develop and exploit, and of the foreign policy decisions finance capital drove.[11] Far from just noting the growth of finance capital as an accelerant in the development of capitalism along the road to the inevitable achievement of socialism, Lenin highlighted the retarding effect of finance capital. His later discussion of rentierism and its social effects—not least the splitting of the working classes in the developed economies—evidenced this concern.[12]

Finally, even if *Imperialism* was an analytical work more than a call to arms, the policy implications of Lenin's thinking are clear. In Lenin's view, finance capital—embodied in the banks, industrial cartels, rentiers, and even finance ministries that both regulated lenders and solicited loans—was the primary engine of the global capitalist system and the driver of the crises tormenting the colonized and downtrodden. Destroying finance capital by controlling the banking system and tearing apart the rentier state on which it depended—including its shares, bonds, and bourses—thus became a top priority of the revolution. Indeed, finance capital and its destruction would become a central theme in Lenin's speeches and writing leading up to the October Revolution in 1917 and in his policy actions in the aftermath of the coup.[13] For Lenin—and, as this book shows, other revolutionaries outside the Bolshevik camp—there was no question: the revolution would be explicitly financial.

International Finance and the Russian Revolution

It is particularly striking, considering all the attention Lenin devoted to finance capital and financiers in *Imperialism*, that questions of finance and the role of international financiers in particular play a peripheral role at best in the mainstream historiography of the Russian Revolution. Over the past two generations, historians of Russia have branched out in a wide range of directions, moving away from questions of high politics and ideology to devote more attention to social, cultural, and even environmental history. Peasant history has been a notable focus of major research by scholars like Orlando Figes and Lynne Viola. The irony is that after decades of the focus on formerly marginalized groups, financiers are now the voiceless and ignored in the grand narratives of the revolution.

Indeed, over time such narratives have deemphasized questions of finance and the role of financiers. Conservative historian Richard Pipes's *The Russian Revolution* (1990) touches on financial issues, but they occupy a secondary place in a narrative focused on politics and ideology, while his contemporary and ideological opposite, radical social historian Sheila Fitzpatrick, devotes even less attention to finance. The paradox is that for all their ideological and historiographical differences, the two historians end up sharing a common interpretation and treatment of key financial questions such as the 5 Percent Russian Government Loan of 1906, which is the focus of Chapter 2.[14] In his otherwise excellent history of the revolution, *A People's Tragedy*, representing a younger generation of scholarship, Figes continued the relative downplaying of financial questions in the broader story of the revolution. To the limited extent that they appear in these grand narratives of the revolution, bankers and finance ministers serve as contemporary observers of politics and even court culture, rather than as historical actors in their own right. The contrast with Lenin's conception of the role of bankers in the world at the time is striking.

True, a second and newer line of more specialized scholarship has shown greater engagement with the financial history of the revolution and early Soviet period. One notable Anglophone scholar in this regard is historian Sean McMeekin, whose work on the early Bolshevik period includes two monographs related to finance—*The Red Millionaire* (2004) and *History's Greatest Heist* (2009).

Russian scholars, too, have been particularly active in this vein. In his 2008 work *Den'gi Russkoi Emigratsii* (Money of the Russian Emigration), Oleg Budnitskii takes up one of the great financial mysteries of the Civil War: the fate of approximately 480 tons of gold, moved in 1915 from the State Bank in Petrograd to Kazan for safekeeping, captured by the anti-Bolsheviks during the Civil War, and ultimately transferred to the White government of Admiral Kolchak in Siberia.[15] Ekaterina Pravilova's *Finansy Imperii* (Finances of Empire) is a recent financial history of Russia over the long nineteenth century.[16]

While McMeekin and Budnitskii deal with colorful financial characters and incidents in Russian history and mined the archives to uncover interesting new evidence, their narratives do not grapple with major questions of Russian financial policy and their relationship to the events of 1917. Pravilova's work, while engaging the theme of public finance in the context of center-periphery relations within the Russian Empire, is less concerned with the revolution per se in the core of the empire.

Jennifer Siegel's *For Peace and Money* (2014) is perhaps the specialist book closest to this one. Siegel's work draws on some of the same archives used in this book but is fundamentally a work of diplomatic history, focused primarily on questions of great power politics rather than the drivers of capital flows and their interplay with the story of the Russian Revolution.

Thus, while this more specialized literature sheds new light on interesting details, notably money laundering and smuggling in the cases of McMeekin and

Budnitskii, or the interplay between diplomacy and high finance in the case of Siegel, the reader looking for a tie-in with the broader arc of Russian history and the revolution itself is likely to be disappointed. The gold reserves McMeekin and Budnitskii both discuss were large; and while both authors stress the size and ultimate fate of the funds, they say little about the factors that created such reserves in the first place, which arguably conditioned the inability of either the Reds or the Whites to utilize the bullion to maximum effect.

Insofar as the narratives of Pipes, Fitzpatrick, and Figes are representative of major narratives of the Russian Revolution, the relative lack of attention to financial questions is also striking. Drawing in part on revolutionary rhetoric of the time, these narratives acknowledge a sense of economic and financial crises in the waning days of the ancien régime, but they are limited in their exploration of the financial and economic factors that led to these crises, and in particular leave crucial financial-historical counterfactuals unexamined. The absence of such discussion in this literature is particularly striking given that the revolutionaries themselves—not least Lenin in *Imperialism*—were obsessed with questions of finance and banking. More recent specialized scholarship touches on financial history in the context of the revolution and Civil War, but leaves unexamined important themes relating to the connections between international finance and the revolution.

The Sociology of Revolution

While a lack of historical literacy often contributes to financial crises, military disaster, and other such dislocations, modern revolutions stand out for the degree to which their participants look to earlier revolutions and revolutionaries in world history. Much of the research for this book took place as the events of the Egyptian Revolution of 2010–11 unfolded, with revolutionaries, figures of the ancien régime, and external commentators all wondering if the events in Cairo would turn the way of those in Tehran in 1979. Russia's revolutionaries were cognizant of the revolutions of 1789 and 1848 in particular; and, indeed, Leon Trotsky's own writings about the course of events in Russia would draw on the terminology of the French Revolution in his adoption of the term "Thermidor" to describe the rise of his rival and ultimate murderer, Joseph Stalin.[17] In the early days of his revolution, Lenin measured himself against the yardstick of the Paris Commune.[18] Revolutions have themselves, in turn, become the subject of comparative scholarship by historians and historical sociologists.

Harvard historian and president of the Society of Fellows Crane Brinton penned one of the classic works on the historical sociology of revolutions, *The Anatomy of Revolution*, in 1938—at a time when, by his own admission, the Russian Revolution was arguably still in progress.[19] Brinton offers what he considers an outline of the "uniformities" observed in revolutions across time and space by drawing on the cases of the English Revolution of the seventeenth century, the American and French revolutions of the eighteenth century, and the Russian Revolution of the twentieth century. Using the analogy of the revolution as a fever—which he employs in a clinical sense and thus without any normative connotations—Brinton walks the reader through the commonalities of the crisis of the ancien régime in his various cases, and then through the different stages of revolution and some of the characteristics shared among the revolutionaries themselves.[20]

In the generations since Briton's classic work on revolutions, scholars in both the West and Russia have grappled with the commonalities, differences, and causes behind the great revolutions of world history. Several central issues and questions appear across this literature. The first is one of scope—both temporal and geographic. Whereas Brinton's work was highly Eurocentric, later work by Theda Skocpol cast a broader net, notably including China.[21] An analogous issue of temporal definition also underscores all these discussions insofar as scholars differ on starting and ending dates of processes they otherwise agree to be revolutions, with often deep analytical consequences. In the case of Russia, even major Russian scholarship in the field of comparative revolutions perpetuates Brinton's focus on the events of 1917 to 1921, comparatively downplaying the events of the 1905 Revolution, which Chapter 2 shows to have been crucial to the broader story of the Russian Revolution.[22]

A second challenge the literature grapples with is definitional. As the Russian economists Vladimir Mau and Irina Starodubrovskaya show in *The Challenge of Revolution* (2001), definitional questions can determine both the subjects of analyses and the results. The authors thus set out to examine the experience of Russia in the 1980s and 1990s within the context of earlier theories of revolution, in the process suggesting ways that the most recent revolution in Russia may modify such theories.[23]

Devoting limited attention to the causal factors driving societies into revolution in the first place, Brinton focused more on the process and stages of the revolution itself. He sought to tease out the "uniformities" among his four cases—uniformities that, if not quite offering a general theory of revolution, still suggested some broad outlines of how revolutions work.[24] Much of the subsequent literature continued this tradition, operating within a social-scientific framework, but also recognizing that unlike comparatively mundane subjects such as recessions or elections, revolutions have deep distinctions and are processes pregnant with historical contingency. A seven-stage schematic of revolution developed by Mau and Starodubrovskaya elaborates from

Brinton, but offers a similar arc that begins with the crisis of the ancien régime, continues through the rule of the moderates and the *dvoevlastie* (dual power) and the rise and crisis of the radical regime, Thermidor, and ends with the consolidation of the postrevolutionary dictatorship.[25]

Questions of economics also course through much of the comparative literature on revolutions. While economic determinism is the bedrock of much classical Marxist literature, narratives stressing mechanistic relationships between economics and political change have been remarkably persistent— witness the myriad commentaries positing a relationship between a spike in global food prices and the Arab Spring. Much of the sociological literature on comparative revolutions jettisons the economic determinism of Marxist or popular journalistic discourse. As Brinton notes, "Our revolutions did not occur in societies with declining economies, or in societies undergoing widespread and long-term economic misery or depression. You will not find in these societies of the old regime anything like unusually widespread economic want."[26] In Briton's telling, "If businessmen in France had kept charts and made graphs, the lines would have mounted with gratifying consistency through most of the period of the French Revolution."[27]

Yet, as much as the sociological literature reflects a more nuanced view of the economic dimensions to revolutions, it may understate economic and especially financial factors. While the literature is rich in discussions of class conflict, much of it is silent on or ignorant of economic matters—especially so on financial matters.[28] Here, the work of Mau and Starodubrovskaya differs from earlier scholarship in that it stresses economic and financial causes and symptoms of revolution, setting it apart from Marxist analyses, in part by arguing that class conflict is not a driver of revolutionary events insofar as a precondition for revolution is the fragmentation of society that sees a breakup of the classes themselves.[29]

The literature on the historical sociology of revolutions is extensive, offering many frameworks within which to consider both historical and contemporary revolutions. The Russian Revolution features prominently in this literature. However, as much as the literature recognizes the broader importance of the events in Russia, it does not adequately frame them.

This book does not pretend to articulate a general theory of revolution applicable to all times and places. It does, however, engage with the literature on comparative revolutions by examining the story of the Russian Revolution—in a decidedly broader temporal scope than the theoretical literature does—in light of the existing models of revolution, and with a focus on many of the financial and economic themes Mau and Starodubrovskaya highlight. In this sense, this project seeks to help social scientists refine their thinking about revolutions.

Financial Globalization and Russia

Over more than three decades, the world has experienced a remarkable degree of globalization, in turn inspiring academic interest among social scientists and historians in the nature and drivers of this phenomenon. A large body of social science research comparing financial globalization in the present to that in the past—especially during what has been called the "first modern age of globalization" of the late nineteenth and early twentieth centuries—is of particular interest. While financial globalization can take a range of forms, the phenomenon of extensive cross-border capital flows is a salient feature of the contemporary global financial order, as it was of that in the late nineteenth and early twentieth centuries.

Economist Moritz Schularick compared both eras of financial globalization in quantitative terms in a 2006 study. He found that while contemporary globalization has seen much greater cross-border capital flow than in the past—with global cross-border investment stocks in 2001 representing 75 percent of world GDP, against 22 percent in 1913–14—the distribution of these investments tells a different story.[30] Specifically, the contemporary era of globalization has seen a higher degree of international investment within the developed world, while the earlier period of globalization witnessed a greater degree of foreign investment flowing from rich countries to poorer ones. As an example, according to Schularick's numbers, Russia was the second largest recipient of foreign investment in 1913–14—accounting for 8.4 percent of total cross-border capital flows, following only the United States, which had already become a major capital exporter.[31] By contrast, in his ranking of 2001 flows, the top eight recipients of cross-border investment were developed economies, with Hong Kong being the top-ranked "emerging market" with only 2.6 percent.[32] As Schularick argued, the contemporary period of globalization has thus been a manifestation of the "Lucas paradox," named after economist Robert Lucas, who observed that capital sometimes fails to flow from rich to poor countries, even though neoclassical growth models would predict that the returns to capital in poor countries would be very high, which would—according to theory—attract large capital inflows, all else equal.[33]

Of course, the 2001 figures Schularick presented in 2006 may now appear somewhat dated and are likely not as representative of rich-poor capital flows today, in light of the rising prominence not only of emerging markets but also of "frontier markets," including those of sub-Saharan Africa, in global portfolios.[34] Still, this trend is relatively recent, and hardly representative of the current era of globalization, which began in the 1980s and 1990s. Indeed, even data on global public offerings of new equity show a marked bias in favor of developed market issuance. Notwithstanding the increased interest

TABLE I.1. Initial public and secondary equity offerings from 1 January 2000 through 28 February 2018

	USD, trillions	% of total
North America	4.21	35
Asia and the Pacific (including Japan)	4.11	34
Europe	2.95	25
Latin America and the Caribbean	0.46	4
Middle East and Africa	0.22	2
Global total	11.96	100

Source: Bloomberg, 20 March 2018.

in emerging markets on the part of institutional investors from the turn of the millennium, the overwhelming amount of new equity capital raised by companies in global markets was raised by those in developed markets (see Table I.1). Equity market investments are of course only a portion of broader portfolio capital flows, but the underrepresentation of emerging markets—particularly in Latin America, the Middle East, and Africa—in this asset class is notable, not least given the increased prominence of equities in the contemporary era of globalization relative to the previous era. This underrepresentation of emerging markets in global equity issuance becomes clearer when taking into consideration that they accounted for approximately 54 percent of PPP-adjusted GDP in 2010, while accounting for only 35 percent of global stock market capitalization—itself a figure three times higher than in 2000.[35] Seen another way, in March 2018, the equity market capitalization represented in the 24-country MSCI Emerging Markets Index was only 14 percent of that of the MSCI World Index, which tracks 23 developed markets.[36] Thus, while less developed economies are increasingly being incorporated into global financial flows, they are still less integrated into global markets than were the poorer economies of the first modern age of globalization. The world is still in important ways not as globalized as it once was.

Russia in particular stands out as a significant player in both the historical and contemporary cases of financial globalization. Notwithstanding recent slowdowns, the Russian Federation is well known to investors today as one of the four BRICs—a term coined in 2001 by Jim O'Neill, then chief economist of Goldman Sachs, in a paper highlighting Brazil, Russia, India, and China as the four key economies that would experience a rapid rise in their share of global income from 8 percent in 2001 to as much as 27 percent over the course of the succeeding decade. Later research highlighted the BRICs as an even more significant driver of global growth, suggesting they would overtake the six leading developed Western economies by 2032.[37] As a BRIC economy, Russia enjoys a position as one of the most prominent "emerging markets" in which investors from "developed" markets invest their capital, accounting in early 2018 for more than 3 percent of the benchmark MSCI Emerging Markets Index. Even after several years of poor performance, Russia is a major component of the major international stock and bond indices against which institutional investors benchmark their performance.

Those with limited historical perspective are often surprised that Russia was in a roughly analogous—if not an even more prominent—position as a destination for foreign investment during the first modern age of globalization. In 1914, on the eve of the First World War, Russia was the largest net international debtor in the world, borrowing more money on international bond markets than Egypt, the Ottoman Empire, and Persia combined, and more than either Brazil or Argentina—all famous and frequently cited cases of debtor economies in history.[38] On a gross basis, Russian borrowing was second only to that of the United States—already a substantial exporter of capital to less developed economies in Latin America and elsewhere.[39] Russia was not only a major borrower, but also one with heavy representation in terms of traded securities on Western financial exchanges. The Paris Bourse—at the time one of the most active and liquid exchanges in the world—was by the closing decades of the nineteenth century a principal center of trading in Russian bonds.

The scale and volatility of global capital flows in both the first and second modern ages of globalization generated a great deal of interest among historically minded social scientists, as well as financial historians, in the key drivers of cross-border capital flows in a globalized world. Two of the leading scholars in the field articulated the puzzle in the following manner:

> Bond prices (or equivalently the corresponding yields premiums or default probabilities) may be seen as the left-hand variable of an implicit equation through which investors priced sovereign risks as a function of a number of variables. This equation serves as an excellent tool to identify the determinants of reputation and to study market perceptions of government policies before WWI. Once its existence in the minds of investors has been recognized, it is possible to use it by retrieving the information available at the time to back up these variables and their influence on bond prices.[40]

In a plethora of research published over the past quarter century, scholars have debated which variables attract investors to or repel them from markets and in turn drive the cost of capital for international borrowers. Although the explanations are multifaceted, it is perhaps useful to think of them as falling into two broad camps: those that stress monetary architecture and those that stress any range of macroeconomic or political fundamentals.

Monetary Architecture and the Gold Standard

Scholars stressing monetary architecture typically focus on fixed exchange rate regimes—represented in the historical case by the gold standard—as a major driver of access to cheap and plentiful capital through the international bond market. In a seminal 1996 paper, economists Michael D. Bordo and Hugh Rockoff spoke of the gold standard as the "Good Housekeeping Seal of Approval" for investors between 1870 and 1914. Using the case of nine "peripheral" borrowing economies, the authors argued that adherence to the gold standard was a signal of financial responsibility by a borrowing government to investors that prompted the latter to lend capital to such governments at more favorable rates than to those with a poor record of adherence to the gold standard.[41] According to Bordo and Rockoff, the value of adherence to gold was substantial, as evidenced in reduced borrowing costs in terms of both gold- and paper-denominated loans. Establishing a risk-free rate of 3 percent for the period, based on the yield of the UK 2.5 percent consol—the benchmark government bond of the time, equivalent in status to the US Treasury bond today—the authors argued that countries with a high, demonstrated commitment to gold convertibility, including Canada, Australia, and the United States, paid an interest premium of roughly only 1 percent over the benchmark rate. In contrast, less credible adherents to the gold standard, such as Argentina, Brazil, and Chile, paid a 2 to 3 percent premium over the benchmark rate on their gold-denominated loans.[42] These differences in rates were magnified in the case of bonds not linked to gold-backed currency. Whereas issuers of paper bonds such as the United States and Italy that showed stronger adherence to the gold standard paid premiums over the UK rate of 1.25 percent and 1.40 percent, respectively, Chile—a less scrupulous adherent to the gold standard—paid a premium of more than 4 percent.[43]

The Bordo-Rockoff work on the gold standard laid the groundwork for a slew of follow-on studies. While engaging with the central empirical question of whether or not adoption of the gold standard influenced borrowing costs, these subsequent works also raised deeper analytical questions that remain relevant to understanding the nature of financial globalization in the late nineteenth century.

On the basic empirical issue of whether or not adherence to the gold standard influenced sovereign borrowing costs, there is reason to believe that Bordo and Rockoff's thesis remains relevant. Drawing on a larger and more varied sample, Maurice Obstfeld and Alan Taylor confirmed Bordo and Rockoff's basic argument, finding that prior to the First World War, adherence to the gold standard reduced a country's sovereign borrowing costs by as much as 30 basis points.[44] Niall Ferguson and Moritz Schularick's subsequent work also concedes this point.[45]

These same follow-on studies that upheld the Bordo-Rockoff argument in a broad sense, however, raised important issues of periodization and location in the core versus periphery. Turning to the period of the interwar gold standard, Obstfeld and Taylor found that contrary to the prewar period, bond markets rewarded devaluers—countries that returned to convertibility at lower levels—rather than those that maintained convertibility at parity. The authors speculated that markets might have been seeing the maintenance of convertibility at parity to be unsustainable in the long run, making devaluation a more credible policy.[46]

Ferguson and Schularick revisited the debate about the gold standard's impact on the cost of capital for international debtors by highlighting development differentials. Distinguishing between advanced economies, colonial borrowers—who, as they rightly pointed out, were in many cases in de facto currency unions with more advanced borrowers and generally subject to strict financial discipline from the metropole—and independent, less developed countries, they argued that investors were able to quickly see beyond the "thin film of gold." In particular, their study found that while the gold standard did impact borrowing costs for more advanced countries, it did little to influence investors vis-à-vis independent developing countries, other than to the extent that monetary stability in core economies facilitated fund flows to the periphery. Ferguson and Schularick further argued that, even in the case of the advanced economies, the gold standard was simply "a proxy for improvements not properly reflected by other covariates; or it may merely capture the effect of low transaction costs." While supporters of the "Good Housekeeping" hypothesis would likely quip that the gold standard as a "proxy" for a range of other factors was part of their original argument, the broader point made by Ferguson and Schularick about the need to take into account the more conflicted evidence with respect to less developed borrowers is an important one.[47]

Macroeconomic and Political Fundamentals

Another body of capital flows scholarship deemphasizes monetary architecture, focusing instead on what can broadly be considered a variety of macroeconomic and political fundamentals. A range of scholarship across the social sciences and history has sought to highlight a variety of variables other than monetary architecture as the ultimate driver of capital flows across borders.

In a landmark 1989 article, economists Douglass North and Barry Weingast argued that political institutions are a key driver of capital flows. The authors contended that the institutions that grew out of the Glorious Revolution of 1688 drove a strengthening of private property rights that translated into lower borrowing costs for the British government, as well as higher economic growth more generally.[48] Specifically, they charted a drop in British government long-term borrowing costs from 14 percent in 1693 to 3 percent in 1739.[49] While North and Weingast admittedly dealt with an even earlier historical time frame, their article made an explicit link to what they at the time called "Third World" debt problems, and their work continues to influence the more recent debate on cross-border capital flows in both the historical and contemporary contexts.[50]

Economist Marc Flandreau has been a particularly prolific scholar of capital flows with respect to the first modern age of globalization. In one of his most widely cited works, coauthored with Frédéric Zumer, the two scholars argued that exchange rate regimes had a negligible effect on risk premiums in the international bond market, and that investors instead focused more heavily on macroeconomic and political fundamentals, specifically debt burdens. Investors today typically calculate debt burdens in terms of the ratio of debt to GDP, but in the historical case they focused on various ratios relating either the stock of nominal debt or the annual servicing costs to exports or tax revenues, as GDP statistics were not available at the time.[51] The authors further pointed out that this earlier period of globalization was not monotonic and that investors' analytical frameworks changed over time.[52] They cited as evidence of the sort of fundamentals investors studied the Service des études financières of Crédit Lyonnais—one of the most prominent financial institutions in the global bond market—and drew on many of this bureau's studies in developing both their conceptual framework and datasets.[53] They also highlighted default history and political instability as significant in the context of their regressions.[54]

Ferguson and Schularick famously argued that geopolitical frameworks were a key driver of the cost of capital during the first modern age of globalization. In their analysis, one of the principal determinants of investor perception of country risk in the London bond market was whether or not a peripheral economy was a member of the British Empire. Specifically, the authors found that peripheral economies that were also British colonies saw an average discount of 100 basis points—in the case of African and Asian colonies, as much as 175 basis points—in the risk premiums charged by the London market.[55]

Political scientist Michael Tomz approached the question of capital flows from the perspective of debtor reputations. Rather than focusing on macroeconomic fundamentals or exchange rate regimes directly, Tomz argued that the reputation of sovereign debtors conditions investors' propensity to lend to the borrowers in question, and the rates at which they lend to them. Drawing on earlier international political economy literature on reputations, Tomz developed a theory of debtor reputation suggesting that countries earn reputations over time, and that their behavior in specific political and economic contexts helps markets place them in one of three creditworthiness categories: stalwarts, fair-weathers, and lemons.[56] In this dynamic model, Tomz suggested that not all payments or defaults are equal—markets reward countries that decide to remain current on external debts in the depths of a crisis to a greater degree than those choosing to pay when times are relatively good; conversely, markets punish countries that default, even in good times, more than those that default in a crisis.

Economists Paulo Mauro, Nathan Sussman, and Yishay Yafeh offered a different story in a series of influential studies highlighting the importance of political violence as an influence on investor decision making. Drawing on a new dataset of bond prices and their automated skimming of the contemporary financial press, this group of authors argued that political stability is in fact the key distinguishing variable that investors in peripheral economy bonds focused on when assessing risk. More specifically, they found that political violence was a variable to which markets were especially sensitive at the time. They took particular issue with the institutional school, arguing that investors did not reward institutional changes, which could only prove their effectiveness over time, as the efficacy of parliaments or central banks is not self-evident at their birth. Markets were quick to overlook such institutional improvements, fixed exchange rate regimes, and other factors in the event of political violence, according to this view.[57]

While the above studies—which represent just a few of the more prominent examples of a rich field of scholarship in economics, history, and political science—offer interesting insights into the drivers of cross-border capital flows in both the historical and the contemporary contexts, they all share some common shortcomings. First, their temporal scope is in many ways artificially constrained. In considering the case of Russia, for example, it is far from evident that financial globalization suddenly stopped in 1914, let alone in 1913, which is a common breaking point in many of these studies. As Chapters 4 and 5 show, even private capital flows to peripheral economies continued in spite of—and indeed in some cases partly because of—the First World War.

Second, the studies broadly share—but rarely explicitly articulate—a common characterization of how bond markets and investor-debtor relations functioned. In essence, much of this scholarship assumes that the decision makers were fairly well informed, rational, individual/retail investors who lent directly to sovereign borrowers in competitive markets. Financial institutions in this schema are largely relegated to a utility-like technical function of merely connecting borrower and creditor. Many of the authors did not employ an analysis of qualitative factors. Those that did limited themselves mainly to the study of the financial press and related specialist publications for investors, like the *Investor's Monthly Manual* and *Fenn's Compendium* or contemporary published accounts. Flandreau and Zumer drew on some archival material from the Crédit Lyonnais archive, but primarily to pull data from the various spreadsheets of the Service des études financières.[58]

This approach is flawed in that it does not reflect how capital markets in fact worked during the first modern age of globalization or, for that matter, how they function in the contemporary era of globalization. At a fundamental level, the assumptions of investor rationality and perfect or near-perfect information are highly questionable. Reliance on the financial press is also not without its problems. Leaving aside the totally corrupt and venal French financial press, even its British counterpart was prone to jingoistic biases and the temptations of playing up political and financial crises.

More importantly, banks played a crucial role in facilitating—or preventing—the flow of capital across borders. Major financial institutions, like Baring Brothers & Co., the various Rothschild houses, and the institutions of the Parisian *haute banque*, were critical players in the bond market not only because they fulfilled the technical role of transferring capital from retail bond investors to sovereign governments, but also because they themselves shaped investor perceptions of risk and opportunities.

In more recent work, Marc Flandreau recognized that "the microeconomics of foreign currency sovereign debt issuance" is an area that "has been relatively underresearched."[59] In his 2009 paper on underwriting in sovereign bond markets, Flandreau and his coauthors Juan Flores, Norbert Gaillard, and Sebastián Nieto-Parra acknowledged the immense power of financial institutions in financial markets, going so far as to call them the "gatekeepers" to the international bond market. This power drew on their broader role that combined the functions of "broker, certifier, and lender of last resort when issues failed."[60] The authors contrasted this to the contemporary markets, where they correctly pointed out that the role of "certifier" has been outsourced to ratings agencies.[61] They found that the most prestigious banks were able to leverage their brand value and thus were associated with the most successful issues—partly because they had a de facto right of first refusal to the business of prospective borrowers eager to win prestige points, and partly because these banks had an interest in maintaining their reputations for success—making the participation of an underwriter, or lack thereof, in a given bond issue a key signal to investors about the issue's desirability.[62] Underwriters in turn used this power to great effect, including, according to recent work by Flandreau and Flores, successfully pressuring governments to implement "pro-peace policies."[63] In this sense, Flandreau's conception of financial gatekeeping is not very different from that of Lenin, when the latter's work is stripped of its ideological vitriol. In short, bankers matter.

The issue of gatekeeper finance reveals another flaw in the assumptions of previous scholarship about sovereign bond markets in the historical case—namely that they were competitive. Partly due to the importance of brands, the market for sovereign lending was extremely concentrated in the past, with the top three lenders in the Paris market from 1895 to 1914 accounting for 65 percent of all new issues, for example.[64] Moreover, many formal and informal arrangements between creditor banks and countries vis-à-vis sovereign lending conditioned such lending during that period. In the case of Latin America, Argentina was considered Barings territory, while Brazil was the domain of the Rothschilds. Many of the regression-based studies in the earlier literature on capital flows did not account for these dynamics operating at the level of the creditor countries and individual banks. If anything, expanding the number of countries in sample sets to include more peripheral economies actually raises the risk of embedding these problems into the analysis.

Finally, much of the earlier literature on capital flows was written from a supply-side perspective. The agents in these stories are the investors who are making the decisions, or—only recently and to a much lesser extent—the banks that are engaging in the lending as "gatekeepers" to the international bond market. The borrowers are largely missing as active agents in these stories. Flandreau and Zumer themselves acknowledged the biases of this framing in their monograph.[65] Tomz's theory of reputation, of course, implies that ongoing decisions by debtor governments do have the power to directly influence investor perceptions, but the bulk of his sources and analysis are devoted to creditors, not debtors. Bignon and Flandreau's article on the Russian and French governments' relations with the French financial press is an important attempt to delve more deeply into the behavior of debtors.[66]

Gatekeeper Finance and the Russian Revolution

This book fills the gaps in the literature on international capital flows, the political economy of revolutions, and indeed the Russian Revolution itself through an exploration of Russia's relationship with international finance in the late nineteenth and early twentieth centuries. Focusing on bankers and finance ministers, it resurrects figures and themes that have received comparatively little attention in major histories of the revolution. Existing theories of revolution in the context of the Russian Revolution—taken in a wider temporal scope—inform it. Last, it explores the capital flows equation from a novel angle—using archives to explore the role and thinking of financial gatekeepers and policymakers on the debtor side. In doing so, it builds on a rich banking history literature, but pushes beyond the traditional limits of the discipline to engage with broader questions about how banks and bankers influenced capital flows and revolution and vice versa. Indeed, this study arguably extends the traditional definition of "gatekeeper" to allow for borrowers' influence upon them. In essence, however, the book retains the core of the original concept, recognizing gatekeepers to be central figures in global finance with immense influence over capital flows.

The study benefits from access to archival material not available to earlier generations of financial historians. Within the context of literature on foreign finance in the Russian milieu, it broadens the scope of a discussion focused largely on Franco-Russian ties to incorporate the growing role of British and American banks in the Russian markets of the early twentieth century.[67]

A study that takes up the case of Russia in particular as a player in global bond markets has several advantages, even for more broadly focused literature on global capital flows that includes developing economies. First, as a market, Russia is inherently interesting. Unlike a small African borrower, Russia was a significant participant in the international bond market—indeed the largest net international borrower by 1914. At the same time, unlike major markets such as Brazil or Argentina, Russia was much more competitive for lenders. All of the major financial houses in the world maintained some engagement with Russia throughout the period. That some of these banks abstained from lending to Russia is itself an interesting phenomenon worthy of exploration. Moreover, an archival approach allows for far deeper insights into the thinking of financial gatekeepers—and, by extension, the drivers of capital flows—than statistical correlations of high-level data or reading of the financial press. The archival sources this book draws on reveal the thinking of some of the most powerful figures in global finance at the time vis-à-vis the Russian markets and international investment more generally. Examining their decision making through the lens of the single but highly significant case of Russia provides insights into the thinking of the most important investors and financiers of the belle époque.

Specifically, a complex but interrelated set of forces—government intervention, competitive dynamics in international finance, and cultural factors—operating at the level of financial gatekeepers facilitated the large capital inflow Russia witnessed through the eve of the Bolshevik Revolution and default. The history of the Russian Revolution is itself intertwined with this investment cycle insofar as the policies of the ancien régime became the focus of attacks from the opposition, who opened a financial front in their fight against the regime—a front that would extend into the period of the Civil War. In this context, just as the political struggle took on a financial dimension, investing in Russia became an act that was not only financial, but also political.

This book tells this story over the course of five chapters. Chapter 1 traces Russia's financial reforms in the late nineteenth century. The chapter puts the reforms associated with Sergei Witte's tenure as finance minister from 1892 to 1903 in a broader context, and also highlights key strategic errors made during his tenure. Chapter 2 focuses on the 1905 Revolution, underscoring the price Russia paid for the strategic errors discussed in Chapter 1, and stressing the important financial-historical legacy of this period within the broader story of the revolution. Chapter 3 explores Russia's rapid recovery from the strains of revolution and war, and the impact of its return to war in 1914. The chapter also adds a financial mirror to a classic debate on the social and political historiography of the revolution. Chapter 4 explores in detail the story of 1917 through the novel perspective of foreign bankers who were on the ground at the time and shows how and why some of the leading financiers in the world remained optimistic about Russia until the very eve of the Bolshevik coup. Finally, Chapter 5 focuses on the 1918 Bolshevik default—the largest in history—and the continuation of the financial struggle by the Bolsheviks after the October Revolution from the perspective of both bankers and Bolsheviks.

1

Fault Lines

THE WITTE SYSTEM AND
MISSED OPPORTUNITIES

IN LATE AUGUST 1892, just before setting off for Poland, Tsar Alexander III
accepted the resignation of Ivan Vyshnegradskii, the Imperial Russian minister of finance. Although the Tsar hesitated, the resignation came as a relief
to both men, and was hardly a surprise to their contemporaries—while
Vyshnegradskii had been an active and reformist minister, he was being held
to account for government policies that exacerbated the disastrous 1891–92
famine and thereby the cholera epidemics it triggered, resulting in the deaths
of some 400,000 people.[1] Among these policies was the raising of consumer
taxes and heavily incentivizing peasants, if not forcing them outright, to sell
more grain. Thus, grain exports, which could have been redirected to feed a
starving peasant population, were initially curtailed, but only in stages and
after delays, ultimately being banned in November 1891, far too late to avert
a human tragedy. Further sealing Vyshnegradskii's fate was his opposition to
the prohibition of grain exports as late as mid-August.[2] The combination of
famine deaths and losses to the Treasury due to the famine's impact on peasant
incomes contributed to the negative publicity that only worsened Vyshnegradskii's own failing health.[3] His term as finance minister, which ended rather
abruptly, was but the last stage of an otherwise highly successful career in
which he amassed a fortune in railroads and finance before transitioning to
government service. Indeed, his January 1887 appointment by the Tsar as a
replacement to Nikolai Bunge—the Tsarist finance minister since 1881—was
initially fêted by some in the business community as the government moving
to put a "practical financier" in charge of the state's finances after a period of
leadership by a "man of theory."[4]

Vyshnegradskii's successor as finance minister, Sergei Witte, was by contrast
a relatively obscure figure to contemporary observers. London's *Economist*

admitted to knowing little about Witte, saying only that he was thought to be an "able financier" and, "if he succeeds in winning the opinion of the banking and operating community to but half the extent his predecessor did, it will be a good thing for Russian financial operations."[5] Gustave Lannes de Montebello, the French ambassador in Saint Petersburg, noted in an 8 September 1892 dispatch to the Quai d'Orsay that the Tsar made his decision only after significant hesitation. The diplomat painted a picture of Witte as a self-made technocrat with a dubious personal life and a prickly personality that had made him many enemies in the Imperial bureaucracy and court.[6] That he chewed gum and, after the death of his first wife, married a converted Jewish divorcée did not endear him to the Tsar.[7] De Montebello went on to acknowledge expectations that Witte would continue in Vyshnegradskii's footsteps and that his doing so would be met with general approval.[8]

Such a lackluster, even apprehensive, response to Witte's appointment is ironic in light of subsequent scholarship making him one of the most famous personalities of late Imperial Russia. Witte, more than any other figure in Russia or the West, is associated with the boom in Russian investment in the late nineteenth and early twentieth centuries. During his tenure as finance minister, from 1892 to 1903, Russia adopted the gold standard in 1897 and repeatedly turned to the foreign capital markets for loans to finance an ambitious program of state-led industrialization. His name was similarly associated with the boom in Russian railroad construction, the Trans-Siberian Railway in particular—an association that began in his earliest days while working in the railroad industry, first in the private sector (initially as a lowly conductor to learn the business) and then in government.

Pro: Witte the Revolutionary

Witte, above all others, personifies the industrialization of nineteenth-century Russia in a range of narratives. Historian Sheila Fitzpatrick portrays him as a technocrat and champion of modernizing reforms who harnessed Russia's engineers and businessmen in his industrialization program but was held back by a civil service elite and a Tsar stuck in the past.[9] Richard Pipes credits Witte with introducing a novel and visionary turn in Russia's financial grand strategy—of initiating the policy, whereby Russia moved to a model of financing industrial growth through aggressive borrowing on international capital markets "rather than squeeze the countryside," as Vyshnegradskii had.[10] Lenin was predictably scathing in his references to the "great acrobat Witte," although this was, of course, because he shared the view later articulated by Fitzpatrick and Pipes that Witte was a key driver of Russia's turn to the global capital markets.[11] This narrative in generalist works, in turn, influenced students of the Russian oil industry, such as Daniel Yergin, whose discussion of Tsarist Russia in his broader global history of the oil business casts Witte as a lone and isolated voice of technocratic reason and reform against the reactionary clique surrounding an incompetent Nicholas II.[12]

Favorable treatments of Witte isolate several factors that supposedly set him apart from his predecessors and successors. His most authoritative recent Russian biographers highlight his "national idea," crediting him with having what some described as "a whole plan."[13] According to them, "not one of the ministers of finance of the post-reform era used such broad means of government intervention in the economy as did Witte."[14] The German economist Friedrich List's 1889 *The National System of Political Economy* particularly influenced Witte.[15] A leading American biographer acknowledges that "the three preceding finance ministers, Reutern, Bunge, and Vyshnegradskii, recognized their country's backwardness and sought to overcome it. They recognized the need for an adequate banking system, a stable currency, and large-scale foreign investment in industry as long as native investors could not provide the necessary capital," but goes on to say, "their achievements fell far short of their goals."[16] Others may have had the right ideas, but only Witte was able to implement them and realize their benefits, according to this view.

At the height of the Cold War, perhaps reflecting awe in certain Western circles of Soviet accomplishments and the Keynesian and statist economic policy paradigm of the times, Witte was favorably cited as the forerunner to twentieth-century industrialization policies in Russia. Thus, one of his most widely cited Western biographers argued that Witte was the first Russian finance minister to make industrialization a priority.[17] Praising Witte's system as the "boldest" yet, Theodore Von Laue credited Witte with "a more rapid pace of industrial advance" relative to his predecessors.[18] Von Laue found something to praise even in Witte's notoriously embroidered budget reports to the Tsar, describing them as an "indispensable morale builder" for achieving his industrialization aims, and the "prelude to the fanfare of statistics blared forth during the early five-year plans."[19] Flirtatious comparisons with Stalin are indeed a salient feature of much of the Witte literature and are not surprising, particularly given the period during which Von Laue was writing.[20]

In the view of other favorably disposed observers, Witte was far from a ham-fisted proponent of government intervention in the economy, and his prior business experience gave him an appreciation for the private sector's potential and importance, as well as the nous to make government interventions in the economy most effective.[21] French historian René Girault credits Witte with a more strategic deployment of Russian government funds abroad to facilitate loan issues, and with the rationalization of the Russian railroad network in the 1880s in a way that not only improved the network but also facilitated railroad bond issues.[22] Witte is also credited in this vein with being a skilled bureaucratic politician who knew how to broaden and leverage his sphere of influence in the bureaucracy, transforming and expanding the remit of departments such as the Institute of Commercial Agents, whose staff he would use to help him tap global capital markets.[23] In this telling, then, Witte was not just a visionary but also a doer who both conceived and implemented a new course in Russian financial policy.

In the same vein, in one of the most reactionary societies in the world, Witte stood out as a skilled and effective, no-nonsense manager who "hired talent over ethnicity" and generally revolutionized the finance ministry with his modern management style and iconoclastic ways.[24] This iconoclasm was not lost on Witte's contemporaries abroad. Niall Ferguson, for example, argues, "It was the appointment of Witte as finance minister which persuaded the Rothschilds to resume financial relations with Russia." He calls attention to Mrs. Witte's Jewish heritage having led the Rothschilds to think that Witte would be more progressive on Jewish affairs.[25] In this sense, there was a silver lining to the tensions Mrs. Witte's background created between her husband and the Tsar. The paradox, in the telling of his most recent American biographer, is that Witte's ability to realize his dreams of accelerating economic growth, rooted in part in his unconventional approach, fed the "military adventurism" of some of the most nationalist and conservative elements of the government that resulted in "foreign entanglement" and ultimately war with Japan.[26]

Witte's own memoirs—both the original Russian edition and the abridged English translation—do much to advance the narrative of a progressive, forward-thinking, and indeed revolutionary technocratic genius who delivered results despite being held back by a Byzantine court and an insecure Tsar. In her preface to his posthumously published memoirs, Witte's widow writes at length about her husband's fear of being censored by the Tsarist authorities. Suspecting his study in Saint Petersburg to be unsafe, he wrote his memoirs exclusively when abroad, keeping drafts in safety deposit boxes at foreign banks overseas that were registered in his wife's name. His widow's recollection of agents from the Okhrana raiding their home after his death in search of these damning documents only sharpens the profile of an iconoclastic reformer persecuted by the forces of reaction.[27]

Contra: Witte the Revolutionary

The notion that Witte represented a breaking point in Russian economic history is not something that emerges only from his memoirs or relatively favorable biographical treatment by later historians. Even his detractors saw Witte's accession as representing a historical discontinuity. Perhaps the most notorious contemporary attacker of Witte's policies was the infamous Elie de Cyon—a gifted but controversial character who himself attracted the scholarly attention of the original cold warrior, George F. Kennan. Born Ilya Fadeyevich Tsion to a Jewish family in Lithuania in 1842 or 1843, by 1873 Tsion was recognized as a gifted physiologist, "Russia's youngest professor, and its first Jewish one."[28] He was also a "strong and confirmed reactionary," which, while odd for a Russian Jewish intellectual of his time, was hardly out of the ordinary for Tsarist society in general and indeed spoke to his strong assimilationist instincts.[29] Within the context of Russia's notoriously radical universities, however, Tsion's views were so controversial that he requested military guards to be posted outside his office and eventually left the Saint Petersburg Medical-Surgical Academy and Russian academia altogether by October 1874.[30]

Eventually settling in Paris and transforming himself into "a well-heeled and cosmopolitan gentleman, installed in a fine apartment in the rue de la Bienfaisance," Tsion—now known as Élie de Cyon—took on a third, French, doctorate and continued his research under Paul Bert, the famous French physiologist. Bert's own left-Republican views—he became minister of education under Léon Gambetta—however proved to be "too much" for Cyon, who left science "frustrated and embittered."[31] Among other things, he developed connections to French military circles—including some notoriously anti-Semitic anti-Dreyfusards—and wrote, at times for Mikhail Katkov's *Moskovskie Vedomosti*, in favor of a Franco-Russian alliance.[32] Katkov, one of the most powerful newspapermen in Russia, in turn introduced Cyon to Vyshnegradskii, at the time Russia's finance minister, who engaged Cyon to help represent the ministry in talks with French and German bankers.[33] According to Kennan, the two fell out over the amount each was entitled to skim off the deal, and Cyon, from that point onward, became a vocal critic of the Russian finance ministry.[34]

Although Kennan rightly points to Cyon's criticism of both Vyshnegradskii and his successor Witte, Cyon was particularly scathing in his critiques of the latter. Some of his pamphlets, including "Où la Dictature de M. Witte Conduit la Russie" (1897), had particularly sharp titles. Others, such as "M. Witte et les Finances Russes" (1895), adopted a less partisan and more technocratic frame; but all were pointed critiques of Russian financial policy in general, and of Witte in particular.[35] Cyon—showing intellectual camaraderie with Katkov—was a vocal critic of the manner in which Vyshnegradskii and Witte sought to introduce the gold standard in Russia.

In 1797, Russia had introduced a silver standard but suffered successive devaluations because of deficit financing during the Turkish and Swedish wars of 1806–12 and 1808–9.[36] After a brief attempt at reducing reliance on money printing to finance deficits by issuing long-term debt, Russia's involvement in the Napoleonic Wars (1812–15) resulted in a new round of printing.[37] By 1815, the silver value of the paper ruble had fallen to just 20 percent of its original value.[38] During the post-Napoleonic era, Russia made strides toward establishing a durable sovereign debt market that would enable the Russian government to fund deficits from the proceeds of foreign and domestic loans without resorting to the printing press. The wars with Persia (1826–28) and Turkey (1828–29), as well as the Polish rebellion (1830–31), were thus financed by a combination of foreign loans and new short-term domestic debt in the form of newly created state Treasury bills.[39] From 1839 to 1843, the government carried out yet another monetary reform, whereby the old paper ruble was devalued into a new partially convertible "credit ruble" at a ratio of 3.5:1.[40] In 1855, in the midst of the Crimean War (1853–56), the Russian government resumed printing money to eventually cover more than 45 percent of total wartime expenses, promising to begin withdrawing the new rubles within three years.[41] Given the huge overhang of paper rubles as a result of the war, the government abolished convertibility altogether in 1858.[42] In the meantime, as a Russian finance ministry report prepared in 1895 under Witte noted, Gresham's Law had kicked in, with silver coin having vanished from domestic circulation and largely having found its way abroad.[43] After some monetary stability was restored during M. K. Reutern's term as finance minister, the Turkish War of 1877–78 saw the printing of more than 1 billion paper rubles, with the paper ruble depreciating by roughly 38 percent from 1879 to 1888.[44] Figures pertaining to depreciation alone, however, tell only part of the story: the currency was not only depreciating, but highly volatile, with realized volatility in some years exceeding 30 percent.[45]

In introducing the gold standard, the Russian government had to decide how to treat the existing paper rubles in circulation. As the 4 February 1895 ministry report noted, the basic theoretical currency of the Russian Empire was the silver ruble, to which the credit ruble was, theoretically, still linked. "Legally," the report acknowledged, "both rubles, silver and credit, are equivalent."[46] In practice, however, the government's collecting of customs duties in gold, the contracting of foreign loans in gold, and the trading of the credit ruble on foreign exchanges created a de facto domestic and foreign market for credit rubles in gold terms, thus creating a gold ruble with a value at the time equivalent to one-fifth of a Demi-Imperial.[47] This in turn implied the de facto existence of three Russian currencies: the silver ruble, the credit ruble, and a de facto gold ruble.

The arguments in favor of adopting a monometallic gold standard while simultaneously engaging in a devaluation and definitive abandonment of silver were several. First, more than half the government's debt, much of it externally held, was denominated in gold.[48] Second, there was the practical consideration that withdrawing the silver and credit notes in circulation would be simply too difficult in a country as vast as Russia; as an earlier finance minister, A. A. Abaza, put it, "notes once in circulation are as difficult to withdraw as it is to separate wine from water."[49] Besides, Russia was not a major silver producer, but in 1895 it did account for 15 percent of global gold production.[50] Indeed, by February 1895 the silver ruble had fallen more against gold than had the credit ruble, the value of which itself likely reflected market expectations of an impending adoption of a monometallic gold standard, as well as of active manipulation of the currency market by the Russian State Bank.[51] Ultimately, the monetary reform saw the credit ruble devalued by two-thirds, making 1.5 credit rubles equal to one new gold ruble.[52]

Cyon's shrill critique echoed the views of many opponents of Witte's policies in the State Council who were open to the adoption of the gold standard, but only if the paper ruble were brought to parity—possible only by increasing gold reserves even more, a slow strengthening of the credit ruble, or reduction in the stock of paper rubles through open-market operations on the part of the government.[53] Such a move would have severely impacted various interests in Russia. The country's export-oriented agriculture would suffer not only from reduced demand overseas, but also from an increase in the real value of agricultural debt—much of it denominated in credit rubles—by a factor of one-third.[54] Indeed, the Russian government itself—also a major player in "credit loans" denominated in the paper rubles—would see those liabilities increase by one-third in real terms.[55] Of course, Cyon saw this all in reverse—as nothing but a transparent attempt by the government to write off its debt on a similar scale.[56] In Cyon's view, the ultimate symbol of government credit was a stable currency, and the government's devaluation was in this sense nothing other than a declaration of state bankruptcy—something that was simply contrary to the "honor and dignity" of Russia.[57] Cyon cast Witte's moves in the monetary sphere as a perversion of an otherwise sane tradition of recent monetary policy in the Ministry of Finance. He specifically pointed to Witte's predecessors Bunge, Reutern, Abaza, and Greig as being extremely cautious on the subject of monetary reforms, and careful to underscore that a rapid introduction of gold into circulation would create counterproductive panics over looming devaluations that would hurt the economy.[58] Cyon acknowledged that Vyshnegradskii was more radical in his approach but nonetheless cast him as, at least initially, holding up a more or less traditional bimetallist line, which Cyon claimed himself to have suggested to the minister in his reports of June 1887 and February 1888.[59] According to Cyon, the real break came much later, in 1890 and 1891, and was furthered by Witte when he assumed the ministry.[60] In monetary affairs, then, Cyon posited a break as occurring in 1890 and thus blamed both Vyshnegradskii and Witte for destroying the Russian currency and, by extension, the credit reputation of Russia itself.

However, as much as Cyon had come to dislike Vyshnegradskii by 1897, he reserved particular hatred for Witte. His pamphlets are riddled with scathing insults of the Russian finance minister. Cyon compared Witte to John Law—the infamous Scottish murderer who wreaked havoc on the finances of eighteenth-century France—singling Witte out for his mismanagement of monetary policy, as well as accusing him of being a particularly corrupt figure of unsavory moral character.[61]

Making reference to Witte's power within the bureaucracy, Cyon portrayed him as reaching dangerously beyond his rightful station. In Cyon's narrative, Nicholas II, like Louis XIV, had every right to say "L'État, c'est moi!" but the nihilist Witte sought to overturn this natural order of things.[62] Witte's rising power, according to Cyon, was not lost to contemporaries. He quoted an anonymous ambassador "who is in particularly intimate relations with our finance minister" as telling his government, "Nicolas II règne, mais Witte gouverne."[63]

Like Witte's admirers, Cyon also saw the Russian finance minister as introducing a more comprehensive and coherent system and holistic program than his predecessors. His assessment of the value of this system was, however, less generous. In Cyon's view, Witte's system, with its emphasis on state intervention in the economy, represented nothing less than the introduction of "state socialism, according to the formula of Marx."[64] Such an accusation, leveled in 1897, was particularly striking in light of future historians' comparisons of Witte to Stalin and his Soviet industrialization drive of the 1930s.

Both favorable and unfavorable narratives of Witte's career from past and present, then, ironically share a common view—that his rise represented a fundamental shift in Russian economic and financial history. Such an opinion is most obviously evident in those works that praise him as a revolutionary reformer in the bureaucracy, but it is also a profile that emerges in the work of his most famous enemy. In its extreme, this view posits 1892 as a turning point in Russian history not unlike 1928—the year of the first five-year plan in the Soviet Union.

However, for all the changes Witte introduced, and for all the ideological coherence he brought to his "system," in examining Witte's policies within a broader scope, and in considering evidence from the capital markets—in terms of financial data, the financial press, and the archival record—it is evident that Witte's time as finance minister represented continuity more than change with regard to his predecessors. Moreover, while he may have been a shrewd tactician in certain areas, Witte's term as finance minister was marked by deficiencies in execution and strategic errors that created financial fault lines in the edifice of the Russian state, which would come home to haunt the government during the crises of 1904 to 1907. These fault lines not only would offer targets of opportunity to the Tsarist regime's opponents, but would themselves constrain the abilities of the regime to respond to crises and challenges.

The Data: A Financial Revolution?

In discussing Witte's tenure as finance minister, scholars frequently make two observations: it saw the introduction of sweeping financial reforms, and because of these reforms, Russia experienced a great inflow of foreign investment. While there is no doubt that the period was marked by a large influx of foreign capital, and especially portfolio capital in the form of investment in Russian securities, the novelty of Witte's reforms and their influence on capital flows is questionable.[65] Indeed, while many of the aforementioned studies engage with economic and financial data to varying degrees, the growth rates they offer for a range of indicators during the Witte period need to be presented within a broader context—both temporally and according to the type of data that are scrutinized.

There is little doubt that the period from 1892 to 1903 saw a boom in foreign investment in Russian securities. According to Girault's estimates, the nominal sum of Russian securities traded in the Paris market increased by 113 percent between 1892 and 1903, while the actual cash value of outstanding stock increased by 75 percent (see Figure 1.1).[66]

This large increase in French investment was not restricted to portfolio flows, however. French FDI in Russia also rose dramatically over the course

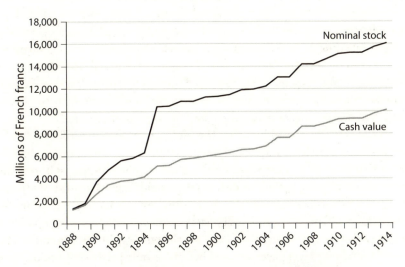

FIGURE 1.1. Estimated nominal and cash value of Russian securities in the Paris market. Source: Girault, *Emprunts Russes*, 84.

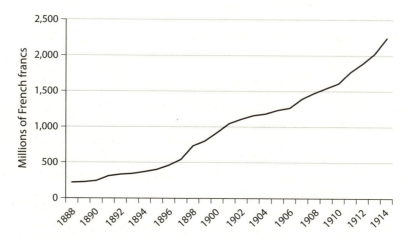

FIGURE 1.2. Estimated French FDI in Russia. Source: Girault, *Emprunts Russes*, 85.

of the closing years of the nineteenth century. According to Girault's numbers, French direct investments in the mining, petroleum, metallurgical, textile, and financial sectors increased at a more rapid rate during this period—by 248 percent, albeit from a lower base (see Figure 1.2).[67]

Economist Paul Gregory's 1982 monograph *Russian National Income, 1885–1913* remains to this day the definitive statistical study on the Russian national income accounts of the late Tsarist period. Gregory's data on net foreign investment show a clear negative bias over the period in question, indicating a strong net inflow of foreign capital (both portfolio and direct), thereby broadly corroborating Girault's more focused picture (see Figure 1.3).[68]

The data thus show a very clear increase in foreign investment—both direct and portfolio—over the course of the last 15 years of the nineteenth century. Moreover—although many of these studies stress this point less than they do movements in the stock of capital—the relative interest rates that Russia was paying to borrow this money were falling throughout this period.

In finance, the spread between the yield on the benchmark bonds of a country and a "risk-free" rate, often represented by the yield on the benchmark bonds of a major core economy, is used to chart the cost of borrowing for a country.[69] The spread, or difference in yield, is used instead of the raw yield, as it normalizes for fluctuations in core economy interest rates.[70] In this sense, Olga Crisp's complimentary assessment of Witte's financial policies, namely, "despite the substantial increase in the public debt Russian state credit abroad reached a level never attained before," is only partly supported by her pointing simply at absolute gains in the prices of Russian bonds.[71] Indeed, as she herself notes, "the relative abundance of capital on the international

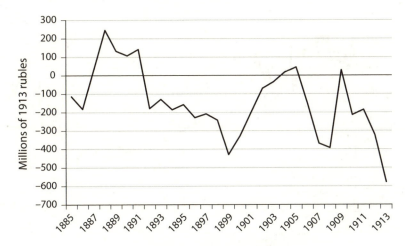

FIGURE 1.3. Net foreign investment in Russia. Source: Gregory,
Russian National Income, 56–58.

money markets" contributed to this increase in bond prices.[72] A falling spread
is indicative of a country's ability to borrow at relatively more favorable rates,
while an increase in spreads indicates that relative borrowing costs are rising.
While adequate liquidity and sufficiently low rates in core economies may
well change the overall risk appetites of investors, dealing with spreads rather
than raw yields helps to isolate relative changes in the markets' valuation of
peripheral country bonds and risk. Crisp's point on Witte's tenure coinciding
with a relative improvement in perceptions of Russian credit would thus have
been made stronger with reference to not only gains in Russian bond prices,
but an assessment of spreads.

Such spread studies, of course, are drawn from prices in the secondary
market—from trades of existing bonds. New issues—in what is called the
primary market—of bonds may occur on terms that diverge from pricing in
the secondary market. Nevertheless, the two markets are connected insofar
as investors and issuers both look to prices prevailing in the secondary market
when considering how to price or bid for new issues. For much of the period
in question, the British government 2.5 percent consol perpetual bond was the
"risk-free" asset against which other financial instruments were measured. The
consol played a role in financial calculations analogous to that of US government treasury bonds today. Considering the spread of the benchmark 5 percent Russian government bond of 1822 over UK 2.5 percent consols (see Figure
1.4) as an indicator for baseline borrowing costs over the period in question,
it is evident that the spread narrowed materially from a peak of more than 300
basis points in the early 1880s to a nadir of only 52 basis points in late 1902.

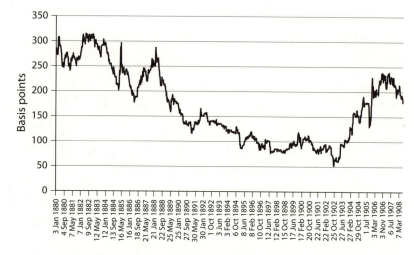

FIGURE 1.4. Spread of the 5 Percent Imperial Russian Government 1822 Bond over British 2.5 percent consols. Source: "GFD Database" (2012), www.globalfinancialdata.com.

The importance of considering yield spreads does not mean that absolute yields do not matter—they are in fact crucial insofar as they are representative of the interest charge the government would pay to service and raise new debt. A government that has experienced falling spreads but rising nominal yields on its traded debt faces the grim prospect of having to roll over existing or issue new debt at increasing interest rates, resulting in a heavier burden of interest payments on its budget. Indeed, economists distinguish between so-called primary and overall budget expenditures, with the former representing government spending before accounting for debt service and the latter incorporating interest payments. A situation whereby a government experiences rising nominal yields even as it tries to improve its primary fiscal balance is every government's fiscal nightmare—spending on debt service (payments to bondholders) is increasing as the government is cutting spending in other areas such as defense, infrastructure, or social services. It is a nightmare pre-revolutionary Russia and countless emerging markets before and since have experienced.

The available financial and economic data show a very clear increase in capital inflows to Russia in the closing decades of the nineteenth century, as well as a reduction in the interest rates international investors on the global capital market charged Russian borrowers. The capital inflow was coincident with relatively rapid economic growth in Russia. According to Gregory's estimates, overall Russian net national product (NNP) grew at a compound annual growth rate of nearly 5 percent from 1892 to 1903. However, in per capita

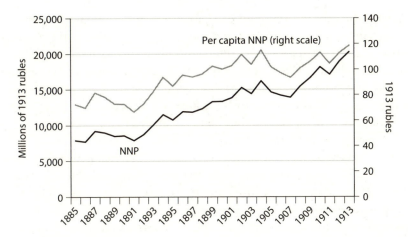

FIGURE 1.5. Russian net national product. Source: Gregory, *Russian National Income*, 56–58.

terms, the increase was just over 3 percent, as Russia's population increased from 120 to 139 million people over the same period (see Figure 1.5).[73] While these figures may not seem impressive in light of recent growth rates posted by so-called emerging markets such as China, or indeed postcommunist Russia, within the context of global growth rates of the late nineteenth century, they were very high.

This growth in turn coincided with a boom across various sectors of the Russian economy. The railroad network and the traffic on it increased at a rapid pace, with the length of the network more than doubling between 1885 and 1900, while total passenger-kilometers rose by 231 percent in the same period.[74] Russian oil production grew by 448 percent between 1885 and 1903, representing an annualized rate of 9.9 percent.[75] Between 1898 and 1902, Russia was the largest oil producer in the world and, with the United States, accounted for more than 95 percent of global oil production.[76] Pig iron production increased by 333 percent between 1887 and 1902, an annualized growth rate of more than 10 percent.[77] Rising domestic consumer demand reflected this growth in the industrial sector. Cotton consumption in Russia increased by 82 percent between 1888 and 1905, with a growing share of it being met by a thriving domestic industry, which provided merely 13 percent of domestic consumption in 1888 but fully 37 percent in 1905.[78]

That the data show substantial inflows of capital, at cheaper rates, coinciding with rapid economic growth in Russia during the closing decades of the nineteenth century is indisputable. There is, however, reason to doubt—on the basis of the data alone—that this marked shift was a result of Witte's activities as finance minister. Considering the data on the stock of Russian securities traded in the Paris market (Figure 1.1), for example, the amount of securities more than tripled in cash terms, and roughly quadrupled in notional terms between 1888 and 1892, the year Witte took office as finance minister. The FDI figures Girault offers (Figure 1.2) show a smaller but still considerable increase of more than 52 percent in the same short period. Clearly, Paris began to warm to Russia before Witte's appointment as finance minister, which was a sudden, not premeditated, move, and thus neither signaled to nor was expected by investors making decisions in, for instance, 1890.

At first glance, Gregory's data seem to cloud the picture in that they show a positive net foreign investment position between 1887 and 1891 (Figure 1.3). The sharp and sustained negative move in the account, implying net borrowings from overseas, ostensibly supports the idea that Witte represented a seismic shift in the Russian government's financial grand strategy. But Gregory's figures need to be taken in context. Specifically, even if Vyshnegradskii infamously strove to maintain grain exports at the time, following the dictum "we ourselves will starve, but we will export,"[79] the 1890–91 famine did negatively impact the Russian balance of payments. The year 1892 is frequently seen as the point at which Russian government policy shifted decisively away from reliance on grain exports and in favor of debt issuance as a means to build gold reserves, with a view to eventually adopting the gold standard. However, Girault notes that already in 1891, the government had drawn down Russian Treasury and State Bank deposits abroad to the tune of approximately 300 million francs.[80] Indeed, Girault refers to the balances accumulated abroad by the Russian state in the 1888 to 1891 period as *"hot-money gouvernementale"* on a short-term rather than investment basis—a liquid rainy day fund to be raided in the event of a poor harvest or other such event that would hurt the trade balance.[81] Given this context for the buildup of Russian assets abroad, the positive net foreign investment position in Gregory's figures between 1888 and 1891 needs to be heavily discounted.

The data pertaining to the real economy similarly do not suggest a clear break between Witte and his predecessors in terms of economic growth. True, the 4.7 percent annualized growth rate for NNP during the 1892 to 1903 period is higher than both the 1.4 percent rate of the previous seven years and the 3.4 percent rate for the entire 1885 to 1913 period.[82] However, the impact of policy on real economic growth is seldom instantaneous, and at least some portion of the higher growth rates of the 1892 to 1903 period is attributable to the policies of Witte's predecessors, to say nothing of exogenous factors. Moreover, from a sectoral perspective, the pre-Witte years can hardly be considered a period of stasis in critical areas of the Russian economy. Russian pig iron production grew at an annualized rate of 12 percent from 1887 to 1892 as against 8.1 percent during Witte's tenure in the finance ministry.[83] The oil industry showed a 13.9

percent annualized growth in production from 1885 to 1892 as compared to a 7.5 percent rate during the Witte era.[84]

Perhaps the clearest evidence that Witte's assumption of the reins in the finance ministry did not represent a major break is reflected in the data on yield spreads (Figure 1.4). The yield data clearly show that investors did not greet Witte's appointment as a positive surprise—indeed, the financial press suggests that in some places, such as Berlin, the reaction was quite the opposite.[85] More significant than the immediate reaction to Witte's appointment are the broader changes in spreads. True, Witte's tenure in the finance ministry coincided with spreads falling as low as 52 basis points over consols, versus 140 basis points when he took office—a reduction of 88 basis points. However, by the time Witte took office, spreads had already fallen dramatically from their highs of 313 basis points in December 1882. That the bulk (66 percent) of Russia's peak-to-trough spread contraction occurred before Witte's 1892 appointment, and well in advance of Witte's introduction of the gold standard in 1897, suggests that, at best, investors were motivated by expectations that Russia would eventually adopt the gold standard, and that the actual fact of gold standard membership itself conferred only marginal benefits vis-à-vis Russia's sovereign borrowing costs.[86]

Historians of late Imperial Russia—who broadly agree that Witte's adoption of the gold standard opened the floodgates to foreign capital—may be surprised to learn that the actual adoption of the gold standard had a relatively small impact on Russia's cost of capital in the international bond market; however, it is less surprising from the standpoint of recent work by economists and historians of finance. Although earlier work by Bordo and Rockoff suggested the gold standard represented a "Good Housekeeping Seal of Approval" in international bond markets, the scholarly consensus over the past 20 years has shifted away from this view to emphasize factors such as geopolitics, institutions, a range of macroeconomic fundamentals, and, most recently, the microeconomics of the sovereign lending business as other influences on capital flows.[87] In this sense, the Russian experience in the late nineteenth century supports skepticism of the Bordo-Rockoff thesis, which much of the historical scholarship on Witte implicitly accepts.

A notable outlier in the work on Witte is economist Paul Gregory's 1979 article "The Russian Balance of Payments, the Gold Standard, and Monetary Policy." Gregory paints a generally positive picture of Witte's decision to adopt the gold standard, arguing on the basis of his net foreign investment calculations that capital inflows were higher than previously thought, and that the gold standard boosted Russian growth rates by about half a percent per annum.[88] Importantly, however, he devotes no attention to bond market time series data on relative spreads, offering instead a comparison of five 5-year averages of discount rates in Saint Petersburg, Berlin, and Paris. Furthermore, only three of the five subperiods he cites cover the pre-1897 period.[89] He acknowledges that if successful adoption of the gold standard had been anticipated before 1897, "the benefits would have begun to accrue well before full convertibility." He notes, however, that "considerable uncertainty continued to prevail until at least 1895, largely due to Russia's past history of unfortunate military ventures which forced the printing of money and the setting aside of notions of convertibility."[90] Again, the yield data (see Figure 1.4) very clearly show a sustained drop in yield spreads for at least a decade prior to the 1897 adoption of the gold standard, suggesting that investors were—whether because of the gold standard or for some other reason—on the margin, viewing Russia as less risky, showing Gregory's skepticism of the gold standard having been "priced in" by markets to be misplaced. That Gregory's conclusions rest on what he himself acknowledges as "the heroic assumption" that the increase in the foreign share of net investment he highlights was due to the adoption of the gold standard brings them further into question in light of the more recent work by economists and economic historians on the influence of the gold standard on global capital flows.[91]

The numerical record, then, shows that Witte's appointment as finance minister in September 1892 was far less of a watershed in Russia's economic and financial history than some would suggest. Whether considering financial market data on foreign capital flows, national income account data, or indicators of industrial production, it is clear that many of the positive developments in Russian economic performance for which Witte receives credit, in fact, preceded him. A comparison of Russian economic and financial policymaking before and after 1892 helps explain why this was the case.

The Evolution of the Witte System

Witte's policies as finance minister became known to historians as the Witte System. Its key components included the expansion and rationalization of ownership in the railroad network—often by bringing private lines into government ownership—the use of protective tariffs to develop domestic industry, and the financing of the state's increased role through indirect taxation and borrowing on the international bond market. With a view to facilitating the latter, adoption of the gold standard, which occurred in 1897, became a foundational element of the system. As much as this complex of policies came to be associated with Witte, it represented little that was new.

Notwithstanding the attention Witte's introduction of the gold standard in 1897 earned him, monetary affairs were probably the least innovative area of his policies. Ukhov ties Russia's first external loan to the Hope & Co. bond issue of 1769.[92] As early as 1839, finance minister G. F. Kankrin, realizing the importance of a stable currency, oversaw the monetary reform that introduced the credit ruble, which would last through Witte's reform of 1897.[93] After the Crimean War, Reutern revived attempts to stabilize the currency, only to see his work set back by the Turkish War of 1877–78.[94] Indeed, Crisp credits Reutern and his decision to require the payment of customs duties in gold as the first major step by the Russian government to adopt the gold standard.[95] Bunge and Vyshnegradskii largely continued this policy.

Ironically, one of the first controversies Witte generated as a newly appointed finance minister was to take steps suggesting he was breaking with his predecessors in the area of monetary policy. Having been under the influence of the Slavophile group, led by the publisher of *Moskovskie Vedomosti*, Mikhail Katkov, and the reactionary Ober-Procurator of the Holy Synod, Konstantin Pobedonostsev, Witte initially favored an inflationary policy and a fiat currency, rather than a fixed exchange rate regime.[96] One of his earliest advisors was A. Ia. Antonovich, a professor of economics at the University of Kiev, whom he knew from his days running the Southwestern Railway, and who was a key figure in the inflationary camp in Russia.[97] It was only after an alarmed senior bureaucrat, A. N. Kulomzin, appealed to the finance ministry agent in Paris, Arthur Raffalovich, for help that the course of policy began to shift. Raffalovich arranged for Bunge and I. P. Shipov to tutor the novice finance minister on monetary policy, even having them translate foreign works on the subject.[98]

The intervention of Raffalovich at this stage is notable and a reminder that the Ministry of Finance maintained a network of agents and active contacts in foreign financial centers well before Witte's arrival as minister. Indeed, it was Vyshnegradskii who oversaw the reorientation in Russian borrowing from Germany to France during Bismarck's infamous *Lombardverbot* of 1887, and the expansion of Russian borrowing in the newly active Parisian market for Russian debt. Acknowledging this, Anan'ich and Ganelin nonetheless credit Witte for revolutionizing the Institute of Commercial Agents of the finance ministry. In their telling, Witte brought life to a sleepy bureaucracy originally established in 1848. He increased ministry control of its agents, broadening their geographical and substantive coverage areas—adding an agent in Washington, DC, in 1893 and thereafter agents in Constantinople, Brussels, and Yokohama. In October 1898, he upgraded their status so that they would be included in the diplomatic lists of Russian outposts abroad.[99]

Anan'ich and Ganelin posit Witte as more than just a skilled bureaucratic infighter quick to expand his agency's influence; they also characterize him as a capable manager of people and a talent scout. In support of this, they cite his appointment of S. S. Tatishchev to the London financial agency, and his appointment of M. V. Rutkovskii, a transport engineer, who had earlier served as the Ministry of Ways and Communications representative in Washington, as the new financial agent in that city.[100] Further evincing his buildup of a cadre of trusted officials, they mention his appointment of M. F. Mering as vice-director of the Credit Chancellery—the key department of the Ministry of Finance that was the interface between the Russian government and financial markets.[101]

The thesis advanced by Anan'ich and Ganelin overstates the quality of the people Witte chose for key posts. Setting aside the potentially disastrous appointment of Antonovich, whom Raffalovich and Bunge quickly sidelined, neither the Washington nor the London financial agent was equal in quality to Raffalovich, who was appointed as ministry agent in Paris by Vyshnegradskii, not Witte. Raffalovich would remain a vocal and extremely effective advocate of the Russian position in Paris financial circles well past Witte's departure from the ministry. The contrast with Tatishchev, for example, could not be starker. Born into an Odessa banking family of Jewish origins, to which Witte was once a tutor, Raffalovich was well known in French financial circles, with several publications on financial matters to his credit, and, as his extensive and direct correspondence with senior French bankers and ministers attests, was arguably more powerful than the Russian ambassador in Paris.[102] Tatishchev, by contrast, was a distinguished diplomatic historian, but hardly a financial wheeler and dealer of Raffalovich's caliber.[103] Indeed, it was particularly telling that, at crucial moments of negotiation with bankers in New York and London in 1898, 1899, and 1906, Witte would send more seasoned figures—including Raffalovich in the latter case—to deal with the American and British banks, or that meetings would happen in Paris.

Moreover, even Witte's appointments in Saint Petersburg were less stellar than Anan'ich and Ganelin suggest. Their praise of Witte's appointment of M. F. Mering to the Credit Chancellery, for example, is particularly curious in view of Witte's own description of him in his memoirs. Mering, the son of a wealthy Kievan doctor, met Witte's stepdaughter through his first wife Sonia while serving as vice-director of the Ministry of Finance's Credit Chancellery. After they were married, Mering moved on to Kiev to take up a position at a commercial bank. He became involved in some speculative positions that went against him, and used Witte's name to fend off creditors. While a group of Kievan businessmen looking to curry favor with the minister of finance ultimately bailed out the bank, Mering eventually fled to Paris, at which point Sonia left him. Witte, incensed over the entire affair, disowned both of them.[104] That the appointment of such a character would be used to make the case that Witte was a fine spotter of talent is striking.

In industrial affairs, Witte rightly gets credit for offering a more comprehensive philosophical basis for his industrial policy than his predecessors did for theirs. Certainly, his pamphlet, "On Nationalism: The National Economy and Friedrich List" (1889), an extensive commentary on the German economist's ideas, did not have any analogues in his predecessors' work. That it lifted much of its material verbatim from List and was likely ghostwritten, however, makes it less impressive as an original manifesto.[105] Indeed, even in terms of industrial policy, Witte's predecessor Vyshnegradskii engaged in much preparatory work. As Stepanov notes, Vyshnegradskii—a mentor to Witte from their time in the railroad industry—came from the same world of entrepreneurship and engineering.[106] Moreover, as early as his December 1886 memo to Alexander III, he emphasized the need to adopt a comprehensive "national economic policy," the foundations of which would be a strengthening of protective tariffs, the adoption of an alcohol and tobacco monopoly, and reform of the railroad system and tariffs, among other things.[107] While Witte implemented many of these policies, then, and was perhaps better suited as a propagandist and politician than his predecessor, his role in conceiving the basic outlines of late nineteenth-century Russia's industrial policy was not pivotal.

That the economic performance of Russia showed continuity before and after Witte's assumption of the reins in the finance ministry in 1892 reflects a general continuity in Russian monetary and industrial policy. Witte's role was largely to refine and implement policies—the basic outlines of which his predecessors had laid out. To this end, his statement in his memoirs, "In a slight measure my immediate predecessors, Bunge and Vyshnegradskii, prepared our finances for the introduction of the gold standard," is indeed grudging.[108] Even in his appointments, he was less revolutionary and less skilled than some suggest.

Good Tactics, Poor Strategy

Of course, even if Witte was less the visionary than he is sometimes made out to be, he did succeed in implementing some of his major policy aims. In the capital markets in particular, he succeeded in both continuing to float new loans and fight detractors of Russian credit. However, his capital markets strategy was also marked by an elementary but costly unforced strategic error that would haunt the regime in the early twentieth century.

Witte is rightly praised for his skilled use of his Paris agent, Arthur Raffalovich—an Odessa-born Jew who spent much of his life in Paris after emigrating from Russia, dividing his time between writing academic tracts on economics and wheeling and dealing on behalf of the Tsarist government, apparently having few qualms about serving as the chief promoter and fundraiser in Paris financial circles for one of the most anti-Semitic regimes in the world.[109] Raffalovich's activities included executing an elaborate propaganda effort on behalf of Witte in France that involved extensive bribery of the financial press. The effort took place with the knowledge and even approval of the French government, and was so successful in perverting news coverage of the Bourse that the government engaged police assets to monitor activity and rumors in the financial markets and report their observations to the government. The archives of the Prefecture de Police de Paris and the police reports it contains on rumors swirling at the Bourse are arguably a more reliable source on happenings in the market than the contemporary French financial press.[110] Tsarist bribery of the French financial press has been the subject of recent scholarship by Marc Flandreau and Vincent Bignon, who found that a racket developed, whereby less scrupulous and opportunistic newspapers sought to use the threat of bad publicity to extract rents from potential bond issuers, including the Russian government.[111] This possible blowback notwithstanding, Witte's energetic and hands-on approach to managing through Raffalovich Russia's relations with the Paris market, and the major heads of the haute banque in particular, was a major contribution on his part. Indeed, his extraordinary enlistment by the Tsar, after he had left the finance ministry, to help put together a major loan in the aftermath of the 1905 Revolution underscores the degree to which Witte's personal relations with Parisian bankers developed into an asset.

Witte also proved to be a smooth operator in the German markets. The most frequently cited manifestation of this speculative genius is his infamous short squeeze on speculators in the Berlin ruble market.[112] As the French consul in Warsaw wrote after the fact on 31 October 1894 to Foreign Minister Hanotaux in Paris, Berlin speculators had built up especially large short positions in the ruble in response to spreading rumors of the Tsar's failing health.[113] Having foreseen this—not least since bearish bets on the ruble were a frequent and popular trade among Berlin speculators—Witte immediately wired Russia's bankers in Berlin, initially to feed the short move by acting as counterparties to short sales.[114] Having encouraged a buildup in ruble short positions, especially on 27 and 28 October, Witte then used his administrative power to prohibit Russian banks from sending credit rubles abroad. The result was a short squeeze as speculators who had built up short positions expecting to easily repurchase rubles in Berlin—where they were usually abundant—found a dearth of rubles, which drove their price higher.[115] The ruble-mark rate rose in a single day from 2.18 marks per ruble to 2.32 and even to 2.34—at more than 7 percent, a truly dramatic intraday move for a currency market—even as the rate in Saint Petersburg and Warsaw remained steady at 2.18.[116] While some smaller Warsaw financiers smuggled rubles into Berlin, the amounts were not sufficient to ease the situation. As the consul remarked, Witte had taught the Berlin market "a lesson"—that they should stop betting on declines in the ruble, because he could at a moment's notice create a short squeeze.[117]

However, for all his skill in talking French markets into continuing to finance his industrialization program and squeezing of the bears in Berlin, Witte was remarkably negligent of the London market, particularly in his early years as finance minister. This was a significant oversight, not only because London was a major financial center in the 1890s, but also because—as Witte and his successors would appreciate in the early twentieth century—relying on a funding base that was too narrow could prove costly in the long run.

Economic historians rightly point to Paris, Berlin, and even New York as major international financial centers during the first modern age of globalization, but it was London that was the true center of global finance in the late nineteenth and early twentieth centuries. While the stock of French capital that was invested abroad—much of it in Russia—nearly tripled between 1875 and 1913, the quantity of British capital nearly quadrupled in the same period.[118] The nominal value of the securities traded on the London Stock Exchange (LSE) rose from £2.3 billion in 1873 to £11.3 billion in 1913, making it more liquid than both the New York Stock Exchange and Paris Bourse combined.[119] With a membership larger than that of its competitors in Paris or New York, the LSE also offered the prospect of more competitive commissions.[120] Yet, despite all the general activity in London, the Russian finance ministry focused far more on Paris and Berlin in terms of the issuance of debt and its relevant public relations efforts.

While the highest levels of the Russian finance ministry may have been blind to opportunities outside the French market, this did not prevent other figures in Russian financial circles from trying to build ties in Anglo-American markets. In what must stand out as one of the most cringeworthy business overtures of the era, Alexander Koch wrote to "J. Purpont [sic!] Morgan" trying to remind one of the most powerful financiers of the age—the "King of America" in his telling—about his own apprenticeship in the Morgan firm three decades prior.[121] Noting that he and his colleague, the Austrian-born banker Adolph Rothstein, had been key players in Russian international bond issues over the past dozen years, Koch informed Morgan of their determination that "the time has come to secure for Russian funds the English market—which, as you know, is the first of the world."[122]

After painting a picture of high demand in London for Russian business by mentioning several unsolicited overtures to the Russian government for London bond deals from a range of bankers, Koch switched to flattery. He claimed he and his partners were "of the opinion that no one could so successfully take in hand the Russian flag as your English firm. You know, better than we do, the English market, and maybe you won't share the opinion that the time is just the right one, still there it is."[123]

Acknowledging that at a time when Russia and Britain were still geopolitical rivals in Central Asia and elsewhere, and that "all depends of political constellations," he nevertheless hoped that "if the right moment is not there yet—it may be about to come."[124] Backtracking from his portrayal of a Russian government besieged by interest in the London market, Koch proceeded to say, "my letter's purpose is to know, if you are willing to take, with us, the leadership of Russian business in London, when the right time comes."[125] Wanting to keep discussions discrete to avoid "useless rumors about Russian business," he said "we don't seek you in order to bring to our Government the help of the large means of your big firm—we want a flag and a name in London and we think that the go and spirit that you have shown everywhere will insure [sic] a glorious success to these transactions."[126]

Despite the groveling tone and clumsy botching of Morgan's name, Koch's overture nevertheless reflected an awareness of the shift of financial power not only across the Channel to London but indeed across the ocean, to New York and the House of Morgan. The approach only underscores the myopia of the Russian finance ministry under Witte for not having made similar moves.

Morgan's response to Koch's overture was unsurprisingly cool. While the American's bank did partake in an issue of Russian 4 percent bonds in March 1898, it was not ready to undertake major underwriting obligations.[127] Writing to Koch on 24 March 1898, the American financier said the moment was not right for him to expand into Russian business in a major way, citing a range of reasons from the death of a relative to "the complicated condition of politics in the United States, as well as in Europe."[128] Nevertheless, that he responded to the Koch overture is telling, as was his comment that "it is not unlikely that something can be done later, but at the moment I must ask you to let the whole matter remain in abeyance until political matters [settle] down somewhat" and Spanish-American tensions eased.[129]

The Koch-Morgan episode does lend credence to the claim by some historians that 1898–99 was a potential turning point in Russian borrowing patterns. Nevertheless, the assertion by Ruth Amende Roosa, in the closing years of the Cold War—a time of extremely limited archival materials—that a "high point" of the Russo-American financial relationship occurred between 1896 and 1906 appears overstated.[130] In her telling, a growing French reluctance to take on more Russian debt and British disinterest rooted in political and economic reasons, coinciding with a rapidly growing American financial sector, led to the strengthening of Russo-American ties.[131] Such an argument exaggerates the depth of ties. It focuses on the activities of the New York Life Insurance Company as a player in the Russian retail financial services market and on J. P. Morgan's role in the market for Russian bonds, but devotes less attention to the First National City Bank of New York—the largest American bank at the time, and one that was "very much interested in Russia."[132] From a global capital flows perspective, the case of New York Life is less noteworthy, since by the admission of proponents of the "high point" thesis it was "never a major force in the Russian bond market," contributing instead to Russian public finances by channeling the savings of Russian policyholders into the domestic money market.[133] Roosa herself acknowledges that in the case of Morgan, relations progressed "in fits and starts" through 1906, but were "largely unproductive."[134]

The notion advanced in some of the literature, that Witte drove early Russian overtures to the American financial market, is particularly curious. Roosa, for example, credits Witte with the earliest Russian attempts to penetrate the American market for sovereign debt issues, claiming that Witte was thinking about this prior to 1892, when he was still minister of ways and communications, but offers no specific evidence to that effect.[135] Her only specific citation in this vein is a November 1898 note to the Tsar from Witte containing a generic comment about the need to ensure the continuation of foreign loans to afford the country "resources against poverty" and pointing to the proposal of an American consular official in Germany, that American banks help provide Russia with funding.[136] The December 1898 visit to New York by the ministry's financial agent in Washington, M. V. Rutkovskii, and a senior ministry official from Saint Petersburg, A. I. Vyshnegradskii, thus marked the first major overture by Russian officials to the American bankers, including Morgan.[137] However, as the Koch episode shows, this was emphatically not the first move by the Russian side toward building ties with the American financial community.

Anan'ich and Bovykin agree with Roosa on the inflection point, dating Witte's first attempts "to open the American market for Russian loans and restore relations with the English market" as occurring in 1898–99.[138] While they acknowledge the London placement of £2,975,000 of state-backed bonds for the Moscow-Vindava-Rybinsk Railway by Schröders, they rightly point out the heavy involvement of Berlin and Amsterdam houses in the deal. Moreover, the placement's limited nature hardly signaled a return of the Russian government to the London bond market along the lines that Witte and some of the British bankers had been contemplating.[139] The $10 million government-backed railway loan issued in the United States similarly fell short of representing a major opening of New York to Russian bonds, given that New York Life, which had a branch in Saint Petersburg, covered 80 percent of the issue, while the Saint Petersburg International Commercial Bank covered 20 percent.[140] Crucially, the negotiations between the International Commercial

Bank, acting as a front for the finance ministry, and J. P. Morgan and National City proved fruitless.[141]

Perhaps more important than the question of who should be credited with making an effort to build Russian-American financial ties in the Witte period is the question of why such ties failed to materialize in any substantial fashion. Taken at face value, Morgan's letter to Koch suggests a reluctance to enter into a new market at a time of personal and political upheaval. In Roosa's narrative, the failure of a great Russo-American deal grew out of Morgan's own extreme caution about risking capital in "a relatively unknown part of the world," as well as tactical errors on the part of the Russians.[142] Writing on 30 December 1898 to the American ambassador in Saint Petersburg E. A. Hitchcock, the New York lawyer William M. Ivens, of Ivens, Kidder, and Melcher, explained that the sudden appearance of the Russian delegation actually backfired in that it "evidenced considerable anxiety on the part of Russia" and constituted "quite a sufficient contradiction of their statement" that Russia was not in dire need of additional foreign capital. That the Russian visit prompted a great deal of talk in the press, and that "strong Jewish and German influences were at work here" did not help matters, in Ivens's account.[143]

Last, and unsurprisingly, internal tensions on the Russian side added to the problems. The Russian ambassador was perturbed that the US embassy in Saint Petersburg gave the deal its initial push and that Vyshnegradskii was being sent directly by the Ministry of Finance, effectively sidelining the embassy in Washington. Rutkovskii for his part resented his own ministry's apparent opinion that their man in America was not up to carrying out the task at hand without direct in-person supervision from a superior in Saint Petersburg.[144] Morgan, roping in Barings through its New York affiliates Baring, Magoun & Co., eventually made the Russians a lowball offer of 92—an 8 percent discount to par value—which they promptly turned down, rightly saying that accepting such a bid would in itself create a panic in the marketplace.[145] The negotiations were restarted in the late spring of 1899 with a 27 April letter from the American chargé in Saint Petersburg to Morgan suggesting that the parties resume the loan talks, but they were ultimately unsuccessful.[146]

The degree to which Witte's finance ministry ignored the London and New York markets is starkly evident from the correspondence in the Baring Archive about a renewed attempt to revive the idea of an Anglo-American deal in 1899. The correspondence, spanning two months in mid-1899, provides insight into how some of the leading financial institutions in the world at the time—banks such as Baring Brothers, J. P. Morgan & Co., First National City Bank of New York, and Mendelssohn & Co, among others—dealt with Russian affairs at the height of Witte's power as Russia's finance minister. While no loan resulted from all the back-and-forth, the episode nevertheless underscores the state of relations between the Russian finance ministry and the London financial community.

On 2 May 1899, Barings in London cabled its New York affiliate Baring, Magoun & Co. a request to probe its New York counterparts about a potential Russian loan. The London headquarters said it was being offered a £10 million loan by the government, with an additional £10 million option. London was planning to offer J. P. Morgan in New York and N. M. Rothschild in London a lead role in the syndicate but first wanted New York to sound out James Stillman at the First National City Bank of New York—forerunner to today's Citigroup—about his interest and to lay out its initial thinking on terms.[147]

In negotiating bond deals, merchant banks such as Barings agreed several deal parameters with the prospective issuer.[148] The first two of these were the coupon interest rate and the underwriters' price. The coupon rate was the interest paid out on the face value of the bond, but underwriters frequently negotiated a wholesale price that represented a discount to the face value, at which they would buy the bond. Such an arrangement would in turn imply a higher effective interest rate for the issuer. Thus, a 5 percent bond bought by the underwriters at 92 would, all else equal, in fact represent an interest rate of 5.43 percent to the issuer. The banks underwriting the deal would in turn offer the loan to the public at a premium to the price they paid to the issuer. Having bought the bond from a government at 92, the banks might, for example, sell the issue to the public at 97, collecting the difference, and passing on an issue with an effective yield of only 5.15 percent to the investor. The banks arranging the deal also frequently negotiated a delayed and stepwise disbursement of funds to the issuer, which further added to their margins and reduced the effective yield of the issue to the borrower. Payments from the issuing syndicate to the borrower frequently occurred over a period of several months, with the balance being held back as deposits at the banks in question. These deposits in turn earned interest at a rate negotiated between the banks and issuer that was typically at a level that would represent another profit stream for the banks.

Contracts frequently included provisions for defraying the advertising and other expenses the banks incurred in undertaking the deal, and options for the banks to issue additional bonds. Finally, the issuer was sometimes contractually allowed to "call" or redeem bonds early, which it might do in the event that rates declined and it decided to convert the existing higher rate bond into one paying a lower rate. In some cases, contracts forbade issuers from engaging in conversion operations that would reduce the effective return to investors; in other cases, issuers were contractually restricted from issuing additional debt that might depress demand for existing bonds in the secondary market and/or raise the default risk of the borrower in question. Today, most investment banks have their own sales forces of retail and institutional brokers; however, in the late nineteenth and early twentieth centuries, the smaller merchant banks, such as Barings and Rothschilds, frequently used third-party brokers. By contrast, larger French banks, for example Crédit Lyonnais, could rely on their extensive retail branch network to distribute loans, at times obviating the need to formally list a security on the Paris Bourse.

In the case of the Russian loan that Barings was contemplating, the bank's initial thinking was to bid 95 for a 4 percent bond, negotiating up to 96, with a plan to float the loan to the public at 98.[149] Within a day of its initial message, on 3 May 1899, Baring, Magoun wired London that National City was indeed interested in the issue—to the tune of as much as $20 million.[150] In a more detailed letter sent on the same day as the initial cable to New York, however, Lord Revelstoke, the head of Barings in London, said that "the whole thing is as yet so vague that we shall not enter into further details unless we succeed in establishing serious and direct negotiations with an accredited agent of the Government."[151] The next day Revelstoke wrote in greater detail to the Dutch merchant bank Hope & Co.—long since overshadowed by its counterparts in London, Paris, and Berlin but still frequently involved in Russian finance because of long-standing historical ties with the government. Revelstoke's letter reveals that a "Mr. H. Muranyi, of the Banque de Commerce Privée of St. Petersburg" approached Barings; however, even this contact was not direct, but rather through a man named W. Betzold who had been passing through London.[152] On 4 May, Barings wrote to Hope saying that Muranyi was headed to Amsterdam and looking to see Hope about the proposed loan, adding that Barings itself was holding off on making any proposals until it could "negotiate direct with the Minister."[153]

In a 4 May letter to Barings, Hope indicated its own skepticism over the entire affair. Showing interest "in principle" in a Russian state loan, Hope were quick to agree with Barings that it made sense to insist on negotiating only with an accredited agent of the Russian finance ministry, adding that, in any case, "we do not think that Mr. Muranyi's Bank has an important political influence in St. Petersburg," before further adding that its representatives would be willing to see Muranyi during his visit to Amsterdam.[154] Hope pointed out that, all else equal, another Russian loan in a Dutch market that had already seen many of them—as part of larger deals centered around the German and French markets—would not excite investors, but a sterling loan offered by a major London house would see demand in Holland. Hope explained that such a loan would simultaneously signal that "the English market would once more be open for Russian Government Bonds" and be read as an event pregnant with political significance.[155] Hope thought a syndicate bid of 96 would be high, assuming a 2.5 percent margin over the wholesale price, but was also conscious that the Russian government would try to drive a hard bargain, even though its representatives coming to Barings was probably an indication of having been turned down in Berlin and Paris.[156]

The next day, Hope wrote Barings immediately after meeting with Muranyi, having concluded that he was not an official agent of the Russian government. Indeed, it was apparent that he had no instructions from the Russian finance ministry whatsoever but was instead fishing for a deal based on talk that an Anglo-Dutch transaction would be "quite agreeable" to Witte were it to happen.[157] Having approached Barings on these thin premises and found the bank to be open in principle to a deal, Muranyi cabled Saint Petersburg trying to drum up firm interest at the finance ministry, not allowing his lack of partners in the Russian capital or Hope's skepticism concerning pricing to deter him.[158] Later the same day, Muranyi rushed back to Hope to say he had heard that Witte's agent was in Paris and willing to see him, and to ask Hope to have Barings send a telegraphic code key so that Muranyi could communicate with the London house about the deal.[159] Revelstoke replied coolly that "if Mr. Muranyi has any definite proposition to make we should prefer him to approach us in the usual way, we do not therefore send him a telegraph code to Paris," adding in a follow-up cable, "we shall not of course think of competing at any price near 97."[160]

Just two days later, Revelstoke wrote to Hope again, saying that Barings received another query on Russian business from a different angle. In this case, Revelstoke related that it was "represented" to Barings that Tatishchev, the Russian finance ministry's official agent in London, wanted to know if Barings would be willing to issue and domicile Russian government Treasury bills with a one-year maturity.[161] Barings replied that "being Agents as we are of the Government in this City, we should of course be glad to attend to any domiciliation they may elect to place under our care," but that, as with the Muranyi approach, Barings refused to enter into any firm discussions until "approached by an accredited Agent."[162] Echoing a comment Hope made in their 5 May note about the "great value" the Russian government would see in a British deal, given that the other major markets were closed to further Russian issues, Barings said, "It is obvious to every person interested in Russian Finance that the Government wants money, and that this is the only open market. They are no doubt endeavoring in a totally irresponsible way to induce the Russians to borrow in London, for the sake of earning a broker's commission."[163] In any case, both banks agreed that while a small Treasury bill issue for £1 million to £2 million at 4 percent was possible, if the Russians were looking to float a larger loan in the near future, it would be advisable not to risk dampening demand for the larger issue by tying up liquidity in a smaller and less critical loan.[164]

In a flurry of cables over the next few days, Barings communicated with its New York affiliates, Baring, Magoun & Co., regarding management of the American side of the potential syndicate. London was keen to prevent an apparently parallel track of talks between G. F. Crane and a certain Bernstein from spoiling an eventual deal, saying that J. S. Morgan in London were being kept appraised; so Barings in London should be allowed to take the lead in any discussions with the Russian government, to which Crane replied that he had suspended his talks.[165] Over the course of the next week, the New York and London outposts of the Barings empire discussed details such as the potential size, price, and distribution among syndicate members of a potential deal.[166] Pricing discussions came to a screeching halt, however, on 19 May, when New York cabled London saying that J. P. Morgan in New York claimed to have been totally unaware of any discussions being led from London about a potential Russian deal. New York wrote: "Strongly urge having interview with J. P. Morgan and explaining entire situation."[167] Morgan had been in contact with Barings in late 1898, but discussions suggesting initial interest from the London representatives of the American house had come to naught after New York brought them to an end.[168]

At this point, the discussions turned toward issues of syndicate membership, with London raising the matter—in response to a telegram from Betzold—of German participation in the syndicate via the houses of Mendelssohn and Speyer.[169] Having sent an agent to Saint Petersburg to speak directly but without commitments to the Russian finance ministry, Revelstoke simultaneously negotiated to provisionally include Mendelssohn, but not Speyer, thus neutralizing a potential rival by including him in the syndicate.[170] The Barings chief next arranged an in-person meeting with J. P. Morgan in London to discuss the Russian loan and reconcile what appeared to have been two parallel tracks of negotiations.[171]

Following the London meeting with Morgan, Revelstoke cabled his New York associates to fill them in on the substance of his chat. The American financier was strongly opposed to the inclusion of Stillman's National City Bank, wanting instead to limit the American participation in the syndicate to that of Barings and Morgan, and offering to take a full half of the issue. Although Revelstoke felt some qualms about doing so in view of Morgan's earlier apparent involvement in the Russian discussions, he insisted that National City remain part of the syndicate, as he sought to build a broader relationship between his firm and the growing American bank. He closed by saying that, according to the latest information he had received, the government was unlikely to negotiate in any case, but he wanted, nonetheless, to make sure Stillman at National City was aware of Barings's loyalty.[172] J. P. Morgan sulked, but stopped short of refusing to join altogether, saying that he was "thinking it over."[173]

In a detailed letter of 26 May, Revelstoke wrote to his counterpart, Stillman, at National City, updating him on a Mexican issue, as well as the ongoing Russian talks. Revelstoke pointed out that Baring, Magoun had felt J. P. Morgan out about a potential Russian deal "some months ago" but that those talks had "ended in nothing."[174] Having been approached most recently "from a totally distinct Russian source," they felt free to talk to National City, and had so informed the House of Morgan through its London outpost, J. S. Morgan. London apparently did not relay the information fully to New York. Meanwhile, the contacts that were dealing with the Baring-Morgan syndicate in the earlier Russian talks reappeared, leading J. P. Morgan in New York to resume discussions. When Morgan met with Revelstoke in London on the way back to New York from Paris, his position showed that he saw the deal through more than a narrow financial lens. In insisting on National City's exclusion from the lead role in New York, and declaring his willingness to take on £5 million of the issue by himself, he, in Revelstoke's view, "made it a point that he laid little stress on the pecuniary advantages of the business."[175] Revelstoke, for his part, also clearly saw the deal at hand in a broader context, stressing to Stillman that he would refuse to give in to Morgan's demand that Barings ditch National City because he felt "bound" to stand by his offer to them, not least because of their "alliance," which he hoped would "become much closer in the future."[176] Moreover, perhaps betraying a little resentment or fear of the growing power not only of New York as a financial center but also of J. P. Morgan as a man and an institution in particular, Revelstoke went on to say that, while Morgan "would seem to dislike this idea . . . it is perhaps as well that a demonstration should now be made, to show him that such possibilities exist. He is, as you know, intolerant of any competition, and while we are sensible of the courtesy and friendship we have constantly experienced at his hands, we are convinced that this point will rise again in the near future, and that it had better be settled definitely without delay."[177] Revelstoke's closing lines underscored that the haggling between banks had taken on a more strategic and symbolic character: "The Russian affair is practically off for the moment: there is much intrigue, but it is quite possible that it may come again to the fore, in a month or six weeks' time."[178]

In a separate letter dated the same day, Thomas Baring scolded G. F. Crane for his role in the misunderstanding that had resulted in the "friction" between Barings and Morgan over the last several days. A "more than ordinarily difficult to deal with" J. P. Morgan had shown the Barings partners in London a letter from Crane. Morgan understood the letter to be an offer to undertake the American portion of the proposed Russian deal on an exclusive basis. The entire affair's deep impact on Morgan personally is clear from Baring's letter expressing his view that Morgan saw the Russian business "as his peculiar property."[179] He went on to say, "in fact his personal pride is touched, and his resentment is of that strong nature which we might expect from him knowing, as we do, his great dislike of any interference with his personal position."[180] The London partners were not seeing this sort of behavior for the first time, and Baring echoed Revelstoke's sentiments regarding Stillman, saying, "We are not disposed to giving in to this feeling, which would mean throwing over our friends, but we intend on the contrary to stick firmly to Stillman, and to try to carry through the business with or without J. P. M.'s assistance."[181] Baring took pains to point out that while his firm was not looking for a fight with Morgan, "it may be as well for him to learn thus early the true state of affairs and to appreciate that an alliance with the City Bank is a factor with which he has to reckon."[182]

By the time an exchange took place between Revelstoke and John Luden in Amsterdam on 29 May, it had become clear that the British-led Russian loan was unlikely to come to fruition in the foreseeable future. As early as 23 May, Fischel of Mendelssohn had met with Revelstoke and mentioned that his firm was arranging a government-backed railroad loan in a move that would prohibitively complicate the flotation of a sovereign bond simultaneously.[183] Betzold wrote Revelstoke from Paris on 31 May, outlining some of the terms of the deal, which was to be led by Mendelssohn, Schröder, and Lippmann, Rosenthal. On a letter of the same day, Luden wrote to Revelstoke to inform him of another offer for Russian business—in this case to help finance, through an issue of both debt and equity on a large scale, including in New York—a "railway somewhere in Siberia," with "full support from the Government."[184]

In August 1899, the Morgan firm was approached in London by the firm of Saunders & Co., export agents for a range of American metals and railroad equipment companies selling into Russia, India, Australia, and Europe.[185] Having heard of the stillborn 1898 and 1899 talks while on a recent trip to Saint Petersburg, the firm's representatives decided to try pitching Morgan on issuing Russian government debt themselves. The archival record in the Morgan Library in New York suggests that they met with some interest from J. P. "Jack" Morgan, Jr., who asked them to write out their views. Saunders & Co. sought to entice Morgan into a Russian deal by mentioning informal understandings with Rothstein for a hypothetical deal and the great potential to use American financing as a mechanism to pry open a major market for American capital goods exports. Saunders & Co. even claimed to have sent a senior partner to the United States to gauge potential interest in Russian paper, reporting "a fair consensus of opinion that the security was good; that Russia had always paid her interest, even in Crimean days, and was as likely to as any other important Government."[186] Admitting that American investors were favoring industrial issues at the moment, and that "it was quite questionable" if they would show preference to a Russian sovereign issue, they proposed issuing Russian railway bonds with government guarantees of interest payments to capitalize on the preference for industrial paper.[187]

Tellingly, however, Saunders & Co. admitted that "M. de Witte has never said, in words, Go [sic] and raise me some money—he has rather indicated I don't want any, but if you choose to offer me some, I will carefully consider it; and M. Rothstein has always talked in the same way."[188] Again, the lack of official sanction was clear, and the source of the proposal to Morgan far less credible than Barings. After months of watching the Barings-led negotiations—however peripherally—it is hardly surprising that Morgan was apparently unimpressed by Saunders's claim to have been given a private codebook by Rothstein and to be able to send someone to Saint Petersburg within 48 hours of an indication of interest.[189] The verdict was clear by mid-August. Apparently tired of engaging in Russia-related discussions dependent on questionable middlemen, the senior Morgan cabled his son, Jack, "Even if Russia Loan practicable, which it is not at the present moment, decidedly unwilling to be associated with Saunders in the matter."[190]

Although all the talk in the summer of 1899 of a Barings- and even Saunders-led Russian loan proved ultimately fruitless vis-à-vis an actual bond issue, its implications are manifold. First, the confused back-and-forth between Barings—not just one of the most powerful financial institutions in the world at the time, which the Duc de Richelieu famously called "the Sixth Great Power," but also one with a long history of being the Russian government's bank in London—and major financiers such as J. P. Morgan, Hope, and Mendelssohn highlighted a remarkable gap in the Russian finance ministry's ties with Western banks and financial centers.[191] Historians frequently portray Witte as a skilled market operator. His short squeeze of the Berlin market and active manipulation of the French press through his Paris agent Arthur Raffalovich, as well as his close contacts with the French haute banque and his counterparts in government, all contribute to the image of a man with a keen sense of markets and a broad base of valuable relationships. In looking at Russian finance from the perspective of the London markets, however, a very different picture emerges.

That leading City or Wall Street figures of Revelstoke's or Morgan's stature would even be in the position of having to consider a meeting with individuals making dubious claims to be acting in the name of the Russian government is remarkable. An analogous situation in Paris is difficult to imagine. Revelstoke and Morgan's French counterparts—Noetzlin of Paribas or Henri Germain of Crédit Lyonnais, for example—were in close and constant contact with Raffalovich, whom they knew to be Witte's personal representative in Paris and, by extension, the most influential Russian in Paris—more so than even the ambassador. Raffalovich's dialogue extended beyond the private banks to frequent contact with the French finance and foreign ministers, who in turn were in close touch with the French bankers.

The contrast with the London and New York markets could not be starker. Throughout the May 1899 discussions, Revelstoke—one of the most powerful financiers of the age—had no direct contact with the Russian financial representative in London. His willingness to see personally a private individual claiming to have a deal from the Russian finance ministry shows just how weak the ties between Witte and the London banks had become and how ineffective the Russian financial representative in London was as an intermediary between the Russian government and the London market. That Jack Morgan was seriously entertaining proposals from import-export middlemen claiming only second-order connections to the Russian finance ministry shows a similar dynamic at play vis-à-vis Russian financial representation on Wall Street.

By contrast, Raffalovich was in regular contact with the French bankers, who knew to look to him or directly to Saint Petersburg for any discussions about Russian business. Particularly revealing is that, at the point that Muranyi indicated to Hope that affairs might crystallize, the meeting with the official representative of the Russian finance ministry was to take place at the Hotel Scribe in Paris, and not in London, even though the issue at hand was being billed as a British-led loan. Moreover, that Barings, Hope, and J. P. Morgan would devote so much time and energy—including a personal meeting between the heads of the British and American firms convened specifically to discuss the Russian business—shows that their internal indications to each other of interest in doing a deal were credible.

As much as the London incident can be read as a tactical failure on the part of the Russian finance ministry and, more specifically, of Tatishchev as the official financial representative in London at the time, it also underscores a broader strategic failure on the part of Witte. The Barings correspondence very clearly shows that Tatishchev was not in regular contact with Barings. The contrast with Raffalovich is not entirely surprising given that the Paris agent was a financier, while Tatishchev's areas of expertise were diplomatic history and journalism. It is curious that, given the importance of London as a financial center, Witte did not send a more seasoned figure like Raffalovich to London. Indeed, he had sent A. I. Vyshnegradskii and M. V. Rutkovskii to New York in late 1898 to begin the earlier round of talks with Morgan's firm, but even they were sent on a specific mission, rather than on a permanent basis, to develop deep ties with the New York financial community.[192] Of course that the ministry's agent in the United States was based in Washington and not New York is itself a testament to how the ministry misdirected its efforts in the American financial community. Yet, even with this minimal American effort on the part of the Russians, the record of the correspondence between Morgan and Rothstein of the Saint Petersburg International Commercial Bank, and between Rothstein and Witte, shows Morgan to have had a closer tie during late 1898 and early 1899 through his intermediary to the Russian finance ministry than Barings did through Muranyi. It is particularly striking that the ministry—through Rothstein—told the American chargé that the rumors of a Barings-led London issue were not true, but did not communicate directly with Revelstoke on the same point.[193]

Another—and potentially more effective—option would have been to broaden the scope of Raffalovich's activities with a view to engaging him more actively in British financial circles according to the manner in which he operated in Paris. After all, Witte had done this in the past with the specific aim of winning over the London Rothschilds—who, horrified by Tsarist anti-Semitism, were reluctant to engage in Russian business—and would do so again in the future during the negotiations over the 1906 loan, which is the subject of Chapter 2.[194] These approaches, however, were limited and, rather than part of a broader strategy to build goodwill in the City, were to some extent cynical attempts to use Raffalovich's Jewish heritage to sweet-talk the London Rothschilds into cooperating in Russian affairs. Certainly, Witte's comments about not thinking it "worthy" of the Russian government to revamp its Jewish policy for the sake of winning Rothschild support for even the critical 1906 loan bring into doubt not only the depth of his commitment or the importance he attached to winning over a major London house but also what historians have often portrayed as a different and progressive stance on the Jewish question in Russia.[195] Ferguson, for example, makes reference to private Rothschild correspondence alluding "to the Jewish origins of Witte's wife" as supporting the notion that the Rothschilds were being won over by Witte.[196] He dismisses the idea that Witte's progressiveness on Jewish issues was the key driver of this shift in Rothschild sentiment, however, pointing instead to the influence of more narrow financial considerations.[197] The evidence from the original Russian version of Witte's memoirs—as opposed to the oft-cited abridged and poorly translated English edition—suggests in contrast that Witte was more of an opportunist than a progressive on Jewish matters. In any case, there is no direct evidence from the archival record that Raffalovich's representations to the Rothschilds to the effect that circumstances were improving for Jews had any sustained impact on their assessment of the issue. To the contrary, within a few years the Rothschilds were dismissing such claims and promises almost out of hand.[198]

Witte's major error, however, was not just in mismanaging his agents abroad and potentially underutilizing Raffalovich outside France. The 1899 loan talks and the neglect they show of London instead reflect a broader shortcoming in

Witte's strategic conception. For all his shrewdness in shaking off Berlin shorts, driving a hard bargain with French bankers, and dealing with a venal and corrupt Paris press, Witte committed the most elementary of financial mistakes—ignoring the importance of a diverse funding base. In pouring most of his attention and resources into the Paris market—while giving some limited attention to Berlin—and in almost totally ignoring London and New York, Witte was in effect making a large, directional, and unhedged bet on the future of Paris as a center of global finance and on the elasticity of demand for Russian debt on the part of French bondholders. That Witte waited for six years before making his overture to the rapidly growing Anglo-American market is also remarkable in that, even prior to his assumption of the post of finance minister, Russia had already become heavily dependent on the French market. As long as Paris was flush with cash and French bondholders and banks were willing to buy Russian loans—whether for political considerations, a lack of attractive alternatives, or other reasons—his strategy of focusing on the French market achieved Witte's aim of using foreign loans to finance Russian industrialization. However, if loan demand were to diminish as the stock of Russian paper trading in Paris increased, if other more attractive investments were to crowd out demand for Russian funds, or if an exogenous shock were to shake the foundations of the Paris market and its role as a major center of global finance, the Russian financial strategy would fail.

Anan'ich and Bovykin conclude their discussion of Witte's 1898–99 attempt to penetrate the New York and London markets by saying the attempt failed "mainly for political reasons," but they offer no specific evidence to detail this claim.[199] Other historians offer more perspective on this point. Russian historian S. K. Lebedev notes that by 1894 Caprivi reversed the 1887 restrictions on the German banking system that barred banks from holding Russian securities as collateral, thereby removing one of the major legal causes of the financial break between Russia and Germany under Bismarck.[200] Ferguson points out that between 1894 and 1896 the German Foreign Office "positively encouraged" lending by German banks to the Russians in an attempt to break the Franco-Russian financial alliance, and that the 1899 idea of a Russian loan in London was "closely linked to a parallel suggestion of a diplomatic deal between Russia and Germany, the implication being that, if Britain refused to lend to Russia, she should turn to Berlin."[201] Ferguson further points out that Russia and Germany would eventually part ways, to some extent over their differing positions on China.[202] Nonetheless, between 1894 and 1900, Mendelssohn participated in no fewer than 19 Russian bond issues in the German market.[203]

Yet, for all the talk about the importance of politics in influencing loan decisions, the Barings correspondence is remarkable for the degree to which the bankers clearly operated independently of political considerations, or, more precisely, for the degree to which Russia's unsure diplomatic position vis-à-vis Britain did not influence Barings's thinking on the loan. Hope was specific in stating to Barings that "a sterling loan . . . offered to the British public by your house . . . would be considered to have a political meaning," to wit, "the English market would once more be open for Russian Government bonds."[204] Revelstoke, for his part, made no indication in his various letters that diplomatic considerations were in any way an obstacle to a successful bond issue. On the contrary, the main hindrances to a deal, in his view, were a lack of direct contact with the Russian government, issues of pricing, and the exact composition of the syndicate. Moreover, Revelstoke was hardly a marginal character in the British establishment. If the Foreign Office objected to a loan, he would have known; indeed, the papers of future loan negotiations—notably those of 1906, discussed in Chapter 2—show him to have been sensitive to political considerations. In contrast to what Anan'ich and Bovykin posit, then, the British market was quite open to a Russian issue during the spring and summer of 1899. That a deal did not happen is more reflective of a lack of effort and poor handling on the Russian side than of political hostility in London.

Conclusion

The late nineteenth century saw a massive influx of foreign investment coincide with dramatic changes in the Russian economy—indeed with changes in the global economy more generally. As noted in the introduction, the world was experiencing the first modern age of globalization, aided by technological change, exogenous shocks to various commodity markets, and the incorporation of vast swathes of the world into global markets through the expansion of European—but also American and Japanese—empires. The changes occurring in Russia should be considered in this broader global context, and the uniqueness of the Russian case or the influence of Russian policymaking on the development of the Russian economy should not be overstated. By the same token, it is precisely the broader context that makes the direction of Russian policymaking at the time such a fascinating subject.

That Russia borrowed on the international bond market during a wave of financial globalization is not particularly remarkable. That it became the largest net international borrower in the world is—doubly so when considering deliberate policies aimed at aggressively tapping such sources of external finance. Analogously, the growth of the Caucasian oil industry and Russian oil production was a function of technological changes and policies in other countries, but was also shaped by the decisions of the Russian Ministry of Finance on taxation—a subject watched keenly by contemporary economic observers.[205] To focus on policy is not to ignore the broader global context but to attempt to understand in which ways the Russian leadership sought to exploit the strategic options presented by exogenous shocks and the extent to which the leadership was successful in doing so.

While many of these policy changes—the adoption of the gold standard, heavy borrowing on the international bond market, the adoption of protective tariffs and a spirits monopoly, and the development of domestic industry— are commonly associated with the tenure of Sergei Witte as finance minister from 1892 to 1903, they in fact represent the culmination of longer running trends in Russian policymaking. Witte was an influential executor of policy, but his tenure in the finance ministry was more representative of continuity than of change.

At the same time, while rightly credited with bringing to fruition important reforms and with skillfully advancing Russian financial interests in Berlin and Paris, Witte's tenure was marked by a major strategic unforced error: a failure to engage the Anglo-American markets. His six-year delay before making a poorly executed overture to some of the most important financiers in the world represented a failure to proactively diversify the Russian government's funding base. Instead, Witte continued along an inherited course, thereby focusing on the French market for loans. This strategy created a fault line in the edifice of Russian finance by exposing Tsarist Russia to the whims of the French market. Engaging with Anglo-American markets would have required the investment of more resources into cultivating the financiers of London and New York. The above-cited archival record of discussions between Russian agents and financiers in Britain and America suggests that Russia would have paid higher rates to borrow there. But seen differently, these costs were the price of hedging Russia's exposure to the French market. As the early years of the new century would show, Witte's failure to invest in such insurance proved to be a nearly fatal gamble.

2

The Loan That Saved Russia?

REASSESSING THE 5 PERCENT RUSSIAN GOVERNMENT LOAN OF 1906

ON 15 FEBRUARY 1906, agents of the Okhrana, the Tsar's secret police, collected their charge from the *Nord Express* at the Saint Petersburg train station and rushed off to the safe house where they would be keeping him, careful to avoid attracting any attention. Their guest was neither a spy nor an unfortunate revolutionary-turned-prisoner but an investment banker traveling incognito under his valet's name at the invitation of the chairman of the Russian Council of Ministers—Count Sergei Witte. The party's destination was Tsarskoe Selo—a village on the outskirts of the Russian capital and the site of one of the Tsar's residences. Edouard Noetzlin, the head of the Banque de Paris et des Pays-Bas, colloquially known as Paribas, was on a secret mission to discuss a planned international loan for the Russian Empire.[1] He and his bank had been involved in more than eight months of delicate negotiations with Witte and his various representatives in both Paris and Saint Petersburg.

The secrecy surrounding Noetzlin's latest trip to Saint Petersburg was well warranted: the political climate in Russia was extremely tense following more than a year of popular unrest and violent repression in what would become known to historians as the Revolution of 1905. Elections were slated to be held in just a few weeks' time for the First State Duma—the first ever legislative assembly of its kind in Tsarist Russia—and the Russian capital was tense with anticipation. Relations between the Tsar's government and liberal constitutional as well as radical elements were particularly strained, as just two months earlier Moscow had been gripped by a strike that saw the revolutionaries nearly take the city.[2] In the repressive counterrevolutionary wave between late October 1905 and the opening of the First Duma on 10 May 1906, the Tsarist regime "executed an estimated 15,000 people, shot or wounded at least 20,000, and deported or exiled another 45,000."[3]

It was against this backdrop of widespread political violence, and in the aftermath of a crushing Russian humiliation in the Russo-Japanese War, that Witte met with his French banker that February. The two men were the lead architects in what was becoming an increasingly sizeable financial undertaking involving some of the largest and most prominent financial institutions in no fewer than eight countries. In most cases, protocol would have dictated that even a senior banker such as Noetzlin see the finance minister, but Witte—himself the Tsarist finance minister from 1892 to 1903—was the chief initiator of a financial grand strategy that saw Russia aggressively tap international bond markets to fund an ambitious program of industrialization over the past decade and, therefore, he frequently dealt directly with bankers. Given the high stakes at play, Witte simply did not trust his novice finance minister Ivan Shipov, or his former finance minister and senior Tsarist bureaucrat Vladimir Kokovtsov, to handle such delicate negotiations.[4] Indeed, while Witte had invited Shipov to the interview, he had initially not even informed Kokovtsov—a frequent envoy to the French bankers—that Noetzlin was in Saint Petersburg.[5] While Noetzlin would stay in the capital for only five days, and leave before signing a final contract, within just two months the two men would be celebrating the success of what some called the largest international bond issue ever floated by any government in the world up to that point—the 2.25-billion-franc 5 Percent Russian Government Loan of 1906.[6]

Given the precarious state in which the Tsarist government found itself in early 1906 and the massive size of the issue, some began to refer to the deal as "the loan that saved Russia."[7] However, an examination of business and government documents from both the Russian and Western sides suggests that such an interpretation is overly generous. Based on materials in European banking archives as well as Russian sources, there is reason to question the idea that the 1906 loan played a stabilizing role, and to think of it instead as a deal that played a destabilizing role in Russia and even abroad in the long run. The loan did not just fail to resolve domestic political tensions, it in fact exacerbated them, exposed the regime to attacks from its enemies abroad, and likely contributed to the roots of the Panic of 1907—a seminal event in the financial history of the twentieth century.

The Background to and Historiography of the Loan That Saved Russia

Most histories of the Russian Revolution understandably focus on the events of 1917. However, they almost always make at least some reference to the Russo-Japanese War of 1904–5 and the Revolution of 1905 in Russia as precursors to the overthrow of the Tsarist regime in the February Revolution of 1917 and the October Revolution of 1917 in which the Bolsheviks took power. Many participants in the events of 1905 would reappear in various roles in 1917. Lenin himself would refer to the 1905 Revolution as a "dress rehearsal" for the events of 1917.[8]

The Financial Impact of War and Domestic Unrest, 1904–5

When the Japanese Navy struck the Russian fleet at Port Arthur on 8 February 1904 in the infamous surprise attack that launched the Russo-Japanese War, it took up arms against a country that was not only militarily unprepared for war, but also suffering a prolonged economic slump. Due in no small part to a challenging global environment, Russia had witnessed a financial downturn and real economic slowdown from 1901 to 1903.[9] According to Gregory's estimates, overall net national product (NNP) fell by 5.6 percent in 1903, the last full year before the war.[10] By late 1903 and early 1904, some observers were finding grounds for optimism, and security prices were showing some recovery; but even those inclined to a positive view kept a wary eye on the increasing tensions in the Far East.[11]

The outbreak of war was a major setback for the nascent and fragile recovery. The need to direct resources and troops to the Asian front tested the limits of the Trans-Siberian Railway—an engineering marvel on paper more than in reality.[12] Among other things, the mobilization created a shortage of rolling stock, which brought Russian grain exports to Germany to a standstill, thus closing off a key source of hard currency less than a month into the war.[13] The monopolization of railroad capacity by the military meant that even as the war stimulated demand in the railroad and armaments industries, it disrupted supply chains and cut off Russian industry dependent on domestic consumer demand from internal markets. The production of woolen goods fell by 15 percent in 1904.[14] The mobilization of 1.2 million reservists—among the most productive workers in the economy—only added to the disruptions.[15] Poland witnessed a particularly sharp crisis, with 25 to 30 percent of industrial workers in the Warsaw *guberniia* losing their jobs and those who managed to keep theirs suffering wage cuts of 33 to 50 percent.[16] Local governments struggling to cope with increased demands turned to the central government in vain for financial help.[17]

The central government, of course, saw the war add to already heavy financial burdens. In the years leading up to 1904 during the slump, the Russian government had extended various subsidies to industry via the State Bank. A poor harvest in 1903 also contributed to a rise in arrears on the part of the peasantry.[18] Even before the war it was evident that Russia would not be able to remain current on its debts without further borrowing.[19] While "rolling over" outstanding debt into new loans is a cornerstone of many sovereign debt management policies, and while governments are in ordinary circumstances able to roll over debt, economic shocks can complicate such a strategy. In Russia's case, the combination of an economic slowdown, which, among other things, hurt tax receipts, and the outbreak of war clearly increased pressures on Russian government finances. Coming as it did on the heels of an economic downturn, the war made contracting a loan an urgent imperative if Russia were to avoid resorting to inflationary policies.

The task of securing a new French loan fell to the novice finance minister, Vladimir Kokovtsov. In spite of some misgivings by the French government—which took umbrage at Kokovtsov's presuming to act like Witte and approaching French bankers directly, and which was concerned about the impact of yet another loan on the fragile market for Russian loans in Paris—Russia secured a loan of 800 million francs (300 million rubles) on 12 May 1904.[20] The financial injection proved to be short-lived, however, as war expenditures for 1904 and 1905 amounted to nearly 1.65 billion rubles, or 40 percent of budgetary revenues, with proceeds from loans furnishing nearly 20 percent of total government revenues.[21] By October 1904, Kokovtsov was once again testing the water with French bankers about another loan without first informing their government.[22] Kokovtsov intended this new loan to raise 500 million rubles, or 1.335 billion francs, to cover the projected war expenses for 1905.[23] Although he would secure a loan of 231.5 million rubles from German banks in early 1905, Russia would not float another major Paris loan until April 1906, by which time the loan size had ballooned to 2.25 billion francs.[24]

"The Loan That Saved Russia"

Almost since the day of the flotation of the loan, the statements and writings of one of its chief architects—Sergei Witte—have shaped the historical narrative surrounding it. Of particular relevance are his memoirs, published posthumously by his wife in 1921.[25] Witte devotes an entire chapter to the flotation of the loan,[26] recounting that the Russo-Japanese War and domestic unrest scared ordinary Russian savers and drove a substantial outflow of capital over the course of 1904 and 1905.[27] He goes on to note that the government's situation became even more desperate in late 1905, and that by the time he and Noetzlin met in Tsarskoe Selo in February 1906 they had determined they would stabilize Russia's financial situation only through a massive single loan that would allow the government not only to avoid tapping capital markets for several years but also to roll over a series of shorter term bonds floated during the war.[28] In the end, after months of delicate negotiations, Witte clinched the deal and, in so doing, in his narrative, managed to preserve the financial architecture—including the gold standard—that he had built in Russia and, more broadly, to provide the financial and economic stability necessary for Russia to achieve a return to relative normality from 1906 to 1910.[29] While Witte proceeds to say that it was Kokovtsov who coined the term "the loan that saved Russia" in a speech to the Duma, taking credit for the negotiations, he largely agrees with this characterization of the loan having been a success and ultimately a stabilizing force.[30]

Subsequent generalist and specialist narratives of the loan by a diverse group of historians share certain broad commonalities that reflect an implicit acceptance of the framework laid out by Witte's account nearly a century ago. The first commonality, of course, is a general acceptance of the premise that the 1906 loan was a victory for the regime insofar as it increased its room for maneuver. Thus, according to the conservative historian Richard Pipes, "[the loan] further freed the Crown for some time from the dependence on the Duma, which was due to open shortly."[31]

A second common theme in the literature is that the unprecedented size of the loan was itself an important vote of confidence from the markets for the regime. Thus, Pipes's ideological near-opposite, Sheila Fitzpatrick, agrees with his characterization, stressing the large size of the deal, the international character of the consortium, and the stabilizing effect on the economy. Showing her revisionist instincts, Fitzpatrick goes on to say, "this meant, of course, that the industrial working class also expanded," but ultimately concedes that the loan—when coupled with the government's violent repression of the workers' movement—laid the groundwork for a period of relative calm that lasted till 1910.[32] In this telling, then, the loan not only solved an immediate crisis but laid the foundations for long-term consolidation of the regime's position.

A third theme running through the work of later generalists, as well as through some of the specialized literature, and complicating the afore- mentioned traditional narrative, is the contested nature of the loan. Thus Orlando Figes, sharing the view that the large loan had a stabilizing influence on public finances, also notes that many at the time "confidently assumed that Russia's dependence on Western finance, renewed in 1906 with the biggest foreign loan in its history, would force [the Tsar] to retain the liberal structure of the state."[33] Figes shows some skepticism for this contemporary view, pointing out that Nicholas II not only looked down on "public opinion" but "had no legal obligation to respect it."[34] Olga Crisp similarly highlights resistance from liberal circles who opposed the loan on the principle that the government would be issuing it without the consent of its people on the very eve of the convocation of an elected legislature.[35] Indeed, Crisp points out that some liberals even threatened to repudiate the debt because the Duma had not approved the loan, thus marking it as an instance of what legal scholars and political economists call "odious debt," or debt incurred by corrupt or repressive regimes "without the consent of the people" or not for their benefit, for which any legitimate successor regimes should therefore not be liable.[36] This point is underscored by one of the leading French scholars of the Franco-Russian investment relationship.[37] Indeed, Russian liberals, and especially the Constitutional Democrat ("Kadet") Vasilii Maklakov, lobbied the French government and even French public opinion against approving the loan, although ultimately distancing themselves from talk of outright repudiation.[38] Franco-Russian tensions in the 1904 to 1906 period surrounding questions of finance are the focus of the scholarship of James William Long.[39] In his telling, the episode "marked the end of 'easy credit' for the Tsarist government in Paris."[40]

However, while acknowledging the contested nature of the loan, these same scholars see the story ultimately resulting in a definitive victory for the government. Girault thus declares that "the political and economic leaders of the Third Republic had not chosen neutrality vis-à-vis the political regime in Russia, they had opted for tsarism." He concludes that they thereby had set in motion a chain of events that, when combined with the effects of the First World War, would lead to the repudiation of Tsarist debts after the Bolshevik Revolution of 1917—the largest and the longest running default in more than 800 years of financial history.[41] Still, in Girault's view, the loan was ultimately "a French financial success, as well as a diplomatic one," in the face of German opposition and difficult circumstances more generally.[42]

Similarly, even as one of the leading American scholars of the 1905 Revolution points to how the opposition "deeply resented" the government's decision unilaterally to contract the loan, as well as the calls of the Social Democrats and Socialist Revolutionaries to repudiate debts,[43] he concludes that "the loan was unquestionably a tremendous boon to the autocracy, without which it might not have survived."[44] While Long's contention that the resistance to the loan was a signal of future intention by Russian opposition forces is convincing, his pointing to a moratorium on Russian issues in Paris between April 1906 and January 1909 as evidence of the deep impact of the opposition is less so.[45] Indeed, the post-1909 period would see Russia return to Paris for several years as an active issuer. In the immediate sense, the loan allowed the regime to maintain the gold standard and cover expenses incurred during the war and revolution.[46] Crisp writes of stepping back from the "verge of financial bankruptcy" in early 1906 to a manifestation "of the immutability of the Franco-Russian alliance."[47]

The diplomatic implications of the loan have indeed been a focus of much scholarly attention. Crisp, for example, points out that beyond the financial gains for Russia, the loan also represented a diplomatic blow to Germany, which, far from breaking the Franco-Russian partnership, also pushed Russia and Britain closer, concluding that "when such important issues were at stake, the wishes of the Russian liberals had to take second place."[48] Nevertheless, Long also points to more narrowly pragmatic rather than geopolitical considerations driving official French government policy: "the French financial market simply could not be inexplicably closed to Russia, nor could the French government treat its ally too brusquely," given the exposure of French investors to Russian securities.[49]

In surveying a broad spectrum of narratives about the loan of 1906, and indeed of the 1905 Revolution, then, it is apparent that there is broad agreement that the loan was a stabilizing influence both in Russia and globally in that it not only stabilized Russian government finances but also strengthened the Franco-Russian alliance and contributed to the Anglo-Russian rapprochement of 1907. Contemporary observers like Witte discussed the loan in these terms—although it was Kokovtsov, not, as many historians incorrectly state, Witte, who used the phrase "the loan that saved Russia" to describe the issue. Subsequent specialist historians generally agreed with this characterization, even if they pointed out that the loan was floated in the face of material opposition by liberal forces in Russia. It is thus unsurprising that in more recent narratives of the Russian Revolution historians continue to write more broadly about the 1906 loan as the one that "saved Russia."

However, there is reason to bring this narrative of the 1906 loan and its broader significance into question. An exploration of 18 months of correspondence between leading members of the issuing syndicate and Russian and Western government officials, as well as other primary sources, suggests a much more complex and conflicted legacy. After examining the almost daily correspondence in French and English between leading financiers— such as John Baring, the second Baron Revelstoke, and head of his family's firm; Edouard Noetzlin of Paribas; as well as figures such as Russian finance minister Vladimir Kokovtsov—it is evident that the 1906 loan served as a catalyst for revolution by opening a new, financial front on which the Tsarist regime had to fight its opponents, and by offering its enemies, both foreign and domestic, a channel through which to apply pressure. Specifically, the loan became a lightning rod for opposition by domestic reformists and revolutionaries and the international Jewish community, which was incensed by Tsarist anti-Semitism. At the same time, the need to support the loan in the secondary market created many new burdens and costs for the Tsarist regime. This more conflicted legacy of the loan is less apparent in previous scholarship, which, by focusing on the Russian or Franco-Russian dimension to the question, misses broader connections.

Starting the Negotiations

Serious discussions of what would eventually become the 5 Percent Russian Government Loan of 1906 can be dated to at least July 1905, when former finance minister Sergei Witte, while en route to Portsmouth, New Hampshire, to lead the Russian delegation in the peace talks that would end the Russo-Japanese War,[50] sounded out French and American bankers about an international loan. By early September, a French consortium, led by Edouard Noetzlin, had approached Revelstoke's Baring Brothers & Co. about joining a syndicate of international banks that would float a large Russian loan simultaneously in Paris, New York, London, and several other Western financial centers.[51] On 15 October, Revelstoke arrived in Russia to represent Barings in discussions with the Russian government and was joined shortly thereafter by a delegation of French bankers, headed by Noetzlin, Arthur Fischel of Mendelssohn & Co., and J. P. "Jack" Morgan, Jr.[52]

Jack Morgan had been sent to Russia by his father to participate in the discussions with the European bankers. Initially, the younger Morgan was skeptical of the entire affair, having been approached by Revelstoke for his thoughts while still in London. He made it clear to his father that he did not think he should get mixed up in existing negotiations, further suggesting a deal was unwise given conditions in the European money markets.[53] His conversations of earlier in the year with Western diplomats and experiences trying to manage Morgan copper interests in the Caucasus in the midst of revolution did not leave him with a favorable impression of the political situation in the empire.[54]

Nevertheless, the senior Morgan smelled opportunity, and enticed by Witte's promises to give his house exclusivity on the American portion of any loan, was even tempted to go to Russia himself.[55] In the end, Morgan decided to dispatch his still-reluctant son to Russia for the experience, sending along his trusted lieutenant, G. W. Perkins, to accompany Jack—no doubt wanting a more seasoned hand by his side.[56] After some delays, Jack Morgan and Perkins set off for Russia from London on the 18th, while Revelstoke departed on the famed—and, to his frustration, fully booked—*Nord Express* from Paris on the 14th, with plans to stay with his friend, the British ambassador to Russia, Charles Hardinge.[57]

The day after Revelstoke's arrival in Saint Petersburg, the city's printers joined a strike movement that Moscow railroad workers had begun days before. Within a few days, the strike had spread and intensified to such an extent that by the time the Union of Unions' considerable membership had joined the striking Moscow railroad workers, much of the city was already cut off from the rest of the country.[58] While Russian cities burned, the bankers in Saint Petersburg bickered in a heated standoff over the division of the underwriting between the French and German banks, and both groups' proxies in Holland. The dispute was so intense that it left Noetzlin bedridden and caused Fischel to have a heart attack in the middle of an afternoon meeting.[59]

Indeed, the bankers seemed thus far unconcerned about the rapidly deteriorating situation in Russia. If anything, being on the ground whet the appetite of the men on the spot—perhaps especially that of Jack Morgan. Whereas the junior Morgan had been skeptical of the entire affair prior to his arrival, by the 21st he was writing home about his "long and most friendly interview" with Kokovtsov and Witte and about Russia's favorable balance of trade underpinning the country's creditworthiness.[60]

It was instead the senior Morgan who was now desperately trying to pull the reins on the firm's participation. Even before Jack and Perkins set off for Saint Petersburg, Morgan was wiring them from New York indicating second thoughts, citing concerns about conditions in the American market and opposition to the deal in New York from Jewish firms incensed by the Tsarist government's anti-Semitic policies.[61] Having received predeparture acknowledgment of his concerns and a promise from Jack and Perkins to act with restraint, the elder Morgan must have been bemused by the bullish cables he received after their arrival.[62]

The senior Morgan tried again to curtail the enthusiasm of his son, stressing the current fragility of the American market, and saying that forcing what could turn into an unsuccessful New York issue "would have a very injurious effect in future upon what we so much desire . . . that is, to open [the] American market to Russian loans."[63] Leaving no ambiguity, he stated that the firm should not continue further discussions "unless our position distinctly understood that we can do nothing at present," adding an instruction to "express to Witte and Minister of Finance deep regrets that circumstances absolutely beyond our control make any other decision impossible."[64]

He got no comfort from subsequent cables. In a wire on the 22nd Jack and Perkins cited strong interest from the other syndicate members for American participation, spoke of the "extremely small" chance of losses, and made the case that "temporary difficulty in selling bonds for an American Syndicate absolutely controlled by us, would be outweighed by great value to J. P. Morgan & Co., G. F. Baker, and friends, of an established position with this international group of leading banking houses in the first completely international transaction in history."[65] Their closing claims that a deal would be of value "not only for future Russian business but for possible affairs in other countries, and American affairs on continent" left little doubt that they had been won over by the other syndicate members and Russian bureaucrats.[66]

The next day, Perkins and Jack Morgan wired home to New York recounting a private conversation they had with Witte at his invitation.[67] Witte was not going to let the House of Morgan off easily, and told the two men to relay to Morgan senior that he had arranged for an international loan largely based on Morgan's advice to the Russian premier regarding the desirability of opening the American market to Russian issues.[68] Witte pleaded with the American financiers to take even a small piece of the deal, citing the symbolic and confidence-boosting effect such a gesture would have on Russian credit internationally.[69]

But Witte also had his pride. As Morgan's emissaries relayed back to him, "If you feel it is utterly impossible[,] he has nothing else to say. [Witte] recommends us [to] go [on] conferences this afternoon and evening on [the] distinct understanding that we shall tomorrow morning be in a position to answer yes or no as to business, and if 'no' advises we should retire entirely from negotiations."[70] Betraying their discomfort at being the dithering bearers of bad news, the men added, "We entirely agree with this as it would be undignified to attempt to continue if we are really going to do nothing."[71] In a last exasperated plug for the deal, they further added, "We cannot overstate [the] kindness and cordiality of our reception by [the] Government and by [the other] groups, nor our unwillingness [to] disappoint them all at present, which certainly would be very prejudicial to our credit all over Europe. Your answer to this cable must definitely settle the matter."[72] To avoid any doubt, they noted, "Our judgment is perfect[ly] clear[:] we ought to join group from [the] standpoint of principle. Witte has told us he would prefer our taking even a very small amount, which [we] suggest we might better lock up ourselves than not go on."[73] Realizing they were pushing hard, they explained, "When the choice is between facing a temporary non-successful issue of [a] small amount and seriously hampering [the] Russian Government in their plan of an international issue undertaken largely because of your advice, we feel your name and credit, and credit of U.S.A., [are] so much involved that we are most unwilling drop [the] business and thereby show ourselves so weak that we disappoint Russian Govt. and [the] strongest financial group ever formed in Europe."[74] Having left no doubt about where they stood on the matter, they promised to "loyally abide by" J. P. Morgan's final decision.[75]

In the face of such a forceful message, J. P. Morgan relented in a cable the next day. He reminded his ambassadors that his objections were rooted not in any problem with Russia, but rather in weak market conditions in the United States that threatened to undermine any Russian bond issue in New York, and thereby the market's perception of Russia's creditworthiness in the future.[76] Saying that he shared the desire to deepen ties with the other banks in the consortium, as well as with the Russian government, and recognizing the substantial risks involved, he authorized the men to partake in the deal for 100 million francs, adding that "we would not for one moment think of a less amount than" the 100 million.[77] The relief of the two American bankers in Petrograd and of Witte and the Russians was evident in the reply thanking Morgan for finally giving in.[78]

By 25 October, as the railways in Saint Petersburg ground to a halt, the Morgan representatives had convinced their boss and the European bankers had sufficiently resolved their differences to offer a provisional term sheet to Vladimir Kokovtsov, the soon to be ex–Russian finance minister, while the headquarters of Barings and Paribas traded cables testifying to the bullish sentiment in their local markets over prospective Russian loans.[79]

As the bankers haggled with the finance minister over the terms of the prospective loan, the strike movement gained strength. On 26 October, the first session of the body that would eventually name itself the Saint Petersburg Soviet took place in the city's Technological Institute.[80] The creation of the Soviet, which would serve as an organizational hub for the strike movement, marked a further escalation of the movement nationwide. As the domestic situation reached new lows, the confidence of the bankers and the government waned. Both sides agreed to finalize a contract, but decided to defer execution of the agreement until such time as the domestic unrest had subsided.

On 30 October, the embattled Tsar finally relented to what liberals had been demanding for months, signing the October Manifesto, laying out a roadmap for a de facto constitutional monarchy in Russia. Reflecting the degree to which financial power had already shifted to the other side of the Atlantic, Perkins had cabled Morgan in New York as early as the 27th with intelligence confirming the imminent proclamation of the manifesto, noting that while rumors were rife, none of the other syndicate members were privy to this inside information.[81]

On the day following the publication of the October Manifesto, Perkins and Jack Morgan left little doubt as to what they thought of the latest developments, cabling New York, "We have seen death of old and birth of new Russia."[82] The same day, Revelstoke set sail for London via Lübeck, followed shortly thereafter by the other syndicate representatives, Perkins and Morgan included.[83]

On his way back, an exhilarated Jack Morgan wrote to his father thanking him for the chance to embark on such a "thrilling and most interesting experience."[84] His letter gushed over the fatherly and solicitous attitude Witte showed toward the younger Morgan, and the obvious importance the Russian premier attached to deepening Russia's financial ties with the United States.[85] Writing to his companion Perkins, he expressed relief that "in view of the general condition in Russia" they were "very fortunate in the way the whole matter worked out," sure "that the Senior will feel the same way."[86] Closing on a note of qualified optimism, he remarked, "At the moment everything seems to be going just as we expected that it would do, and Witte appears to be holding his own, though how long that can last I do not quite see in view of the strains on his health."[87]

Domestic Opposition

As the bankers headed home, having put their talks with the Russian government on ice, the loan only gained prominence as an issue of domestic politics. By mid-November 1906, government crackdowns in Poland and against a mutiny at the Kronstadt naval base near Saint Petersburg revived the strike movement. This second stage of strikes saw an evolution of tactics that combined earlier violence with a newer focus on financial attacks against the state. In a letter to Revelstoke in early December, Cecil Spring Rice—the chargé d'affaires at the British embassy in Saint Petersburg, a former commissioner of the public debt in Egypt, the future ambassador to Washington, and one of the most perceptive Western observers of the Russian scene at the time— noted that the Social Democrats were engaged in a serious financial boycott of the state that involved everything from the nonpurchase of liquor, the sale of which was a lucrative government monopoly, to the nonpayment of taxes. He went on to report that the revolutionaries were openly declaring—most recently in the Peasants' Congress—that the people would not tolerate the further issuance of loans and would refuse to pay interest on any loans the government issued, and were making these declarations in an effort to deliberately ruin Russian credit internationally.[88]

After the head of the Saint Petersburg Soviet, Nosar, was arrested on 9 December, a troika of leaders, including Lev Bronshtein—better known in revolutionary circles as Leon Trotsky—took over. One of the last and only acts of the new leadership was to formally issue a Financial Manifesto on 14 December. The document was a scathing critique of the government's financial position and policies. It began by declaring, "The government is on the brink of bankruptcy," and went on to point out, "The government's struggle against revolution is causing uninterrupted unrest. No one is any longer sure what the morrow will bring. Foreign capital is going home. 'Purely Russian' capital is also flowing into foreign banks. The rich are selling their property and going abroad in search of safety. The birds of prey are fleeing the country and taking the people's property with them."[89]

The manifesto went on to critique the government's policy of borrowing from the international bond market, pointing out that loan proceeds were being spent on railroads and the military, but that "there are no schools. Roads have been neglected."[90] The manifesto continued, saying that even the military outlay had been of dubious utility, since, in spite of all the spending on the army and navy, the Tsar's soldiers were remarkably poorly equipped—something reflected not only in revolts within the military but also in the broader defeat at the hands of the Japanese.[91]

The manifesto next shifted to a much more specific critique of government finances and financial policies. First, it attacked government support of private banks linked to industrialists, arguing that the government was in effect engaging in financial repression that saw small savers' capital rerouted to bailouts of private banks and industrial conglomerates. Next, it questioned the State Bank's monetary discipline, claiming that commitments had far outstripped the bank's gold reserves, and suggesting that the government's ability to maintain the gold standard—one of the linchpins of Russia's industrial boom since its adoption in 1897—was questionable.[92] The manifesto went on to mount yet another critique of the government's policy of borrowing on the international bond market—this time focusing less on the use of the proceeds, and concentrating instead on the increasing nominal burden, claiming that new loans were being floated merely to cover interest payments.[93] It continued its critique, alleging that "the government prepares false estimates of revenues and expenditures, showing both to be less than they are in reality and fleecing indiscriminately so as to show a surplus instead of an annual deficit."[94]

Up to this point, the manifesto, if at times shrill, hardly struck a revolutionary stance. In its calls for fiscal and monetary discipline, for more equitable treatment of small savers' capital, and for an end to bailouts of crony capitalist industrialists and financiers, it can indeed be read as a fairly conservative tract, and one that reflected the concerns of the property-owning bourgeoisie as much as, if not more than, those of workers or peasants. Moreover, many of the assessments and critiques of the government's financial position and policies were arguably legitimate.

Given the rapid increase in the circulation of paper money (see Figure 2.1) starting in 1904, questions as to the sustainability of gold convertibility were not unreasonable. Moreover, after having steadily fallen from a peak of more than 70 percent in 1895 to a prewar trough of slightly more than 50 percent in 1904, the ratio of government debt to NNP was nearly 60 percent by the time the manifesto was issued.[95] The bond market, where Russian spreads relative to benchmark British consols exploded during the war and revolution (see Figure 2.2) to more than twice prewar levels, reflected these financial strains. The banking system was becoming increasingly concentrated, with the major Saint Petersburg private joint-stock commercial banks enjoying an increasingly large market share—their share of Russian banking system assets grew from 13.7 percent in 1900 to nearly 30 percent in 1908 (see Figure 2.3).[96] Moreover, concerns about Russian fiscal accounting were widespread in the investing community. The *Economist*, for example,

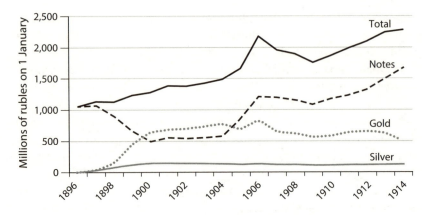

FIGURE 2.1. Money and specie in circulation in Russia.
Source: Crisp, *Studies in the Russian Economy*, 138–39.

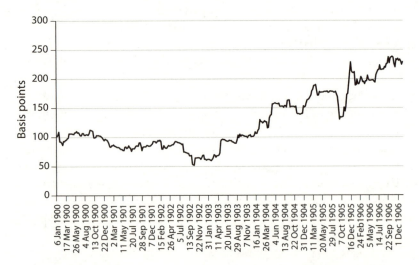

FIGURE 2.2. Spread of the 5 Percent Imperial Russian Government 1822 Bond over British
2.5 percent consols. Source: "GFD Database" (2012), www.globalfinancialdata.com.

was a frequent critic of Russian budgetary accounting conventions, such
as the arbitrarily drawn division between "ordinary" and "extraordinary"
expenditures, but also frequently flagged what it thought were cases of data
missing from budgetary reports altogether, or instances of provisioning and
estimates being totally unrealistic.[97] Where the Financial Manifesto was critical of the Tsarist government's policies, questioning their equity and effectiveness, it thus reflected a mainstream, even bourgeois, consensus shared
by many investors.

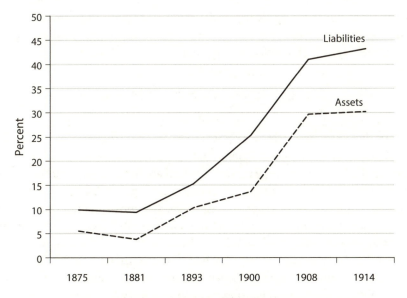

FIGURE 2.3. Share of Saint Petersburg joint-stock commercial banks
in the total assets and liabilities of the commercial credit system,
1875–1914. Source: Crisp, *Studies in the Russian Economy*, 119.

The manifesto marked a sharp departure from the political center, however, in what amounted to its declaration of financial war on the government.
Having laid out its critique of the government's finances and financial policy,
the manifesto claimed, "In order to safeguard its rapacious activities the government forces the people to engage in a deadly struggle with it. Hundreds of
thousands of citizens are perishing and are ruined in this fight." It went on to
declare, "There is only one way out—to overthrow the government, to deprive
it of its last forces. It is necessary to cut the government off from the last source
of its existence: financial revenue. This is necessary not only for the country's
political and economic liberation but also, more particularly, to restore order
in government finances."[98]

Having thereby declared war on the government within the realm of
finances, the revolutionaries articulated their strategy in the manifesto. Specifically, they would refuse "to make redemption payments and all other payments to the Treasury," would require payment in gold for all transactions,
including in the payment of wages and salaries, and would withdraw all deposits from the state savings banks and State Bank, again demanding payment
in gold.[99] In doing so, they would seek to drive the government off the gold
standard. Moreover, the manifesto ended by explicitly stating, "We have . . .
decided not to permit the repayment of loans which the Tsarist government

contracted while it was clearly and openly waging war against the entire people."[100] Within two days, the papers that published the manifesto were shut down and all of their leaders arrested.

The Impact of the Financial Manifesto

The manifesto has received little scholarly attention, and to the degree that it has, there is controversy as to how much effect it actually had in both the financial markets and government circles. George Garvy, an émigré economist at the US Federal Reserve, was skeptical about the ultimate influence of the manifesto, arguing, "under the circumstances prevailing at the time, it is well-nigh impossible to assign the rise of [bank deposit] withdrawals to any single factor." He further noted that immediately after the 1905 Revolution, Russian socialists abroad downplayed the influence of the manifesto, as did later official Soviet historiography, which characterized it as only a "preparatory step"—one that Lenin described as merely a partial and nascent instance of cooperation between the proletariat and peasantry.[101]

Ascher, citing Garvy's account, added that the ability of the revolutionaries to spread the manifesto's message was limited.[102] The breakdown in telegraphic and postal communications for much of December due to strikes ironically worked against the revolutionaries' attempts to spread the word from Saint Petersburg to other major cities.[103] Government attempts to muzzle the press also saw divisions emerge between various newspapers over both their attitudes toward the manifesto and reaction to government actions, in what could be seen as a victory for the government.[104]

There are, however, several flaws in this view that the manifesto was of little real consequence at the time. First, it is not surprising that Soviet writers, and Lenin in particular, would attempt to downplay an instance where Trotsky was in a very visible role, while the father of Bolshevism was in comparative obscurity. Moreover, the tactics advocated by the manifesto, although extreme in essentially seeking to bring down the regime by creating a financial crisis with wide-ranging consequences, fell short of calls for the violent methods—notably including bank robberies—that Lenin was already advocating at the time.[105] In this sense, the critiques of Soviet historians must be heavily discounted due to ideological considerations.

Second, contemporary sources very clearly testify to the alarm that the Saint Petersburg Soviet, and the Financial Manifesto in particular, generated in official circles. The unabridged Russian edition of Witte's memoirs contains one such instance. Early in his chapter on the 1906 loan, Witte specifically notes that "revolutionary-anarchists," whom he distinguishes from Kadets, actively sought to turn opinion both in Russia and France against the loan. He notes that the Russian press's publication of the manifesto dealt a serious blow to the government's efforts to float the loan, not least since it further eroded foreign investors' confidence in the project. Indeed, he was sufficiently worried about the negative impact of news of the manifesto spreading that he called the editor of *Novoe Vremia*—a generally conservative paper that distanced itself from the government in December 1905[106]—at 2 AM, threatening him with the newspaper's closure to prevent its publication.[107] Foreign papers of record also picked up on the manifesto and even published it in full.[108]

Moreover, a 5/18 December 1905 report to Tsar Nicholas II from the government's Committee of Finance highlights accelerated depletion of the state gold reserves in December and points to a panicked discussion at the highest levels about withdrawals from the banking system (see Figures 2.4 and 2.5) and a possible devaluation.[109] The next report, dated 14/27 December 1905, stated that the State Bank was reaching its legal limits in terms of currency issuance, and that the government would need to amend the State Bank statute if it were to continue printing money. The report goes on to discuss the pros and cons of suspending convertibility to preserve rapidly dwindling reserves.[110] The panic in government financial policymaking circles is most clearly reflected in the State Bank refinancing rate (see Figure 2.6), which the bank increased by 250 basis points in just a few weeks in late 1905 and early 1906 to 8 percent—the highest level since at least 1892, and indeed through 1917—in an attempt to stem the capital outflow.[111]

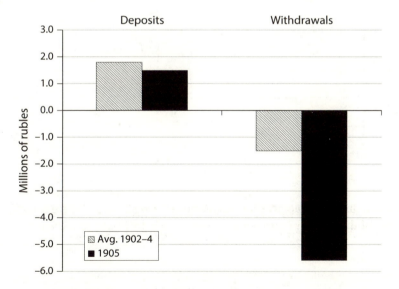

FIGURE 2.4. Changes in deposits in Russian government savings banks *in* Saint Petersburg during the month of December. Source: Garvy, "Financial Manifesto," 26.

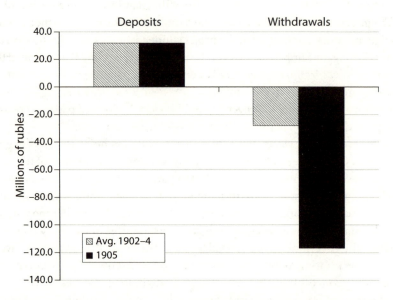

FIGURE 2.5. Changes in deposits in government savings banks *outside* Saint Petersburg during the month of December. Source: Garvy, "Financial Manifesto," 26.

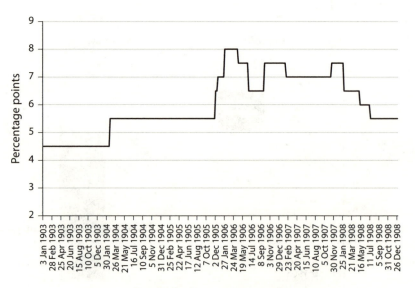

FIGURE 2.6. State Bank of Russian Empire refinancing rate.
Source: "GFD Database" (2012), www.globalfinancialdata.com.

The speed with which the Soviet was closed after the manifesto's issuance gives credence to the view that the arrests were motivated by the government's fear of being driven to bankruptcy by the financial boycott. Witte's account of having called the editor of a major newspaper in the middle of the night to pressure him into refusing to publish the document underscores the alarm the document generated in official circles.[112] The evidence from financial market data, as well as from internal reports drawn up by Russian government financial policymakers, further supports the view that the manifesto—whether directly or indirectly—did increase the financial strain on the government.

The reports of the foreign press offer some of the clearest evidence that the manifesto did have a material impact. The local Russian press is problematic as a source because so many papers were shut down before or because they printed the manifesto, with the government further removing from newsstands copies of the papers that printed or covered it.[113] Thus, a certain degree of self-censorship must be assumed. The *Times* of London, however, clearly indicated the manifesto's impact in its coverage of Russia. In its lead Russia-related story of 4 January 1906, the paper reported that the government was clinging to Witte above all else because it was "most vulnerable" in financial matters since "the vast majority" of the population was unable to pay taxes because of the economic downturn associated with the revolution, or unwilling to pay because of "the revolutionary propaganda."[114] Just over a week later, the same paper noted, "it is notorious that the peasants refuse to pay taxes," and that there were "good ground[s] for the contention of the Liberals that financial difficulties are inevitable and that the Government will thus be compelled in the end to make further concessions."[115]

The clearest indication in the foreign press of the manifesto's impact came from the government itself. Reporting on a statement about public finances by Shipov, the finance minister, the *Times* commented that the minister's report referred to "panic induced by the seditious propaganda" of the revolutionaries having "led to realizations and a transfer abroad and the conversion of paper into gold, as well as withdrawals from the savings banks."[116] Shipov made his statement in the context of the latest State Bank reports, for the weeks ended 21 and 29 December 1905.[117] The *Economist* flagged the former as proof of the government having violated the legal minimum of reserves and justification for having declared in December that Russia had moved off the gold standard.[118]

Looking back on events, the Saint Petersburg correspondent of the *Times* commented on 20 January 1906: "During the last two months, influenced by the efforts of the revolutionaries to bring about the economic ruin of the country and thus incite the people to desperate acts, many private persons and Russian commercial firms have been taking their capital abroad. This movement has been taken advantage of for speculation on the Bourse for a fall in funds and in the rouble exchange."[119] Even as Ministry of Finance officials expected and hoped that stabilization in the domestic situation would lead to a short squeeze driving a rebound in prices, the correspondent clearly saw the revolutionaries as having succeeded in applying financial pressure on the regime.[120] Indeed, as some argue, it would not be until 1907 that the domestic situation stabilized.[121] In the meantime, the refusal to pay taxes would continue to be a major instrument of dissent, not least among the peasantry.[122] Moreover, the aftershocks of the manifesto would continue to echo in the political realm as well. The sentencing of Aleksei Suvorin—the editor of the newspaper *Rus'* who had been jailed for publishing the manifesto—unified opposition voices just as the initial government response had divided various papers.[123] Thus the Kadets seized on the sentencing to issue a resolution condemning the government's sentence and its strong-armed response to the Moscow uprising.[124]

Ultimately, the closure of the Saint Petersburg Soviet, the surrender of the Moscow Soviet in late December, and Mendelssohn & Co.'s liquidity injection to the government through a crucially timed rollover of existing debt all dealt a blow to the revolutionary movement, and bought the government time. However, the events of 1905 clearly marked Tsarist debts as a key focus of revolutionary anger.

Furthermore, over time, the anger tied to the financial question would only increase. On 22 July 1906, the day of the closure of the First Duma, 178 former deputies—approximately one-third of the Duma—gathered in the Finnish town of Vyborg, an hour and a half by train from Saint Petersburg, at the initiative of the Kadets.[125] The next day, the remaining 152 deputies adopted what became known as the Vyborg Manifesto.[126] The manifesto appears in various narratives of 1905 in the context of the closure of the First Duma but, until more recent work by Shmuel Galai, had been poorly studied—some scholars even incorrectly identify the date of its adoption as 22 July 1906, rather than 23 July.[127]

The manifesto was a striking document in that it marked a sharply radical turn in the Kadets' position—indeed one that Galai argues doomed this otherwise viable constitutional alternative to Tsarism in Russia.[128] Most controversial was the manifesto's closing call to action:

> The government does not have the right either to collect taxes from the people or to call the people to military service without the consent of the people's representation. And so now, when the government has dissolved the State Duma, you have the right to give neither soldiers nor money. If the government, in order to get means for itself, begins to borrow money, these loans, concluded without the consent of the people's representation,

are henceforth not valid, and the Russian people will never recognize or pay them. And so, before the people's representation is convened, don't give a kopeck to the treasury or a soldier to the army.[129]

The parallels with the Financial Manifesto are striking, as was the identity of the author: the historian and Kadet leader Paul Miliukov.[130] The Kadets, who had previously shied away from talk of repudiation, were now leading the call for it. Signatories included Vladimir Nabokov's father, who would later spend three months in jail for his participation in the affair.[131] Long and Ascher are quick to note that the Kadets' Fourth Party Congress renounced the Vyborg Manifesto in September 1906.[132] Subsequent attempts by the Kadets to downplay the event no doubt contributed to this narrative.[133] Nevertheless, the act itself was a sign of radicalization. Moreover, the debates within the party's Central Committee after the Vyborg declaration showed trends toward even more, not less, radicalization in a financial vein. Thus, on 30 July 1906 the Central Committee decided to add a provision to the manifesto calling on the population to withdraw deposits from the banking system.[134]

The committee subsequently reversed this decision, but the Kadets' actions during the summer of 1906 nevertheless show that the Financial Manifesto and associated strategy of financial war against the government continued to resonate long after the closure of the Saint Petersburg Soviet, and that the flotation of the 1906 loan had only aggravated and radicalized the opposition. Indeed, as Spring Rice warned in a memo forwarded to Revelstoke before the loan was issued, "It should . . . be borne in mind that the parties in Russia who are opposed to the present Govt. would bitterly resent any active foreign assistance and they have declared that no further loan will be allowed. Should a loan be issued without the previous consent of the representatives of the people, it will be repudiated."[135] His words were to prove all too prescient in 1918.

International Opposition

By early 1906, officials in the Russian government were breathing a collective sigh of relief, having overcome the revolts in Saint Petersburg, Moscow, and elsewhere. Although the situation in Russia was still precarious, the government's bankers were sufficiently confident to contemplate a small short-term loan in January as a "prelude" to a bigger operation later in the year.[136] However, having achieved a modicum of improvement in its domestic affairs, the government now faced new external obstacles to its attempts to secure a loan and, through it, financial and political stability.

The new delays stemmed from the First Moroccan Crisis, sparked by the visit of Kaiser Wilhelm II of Germany to Tangier—seen at the time as a challenge to French predominance in the country. A diplomatic conference convened at Algeciras in January 1906 to resolve the dispute, and the French government had made their approval of a Russian loan being floated by French banks in the Paris market contingent on a favorable outcome at the conference.[137] Witte had for a long time sought to broaden the Franco-Russian alliance to include Germany, and still held out hope that Algeciras might in some way actually represent a step toward the establishment of such a partnership.[138]

However, formation of a triple alliance required cooperation from both the French and Germans, and neither was forthcoming in offering it. Witte's diplomatic hopes were dashed by two factors. First, continued mutual hostility between the French and Germans hindered progress. Second, as Witte himself grew to appreciate, the Germans were aware of Russia's troubled financial position and the Morocco-related conditions the French attached to the Russian loan. Even if Germany had wanted to step in and take France's place as Russia's financial patron, the sums the country now required after two tumultuous years were so large it was doubtful the German banks would be able to meet this demand, especially in light of considerable demand for credit domestically.[139] Indeed, the average three-month discount rates on the German money market had risen from 2.43 percent in the third quarter of 1905 to 4.51 percent in the fourth quarter.[140] As Witte began to notice, German financial diplomacy was starting to shift into the role of a spoiler with respect to the Franco-Russian alliance. Algeciras served this purpose, as Germany began to play for time, realizing that the longer it delayed, the longer Russia would have to wait for French approval of the loan, straining ties between the two.[141] It was during this time that Witte requested Noetzlin to visit Saint Petersburg so that the two could agree on the general terms of the loan, pending a final settlement at Algeciras.

During their meeting, Noetzlin questioned the legality of contracting a loan before the convocation of the Duma. Witte brushed this concern off, saying that the legalistic arguments about needing Duma approval were a smokescreen for attempts by the liberals to hold the current government hostage over previous decisions and failures like the Russo-Japanese War, and that waiting for the Duma would mean further disastrous delays for all involved.[142] In the face of later French government pressure, Witte would commission Russian international jurist F. F. Martens to issue a legal opinion supporting the Russian government's position.[143]

While both the French government and Noetzlin yielded in early 1906 on the point of Duma approval, they did so with minimal resistance and with no effort to secure guarantees—what financiers today refer to as "conditionality"—from the regime that it would adopt a more reformist, conciliatory posture vis-à-vis at least those liberals who were of a moderate persuasion. In doing so, the French did more than just—in Girault's characterization—side with Tsarism and thus help float an "odious debt." They missed an important moment, when they could have pushed for a change of direction in regime policy. Of course, after the bloodshed of 1905, the prospects for reconciliation between the regime and even moderate liberals had narrowed, and given their existing exposure to Russian debt, French threats to walk away from Russia entirely would not have been credible.

On the other hand, the French use of conditionality on issues like Russian military orders and the Moroccan Crisis showed that they were willing to push the Russians when motivated to do so. In this sense, by caving in so quickly to Witte's position on the Duma, the French missed a real opportunity to change the course of Russian policy and indeed history.

Having resolved the outstanding major issues to their mutual satisfaction, Witte and Noetzlin proceeded to agree on the outlines of a deal. The syndicate would raise a loan for a nominal amount of 2.25 billion French francs at 6 percent net, which would not be callable for at least ten years.[144] The syndicate would agree to underwrite half of the loan on a firm basis. According to custom at the time, the loan proceeds would be disbursed to the Russian government in installments. While on deposit at the issuing banks, the funds would earn interest at a rate of 1.25 percent.[145] With a final settlement at Algeciras that was acceptable to the French in sight, the French government finally gave Noetzlin approval to enter into final negotiations with the Russian government on 31 March 1906.[146]

No sooner had Russia and its French bankers secured the blessing of the French government than the German government indicated that it would not allow its banks to engage in Russian business in a thinly veiled punishment for Russia's support of the French during the Moroccan Crisis. The withdrawal of Germany was a blow to Russian designs, in that the experience of French vacillations and delays over questions of loans during the war and revolution highlighted the importance of a diverse funding base for Russia.

Yet the most painful blow was to come from the House of Morgan. Witte had cabled Morgan in early April saying he hoped the old man would show the "same goodwill" he had extended during the 1905 talks, adding that he had sent "a friend" of Jack's to London to discuss matters in detail with the younger Morgan.[147] The latter's views had markedly soured, largely due to conditions in the British money market. As he wrote to his father from London:

> Hope very much Russian business will be turned down again for present, as under present circumstances here it would be most impolitic and very injurious to us to offer any foreign bonds, and we do not believe it would

be possible to form syndicate to carry them at present as proposed last autumn. Bond market is absolutely dead and everyone is carrying their full quota or more of first class securities. The investment demand does not seem to improve in the least, and everyone is in state of mind to refuse everything in the way of new business or participations no matter how good. Bank statement with reserves under 25% limit not calculated to help, and loss of cash this week 7,900,000 is serious.[148]

Still, the elder Morgan, already in Europe, felt obliged to go to Paris to meet with the syndicate for talks.[149] In an almost comic twist, it was now the father who seemed to have been seduced by the syndicate members and Russian representatives. Acknowledging that "it has been difficult [to] make [the Russians] understand their credit in open market much greater than it is in reality" and adding that "I have given them no encouragement," he nevertheless felt "in view of what has already transpired, as well as our future relations with Russia and with the financiers we have been in associate with, make it desirable we should at least give nominal support."[150] Still, perhaps reflecting memories of trying to restrain his men on the spot in 1905, he concluded, "I am not willing [to] act unless you all approve."[151]

Perkins and Jack Morgan cabled back in no uncertain terms that "the business proposed would be absolutely unwise at present."[152] They repeated Jack's earlier concerns over market conditions, noting that since the start of the year they had already bought a great number of bonds that they had been unable to unload on a saturated market.[153] They were also mindful of the "unpopular" nature of the business, and relayed Morgan associate G. F. Baker's strong opposition and warning that if the Morgan firm were to take a portion of the Russian deal, Baker would be unwilling to publicly partake on his own or on his bank's account in any portion of the deal.[154] In closing, they remarked, "We are all greatly distressed at declining business, especially after your consideration last October, but we know we do not exaggerate difficulties, dangers. It is not [a] question of money but of public hostility which we ought not provoke."[155]

Having received the counsel of his son and partner, Morgan delivered the bad news to the syndicate and Russians on 11 April, "as kindly as possible," relaying the Russians' disappointment to his partners.[156] Whatever his reasons, J. P. Morgan's cancellation of his firm's participation was a serious blow, to which Witte took personal offense after the two men had reached what Witte thought was a firm agreement during his visit to the United States to negotiate the Portsmouth Peace Treaty.[157]

In seeking to make the 1906 loan a truly international issue that would be traded actively in a number of international financial centers outside Paris, the

Russian government was deliberately trying to establish itself in new markets to avoid future overreliance on the French.[158]

Witte highlighted the importance of this issue to Joseph Dillon, the *Daily Telegraph* correspondent in Russia, who had "gone native" and served as a public relations consultant of sorts for the Russian prime minister.[159] Dillon in turn frequently spoke with Spring Rice, who recounted an early January 1906 conversation between the two men about Witte's desires to British foreign secretary Sir Edward Grey:

> During the war what Russia had needed was a strong military friend on her border. This Germany had supplied. But now what Russia needed was not so much the support of a military power as that of a great liberal and commercial power. England's sympathy if afforded in some open and evident form would be of the very greatest service to the party of order. . . . Germany could give a finger's length of help and England an arm's length. France was so deeply implicated in Russia's financial situation that her opinion was discounted. But England was entirely independent of these considerations.[160]

Although Dillon and Spring Rice spoke of Witte's attempt to win the favor of England, the comments about "a great liberal and commercial power" show how American support—even if not explicitly mentioned—was equally valuable. Prodded by Spring Rice about the form in which Witte desired this stamp of approval, Dillon indicated that the Russian premier sought British participation in a loan.[161]

The tragedy, of course, was that Witte sought to internationalize the market for Russian loans in the worst circumstances: when Russia was on its knees, and without having established an Anglo-American investor base in good times. As Spring Rice reminded Dillon, "a loan depended not on the will of our government but on the disposition of the City."[162] Earning the trust of the City and Wall Street—markets Witte had largely ignored for much of his tenure as finance minister—would be challenging in the midst of a revolution. In this sense, his failure to engage with the Anglo-American financial markets in the late 1890s, documented in Chapter 1, proved to be a costly oversight.

At the same time, by seeking to engage in new markets, the Russian government increased its exposure to active resistance from Jewish financial houses that vocally protested the Tsarist regime's anti-Semitic policies and support of pogroms. Apart from some warnings from Spring Rice in Saint Petersburg, this Jewish opposition in the new target markets did not initially attract much attention in syndicate correspondence.[163] In 1905, Witte had sent the Russian financial agent in Paris, Raffalovich, to London to meet with the English Rothschilds, who said their participation in any Russian loan would be contingent upon the undertaking of concrete steps to improve the condition of Jews in Russia—something Witte refused to entertain at the time.[164] When Wilhelm II later told the Tsar that the Jewish issue would be an impediment to the success of the loan, Witte again dismissed such claims as a German red herring, saying that Jewish financiers would not publicly participate but would, in the end, buy into a successful deal secretly through the secondary market. Having thus convinced themselves that all was in order, and having cleared the Algeciras hurdle, the Russian government and the syndicate moved quickly to sign a loan contract for 2.25 billion francs on 16 April 1906.[165]

Following what at first glance was a highly successful initial offering, however, the performance of the bonds in the secondary market began to falter within days of their issuance. Although the syndicate decided to proceed with the loan in spite of the California earthquake of 18 April 1906, the disaster did have a depressive effect on the market and on Russian bonds in London.[166] Contrary to Witte's expectations, the London Rothschilds did not participate in the loan even secretly, thinking it far too richly priced, and predicting difficulty for it in the near future. Indeed, a generally tight money market soon combined with renewed political fears over the opening of the new Duma on 10 May to depress the market for Russian bonds.[167] By late May, the tensions between Tsar and Duma had affected Russian bonds enough to weigh on the broader Paris market, which in turn pushed London lower, according to the Rothschilds' internal reading of events.[168] Amid the turmoil, one of the American managers of a Morgan-affiliated business in the Caucasus, who was also serving as a US consul, was murdered in Batumi—a grim reminder to the New York house of the wisdom of having limited their Russian involvement.[169]

By mid-June—less than two months after what had initially seemed to be a successful offering—the Russian financial cancer appeared to be spreading. The London Rothschilds wrote to their cousins in Paris, "the Russian loan, which was written for more than 100 times, and supposed to be the greatest financial success in the world is 2 to 1 3/4 discount. This is undoubtedly a disturbing element in international finance, and this Russian unrest may produce events in other countries which it is difficult at present to gauge."[170] Revelstoke and Noetzlin, as the lead bankers for the deal in their respective markets, went into crisis management mode.

Kokovtsov, having been reappointed finance minister in April, wrote to Revelstoke on 17 June, saying that he was aware of weakness in Russian bonds and asking for advice. Revelstoke replied, suggesting they support the bonds by making purchases in the secondary market with a fund of £2 to 3 million to be spent on an opportunistic, discretionary basis by Barings. In Revelstoke's estimation, buying £500,000 worth of bonds in nominal terms would suffice to stabilize the market.[171]

As the markets continued to fall, strains began to show in the usually collegial correspondence between Noetzlin and Revelstoke. The placement of significant portions of the Russian issue in the English market naturally heightened the attention of the financial and broader press to Russian affairs in a manner that was not always as flattering as that of the French press, which was notoriously susceptible to outright bribery.[172] This difference became a source of some tension between the British and French syndicate members, with Noetzlin, on 18 June, writing a lengthy complaint to Revelstoke about an article in the *Times* on Russia, asserting that the article was full of "tendentious" and baseless claims, before going on to say how shocked he was that "your premier newspaper engages in such fanciful and malicious assessments." Noetzlin went on to complain that the *Times* articles were doubly damaging because they were reprinted by Parisian papers, suggesting that Revelstoke try to "end the campaign" in the London press against the Russian bonds.[173] Revelstoke replied by pointedly reminding Noetzlin that negative stories about Russia in the British press were reflective of events in Russia rather than bad journalism.[174]

By 20 June, Revelstoke and Noetzlin had convinced Kokovtsov to create a Russian government-backed fund to actively support the loan in the secondary market. The fund in the London market alone was initially £300,000, eventually growing to £400,000 as the situation worsened.[175] In spite of the support funds in the British and French markets, however, the souring political situation in Russia and the broader context of the California earthquake aftermath combined to drive Russian bond prices lower. On the eve of the dissolution of the First Duma on 21 July, the situation in Russia dominated global markets with heavy bear activity in Russian securities driving down the broader market in both London and Paris.[176]

Significantly, the London Rothschilds attributed the general depression in the market more to the "heavy cloud" of Russian bonds than to selling by insurers to help pay for claims from the California earthquake.[177] This is a particularly interesting remark, given that some, including Robert F. Bruner and Sean D. Carr, cite a lack of liquidity in global credit markets as a root cause of the Panic of 1907—one of the most significant financial crises in modern history, which, among other things, led to the creation of the US Federal Reserve in 1913.[178] Bruner and Carr attribute the global liquidity crunch in 1906 to the California earthquake, which struck just two days after the contracts for the Russian loan had been signed. Given the close temporal proximity of both events, disaggregating the effects of the two to any exact degree is impossible. Nevertheless, the observations of the Rothschilds and other well-connected contemporary observers suggest that the liquidity crunch was at least in part—and possibly largely—due to the failure of the Russian loan, which in turn implies that the global panic was rooted partly in events in Russia.

By mid-1906, Jewish opposition to the Russian loan gained prominence as a source of weakness in Russian securities. While Jacob Schiff of Kuhn, Loeb famously went out of his way to aid Japanese war finance during the Russo-Japanese War as a form of fighting Russian anti-Semitism, there is in fact little evidence in the files of the Rothschild bank's London archive to suggest an active manipulation by that house of the 1906 Russian loan.[179] However, the syndicate members, such as Barings, as well as diplomats, such as Spring Rice, attributed much of the negative press coverage of Russian financial and political affairs to Jewish figures opposed to official Russian anti-Semitism. The sentiment was confirmed to a degree by the heated exchange between Rutkovskii, who was the Russian government's financial agent, and Lord Rothschild in November 1906 over the appearance of an article in the *Times* quoting the *Jewish Chronicle* as saying that the Russian government was spreading false rumors about the Rothschilds ending their financial boycott of Russia. The acerbic correspondence between Rutkovskii and Rothschild in the aftermath of the publication of the articles suggests that the Rothschilds were not averse to and likely complicit in the embarrassing coverage the Russian government received.[180] Of course, there is little doubt that the Russian government would have encouraged rumors that the Rothschilds were abandoning their boycott—such an event would have almost certainly helped Russian security prices; and indeed the government had for some time been trying to woo the Rothschilds to do this, without making any tangible concessions on official anti-Semitism.[181]

In pushing for a truly international issue, the Russian government did diversify its funding base, reduce its dependence on what had proven to be fickle French markets, and even planted the seeds for the 1907 Anglo-Russian diplomatic rapprochement.[182] The urgent attempt by the government to internationalize the issue in 1906 only highlights Witte's failure, discussed in Chapter 1, in the late 1890s to invest in developing Russia's ties with the Anglo-American markets. Moreover, as its experience in the British markets—which it reentered through the 1906 loan—showed, the international character of the loan came at a cost. In hastily reentering the British market, the Russian government was engaging a market that was arguably harder to manipulate and created—in the form of the 1906 loan—an easy site of attack against the regime. At the same time, the loan proved to be a destabilizing influence in global markets, possibly contributing to one of the greatest financial crises of the twentieth century.

Of course proponents of the narrative that the loan saved Russia would argue that the proximate impact of the loan was to extend a financial lifeline to the Tsarist regime. In a similar vein, it could be argued that heightened vulnerabilities are inherent in the act of taking on a loan. While both points are to some extent true, such arguments miss the context in which the loan was floated. They also grossly understate the degree to which key players in the loan saga took actions and made clear choices that resulted in the loan raising vulnerabilities and risks beyond those that would have been inherent in a loan raised in a different context.

The decision to first close the Duma and then proceed with the loan without any attempt to involve opposition forces in the planning, for example, was a choice the Tsarist regime made. It was part of a policy course that even relatively liberal figures such as Kokovtsov and Witte helped execute. Foreign participants in the loan saga, too, made decisions pregnant with consequences in the loan discussions. The failure of both the French government and French bankers to make approval of the loan conditional on a more inclusive domestic political path was a missed opportunity to float the loan in a less contentious manner. That the French did force conditionality on the Russians vis-à-vis the Moroccan Crisis only underscores the degree to which such a path was open—but not taken—by the French financial community. The decision by potentially new entrants into the Russian sovereign lending business, such as J. P. Morgan, to ultimately decline participation in the loan further highlights the leverage the French had but failed to exercise over Russia.[183] It would thus be a mistake to see the increased vulnerabilities of the Tsarist regime to financial attack after the 1906 loan as inherent in the act of borrowing. While some degree of heightened vulnerability was indeed inevitable, the manner in which the loan was floated served to materially exacerbate it.

Conclusion

In writing the story of the Russian Revolution, historians frequently adopt—implicitly or explicitly—the triumphalist Witte-Kokovtsov narrative of the 1906 Russian Government Loan as the loan that saved Russia. While the loan was certainly large and required a great deal of coordination and cooperation among the various issuing houses and governments, it was far from the unqualified success and stabilizing influence it is often assumed to have been, and is better seen as a Pyrrhic victory. Correspondence between key business and government leaders involved in the deal suggests a far more complex and conflicted legacy.

Domestically, the loan served as a lightning rod of opposition for opponents of the regime, ranging from moderate constitutionalist forces to the radical Social Democrats. The notion that the Tsarist regime would try to push through a loan without the prior approval of the Duma angered large segments of the political spectrum and reinvigorated the opposition, as evidenced not only in the Financial Manifesto of the Saint Petersburg Soviet but also in the

Vyborg Manifesto of 1906, which was signed in July by members of the just-dissolved First Duma in a conscious echo of the Financial Manifesto. Indeed, the fury of the Duma deputies vis-à-vis the 1906 loan is palpable in the calls of the Vyborg Manifesto for the citizenry to withhold taxes and the threat to repudiate any and all loans contracted without the approval of the Russian population.

From an international perspective, the loan showed that the Russian government was able to diversify its funding base beyond France, which had proved to be a less than ideal ally in its reluctance to lend to Russia during the difficult periods of 1904 and 1905. At the same time, the sudden move to internationalize the market for Russian debt highlights the failure of Witte to engage the Anglo-American financial markets in the late 1890s as a major strategic error. Moreover, in reaching out to the British market, the Russian government also exposed itself to attacks in the financial markets through devastating press coverage generated by its opponents. At a time when global markets were already reeling from the impact of the California earthquake—cited by some as the root cause of the Panic of 1907 in the United States—the decision to issue a massive loan created an easy opportunity for the regime's opponents to talk down a benchmark loan, damaging Russian credibility in the markets and thus dealing a financial blow to the regime.

As 1906 drew to a close, the Russian government's problems were far from over, and while the loan had relieved some of them, it had created and exacerbated others—both within Russia and abroad. Even as the barricades were being torn down, and the fires of peasant revolt extinguished, the financial front remained open.

3

The Interrevolutionary
Recovery and Rally

ROUGHLY MIDWAY BETWEEN the Moscow Station—Saint Petersburg's oldest and busiest rail terminal—and the golden-spired Admiralty, sandwiched between a fast-food sushi outlet and a popular local coffee shop, stands No. 62 Nevsky Prospekt. Until recently, the building housed the Saint Petersburg flagship store of the Spanish clothing retailer Zara, which, prominently positioned on the northern capital's main thoroughfare, was doing a brisk business catering to Russia's middle class. Like much of the city's commercial real estate, No. 62 is constructed in the imposing and ornate style of the late Tsarist era and has clearly seen better days. At first glance, it is otherwise unremarkable in a city full of such structures, but engraved on the balcony just above the main entrance are the letters "БАНКЪ," revealing in prerevolutionary spelling the building's original purpose as that of a bank. Indeed, this now-vacant clothing store once housed one of the most influential financial institutions of the Russian Empire—the Banque du Nord, a Russian joint venture of the Société Générale and the Banque de l'Union Parisienne (BUP) which, after its merger with the Russo-Chinese Bank in 1910, became the Russo-Asiatic Bank.[1]

It was through the window recently displaying mannequins clad in miniskirts that Théophile Lombardo looked as he penned a letter to Paris on 28 September 1907. A Frenchman, Lombardo had been in Saint Petersburg for some time, serving as a senior manager of the Banque du Nord. He had witnessed the recent political turmoil play out on Nevsky Prospekt and elsewhere in the capital. Even so, the picture he painted, of political tranquility and of financial and industrial affairs being "ultra calm," was optimistic.[2] In light of both prior and subsequent events, Lombardo's upbeat interpretation seems remarkable, and yet it was well timed: the decade between 1906 and 1916 witnessed a striking recovery in the market for Russian securities, reflected also in a range of indicators in the Russian real economy. The sharp rebound in Russian security prices would be noteworthy in ordinary circumstances. That this positive turn in financial markets' perceptions of Russia took place in the aftermath of a revolution, in spite of the outbreak of a world war, and on the eve of one of the greatest revolutions in modern history makes the phenomenon even more curious.

The political realm was far from uneventful between 1906 and 1916. Setting aside the outbreak of world war in 1914, Russia did not see even the superficial political calm that prevailed in other countries. The assassination of the reformist prime minister Pyotr Stolypin in 1911, the 1912 Lena Goldfields Massacre, and the anti-Semitic Beilis affair of 1913 underscored significant social and political tensions persisting in pre-1914 Russia. International relations in the interrevolutionary years also saw various crises and confrontations. The Second Morocco Crisis of 1911 between France and Germany, and events culminating in the Balkan Wars of 1912 and 1913, reflected significant geopolitical tension in Europe.

Financial markets, too, witnessed dislocations. The Panic of 1907, touched upon in Chapter 2, is the most notorious financial crisis of this period. Peripheral economies also had their share of problems. Latin America, for example, was in the midst of a debt crisis. After the Colombian and Costa Rican defaults of 1900 and 1901, respectively, Brazil—a much more prominent international debtor, particularly in London—defaulted in 1902 and then again in 1914. Ecuador defaulted no fewer than three times: in 1906, 1909, and 1914.[3] One of the biggest sources of headache to the financial markets, however, was Mexico, which was in the throes of a decade-long revolution and would default in 1914.[4]

Yet, despite the continued domestic political instability, regional geopolitical tensions, and multiple shocks to the international capital markets, market perceptions of Russian risk continued to fall consistently over the course of the decade. By the outbreak of war in the summer of 1914, the spread of benchmark Russian government debt over British consols stood near multiyear lows. By late 1916, the spreads would contract to levels lower even than those in peacetime (see Figure 3.1 and Chapter 4). Investors were apparently quick to shrug off the memory of the strikes, violence, and destruction of property that occurred in Russia during the 1905 Revolution, as well as the various war scares, and even the subsequent outbreak of a global conflict of unprecedented destruction. Moreover, they moved back into the Russian market on a large scale—Russia's net foreign investment account was approximately −153 million rubles in 1906, rising to −369 million in 1907, versus +45 million in 1905 and −242 million in 1898, the year after Russia's adoption of the gold standard.[5] In 1913, Russia saw the largest capital inflow in at least 28 years (see Figure 1.3).[6]

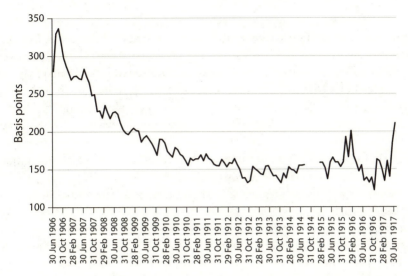

FIGURE 3.1. Spread of Imperial Russian Government 1906 bond over British consols. Source: "GFD Database" (2012), www.globalfinancialdata.com.

The interrevolutionary rally, thus, is a striking and curious phenomenon that flies in the face of existing theories that suggest political instability and violence are bad for markets.[7]

In exploring the archival record, it is evident that investor perceptions of improvements in the real economy, a geopolitical realignment, and factors operating at the level of financial gatekeepers all contributed to the interrevolutionary rally. Yet despite the improving economic indicators and rising security prices, Russia's economy and financial system became increasingly fragile in the decade from 1906 to 1916.[8] Paradoxically, were it not for the fiscal stimulus provided by the armaments buildup that preceded the First World War and the outbreak of the war itself, the Tsarist regime could have faced a potentially disastrous financial crisis in 1913–14.

Economic Drivers of the Rally

Russia in early 1907 was spent. The previous three years witnessed humiliating defeat in the Russo-Japanese War of 1904–5, only worsening the popular discontent that erupted in the Revolution of 1905 and, in fact, stretched well into 1907.[9] Violent urban strikes and peasant unrest in the provinces at once fed the drama of high politics and were nourished by it—the long-awaited First Duma lasted a mere 72 days before being dissolved on 21 July 1906, exacerbating political tensions.[10]

As the Second Duma prepared to convene on 5 March 1907, Russia remained on a knife edge. Yet as the correspondent of the *Times* of London reported, "a singular calm prevails on the eve of the Duma."[11] True, just over a week earlier, revolutionary terrorists had attempted to assassinate Grand Duke Nicholas Nikolaevich while he was en route from the Imperial retreat at Tsarskoe Selo to the capital—a stark reminder that Russia's political problems were far from resolved.[12] Still, the *Times* correspondent noted, "The contrast with the corresponding period last year is complete."[13] Even if the calm was merely "superficial" as the various parties distrustfully eyed each other, outright violence seemed to be finally receding.[14]

Even the *Economist*—a publication that had maintained a witheringly critical and bearish stance on Russia for decades—betrayed a few rays of optimism in February 1907. It found in the makeup of the opposition reasons to be "even more hopeful for the cause of reform," finding the most radical of the socialists to be in too weak "a condition to alarm even the more timid among the *bourgeoisie*."[15] The cautiously optimistic picture extended from the halls of power in Saint Petersburg to the towns and fields of provincial Russia. As the *Economist* pointed out, "the revolutionary elements seem to have undergone a marked decline. Terrorist outrages continue, but they are, on the whole, individual and sporadic."[16] Poland, the Baltic provinces, even the Caucasus and Moscow—the site of particularly bloody violence—all exhibited a noticeable decline in revolutionary activity. To be sure, the people still wanted change, but the results of this most recent election suggested to the *Economist* that Russians were willing to seek it through peaceful, parliamentary means. The revolution was over. Russia was turning into a liberal democracy.

Of course the Second Duma outlasted the First by a mere month, having been shut down in an early morning raid by the Okhrana on Sunday, 16 June 1907.[17] Yet even as supporters of the opposition howled of a coup d'état, and even though the army was put on alert, the event did not reignite the flames of 1905.[18] That the dissolution decree set a timetable for the new, Third Duma to meet on 14 November, and provided general guidelines for its composition, helped smooth the transition.[19]

The closure of the Second Duma actually came as a relief to some outside the Winter Palace. As Lion, an engineer and one of the BUP's local expatriate correspondents in Saint Petersburg, said in his letter to the bank's president, R. Villars, "there is in business circles, satisfaction at the dissolution of the Duma. It was a real relief."[20] Lion proceeded to say that he did not anticipate any trouble—that one could count on the army, notwithstanding some potential minor disturbances in Poland.[21]

It was no accident that Lion found himself in Saint Petersburg on the day of the Duma's closure. As the representative of a major French financial institution, he had spent the past several days meeting with various industrialists, diplomats, and government ministers—indeed he saw the minister of finance, Kokovtsov, that very afternoon.[22] Just as the political situation appeared to be stabilizing—if only in fits and starts—in Russia by mid-1907, key contemporary observers perceived signs of stability and growth in the economy too. The interest of foreign banks in Russian deals was consequently reviving.

As early as 15 January 1907, a high-level meeting of top French and Russian bankers convened at the Grand Hotel in Paris at the initiative of Maurice de Verneuil, the head of the Paris stockbrokers' association, to discuss Franco-Russian financial relations. The Paris Bourse operated a dual market, whereby the official *parquet* consisted of listed securities traded by a monopoly of stockbrokers, or *agents de change*, while the *coulisse* was a free market open to all. Since at least the 1890s, Russian securities were generally officially listed on the *parquet*. Obtaining listings for individual security issues was thus a major negotiating point in deals between Russian issuers and French bankers. De Verneuil, occupying a semiofficial role straddling the public and private sectors, was a key gatekeeper figure in this process.[23]

The minutes of the early meetings between these French and Russian bankers show de Verneuil initially to have had defensive intent. Coordinating the activities of the major French and Russian banks would allow them to share information, as well as the costs of sourcing and evaluating deals. More to the point of French interests, centralizing deal negotiations would help focus the flow of Russian securities being floated on the Paris market. De Verneuil's stress on the need to coordinate the financial and commercial aspects of foreign lending was a thinly veiled attempt to secure orders for French industry from the Russian firms financing their projects with French capital. While the Russian bankers deferred to their finance ministry on this issue, they acknowledged as legitimate French expectations that loans be reciprocated with orders for industrial goods.[24]

At the same time, the meetings revealed that the consortium could not merely protect French interests, but also feed a reviving demand for investment on the part of the Russians. P. L. Bark, the representative of the Volga-Kama Bank and later the last finance minister of Imperial Russia, said that Russian industry was hungry for capital and that this demand was not being satisfied.[25] Indeed, by 1907, the Russian economy was showing signs of a rebound from the depths of a prolonged industrial slump.

This slump was not just a product of the dislocations of the Russo-Japanese War and 1905 Revolution—it was also cyclical in nature. The Second Boer War of 1899–1902, an accelerating American economy, and bullion outflows to Japan contributed to a monetary tightening in Europe that hurt growth, including in capital-hungry Russia.[26] The further pressures of war and revolution only added to the strains of the economy. Indeed, the strife of 1905 hit certain heavy industries particularly hard. After peaking in 1901, oil production, concentrated around Baku, a center of revolutionary activity, fell 8 percent by 1904, and would drop to 64 percent of its peak in 1905.[27] Russian oil production would not rebound to its 1904 levels until well after 1917.[28] Alexander Gerschenkron argued that a recovery in the overall economy began in 1903, but was strangled by the war and revolution.[29]

Having suffered the triple blows of a cyclical downturn, defeat in war, and revolution, the Russian economy was operating from a low base in 1906 as recovery slowly began. Having fallen by 81 percent in 1905 to the lowest levels since 1890, net investment increased sharply, by 78 percent, in 1906.[30] Even as iron and steel production fell by 11.1 percent, overall gross industrial production bounced back by 8.6 percent in 1906 as compared to 1905.[31] In 1907, net investment in structures increased by 91 percent.[32] Thus, even as overall net national product continued to decline through 1907, according to Gregory's estimates, there were signs of an emerging recovery in certain sectors as early as 1906.[33]

Perceptions of a Revival in Agriculture

As industry was emerging from the cyclical-revolutionary slump, key foreign financial observers also perceived an improvement in Russian agriculture. Of course the emancipation of the serfs in 1861 disappointed those who saw in it a chance to modernize rural Russia by freeing labor markets and redistributing land. Notwithstanding the formal freedoms emancipation granted erstwhile serfs, it consolidated the power of the rural commune, which served as the link between the central government and individual peasants.[34] Beyond facilitating government collection of onerous redemption payments and land taxes, communes perpetuated agricultural practices that prevented economies of scale in farming. Some 80 percent of communes frequently redistributed and reapportioned land between peasant families.[35] The nearly 40 percent increase in the Russian population from 1861 to 1905 only aggravated the situation, shrinking the average communal allotment by 25 percent.[36] Russian mortality rates—nearly double those in England—and the fourfold rise in emancipation payment arrears between 1875 and 1895 underscored the failures of post-emancipation Russian agriculture.[37]

While Stolypin's name is most closely associated with attempts to break the commune's hold on the Russian peasantry, his biographer, Abraham Ascher, argued the agrarian reforms were not "his brainchild."[38] Still, Ascher rightly credits Stolypin with translating "the abstract ideas on agrarian reform into reality" in the face of significant opposition, not least from "nostalgic"

Slavophiles.[39] That a figure like Kokovtsov—from the generally progressive finance ministry—also opposed the reform underscores the depth of opposition Stolypin faced.[40] The law of 22 November 1906 allowed peasants to break free of the commune by converting their strips to private consolidated holdings either within or outside the village.[41] Still, there remained a significant gap between the legal rights peasants gained and the reality on the ground—between what the government sought to achieve and the persistence of communal power, which frequently repressed entrepreneurial peasants.[42] Of course, it was not just peasants seeking to break free of the rural commune who faced intimidation. The events of 1905 were unsettling enough that the rural gentry sold 20 percent of its landholdings to the peasantry between 1906 and 1914, with the proportion rising to one-third in those areas that had been particularly restive.[43]

Nevertheless, foreign investors and other observers influential in financial circles did perceive improvements in Russian agriculture—whether because of or independent of the Stolypin reforms. These perceptions contributed to their optimism regarding Russia. In his 28 September 1907 letter to Paris, Lombardo reported that while the most recent harvest was only slightly higher than average, weak harvests elsewhere boosted Russian prices.[44] In his view, a merely average upcoming harvest would be better even than an excellent harvest during a period of average prices. He suggested that the BUP consider advancing funds against wheat.[45] Lombardo sounded an increasingly optimistic tone through the course of the fall of 1907, remarking on 28 October that he expected the Third Duma to be significantly more conservative and thus more cooperative with the government.[46] Encouraged by trends in agriculture and politics, he expected the start of "a very significant recovery" in Russian securities, provided Western money markets remained calm. He attributed a tightening of liquidity conditions in Saint Petersburg to an unusually large number of grain transactions, casting agriculture as a key driver of this recovery, not least since grain prices were the highest he had ever seen in Russia.[47]

Not all observers agreed with Lombardo's positive spin on the situation in late 1907. In its review of 1907, the State Bank's Moscow office acknowledged the rise in grain prices, but placed more emphasis on low volumes as a driver than did Lombardo. Accordingly, it blamed the Panic of 1907 in the United States rather than agriculture for the tighter liquidity conditions.[48]

Nevertheless, by the 1908 harvest season, key members of the international financial community perceived a major improvement in Russian agriculture. Writing in late 1908, Victor Davydov, one of the local agents for Paribas, cast a favorable light on the government's agrarian reforms, the decree of 22 November in particular, and the ability of the government to continue to work with the Third Duma to turn the decree into permanent legislation in spite of their relations being stormier at times than Lombardo had anticipated in 1907. Davydov noted that beyond the 3.2 million *desiatinas* acquired by 422,000 new landowners leaving communes in the short period since the law was passed, the weakening of the commune would have a significant multiplier effect.[49] Davydov observed that the reforms would probably improve agricultural output—expecting an increase of 400,000 rubles per annum in grain sales from European Russia—and a freer peasantry would facilitate the government's resettlement efforts in Siberia.[50]

In early 1909, Davydov outlined what he saw as transformative changes in Russian agriculture. He acknowledged the empire suffered from lean harvests in 1907 and 1908, which in turn only raised peasant indebtedness. Nevertheless, he maintained that both years witnessed improvement on the ground. Producers were responding to price signals by shifting the mix of land use in favorable directions, often in favor of dairy. The South and Southwest in particular showed a boom in poultry production, driving a 100 to 200 percent increase in production, with German and British imports of Russian geese and chickens being a primary driver of this expansion.[51] Even though this growth occurred off of a low base, in Davydov's view the rate was sufficiently high for poultry to have become a significant portion of the peasant economy and rural market. He stressed that the shift in the mix of output in the Russian countryside was something that the figures on grain production missed.[52]

More interesting—and convincing as evidence for his bullish case, given that an emerging boom in goose production was hardly going to replace grain exports—was Davydov's description of labor markets as they related to the mix in agricultural production. He observed that seasonal nomadic labor was an important input in the major grain producing regions in the southern empire and that, in the North, as much as 88 percent of the male workforce participated in this seasonal nomadic labor market.[53] Davydov claimed that with the rapid growth of the dairy economy in Russia, this proportion fell to 20 percent in 1907 and 15 percent in 1908.[54] The Baltics, typically a source of migrant labor, were now witnessing a shortage of unskilled labor themselves, such was the pickup in activity.[55] Davydov reported an increased use of artificial fertilizer and more strategic deployment of fallow land as a further indication of changing agricultural patterns.[56] To observers at the time, there was evidence of rural dynamism as early as 1908, then, even if the headline figures on grain output continued to disappoint.

In 1909, a strong harvest built on the modernizing and market-oriented changes Davydov highlighted to amplify perceptions in foreign financial circles of upside in Russia. Even the *Economist* admitted by early August 1909 that Russia would likely produce "one of the greatest crops on record" that year.[57] The magazine began the year with a characteristically skeptical stance on the emerging Russian rally. It acknowledged a 21.5 percent rally of the 1906 loan off its 1907 low. Nevertheless, it argued that a weak Duma, inept bureaucracy, money-hungry defense establishment, and sensitivity to harvests prevented sustained improvement in Russia's political and economic situation, and found Kokovtsov's 1909 budget proposal to be grossly optimistic.[58] By the fall, however, even the *Economist* conceded that while markets were "by no means infallible," they were led by "those who have developed an instinct for gauging the temper and prospects of foreign countries," and by this standard the recent Russian rally did suggest the basis for some optimism.[59] Grudgingly, the magazine that for years excoriated the financial policies of Witte and Kokovtsov and the backwardness of Imperial Russia admitted: "The present situation in Russia is one of hopeful suspense. Just now there is a lull in the revolutionary activity, and the country is quiet. The Duma, it seems, has really come to stay, and though its discussions are still of the academic order rather than the practical, it is beginning to make its influence felt on the administration. Internal conditions in the country are almost entirely dependent on the state of the harvest, and this year the yield is exceeding all records."[60] Although qualified, this was an extraordinary endorsement from the magazine, given its typical stance. In a thinly veiled hedge against further upside, the magazine closed by remarking, "Russia, in spite of the grossest mismanagement, has, so far, always succeeded in weathering the worst financial storms."[61]

By the fall of 1909, then, even those observers who were typically skeptical on Russian affairs began to see grounds for optimism. In the eyes of foreign financial observers, the nascent recovery began at a time of political strife and poor harvests with the early stages of an industrial rebound off of a low base. Changes in Russian agriculture, partly associated with the Stolypin reforms, helped the recovery along. Even if these changes did not result in major shifts at the level of national accounts, which continued to show weakness on an aggregate level, financiers and other observers of the Russian scene perceived a change. The strong harvest of 1909 and the bumper crop that followed in 1910 served as additional agrarian shocks that further boosted perceptions of a Russian recovery—driving a return in ever greater numbers of financiers seeking opportunity in Russia.

Of course much of the above-cited commentary is drawn from the contemporary accounts of a handful of foreign financiers or local agents of foreign banks. Many of these observers relied on anecdotal evidence or reflected cognitive biases in the choice of indicators they followed or the sources they used. Such accounts cannot be read as an authoritative macroeconomic bill of health for the Russian economy in the years in question.

Nevertheless, the data collected by subsequent scholars suggest a favorable global backdrop to Russian agriculture in the early years of the twentieth

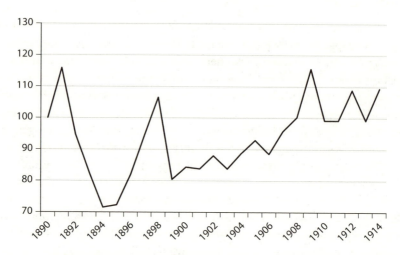

FIGURE 3.2. Index of wheat prices in Britain based at 100 in 1890. Source: Clark, "Price History of English Agriculture," http://faculty.econ.ucdavis.edu/faculty/gclark/data.html.

century. Lombardo's comments about strong prices in 1907 are supported by Clark's price data from the British wheat market (Figure 3.2). British wheat prices showed a steady upward trajectory since bottoming in 1899, and a particularly sharp upturn in the years immediately following the turmoil of 1904 to 1906. The marked rise in Russian grain exports suggests that Russian farmers were indeed taking advantage of this favorable global price environment. Cereal exports rose from 7.9 million tons between 1899 and 1903 to nearly 12 million tons in the period from 1909 to 1913.[62] Such a rise in exports itself reflected favorable productivity trends, with Russia seeing periods of surplus from 1902 to 1904, from 1907 to 1911, and from 1912 through the start of the war.[63] The rise in output was a function of improved yields, as well as an increase in the amount of land under cultivation.[64] The latter grew by 6 percent in the agricultural belt of European Russia and by more than 70 percent in Siberia between 1904 and 1914.[65] The Soviet Union would reach the Russian Empire's 1912–13 cereal output levels only in the early 1950s.[66]

Of course, subsequent scholarship—operating with the benefit of hindsight if not flawless data—has also challenged the picture painted by some of the rosiest commentary of contemporary financial observers. Notwithstanding the headline output increases and favorable commentary of bankers, cereal yields of 0.6 to 0.7 tons per hectare on the eve of the war remained very low by contemporary international standards, for example.[67]

These considerations do not, however, make the perceptions of contemporary financial observers of the Russian scene irrelevant to the financial historian. In financial markets, as the case of Russia shows, perceptions—especially those of key figures with a disproportionate influence on the allocation of capital—can influence reality insofar as they color investor behavior and capital allocation decisions.[68] Studying the narratives—however flawed—of contemporary observers in privileged positions in the journalistic, diplomatic, and banking communities helps distill the rationale behind foreign investors' increasing interest in Russia in the aftermath of the cataclysms of the Russo-Japanese War and Revolution of 1905.

Bond Market Comeback: The 1909 Conversion Loan

Perhaps the greatest testament to the international financial community's belief that things were turning in Russia was the flotation of the 1909 loan in Paris. The loan marked Russia's return through a major issue to the Paris market—a visible vote of confidence from the French haute banque.

Under a deal between the French and Russian finance ministers at the time of the 1906 loan, Russia agreed to refrain from further issuance in the Paris market for two years.[69] By early 1909, the Russian government was able to return to the Paris market for a loan to roll over the State Treasury bonds it floated in 1904.[70] According to Kokovtsov's memoirs, the negotiations for the loan began when he met Noetzlin of Paribas in Homburg in August 1908, making clear he expected the banks to recognize that Russia was no longer in the position it had been when floating the infamous 5 Percent Loan of 1906 amid the turmoil of the 1905 Revolution.[71] Basing his talks on a 4.5 percent coupon, Kokovtsov found Noetzlin to be very receptive, with size and price being of lesser issue than technical matters relating to the placement and listing of the bonds.[72]

Kokovtsov's memoirs further reveal that he was concerned over the listing when he met Noetzlin.[73] French radicals were angered by their government's support of Tsarist autocracy against a reform movement through the flotation of the 1906 loan, and shamed by Russian liberal politicians and intellectuals—not least by Maxim Gorkii's pamphlet, "La Belle France" (1906)—for allowing the loan to proceed. They now sought to prevent another loan from being issued until tangible reforms in Russia had taken place. Thus, in February 1907, a radical deputy, incensed by talk of Russian loans, interrupted French foreign minister Pichon's speech in the Chamber of Deputies, screaming, "Le peuple russe est notre ami, et le tsar est un assassin!"[74] The minister coolly replied that he was happy to see a strengthening of Franco-Russian commercial and industrial bonds, adding, "Russia, gentlemen, has always honored its financial signature."[75] Cognizant of the risk of French radicals derailing Russian borrowing abroad, Kokovtsov made a point of personally thanking Pichon for his public support.[76] Even while denying rumors that Russia needed another loan,

Kokovtsov jealously reserved the right of the Tsarist government to float one without Duma consent, stressing this in interviews publicizing the improving situation in Russia.[77] The issue remained sensitive a year later, and Kokovtsov was pleased to hear from Noetzlin in August 1908 that the French government would not block a loan.[78]

The pricing agreed and a French government veto avoided, the loan was finally issued in January 1909.[79] The flotation, naturally, was of much greater value to the Russian government than the sum of the funds it raised and the reduction in interest charges it bequeathed to the Treasury. In issuing a loan on the primary market in Paris with the backing of the French haute banque, Russia was doing much more than raising money. For the French government to allow the loan was a powerful signal of the legitimacy in the international market of the Tsarist government after the Revolution of 1905. The price of the loan—a far cry from the comparatively humiliating terms of 1906—and the active participation of major banks served to legitimize Russia as an investment, rescuing it from the pool of speculative peripheral economies where detractors such as the *Economist* often argued it belonged.

The Influence of Geopolitics on Capital Flows

The interrevolutionary rally gained momentum from and reflected investor perceptions of an improving situation in Russia. Investors were encouraged by what they saw as a reviving real economy, but also by several exogenous factors in the realms of politics and finance. Geopolitics in particular served as a powerful influence on capital flows and the decision making of financial gatekeepers in the interrevolutionary decade. The 1909 loan demonstrated that home governments of creditor banks could act as spoilers or enablers of Russian deals, making Russia's diplomatic relations highly relevant to the trajectory of Russian finance in the period.

Two notable features of the interrevolutionary decade are the improvement in Anglo-Russian diplomatic relations, and the increased participation of British capital in Russian finance and industry. On 31 August 1907, the British and Russian governments signed what became known as the Anglo-Russian Convention of 1907.[80] There is debate as to whether Central Asian affairs—the focus of the document itself—were merely a pretext to reach a truce between the two powers in Europe.[81] Whatever the motives, the agreement marked a sea change in international relations, with Britain and Russia taking steps to end the "Great Game" in Asia and their more general rivalry, shifting from animosity to partnership.

To say that the 1907 agreement allowed British capital to enter Russia, or Russia to turn to the London bond market, would, of course, be false. As the example of the 1906 loan discussed in Chapter 2 showed, British markets were open to Russia before 1907, and indeed it was arguably the 1906 loan that helped drive the diplomatic rapprochement. At the same time, the convention did make British and other foreign investors more receptive to Russian investments. The *Investor's Monthly Manual* reported, "The publication of the Anglo-Russian Treaty was well received in this country and on the Continent, and its reception was followed by renewed interest in Russian loans."[82] While noting that volumes were not very heavy and that most of the support came from continental bourses, it reported a 3.5-point increase in the price of the 1906 bond.[83]

The next month's issue—marked by talk of the Panic of 1907 that was then gripping the United States—noted, "The weakness of several of the foreign bourses was reflected throughout October in our own foreign market," pointing to a Dutch banking crisis and the American troubles.[84] Amid this chaos, it was striking then that "throughout the greater part of the month Russians were rather steadier than other securities in the market."[85] Another article related the poor performance of English companies operating in the Baku oil fields, praising Russian managers, while critiquing the expatriates. The article blamed the latter for the failures of British concerns, rather than the political instability in Russia. Ending on a hopeful note, it argued that the problem was not Russia but bad English management, and that replacing the latter could achieve a turnaround.[86]

The optimism associated with improved Anglo-Russian relations was manifest not just in the financial press. Lord Revelstoke of Barings had gone to Paris for two days in early October for talks with Kokovtsov, who was visiting the city and also meeting with Mendelssohn's Fischel. This meeting—uniting three of the key players in the 1906 loan talks—immediately stoked rumors of an impending Russian deal, which Kokovtsov vigorously denied, saying that Russia did not need another foreign loan, and that he was merely in town on holiday. Discussing the 1906 loan, both Fischel and Revelstoke acknowledged that demand had recently picked up, especially after the Anglo-Russian agreement. While Fischel could not convince Revelstoke to create a pool to support and profit from a rise in the price of the 1906 bond, the latter's reluctance to do so stemmed from his pessimism on American affairs and a desire to see that Russia be allowed back into the Paris market rather than from any deep wariness over Russia.[87] Revelstoke would underscore the value of the Anglo-Russian rapprochement to Russian finance in his cable to Kokovtsov after the 1909 loan, when he noted that improved diplomatic relations between their countries likely fed the surge in retail investor interest they witnessed.[88]

The most obvious and arguably consistent geopolitical support of the rally was of course the Franco-Russian alliance, which stretched back to the nineteenth century and, in 1906, helped Russia secure its 5 Percent Loan on the Paris market despite vocal opposition from both Russian liberals and French radicals. Pichon's line against the radical deputies in 1907 was just a continuation of this trend, and the decision to turn a blind eye to Russia's persistent domestic political troubles in granting a listing to the 1909 loan underscored the importance of the alliance to the French.

This interconnection between geopolitics and financial markets became particularly clear in later years, especially in 1913, when the French and Russian governments agreed on an arrangement explicitly linking bond listings in Paris to Russian actions in the military sphere. That de Verneuil, a stock broker, not a military man, went to Saint Petersburg to negotiate with Kokovtsov—by then de facto prime minister—was telling. The deal tied Russian access to the Paris bond market to Russian commitments to build strategic railways according to the preferences of the French General Staff, and to boost the strength of its peacetime army.[89] That a financier negotiated an agreement so closely tying financial and military concerns highlights the importance of geopolitics to Russian finance in this period.

A perception of geopolitical stability also encouraged investment in Russia. The period from 1906 through the first half of 1914 was peaceful for Russia from an external standpoint. Russia avoided outright conflict despite numerous war scares and crises in the Balkans and elsewhere. Indeed, investors overwhelmingly failed to anticipate the outbreak of war in 1914.[90] In the prewar era, financial and economic arguments against the war—not least Norman Angell's *The Great Illusion* (1910)—proved particularly seductive.[91] Of particular note was financier Ivan Stanislavovich Bloch's *Is War Now Impossible?* (1899), which advanced an economic argument against the war that, in turn, helped inspire Nicholas II's Hague Peace Conference initiative.[92] Bloch's work is particularly interesting from the standpoint of Russian financial history, given that he was an early employer of Witte's when, after the Russo-Turkish War, his Southwestern Railroad acquired the Odessa Railroad, where Witte had been working.[93] Bloch's vice president, I. A. Vyshnegradskii, who would himself become finance minister, was in charge of actually running the railroad and became one of the patrons of the young Witte at the line.[94] In this context of influential thinkers and financiers in both Russia and Western Europe rating the chances of a pan-European war to be unlikely, the 1907 Anglo-Russian entente was a sign of stability, and the continuation of French desire to maintain the diplomatic alliance with Russia a reassuring sign to investors that the Paris bourse would remain open to Russian bonds, thus providing a financial cushion to the Russian government. Of course, for those with patriotic considerations in mind, alliances between governments only added a reason to invest.

Cartels and Distressed Opportunities:
Reassuring and Attracting Investors

The interrevolutionary Russian rally was not simply a product of macro-economic recovery, patriotic impulses, and—however false it would prove to be—a perception that there was little likelihood of Russia entering a major conflict. Industry- and firm-level factors also pushed financiers to look to Russia. Specifically, a large number of distressed investment opportunities and competitive pressures attracted gatekeepers to Russian markets.

Of course, the notion of "gatekeepers" in financial markets as initially developed by Marc Flandreau, Juan Flores, Norbert Gaillard, and Sebastián Nieto-Parra was one in which the underwriters acted as the "gatekeepers" for countries seeking to tap sovereign debt markets.[95] In this conception, the gatekeepers were the ultimate agents and decision makers. The picture emerging from the Russian case is one in which the so-called gatekeepers were in fact themselves influenced and drawn in by perceived developments in the Russian economy and by competitive pressures within their industry. While these considerations may suggest a refinement—and humanization—of the definition of gatekeeping, they do not imply that gatekeepers were materially less important or central to sovereign debt markets in the late nineteenth and early twentieth centuries than Flandreau and his coauthors suggest.

Protecting Investors from the Slump through Market Coordination

Efforts to coordinate markets—with Russian help—reassured foreign investors. The strains of the cyclical downturn that began in 1901, coupled with the added pressures of the war and especially the Revolution of 1905, squeezed Russian commerce and industry. Foreign investments—often in the form of what today would be considered private equity stakes—were especially concentrated in heavy industry, which was particularly vulnerable. Girault estimates, for example, that more than a third of all French investment in Russian industry in 1900 was in the metallurgical sector, with nearly a further third in coal mining.[96] Thus, even though Russia remained an overwhelmingly agrarian-driven economy at the time, the high concentration of foreign capital in heavy industry makes industrial trends significant from the standpoint of understanding the decision making of foreign investors regarding Russia. The French banks behind these firms were already worrying about their vulnerability to an industrial slump when on 11 November 1900 they held one of their earliest meetings at Paribas to discuss a cartel arrangement in Russia.[97]

With Witte hesitant to allow a foreign cartel to dominate the Russian market for key industries like metallurgy and coal mining, but also keen to prop up their Russian investments, the banks tried another tack. Through the first half of 1901, the Société Générale elaborated its plan for what would become known as the Banque du Nord in discussions with the French and Russian governments. Seeded with French capital, but also able to accept deposits in Russia, the bank would be a "universal bank," engaging in both commercial and investment banking activities. Its key aim would be to help Russian heavy industry in particular overcome a difficult period of low prices and overproduction.[98] In an indication of the public-private partnership the creators of the project envisioned, Maurice Verstraete, a Ministry of Foreign Affairs diplomat who had served in the consulate in Moscow and embassy in Saint Petersburg, was seconded to the bank. By late July, the Russian government had approved the bank's charter.[99]

The Banque du Nord alone, however, could not stop the crisis from accelerating. Leaving aside the consideration that the Société Générale intended to use the bank as a vehicle to support its own interests in Russia, rather than as a broader public-private support mechanism, the crisis rapidly deepened in 1901.[100] In June, the Russian business world was shocked to learn of the bankruptcy of A. K. Altchevskii, a prominent industrialist who, through the Kharkov Land Bank, which he founded in 1871, built up a vast business empire straddling the financial and mining sectors.[101] Upon his suicide in 1901, it was discovered that his overleveraged empire's balance sheet had assets of only 250,000 rubles against liabilities of 19 million.[102]

As the scale of the potential problems became clearer, calls for the Russian government to more actively support industry—both domestic- and foreign-owned—became more insistent. As late as mid-September, Witte was holding a firm line, telling French finance minister Joseph Caillaux that he could not allow French cartels to form in Russia.[103] By mid-October, however, he had changed his tune, offering state aid for the Kerch and Briansk steel mills that had been the subject of many of these discussions.[104]

As the crisis showed no sign of abating, a conference of 60 delegates representing 18 metallurgical firms took place in Saint Petersburg on 2 February 1902 to discuss ways in which they could cooperate to rationalize production in the hopes of preserving prices.[105] By July 1902, the Russian government approved the charter of the Obshchestvo dlia Prodazhi Izdelii Russkikh Metallurgicheskikh Zavodov (Society for the Sale of the Output of Russian Metallurgical Factories), known by its acronym Prodamet.[106] While the first agreements were limited to sheet iron, by 1909 the syndicate had agreements on pipe and rails, among other things. Members of the syndicate were obligated to sell their output of the relevant good exclusively through Prodamet, subject to financial penalties.[107] Despite problems stemming from differences in productivity between member firms, Prodamet achieved its price stability objective and indeed price increases for the industry.[108]

The success of Prodamet was not lost on other industries. As early as December 1901, six locomotive producers formed a looser syndicate, known by its Russian acronym Prodparovoz, which was ultimately denied official sanction in 1908.[109] Prodvagon resulted from an agreement in March 1903 between eleven railroad car producers, but remained largely dormant until 1906 and only adopted a formal quota system in 1908.[110] The Donets coal mines formed their own syndicate, Produgol', in March 1906.[111] As Gatrell notes, the syndicate system both comforted investors in Russian industry about future pricing and allowed Witte to show the foreigners among them that the Russian state would not use the slump to buy up foreigners' Russian investments at fire-sale prices.[112] If anything, as events in the banking sector would show, it would be the foreigners who would see the crisis as an opportunity for investing in distressed situations—in banks themselves.

The Poliakov Affair

Despite all the attempts to manage the industrial sector crisis through cartels, Russia still witnessed some spectacular bankruptcies. If that of Altchevskii was the most jarring, the case of the Poliakov banks was the most significant from the standpoint of foreign financiers. In the Poliakov episode, the economic crisis in Russia resulted in distressed investment opportunities that enticed foreign investors into the market.

Lazar Solomonovich Poliakov was the wealthiest of three brothers engaged across a range of industries. Seeded with capital from his father, Solomon Lazarevich, a merchant of the First Guild, Lazar Solomonovich began his own mercantile career in the 1860s.[113] By 1898, after 25 years in business, Poliakov could look back on the slew of government medals and awards testifying to his charitable and business activities.[114] Among other positions, he was the chairman of the Petersburg-Moscow Bank and the founder and principal shareholder of the Moscow Industrial Trade, South-Russian Industrial, Orel Commercial, Moscow Land, and Yaroslavl-Kostroma Land banks.[115]

Beyond owning this roster of banks, Poliakov had extensive investments in industry. The list of businesses in which he was involved included rubber manufacture, forestry, construction, railroads, and insurance. In the 1890s, he looked abroad to exploit opportunities in Persia.[116] When these ventures produced losses, he engaged in fraud to mask them.[117] In 1893, Poliakov used his Moscow International Bank to finance his failing Persian cotton operations. He further tried to recover the losses by speculating on the international cotton market.[118] After initial gains, by 1900 and 1901 the trades turned sour, only compounding the previous hits the bank had incurred. Shareholders turned for redress to the Credit Chancellery of the finance ministry.[119]

Poliakov's shady deals between his Moscow bank and Persian businesses were just the tip of an iceberg of fraudulent and questionable transactions and practices involving his complex web of businesses and banks. Although the web held for years, it did not survive the economic crisis that hit Russia in the early twentieth century.[120] As early as the summer of 1900, Witte reported to Nicholas II his concerns about the solvency of the Poliakov banks and the stability of the businesses with which they were connected.[121]

In a late 1901 report to the Tsar, Witte detailed how he estimated that the losses at the three key Poliakov banks—the Moscow International, the South Russian, and the Orel—were sufficiently large to have rendered them effectively bankrupt. Beyond the losses suffered by their shareholders, the banks were large holders of private deposits. A failure of these banks not only would result in losses to retail shareholders—estimated by Anan'ich to own three-fourths of the Moscow International's shares—but also would trigger a run on the banking system and destroy market confidence.[122] Poliakov was too big to fail.

After much discussion within the higher echelons of the Tsarist government—that Poliakov was a Jew did not help his case—the government decided to seize Poliakov's shares and put the three banks on financial life support via temporary loans. This allowed the banks to remain current on debts, pending a final decision about whether to push for a bankruptcy or recapitalization.[123]

By late 1905, Western financiers had taken notice and were interested. Lombardo wrote to Villars, the president of the BUP, on 17 December 1905—the day after Tsarist authorities raided the Saint Petersburg Soviet—on the future course that the Banque du Nord, and the French in general, should take vis-à-vis Russian investments.[124] Acknowledging that until the recent unrest abated all investments in Russia were unadvisable, Lombardo nevertheless proceeded to make the case for an expansion of the Banque du Nord's operations. He vented his frustration over the risk-averse behavior of his fellow Frenchmen on the board and at the Société Générale, which was loath to invest more into the Banque du Nord. Lombardo argued it was nevertheless difficult to engage in any serious business in Russia without an adequate capital base and a more substantial operation on the ground. Absent a research department comparable to that of Crédit Lyonnais, the risk to the bank of entering poorly studied deals would be too high, in his view. Having made the case for an expanded presence in Russia, he argued further—without irony—that a merger with two of the three zombie banks of Poliakov's erstwhile business empire was the ideal way for the Banque du Nord to expand its operations.[125]

The Poliakov saga dragged on into 1909, despite various attempts by French and other banks to do a deal. By September 1909, the London City and Midland

Bank—one of the largest in the world—was considering an acquisition as a potential expansion into the Russian market. Dealings with unreliable and demanding correspondents had frustrated the bank's earlier attempts to engage in Russian business, including the origination of municipal loans, crystalizing the advantages of having a direct local presence.[126] A September 1909 memo reveals that the bank's attempts to enter the market via the creation of a new and separate "Anglo-Russian Bank" proved difficult, due in large part to a Byzantine local regulatory environment. Cognizant of the time that would be wasted in trying to secure a new bank charter, the memo advocated acquiring the distressed Poliakov banks, which had been merged in May 1908 into the so-called Union Bank.[127] As the memo noted—and the bank's competitors recognized—in buying the Poliakov banks, Midland stood to gain a banking charter without the hassle of an application from scratch, as well as the merged banks' network of 68 regional branches. That the banking license and branch network would be acquired at a presumably distressed price at a time when the bankers perceived a recovery in Russia only added to the attractiveness of the deal.[128]

In the end, after years of talks in which numerous foreign suitors considered various types of deals for purchasing the Poliakov banks, the Russian government ultimately disposed of its stake through a combination of share sales in the open market and backing the reorganization of the banks by local financiers in early 1908.[129] The newly merged bank initially prospered, managing to pay a dividend of 7 percent by 1909, but soon ran short of capital and turned to the BUP, which, in 1910, finally injected 5 million rubles in exchange for a stake and board representation.[130] This episode did not end happily for the French bankers, however, who, as if haunted by the corporate ghost of Poliakov, found themselves unable to control shady and questionable lending practices and under constant pressure for new capital infusions. They finally decided that it would be better to break with Union Bank than to continue caving to the repeated capital requests of a duplicitous partner.[131]

For its part, the government had to fend off a range of critics of the affair well into 1913—from right-wing anti-Semites to liberals who read the state's support of the banks and the ease with which Poliakov escaped serious punishment as a manifestation of Tsarist crony capitalism.[132] Kokovtsov successfully resisted the persistent pressure from Stolypin and others within the government to force an early resolution of the situation. He maintained that to do so would jeopardize the financial stability of Russia and claimed to have had the State Bank sell off the last shares in 1912, resulting in the government pocketing a profit of 3 million rubles through its involvement in the affair.[133]

Lombardo's Banque du Nord—one of the original suitors to the Poliakov banks—ultimately merged with another distressed bank: the Russo-Chinese. The latter, founded in July 1895, was the brainchild of Witte, who had convinced French private banks, including the Comptoir d'Escompte, Crédit Lyonnais, and Paribas, to provide much of the seed capital.[134] As Russia became increasingly aggressive in Far Eastern geopolitics, it used the Russo-Chinese as a vehicle to advance its political interests more than its commercial interests, resulting in significant losses that necessitated a recapitalization or merger.[135] An attempt to merge the bank with the Bank of Siberia fell through by late 1909.[136] The difficulty of the turnaround was apparent to the French foreign minister, who noted that the bank had no fewer than 52 branches, most of them unproductive, located not just in Siberia and the Far East but around the rest of Asia, including in the East Indies, Europe, and even New York and San Francisco.[137] Nonetheless, by December 1909, the Banque du Nord was preparing to conduct due diligence on the Russo-Chinese,[138] whose share-holders finally approved the merger on 6 March 1910.[139]

The troubles of the Russo-Chinese and Poliakov banks are significant because of their role in reviving foreign investors' interest in the Russian market. The prospect of taking advantage of the distressed condition of the banks to acquire their extensive branch networks enticed foreigners back into Russia after the slump of 1901–3 and the political turmoil of 1904–6. The interest was of course predicated on the perception that Russia had already hit rock bottom. The case of Midland Bank's abortive talks to acquire Union Bank was particularly striking as an instance of a foreign bank looking to gain a foothold in Russia through the purchase of a distressed asset.

True, Midland's initial foray into the Russian market took place before it entered discussions about acquiring a Russian bank. Its first deal was a £3.4 million loan at 4.5 percent, with a Russian government guarantee on behalf of the Armavir-Touapsé Railroad in Southern Russia and the Caucasus.[140] The loan was in fact Midland's first venture into the world of foreign (i.e., non-British and non-colonial) loans. The deal was also a landmark transaction insofar as it represented the entry of a major British joint-stock bank into the market for Russian bonds, which—to the extent that it saw British participation—merchant banks like Barings and Rothschilds dominated hitherto.[141]

The entry of a joint-stock bank into markets previously dominated by merchant banks also reflected a broader shift in global finance taking place at the time, whereby joint-stock banks with large and increasing capital bases were becoming a formidable force in international finance. In England and Wales, the ten largest banks held 46 percent of deposits in 1900, but would increase their deposit share to 97 percent by 1920.[142] As these banks grew larger, they also entered new markets, including that for foreign loans and branch banking.

However, it was only after the Armavir-Touapsé flotation, when considering the Union Bank deal, that Midland devoted significant resources to exploring Russian opportunities. In an April 1909 memorandum, Sir Henry

Burdett laid out his proposal for an Anglo-Russian Bank that could facilitate Russo-British commercial and financial transactions by acquiring Union Bank. Among other things, his proposal noted that the bank could profit from an estimated 1 to 1.5 percent rate spread between its projected cost of borrowing and high-grade loan rates in Russia.[143] While David Miller, of Midland's new foreign exchange department, visited as early as 1907, by 1909 Midland showed a deeper engagement with Russia. Miller visited Saint Petersburg in the summer of 1909 to fish for deals but found the city suffering from a cholera outbreak. Many of the people he sought were in any case away at their dachas in the country, and he was sensitive to indications that those who remained did not take his overtures seriously.[144]

By September 1909, Midland chairman Edward Holden was ready to do a deal for Union Bank, even independent of a British syndicate. Signaling the seriousness with which Midland was approaching Russian matters, Sir Edward sent his son Norman to accompany his closest confidant, Samuel B. Murray, on a mission to Moscow and Saint Petersburg.[145] The two men arrived in Moscow on 23 September 1909, and immediately began seeing people over the Union Bank affair.[146] They received a cold reception from Count Tatishchev, the head of Union Bank, and heard that L. Davydov at the Credit Chancellery in Saint Petersburg was not pleased with Midland's overture, given that he was partial to a German bank.[147] As the de facto banking regulator, he held great power in the matter. Davydov gave them a cordial but noncommittal reception when they met a few days later, on the 28th, recalling the government's long relations with Barings, and saying that the Union Bank matter would not be decided for another year or so.[148] The next day, Davydov was more openly hostile, claiming to the Midland men that, among other things, he heard the Bank of England is "no friend of yours," and reiterating the Russian government's loyalty to Barings.[149]

The Union Bank deal ultimately fell through for Midland—partly because of continued obstruction from Davydov, who convinced the cabinet that the bank was now adequately capitalized, and partly because Midland's due diligence heightened its own concerns.[150] The mission and all that his son and Murray had told him about their meetings with business and government figures in Russia while exploring the Union Bank deal piqued Edward Holden's interest, however. By late October, Holden had decided that a more permanent presence for the bank in Russia would be advisable, and sent Miller to Saint Petersburg to take up residence there for an initial period of six months.[151] Miller's immediate task was to gain a foothold in the issuance of Russian municipal debt, which was becoming increasingly common, but neither he nor Holden ever abandoned the idea of a direct presence for Midland in Russia.[152] As Chapter 4 shows, they eventually realized this dream—in 1917.

The Poliakov and Union Bank episodes thus show that in the view of key foreign financiers, the dark cloud of slowdowns, bankruptcies, and general turmoil produced by the cyclical slump and revolutionary unrest of 1901 to 1906 had a silver lining. Foreign investors—including some of the world's largest banks—were quick to smell opportunity amid the financial ruins, particularly in the banking sector. While in the case of the Poliakov banks and others these opportunities ultimately appeared to be an illusion, they nonetheless drew foreign financiers into Russia for closer examination. This process created its own momentum, which Russian government officials as well as businessmen were shrewd in exploiting to meet their ever expanding appetite for capital.

Competition as a Driver of Foreign Investment

Competitive dynamics between bankers also influenced their behavior, and were in turn leveraged by the Russian government to entice them. As Murray's conversation with Davydov at the Credit Chancellery made clear, Midland was not the first bank to express interest in Union Bank. By 1909, a range of foreign bankers were making the pilgrimage to Saint Petersburg in search of deals and to foster relationships with the officials in the finance ministry and the Credit Chancellery.

Although activity had been increasing for some time, 1909 was a key year. On 13 January, de Verneuil indicated to the finance ministry that, in principle, a listing of the 4.5 percent loan that the Russian government and its bankers were discussing was possible.[153] While the French banks could have placed a loan among their large retail clientele directly, a formal listing on the Paris Bourse was an important stamp of approval, and fed the existing momentum in financial circles.

Noetzlin and Revelstoke had been carrying on a regular and bullish correspondence on Russian affairs for much of 1908. In June, Revelstoke was telling Noetzlin, "I feel happy about Russia" and noting strong demand in London for Russian gold-backed bonds.[154] Noetzlin made it clear in the summer of 1908 that he was looking for a chance to do another Russian deal, and Revelstoke was in agreement, observing in a letter to Kokovtsov that abundant liquidity in London was driving investor interest in sovereign bonds, "especially in those of the Imperial Government."[155] Underscoring the degree to which the outlook for Russia had turned, he closed with the remark that "the work of the last two years, therefore, has not been in vain; and Your Excellency may rest assured that the efforts which were initiated under your auspices will lead to a growing interest being taken in Russian affairs."[156]

Bankers were thus quick to respond to confirmation that the Paris market was once again open to Russian securities. Noetzlin wrote to Kokovtsov in early February that he was planning a trip to Saint Petersburg to see him, but also to more closely examine the Russo-Chinese deal and to meet with clients, including Putilov.[157] Revelstoke notably arrived in Saint Petersburg to meet with Kokovtsov the very same week that Midland's Murray and Holden were in town.[158] Moreover, the archives of the French banks show their representatives to have been pitching their offices with various deals through the course of the year.

The finance ministry and its Credit Chancellery were quick to pick up on this increased foreign interest, exploiting the bankers' competition to secure more favorable terms. Of course, critics accused Kokovtsov of giving in too easily to the banks, and his memoirs reveal his sensitivity to this charge.

Bankers' views on this question differed from those of Kokovtsov's detractors. Referring to the Russian finance minister's relations with Crédit Lyonnais, Revelstoke complained to his partners at Barings that Kokovtsov was "entirely in their hands and is powerless to dictate."[159] Painting a very different picture, Noetzlin complained to Revelstoke during the 1909 loan negotiations, "My existence has become almost intolerable during these last few days, placed as I am between my six constituents, on the one side, and Mr. Kokovtsov and his lieutenants on the other side, who send me at his order all sort of 'love messages.'"[160] Kokovtsov's lieutenants certainly added their sting to these messages. As Revelstoke related during the same negotiations, Kokovtsov's representative, Davydov, "is in fact enjoying himself with Noetzlin."[161] He would later praise Davydov to Kokovtsov for his "tact and firmness" in driving a hard bargain that "a less determined and less dexterous representative" would have struggled to achieve.[162]

Transcripts of a Budget Commission meeting from early 1909 show that while Kokovtsov's memoirs may have overstated the ease with which he dictated terms to Noetzlin at Homberg in 1908, the finance minister indeed understood the leverage Russia held over its bankers. Responding during the meeting to Russian criticism over the 1909 loan, Kokovtsov argued that the critics' fixation on the 4.5 percent coupon of 1909 was irrational.[163] However small, the headline coupon rate was a 50 basis-point improvement over that of the 1906 loan; moreover, Germany had seen the coupons on domestic debt it floated rise from 3 to 3.5 percent in 1907, and to 4 percent in 1908.[164] The 4.5 percent coupon Russia was paying was partly due to an increase in global rates, making its 50 basis-point reduction in the coupon relative to the 1906 loan more significant. As Revelstoke had explained to Kokovtsov, however, the French bankers found a half percentage point rate odd—"un type bâtard"— and more common to the German than French or British markets.[165]

If anything, judging by Noetzlin's earlier comments to Kokovtsov on Davydov's negotiating behavior, Russia may have been overplaying its cards in talks with the French banks.[166] Kokovtsov shows that he was conscious of the difference in bargaining power between the large French deposit banks, such as Crédit Lyonnais and Société Générale, which had the ability to place bonds directly within their extensive retail networks, and the merchant banks with smaller footprints.[167] Stating that, in any case, what mattered was the effective interest rate the government paid after discounts rather than the nominal coupon, he reiterated that the 1909 loan was floated at a favorable rate in a rising rate environment, and that the very fact that Paris had allowed a loan spoke for itself. He closed by declaring, "feci quod potui, faciant meliora potentes."[168]

Bankers were acutely aware of the increasing competition. During his July 1909 visit to Saint Petersburg, Midland's D. A. Miller was insecure about his deep-pocketed, but—at least relative to Barings—less prestigious bank's position and chances for winning further Russian business. As he wrote to London: "The importance of Sir Edward coming out here with me in Sept/Oct (when the Municipal Loan will be talked about) cannot be overestimated. Big names are thought much of here and the French, for example, have a certain Marquis de Beauvoir pushing their interests. I do my little best to uphold the dignity of the Bank; but after all it requires a more imposing personality than mine."[169] Later that same day, he wrote, "This place is *full* of all sorts of people nibbling after the Municipal business."[170]

The Russian government took full advantage of these insecurities. During his July trip, Miller met with an unnamed man "practically appointed by the Govt. to rehabilitate the Private Bank," another failing financial institution in which the government was trying to secure the investment of a major foreign bank.[171] Miller took at face value the man's claim: "The *Govt. will not allow it* to fall. It is a question of new capital and that once obtained the Govt. will help it in every way—will deposit some millions of Roubles with it—will give it the next railway issue and will practically take it under its wing. . . . It is a really serious & good thing. Pourparlers with a German group have already gone pretty far but we should have the choice."[172] This mentioning of third-country foreign banks' interest in deals was a frequent feature of many Russian government overtures to foreign investors.

The growing British interest in Russia played into French insecurities. Less than a month after Miller sent his cables to London from Saint Petersburg, the local Paribas agent, Victor Davydov, wrote to Paris, highlighting the risk of railroad concessions in Moscow and Petersburg being awarded to British groups.[173] The French government, too, picked up what it felt were signals of the Russians turning elsewhere. Newly reappointed French finance minister Georges Cochery complained to Pichon, the foreign minister, about Russia's lack of loyalty in the financial and commercial spheres. Citing press reports, he repeated the now familiar refrain that, having taken French money when times were tough and it was desperate, Russia was now turning to other jurisdictions with its bond offerings and industrial concessions. Acknowledging that competitors included friendly countries, Cochery nevertheless argued that France should enjoy a privileged position.[174] He pressed for the French ambassador to push the Russian government to show the same favor to French industry that it enjoyed from French banks.[175]

Pichon's reply revealed differences within the French camp. While the foreign minister agreed to have the ambassador press Cochery's concerns, he questioned the accuracy of the cited reports. He particularly highlighted his apprehension that the Russians saw in British capital and industrial expertise something the French could not provide, and that the matter was not one of the Russians according special rights and privileges to the British, but rather of the latter winning in fair competition.[176]

This diversity of interpretations of Russian statements and actions was evident in the French private sector as well. In September 1909, Bethenod of Crédit Lyonnais recounted a conversation with an insecure Noetzlin. The latter had received a cable from L. Davydov, head of the Credit Chancellery, in response to a discussion the two had been having about the Municipal Credit Bank. Davydov replied that he would respond in a separate letter to his questions. Bethenod did not find it unusual that one of the most powerful bureaucrats in the Russian government—in charge of not only managing one of the largest public debts in the world, but also helping to oversee the Russian banking system—decided to write in more detail later. Noetzlin thought otherwise, saying, "what bothers me, is this future; when a Russian talks about the future, the thing is not going to happen."[177] He proceeded to fret over their mutual decision to have waited for State Bank clarifications on the deal, "while others took the lead."[178] Bethenod protested, "We are not in the presence of the Oyster of the Pleaders, which not one [of the Pleaders] managed to swallow, but rather in the presence of a cake that everyone can eat until they are full."[179] Noetzlin nevertheless maintained that those who were able to set terms, nominate board members, and gain other rights in such affairs would seize the best opportunities for themselves to the detriment of Paribas.[180]

Such insecurities only aided Russian efforts to broaden both their funding base and the ends to which foreign capital could be deployed. Just days after Noetzlin's hysterical reaction to Davydov's one-line cable, the French chargé in Saint Petersburg, de Panafieu, responded to Cochery and Pichon's comments about a Russian pivot to Britain. He dismissed many of the rumors as an exaggeration of reality, seeing market reactions to the rumors the ministers quoted as overblown. He nevertheless reported a genuine and organized attempt by the Russians to attract British investment, particularly to Western Siberian railroads and mining. The diplomat noted that the French had not shown great interest in Siberia, and that since the British had, Kokovtsov likely saw British capital as easier to procure for the Siberian development plans he favored. De Panafieu doubted that the finance ministry's alleged preference for British firms had any basis in fact, but thought rumors to this effect encouraged British firms to bid on concessions. Such dynamics, in his view, explained negotiations involving British banks to accelerate railroad construction in Siberia and Central Asia. He closed by speculating that the Russians were also keen to wean themselves off overdependence on the French—something Witte in particular had failed to do, and for which Russia had paid a heavy price in 1906. German and British capital was a means to this end.[181]

The dance between Midland, the French banks, and the Russian finance ministry underscores how changes and competitive dynamics within the banking industry itself were a powerful driver of foreign capital to Russia in the interrevolutionary years. Joint-stock banks were emerging as a new force in global finance—including in the sovereign lending business. French banks faced increasing competition from their English counterparts in markets including Russia. The shrewd officials of the Russian Ministry of Finance were all too cognizant of such dynamics, playing on the competition between bankers to Russia's advantage by luring foreign capital into a broader array of geographies and sectors within Russia. In addition to leveraging the competition between banks to lure foreign capital into a wider range of regions and sectors within Russia, the government facilitated new types of lending altogether. This trend was particularly important with respect to municipal finance.

———

Since the turn of the century, Russian cities had become increasingly prominent issuers in the bond market, reflective of the deep societal changes taking place in the empire. Cities were struggling to keep up with the rapid growth of their populations, which demanded investment in various areas of the urban infrastructure—from lighting to transport. The cholera epidemic that Miller struggled to avoid in Saint Petersburg on his visit in July 1909 was but a symptom of the rapidly growing city's inadequate sewage system.

A 1911 report by the French consul in Kharkov provides insights into the problems facing boomtowns in the industrial and agricultural belts of Ukraine and southern Russia. In the space of a single year, the city's operating expenses increased by 17 percent; fire department costs alone rose 60 percent over the preceding decade.[182] Peculiarities of Russian legislation capped the amount the city could raise from most sources of income, forcing it to rely on taxes from hotels, cafés, restaurants, and cabarets, as well as income

from municipality-owned property and businesses for most incremental revenues.[183] The resulting deficit was projected to rise from 398,666 rubles in 1908
to more than 600,000 in 1911.[184] Kharkov financed these deficits through sales
of bonds locally, as well as in Saint Petersburg. Between 1902 and early 1911,
the debt nearly doubled to 6,868,559 rubles.[185]

The situation in Kharkov mirrored that of many municipalities across the
empire. By the time of the Kharkov consul's report, the Russian Ministry of
Finance was becoming alarmed that the municipal bond issuance boom would
cannibalize markets for bonds of the central government and other imperial
issuers. Revelstoke was complaining to Noetzlin and Kokovtsov about the
potential for second-tier bonds to hinder central government debt flotation
as early as 1908.[186] Plans for a Finnish bond issue, for example, interfered with
the 1909 central government loan.[187] Municipalities' finances indicated more
paper to come: Saint Petersburg's budget more than doubled between 1904
and 1909 alone, while Moscow's increased by 55 percent.[188]

The growing competition among bankers enabled the ongoing expansion of Russian cities, or as one financier put it, "l'Haussmanisation de St.
Pétersbourg," to continue.[189] Midland was chasing municipal deals when
breaking into the Russian market in late 1909, and it was for the purpose
of winning municipal business that Holden sent Miller to live in Russia for
six months. The London Rothschilds, too, commented in their daily letters to Paris on the fierce competition for municipal loan business between
the house of Speyer and their rivals in Europe.[190] In cables to Paris in 1912,
Georges Louis, the French ambassador to Russia, bemoaned the unequal
bargaining position of the Russian government and French banks in an environment whereby the Russians could reduce the bankers to the position of
supplicants.[191]

French regulators also worried about the flood of municipal bonds from,
at times, obscure municipalities making it onto the Bourse; but competitive
considerations continued to win the argument. In late 1913, the Ministry of
Finance raised concerns about a 180 million ruble Saint Petersburg municipal
bond that Crédit Lyonnais was bidding on, because the municipal government had outstanding disputes with a French contracting firm. The chargé
d'affaires in Saint Petersburg lobbied Paris to allow the loan, arguing that if
Crédit Lyonnais withdrew from the bidding, it would only open the way for
the Germans, without resolving the dispute between the municipality and the
contractor. Ultimately, a compromise was worked out whereby the loan would
be allowed but the listing on the Bourse withheld pending a resolution of the
issues between the city and contractor. This stipulation was ostensibly a sign
of the French regulator forcing conditionality into a loan agreement. However,
the restriction was hardly a major headache for the municipal government,

insofar as Crédit Lyonnais's network of retail branches allowed it to conduct private placements without involving the Bourse. Competition had prevailed over prudence.

By 1914, then, a range of financiers perceived that Russia had recovered from the triple blow dealt by the cyclical industrial slump of 1901–3, the Russo-Japanese War of 1904–5, and the Revolution of 1905, the aftershocks of which were felt well into 1907. An industrial rebound from a low base gained momentum as some benefits accrued to Russian agriculture from the Stolypin reforms. The strong harvests of 1909 and 1910 only added to perceptions of a recovery. The Anglo-Russian entente of 1907, coupled with a continuation of the Franco-Russian alliance, provided geopolitical support that resulted in both direct and indirect promotion of British and French investment in Russia.

Beyond these macro-level shifts, two micro-level changes served as powerful magnets of foreign capital. First, the severity of the industrial slump and political turmoil resulted in a number of bankruptcies that offered foreign investors opportunities that were—at least superficially—good chances to buy up assets at distressed prices, generating interest among some of the largest banks and financial groups in the world, not least Midland Bank. The process of evaluating these deals itself generated more interest in Russia, and in the case of Midland, would eventually result in a much more direct commitment in 1917. Second, competition, including that from new entrants into the world of Russian investment, pushed banks to loosen lending standards—reflected not only in lower interest rates in the primary and secondary markets for Russian sovereign debt, but also in the wider access to global capital markets for a broader group of Russian issuers including, notably, municipalities.

An Increasingly Fragile System

Yet, for all these superficial signs of improvement and progress, Russia was in fact growing more fragile, not more robust, on the eve of the First World War. Political and financial fault lines in the Tsarist edifice emerged and remained unresolved as war broke out. Partly because of the speed of the rebound, the Tsarist government never resolved its political differences with the opposition—so painfully clear in 1905 and 1906—over financial policy. If anything, the boom only deepened the political divide. In the financial realm, Russia was becoming increasingly vulnerable to a financial crisis because of an increasingly levered financial system. Ironically, it was the First World War that papered over these fissures in the short term, preventing—at least temporarily—a potentially severe political and financial crisis.

*Deepening the Financial Front: The Politics of Finance
and Social Implications of Foreign Investment*

In some ways, pointing to political fissures in Russia between 1905 and 1914 as a sign of Russia's fragility is to state the obvious, and to risk falling into the teleological. Both the First and Second Dumas were short-lived affairs. While the Third (1907–12) and Fourth Dumas (1912–17) lasted longer, they too saw their share of conflict with the court. The assassination of Stolypin in 1911 was a rude reminder that the revolutionary movement was alive and well in Russia. Pogroms and other such violence similarly were manifestations of the thriving reactionary element in Russian politics.

Yet, to focus on these most visible manifestations of discord and dissent in Russian politics is to miss the persistence of important fissures in the Russian body politic—and indeed society at large—around questions of Tsarist financial policy. A closer examination of the 1906 to 1914 period shows that the financial front along which the regime and opposition fought did not collapse with the closure of the Saint Petersburg Soviet in 1905, nor with the flotation of "the loan that saved Russia" in 1906. Instead, the regime's financial policies continued to be a source of considerable resentment across a range of groups, from those of the parliamentary opposition to the radical revolutionaries and ordinary people, throughout the 1906 to 1914 period.

Kokovtsov's memoirs document the persistence of a fundamental fissure between the regime and the parliamentary opposition over financial affairs. They reveal that, even as the financial fault line in the Tsarist edifice was widening, he, as the minister of finance and later the chairman of the Council of Ministers, remained blissfully unaware of the depth of this problem. His memoirs relate in detail all the battles he fought in both of those roles during his time in government. He devotes considerable attention to issues of finance, as well as to his battles over the budget and regulation of the banking sector, which included his handling of the Poliakov affair.

Kokovtsov's accounts of his Duma battles make clear that, as far as financial affairs were concerned, the regime and opposition were talking past each other to such a degree that Kokovtsov was unaware of the extent to which his financial policies were deepening the divide. Kokovtsov's general line in discussing Duma debates over finance was that the opposition was simply uneducated in such matters. Thus, with respect to the early debates of the Third Duma, he claims that the historian and Kadet leader Miliukov "had never studied budgeting, and was not at all prepared to fight the government on that ground," before dismissing his critiques as revolving around "the already too familiar theme of the insufficiency of the Duma's budget rights."[192]

In speaking of Andrei Ivanovich Shingarev, Kokovtsov showed more respect, notwithstanding Figes's claim that "even his closest friends were forced to admit that he was little more than a decent mediocrity."[193] Initially acknowledging "no one in the government knew anything about Shingarev," Kokovtsov said that, after an initial period during which the Kadets thought him "not formidable enough to battle the government" on financial policies, "in the six years that followed, Shingarev was the outstanding exponent of the Cadet [*sic*] credo and my invariable opponent. . . . The deputies from the guberniia of Voronezh . . . reported that in zemstvo assemblies he had been regarded as a specialist in budget matters and a forceful and clever debater."[194]

However much Kokovtsov respected Shingarev—a future minister of agriculture and later minister of finance—as debating partner, Kokovtsov was just as dismissive of Shingarev's arguments as he was of Miliukov's. In discussing the 1909 loan, Kokovtsov recalled how the opposition critiqued it in Duma debates on the 1909 budget bill, pushing the case that the government's actions were "illegal."[195] He then proceeded to recount how he undermined Shingarev's argument—that the 1909 loan would weaken Russian credit internationally instead of strengthen it—by showing himself to be more well versed in financial affairs and the technicalities of the bond market. Kokovtsov described how, during the budget debate, Shingarev "avoided all discussions of the budget itself and read a wholesale indictment of the government's entire program."[196] Kokovtsov proceeded to list the ways in which Shingarev was wrong about the details, lamenting the favorable press coverage the latter received, not least from the Kadet newspaper *Rech'*.[197]

Kokovtsov repeated this pattern—of recounting the opposition's government policy critiques, dismissing them as inconsistent with the data and/or betraying a lack of financial literacy, and bemoaning throughout discussion of the Duma debates the favorable press coverage given to the opposition's stance. Ironically, this pattern reveals how poorly Kokovtsov understood and responded to the opposition's position on financial affairs. Kokovtsov's responses reveal him to have thought that he was debating the details of policy, whereas his citation of the opposition's focus on the legality of government financial policies and their unfairness—echoed favorably in the press—shows that the debate was in fact taking place on a much higher level than he realized. As in 1905, the opposition was still arguing that the government had no right to make the decisions it was making in the financial realm. Miliukov specifically adopted the stratagem of blocking the government on budget questions as part of his strategy of "declarative opposition" that marked a radical shift in Kadet politics in the fall of 1912.[198] The tension was evident to British diplomats, who in the lead-up to the 1909 loan issuance were warning Revelstoke to be skeptical of claims by Kokovtsov that the Duma would speedily approve borrowing plans.[199]

By allowing himself to get caught up in the numerical details of the opposition's critique and, no doubt, hearing these arguments articulated in a debating chamber rather than in the streets, Kokovtsov failed to appreciate the revolutionary nature of the opposition's protests. In dismissing the press reports on the Duma debates as hopelessly biased, he demonstrated his failure to grasp the need to vigorously defend the legitimate right of the government to make even major financial decisions without Duma approval. That local government bodies with reactionary leanings—such as the Odessa municipality—would get favorable treatment from the central government regarding, for example, approval of municipal loan issuance did not help bridge the divide over financial policy between the regime and opposition.[200]

It was not only those in the liberal opposition who continued to object to government financial policies enacted between 1905 and 1914. Lenin—in a withering critique of both the government and the Kadets, "The Cadet [sic] Duma Grants Money to the Pogrom-Mongers' Government" (1906)—again articulated a rights-based critique of the government's approach to financial policy. First excoriating the Kadets for legitimizing the government's financial policies by granting approval to government requests for initiatives such as famine relief, he proceeded to articulate a critique very much along Kadet lines—namely, that the government violated the basic political compromise reached in creating the Duma by claiming that it did not need Duma approval to raise or spend money, because such decisions were "determined by the supreme power."[201] In this sense, the opening of the Duma added another dimension to radical criticism of the government's approach to financial policy, which went above and beyond the traditional—and ongoing—rants against misleading salesmanship by the finance ministry.[202]

Less obvious, but arguably more pernicious insofar as it touched people in everyday interactions, was the growing popular resentment along more nationalistic lines against foreign finance and the expatriates involved. A classic manifestation of this was an incident in 1910, played up by the nationalist newspaper *Novoe Vremia*, in which it claimed to have sent a check to its Paris correspondent through Crédit Lyonnais—the only foreign bank in Russia with a network of branches operating under the same name as the parent—only to have the check lost or stolen. A forger eventually found and cashed the check. When the paper was unsuccessful in getting redress from the bank, it launched an attack on banks such as Crédit Lyonnais and—through its Banque du Nord subsidiary—Société Générale, which ran operations in Russia, claiming that they were all "feeding on Russian money."[203]

The French ambassador, who related the incident, acknowledged that the newspaper blew it out of all proportion, but nonetheless admitted that he detected a hint of truth in the allegations. He sensed a divide between the policymakers looking to attract foreign capital and a growing share of public opinion that resented the perceived exploitation of poor Russians—a theme the press was skilled at playing up. The ambassador cited the negative views appearing in the popular press at the time about tramways—a common municipal infrastructure project—as an example of this discontent. Most interestingly, the ambassador pointed to a growing cadre of unemployed and underemployed Russian technicians as problematic. He noted that foreign banks and factories preferred to bring in French workers to fill many managerial and other white-collar posts, creating what he called an "intellectual proletariat."[204] He went on to say, "It would be a mistake to think that it is just a small portion of the public and press that cultivate[s] these xenophobic tendencies. Frankly, it is more or less widespread."[205]

Notwithstanding improvements in Russian bond prices, and indeed in the real economy, then, the 1906 to 1914 period was one of a persisting divide between the regime, the opposition, and a large portion of the public, over issues of financial policy. The tragedy of Kokovtsov was that he continued to fight along the financial front of 1905—attempting to build up reserves and reduce interest costs, and measuring success in terms of his ability to strengthen the finances of the Russian state. His dismissal of opposition concerns about the legitimacy of the government's financial policies, however, shows him to have failed to learn the other lesson of 1905—that to truly secure the state's finances for the long run, the government needed not only to enact judicious financial policies, but convince the people of their right to do so as well. Foreign financiers, too, contributed to this political and social divide through their often high-handed behavior, which has since been unwittingly imitated by generations of expatriates in developing countries.

Financial and Operational Leverage

A second area of fragility in Russia could be found in the financial system. Although the period of recovery from 1906 to 1914 was characterized by a rapid rebound in both the real economy and the markets for Russian securities, Russia was by 1914 a highly levered economy with a vulnerable banking system teetering on the brink of what could have been a disastrous financial crisis. That this crisis was averted had much to do with stimulus associated with the buildup to and outbreak of the First World War.

At first glance, Russia's debt profile on the eve of the war seems favorable. True, Russia was the largest net international debtor in the world by this time,

TABLE 3.1. National debt as a percentage of net national product, 1887–1913

	France	Britain	Germany[a]	Russia
1887	119.3	55.3	50.0	65.0
1890	—	44.6	51.2	77.1
1913	86.5	27.6	44.4	47.3

Source: Ferguson, *House of Rothschild*, 416.
a. Germany = Reich plus federal states.

and its central government debt had grown by 137 percent in sterling terms over a quarter century of state-led industrialization. The relative burden of central government debt as a percentage of net national product, however, had fallen, from 65 to 47.3 percent, and compared favorably to contemporary powers, to say nothing of more recent times (see Table 3.1).[206] In the four years leading up to the war, even Russia's nominal debt dropped slightly, due to amortization.[207] The last full prewar fiscal year, 1913, showed a total fiscal surplus, including both ordinary and extraordinary budgets, of 69.6 million rubles.[208]

The problem with focusing purely on the central government debt, as entered in the *Gosudarstvennaia Dolgovaia Kniga* (Public Debt Book), is that doing so misses both the substantial semiofficial guaranteed loans for which the government was liable, as well as the considerable shift in the mix of overall Russian debt in the years leading up to the war. Specifically, the figures in Table 3.1 that show a drop in Russia's public debt burden, to 47.3 percent, account only for the debt carried on the Public Debt Book. If one were to add to this figure the amount of mortgage debt the government guaranteed for the Bank of the Nobility and for the Peasants' Land Bank, as well as for other guaranteed railroad debt, the figure of nominal government indebtedness would rise substantially. At the start of 1914, for example, the sum of government-guaranteed debentures and certificates of the Nobles' and Peasants' banks alone totaled 2.2 billion rubles, versus a central government debt estimate of 8.8 billion rubles.[209]

Beyond the liabilities that the government assumed, but which were not reflected in the central government debt figure, the prewar years also saw a shift in the mix of debt being issued by Russian entities. As Apostol—a lieutenant of Raffalovich in Paris who coauthored one of the key studies of Russian public finance on the eve of the Bolshevik Revolution—noted, private-sector debt issuance largely stopped during the twin shocks of war and revolution and difficult market conditions from 1904 to 1906.[210] What he calls "issues for productive purposes" began to pick up in 1907, at a time when the rate of increase in general government loans was slowing.[211] Not only did the amount of central government debt issuance from 1909 to 1913 drop to less than a tenth

TABLE 3.2. Breakdown of securities issued in Russia and abroad, 1904–8 and 1909–13 (rubles, millions)

	1904–8	1909–13	Percentage of 1904–8 total	Percentage of 1909–13 total
Government loans	2,143.2	175.0	49.0	3.1
Mortgage loans	1,279.3	2,475.4	29.2	44.5
Municipal loans	86.2	226.4	2.0	4.1
Railway stocks and bonds	207.4	847.2	4.7	15.2
Shares of commercial and land banks	64.5	456.2	1.5	8.2
Industrial and commercial stocks and bonds	596.7	1,378.4	13.6	24.8

Source: Michelson, Apostol, and Bernatzky, *Russian Public Finance during the War*, 237.

of its 1904 to 1908 high (see Table 3.2), but the share it represented of all Russian security issuances dropped from 49 percent in the earlier period to just 3.1 percent in the later period.[212] Mortgage loans, the issuance of which nearly doubled between the first and second periods, became the most prominent type of new issue in the later period.

Railway and municipal loans, too, showed strong growth. Perhaps the most striking growth, however, occurred in the issuance of industrial and commercial stocks and bonds, which boomed from 1909 to 1913, more than doubling the levels achieved during the period from 1904 to 1908, and rising from the third to the second most prevalent type of new issue.[213] Beyond the nearly 27 percent increase in total securities issued between the 1904–8 and 1909–13 periods, the securities data thus show a significant shift in the mix of new issues. The shift was unquestionably toward a more risky asset mix. Whereas municipal and railroad loans often, but not always, enjoyed an implicit or explicit government guarantee, such was not as frequently the case for industrial securities. Moreover, even though foreign issues increased by 13 percent between the two periods, the share of domestic markets in the incremental issues increased from 65 to 88 percent (see Table 3.3).[214] The data on securities issuance, of course, do not include bank loans issued directly to companies. Given the general loosening in credit conditions, it is reasonable to assume that bank loans too increased along a similar pattern, and that Apostol's already striking figures thus should be read as a lower bound vis-à-vis the total amount of loans Russian borrowers contracted.

Beyond the lack of direct state support was the issue of operational leverage embedded in many of the industrial enterprises that were engaged in the borrowing binge of the late prewar years. Most of the businesses issuing these

TABLE 3.3. Securities issued in Russia and abroad, 1904–8 and 1909–13 (rubles, millions)

	1904–8	1909–13	Percentage of 1904–8 total	Percentage of 1909–13 total
Securities issued within Russia	2,861.8	3,840.4	65.4	87.7
Securities issued abroad	1,517.30	1,718.40	34.6	39.2

Source: Michelson, Apostol, and Bernatzky, *Russian Public Finance during the War*, 238.

securities were by their very nature high fixed-cost enterprises. Railroads, steel mills, coal mines, and other such businesses that accounted for much of the incremental borrowing require large up-front investment and have high overheads, but benefit from large economies of scale. They benefitted—or suffered—from what is known in financial accounting as high operating leverage. Thus, for example, for a railroad operating a train pulling a long chain of railcars to carry an additional carload of grain creates little in the way of additional cost, as the costs of running a train are largely fixed. In good times, high operational leverage is good for a business, because any marginal revenue largely falls to the bottom line without having led to a proportionate rise in costs. In bad times, however, the reverse is true, and revenues fall at a higher rate than costs, thus magnifying losses. The greater prevalence of securities from the railroad and heavy industrial sectors in Russia's public and private debt profile suggested a high degree of embedded operational leverage— leverage that currency-based figures on debt in Russia do not capture.

Of course, it could be argued that leverage in and of itself is not a bad thing insofar as there is an optimal amount that could promote output. In this view, an overcapitalized entity or economy forgoes growth by keeping leverage below this optimal point. A historical econometrics exercise of determining what such an optimal point may have been in Russia at the time is beyond the scope of this study. What is evident, however, is that directionally, leverage— as defined in a broader sense—was increasing in Russia. Even accepting the notion of an optimal amount of leverage, arithmetically leverage works both ways, with attendant trade-offs. In this sense, while lower leverage may have entailed lower growth, it would also be associated with lower losses in a downturn.

Economists may quip that the focus on operating leverage specifically reveals an ignorance of the concept of sunk costs—that having invested in fixed capital, a business should not be influenced by its previous investments, and may actually benefit from having done so insofar as they create barriers to entry for potential competitors. This view has its merits, but understates the significance of accounting realities on the decisions of both business owners and investors. From a strictly accounting standpoint, the losses incurred by high fixed-cost businesses appear in the income statement and balance sheet, influencing metrics that investors in the past considered—as today—when evaluating the creditworthiness or equity value of a firm. The sunk cost perspective also underestimates the influence of cash and accrual accounting losses on the behavior of business owners and market participants that were and often are less than fully rational. From a national perspective, the increased prevalence of firms and industries with high operational leverage both in national output and in the outstanding stock of Russian debt issues exposed both reported corporate profits and investors in Russian debt securities to this greater volatility.

The combination of an improving economy and more willing lenders fueled a boom in agricultural borrowing as well. Much of the increase in mortgage debt reflected land purchases by peasants. It was this debt-fueled boom that raised the risk of a sharp downturn in Russia, which would hit both town and country. A French consular report from Odessa in mid-1913 noted worries about the harvest—that of 1912 had not been strong—with dire implications for the estimated 100 million Russians still living solely off the land who, in the most recent year, generated enough only for their subsistence.[215] Spikes in freight rates and war insurance costs tied to the Italo-Turkish and Balkan Wars squeezed exports, magnifying such problems. The report argued a calamity was averted because traders and industrialists involved in the grain trade enjoyed access to credit—a potentially dangerous trend if the 1913 harvest was not as strong as forecast. Turning to the Russian banking system, the report highlighted concerns over the quality of loan books. Beyond issues of asset quality, banks were also in a "hunt for deposits," with the largest banks paying 4.5 to 5.5 percent for deposits, while their cost of borrowing from the State Bank was 6 to 6.5 percent.[216] There was, furthermore, little hope of a near-term drop in rates, given how busy European governments had been in issuing debt as of late.

The consul went on to note that it was not just bank balance sheets that were under strain, but those of individuals as well: "During the last six years following the Russo-Japanese War, Russian banks made the mistake of engaging all classes of the population, from the high lord to the common domestic servant, in speculation. People who have nothing to lose are quickly brought to speculation; but just as quick to spend their winnings, they are not able to withstand the smallest crisis."[217] Moreover, he highlighted widespread land speculation as representing an even greater danger than did the Bourse. He related how a plot of agricultural land worth 200 rubles per *desiatina* prior to the Russo-Japanese war was now selling for 600 rubles,[218] adding that peasants struggled to support such prices, which they in any case paid with the help of mortgages, given that they were still operating with such primitive methods and infrastructure whereby "the average yield of a hectare is not even half that in France."[219]

After finding some solace in the large size of Russian government reserves, the consul commented on manufactured causes of bad harvests. He pointed in particular to 15 years of deforestation lowering soil humidity. One major source of Russia's export earnings was a thriving timber trade. As the consul reported, there had been so much harvesting of timber, and so much export of it to meet booming European demand, that the state railroads were unable to find wooden ties for their own construction needs. To discourage the export of timber, and especially railroad ties, the state railroad raised the transport tariff on ties to 10 kopecks per piece.[220]

An endogenous tension and potential point of diminishing returns was, thus, emerging within Russia's growth model. The very export-oriented behavior of certain sectors, such as timber, required to earn the foreign currency necessary to service Russia's external debts undermined other key sectors such as agriculture and railroad construction. The fuel inefficiency of industry and municipalities added further strains. Due to globally elevated energy prices and the domestic timber shortage, the consul in Odessa expected that Russia—itself a major producer of coal in the Donets basin—would have to import materially significant quantities of coal in the future.[221]

In addition to the high degree of leverage in the countryside, by as early as 1912 signs of a renewed industrial slump were apparent to French observers. The consul in Warsaw painted a truly disconcerting picture in a dispatch sent to the Quai d'Orsay in late June. Even as Polish industry speedily rebounded after the turmoil of 1904 to 1908, the consul noted that the end of reconstruction eliminated a source of demand. The textile industry was also a source of concern. The Łódź region—the "Polish Manchester"—accounted for some 800 factories employing 150,000 workers, including two French operations with a workforce of 2,500.[222] Having already experienced a demand slump, firms were cutting hours, with some factories not even working a full week, but rather four days out of seven.[223] This Łódź industrial belt was the site of significant unrest in 1905, and would remain important in future events.[224]

The consul attributed the textile slump to several factors. Bumper harvests, coupled with the expulsion of the Jews from Lithuania drove overinvestment in the textile industry. Lackluster Volga and Siberian harvests in 1911 hurt peasant incomes, thereby cutting demand. A late winter cut into the demand for warmer fabrics. During the Second Morocco Crisis in 1911, German firms that were important sources of credit to the Łódź factories cut their lines of credit. All these headwinds combined to drive a rise in both shop inventories and bankruptcies. Indeed, before remarking on the flagging sugar industry, the consul reported that the total number of bankruptcies in the area, which stood at 42 in 1906, had increased to 145 in 1911, and had already reached 52 in the first quarter of 1912 alone.[225]

Despite improvement in the Russian economy in the years between the end of the 1905 Revolution and the start of the First World War, then, contemporary observers perceived signs of fragility. Financial leverage remained high in both the public sector—when government-guaranteed bonds are included—and the private sector. Moreover, the high degree of operational leverage embedded in many of the private- and public-sector loans only magnified the financial leverage in the economy. That the countryside and key sectors of the economy, such as textiles, still depended so much on good harvests left little doubt as to the still truthful ring of "His Majesty the Harvest" ruling Russia.[226] As even Gatrell acknowledged in his otherwise positive assessment of prerevolutionary Russian agriculture, sharp annual fluctuations in grain production remained a problem well into the twentieth century.[227] While such trends were highly significant from the standpoint of the Russian economy, they were fed to a significant degree by foreign investors and financiers. In this sense, the growing leverage in Russia was not only a source of fragility for the Tsarist economy, but also a concern to foreign banking systems and international markets increasingly tied into Russian finance and thus increasingly invested in the stability and growth of Russia. This trend was itself an echo of the potential contribution of the Russian Loan of 1906 described in Chapter 2 to the Panic of 1907.

By late 1913, the signs of trouble were only growing, not least in the eyes of French observers. On 27 October, the French foreign minister wrote to the finance minister with concerns over strikes in Riga that were prompting foreign banks to cut lines of credit, aggravating the situation and threatening to undermine a municipal loan of 10.5 million rubles that the government was planning to float.[228] The year had seen Moscow Union Bank face a capital call from the State Bank, which wanted it to raise 30 to 40 million rubles of equity immediately.[229] Changing their previous behavior, the bank's French backers, BUP, turned down its request and disengaged themselves from the board and branch network of the overleveraged institution.[230] The French commercial attaché's review of 1913 noted that volatility on the Saint Petersburg Bourse had increased, with a downward bias in prices.[231] By 4 April 1914, Paléologue, the French ambassador in Saint Petersburg, was writing to Doumergue, the French foreign minister, about a weak and unsettled local market, although he was at a loss to describe it using traditional political and economic explanations. He instead suggested that the radical increase in government interventions in the economy and uncertainty over the future policies of the newly appointed finance minister, Bark, unsettled markets. He added that Russian industry had seen several good years, fed by easy credit, and "the least aggravation of any one of them could be fatal to a large number of them," but concluded by hedging with a comment about the Bourse not reflecting reality and Russia having many resources.[232]

The Defense Stimulus

For all the leverage building up in the Tsarist economy, however, and as much as its manifestation as increased government intervention in the economy may have unsettled markets in the short term, the stimulus from the contemporaneous defense buildup served as a timely intervention on the part of the government. Specifically, defense spending had the effect—whether intentional or not—of supporting industry and staving off what could have become a devastating financial crisis. In this sense, the approach of world war served to actually shore up the Tsarist regime, rather than hasten its demise.

To this end, the one bright sign amid all the gloom of the 25 June 1912 report of the French consul in Warsaw was the boost in demand that the metals and mining industry received from the Russian naval rearmament program. The Duma had just approved a credit of 502 million rubles for the industry, which the consul said would compensate for its flagging construction orders.[233] Starting in 1911, the government also sharply accelerated spending on the railroads (see Table 3.4). The increased spending, particularly in 1913, occurred in the context of the aforementioned moves by the French government to link further loans for Russia to its meeting certain targets vis-à-vis strategic—as defined by the French and Russian general staffs—railroad construction. On

TABLE 3.4. Expenditure on railway construction, 1905–14 (rubles, millions, current prices)

	Construction of new lines	Improving of existing track	Total state outlays
1905	73	82	155
1906	41	71	112
1907	49	75	124
1908	60	74	134
1909	60	71	131
1910	63	65	128
1911	96	68	164
1912	111	66	177
1913	133	87	220
1914	93	95	188

Source: Gatrell, *Tsarist Economy*, 174.

TABLE 3.5. Defense production, 1908–14

	Index of defense spending	Value of defense production (rubles, millions)
1908	69	269
1909	71	277
1910	73	285
1911	73	285
1912	87	339
1913	100	390

Source: Gatrell, *Government, Industry, and Rearmament in Russia*, 255.

the eve of his dismissal in 1914, Kokovtsov had been trying to arrange a loan of 500 to 600 million francs within the framework of this arrangement.[234]

The role of the defense industry in the late Tsarist industrial boom is, of course, well documented. Gatrell's *Government, Industry, and Rearmament in Russia, 1900–1914* remains the classic work on the subject. Among other things, he charts how the labor force in the armaments industry increased by 40 percent between 1908 and 1913.[235] However, Gatrell is arguably too modest in his claim that rearmament was "the mainspring of industrial growth" that offered a recovery that was faster than the normal cyclical recovery Russia would have eventually entered.[236] As the index on defense spending he constructed shows, the increase in defense spending was not gradual but weighted toward the years after 1911—with flat to single-digit percentage growth before then, followed by jumps of 19 percent and 15 percent in the years immediately following (see Table 3.5). In this sense, the defense spending Gatrell charted began to increase significantly at the point when various observers started to recognize signs of fragility in the industrial and agrarian economy.

Of course, it would be a mistake to see in the rearmament program a targeted or efficient form of stimulus. Gatrell rightly argues the industrial revival "occurred in a fit of absence of mind" rather than through a concerted attempt to link defense and private industry.[237] To the contrary, Russian defense procurement stifled the private sector in many ways.[238] Furthermore, neither the naval rearmament nor the strategic railroad construction that were so central to prewar defense spending could be said to be the most logical or efficacious programs. Gatrell rightly questions the military logic of spending so much on building up a navy that could not credibly achieve dominance in the Baltic, the Black Sea, or the Pacific.[239] Moreover, the strategic railroad program threw capital at a problem that was more likely operational in nature. Witte himself devoted his earlier career to operational issues, and decades after his work in the railroad industry, Russian railroads were still in a sorry state. While key lines—not least the Trans-Siberian—were single-track affairs, imbalances between rolling stock and locomotives and general misallocation of resources were major drivers of delays and waste. Additionally, for all its stimulative effects, the increase in defense spending only added to the empire's debt.

Still, blunt, inefficient, and unintended as it may have been, the increase in defense spending did provide stimulus to key sectors of the economy and in key geographies, such as the Polish industrial belt and Saint Petersburg itself. By taking a broader view that encompasses the banking system in particular, then, it is apparent that Gatrell was too limited in his characterization of the impact of defense spending on the eve of the war. Tsarist rearmament did not merely speed up an industrial recovery that would likely have come anyway; it also drove an increase in defense spending at precisely the time when and in the places where the empire was becoming most vulnerable to an industrial slump that—because of the high degree of leverage in the system—could have triggered a financial crisis. Even if such spending increased leverage in the long run, it nevertheless sustained and stimulated growth in the near term. As a result, the Tsarist regime avoided a potentially severe financial crisis, even as the potential gravity of a future crisis grew.

Of course, to note that the Tsarist economy was growing more fragile due to increased leverage and slowdowns in key areas of industry is not to argue that a financial crisis—to say nothing of a revolution—would have occurred in mid-1914. Both financial crises and revolutions are highly contingent events, and both economic imbalances and political tensions can build for extended periods of time before moments of sharp adjustment take place—if they do at all. To make the historical claim that the Tsarist economy was growing more fragile is not to make a precise prediction of a financial crisis and/or revolution in a counterfactual scenario. The aforementioned weather-dependent nature of Russian agriculture, which remained a key driver of the overall economy, could deliver positive as well as negative shocks, for example. Nevertheless, the increased leverage and the signs of industrial slowdown combined to suggest increased vulnerability—fragility—in the Tsarist economy in the years in question.

The Historical Significance of the Prewar
Crisis and the Haimson Debate

Whether or not the brewing financial crisis that the rearmament program and war forestalled would have resulted in a Bolshevik takeover in 1914 is, then, impossible to determine. Nevertheless, this picture of growing economic and financial fragility and buildup to crisis resonates with the classic debate among social and political historians about the role of the outbreak of war in the broader historical arc of the Russian Revolution.

More than fifty years ago, Leopold Haimson, Arthur Mendel, and Theodore Von Laue debated the degree to which, from a social and political perspective, Russia was primed for revolution on the eve of the First World War.[240] In Haimson's telling, a traditional Soviet view held that but for the start of the war and the associated rise in "chauvinistic" tendencies, Russia would have seen a revolution as early as 1914.[241] In contrast, many Western scholars argued that it was the war that turned Russia off a stabilizing and reformist, rather than revolutionary, path.[242] This line of argument brings to mind the counterfactual implicit in Stolypin's famous quote, "Give the state twenty years of internal and external peace, and you will not recognize present-day Russia."[243]

Haimson controversially argued that the Russian working class was growing less, not more, moderate from the summer of 1912, as evidenced by Bolshevism's growing popularity.[244] At the same time as workers and the privileged were becoming polarized, in Haimson's narrative, so were the privileged and the Tsarist regime.[245] It was this dual process of polarization that brought Russia to the point that "by the beginning of 1914 any hope of avoiding a revolutionary crisis appeared to be evaporating even among the more moderate representatives of liberal opinion."[246]

The picture emerging from the perspective of financial history of Russia being on the verge of a financial crisis, which the defense buildup and the war forestalled, resonates with that which Haimson draws from the sociopolitical perspective. There is a distinction, however. Haimson's argument was, as he later recalled, that "even in the absence of war, Russia's body politic would have been subjected to revolutionary turmoil comparable to those it experienced in 1917" and that the war would "accelerate substantially" the revolutionary process. The financial history perspective suggests that the buildup to war played a stabilizing role. In this latter view, the rearmament period and then the initial years of war actually delayed a crisis because of the fiscal stimulus such circumstances provided to the economy, and the greater flexibility the war gave economic policymakers, even if—as Chapters 4 and 5 will show—the later years of Russia's war did ultimately considerably accelerate the collapse.

If anything, against the background of Haimson's narrative, the impact of the fiscal stimulus of the armaments drive and start of war become doubly significant. In the context of the labor unrest to which Haimson points—with larger, more frequent, and increasingly radical strikes—an industrial slump would have only added fuel to an already raging fire.[247] Of course, agriculture remained arguably more significant to overall economic output than did industry. However, the events of 1905 showed that the industrial sector—and industrial unrest—had a disproportionately high degree of influence on political developments. The significance of any industrial slowdowns in the empire was thus much greater than their impact on imperial economic output. Defense-related orders helped avert such an industrial slump. Similarly, the wave of foreclosures that could have resulted from a crisis in the increasingly leveraged countryside—either because of a poor harvest, to which Russia was still very vulnerable, or because of a real economic downturn—would have done nothing to moderate discontent either in the countryside or among the urban working class, which retained ties to the village. In his updated view, published in 2000, Haimson articulates his main modification to his prior views as being that "the most striking feature of this crisis on the eve of the war was its largely suspended character" as "most of the major individual and collective actors involved in the unfolding crisis in urban Russia recoiled from any decisive actions."[248] In this framework, a financial crisis may well have been the factor pushing them over the edge.

Conclusion

The period between the 1905 Revolution and the start of the First World War saw a remarkable rebound in the Russian economy. After suffering the triple blows of a sustained cyclical downturn, a humiliating wartime defeat, and a revolution, financial markets perceived accelerating real economic growth, and reopened for Russia. Financiers were at first drawn back to Russia by the nascent recovery in the real economy, as well as by the opportunity to invest in distressed assets. Geopolitics were incrementally encouraging, with the Anglo-Russian Agreement of 1907 building on the continuity of the Franco-Russian entente, which would indeed grow stronger in the financial sphere with the agreement on strategic railroads in 1913. Once the recovery was under way, competitive dynamics between financiers became a further driver of investment, and shifted the debtor-creditor power balance in favor of the Russians, in turn encouraging further lending.

By 1912 the Russian empire was booming, but at the same time it was also growing more fragile. The financial front remained very much open in the political realm, as many of the conflicts of 1905 remained unresolved, and in some ways gained new sharpness with the opening of the Duma. Leverage was increasing, and the mix of securities and loans floated by Russian issuers was shifting in the direction of a higher risk profile. The Russian growth outlook continued to depend throughout this period on the harvest—with ever-greater risks as the issuance of mortgage debt skyrocketed. It was precisely at this time, when the system was at its most fragile, that the naval rearmament program and the understanding with the French to accelerate railroad construction provided an added boost to an economy that had already shown evidence of being susceptible to a potentially disastrous slowdown.

Once the war began in 1914, the Russian and other governments gained additional breathing space. The war changed the dynamics of public finance for Russia—it was able to borrow directly from Allied governments on generous terms, and the suspension of convertibility gave further flexibility on the monetary front. At least for a time, then, the war eased the pressures of public finance on Russia. In this sense, the buildup to war and its start in 1914 actually averted a potentially disastrous financial crisis and bought the regime time.

4

Investing in the Revolution

ON 15 JANUARY 1917, the First National City Bank of New York—forerunner to today's Citigroup—opened its inaugural office in the Russian Empire in a regal building that once housed the Ottoman embassy.[1] The branch opening in Petrograd marked the culmination of a long period of study of the Russian market and courtship of Russian government and business leaders by National City's New York–based senior management and its agent in Russia, H. Fessenden Meserve. While the bank had been active in Russia prior to opening the Petrograd branch—agreeing to a loan of $5 million at 6 percent with Tsarist finance minister P. L. Bark through its London representative in 1914, for example—the move to formally establish a physical branch in the Russian Empire marked a new level of commitment to Russia.[2] Before the year ended, however, the bank had been raided by agents of the—now Bolshevik—Russian government, who claimed it had failed to properly report on its business activities to the State Bank, and proceeded to seize its documents and vault keys. The Bolsheviks eventually released the branch manager, R. R. Stevens, but there remained little doubt that National City's Russian experiment had not gone according to plan.[3]

While National City's experience in Russia is a particularly dramatic case of a poorly timed business move, in many ways it more generally symbolizes the decisions of Western investors vis-à-vis the Russian markets at the height of the First World War. An examination of bond market data shows, for example, a sharp decline in yield spreads of Russian government bonds relative to comparable British consols (see Figures 3.1 and 4.1) from the time of the 1905 Revolution to the eve of the October Revolution of 1917. Indeed, the risk premiums on Russian debt relative to Western benchmarks approached multiyear lows in early 1917—in spite of the political instability and severe war-related strains the Russian economy and society were experiencing. While the behavior and subsequent losses of high financiers—whether in the strategic decisions of banks or the trades of bond traders—very clearly suggest a failure to accurately forecast future events in Russia, such failures are not intrinsically

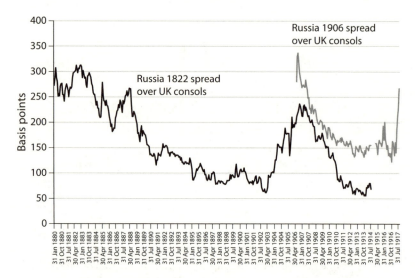

FIGURE 4.1. Spread of Imperial Russian Government 1822 and 1906 bonds over British consols. Source: "GFD Database" (2012), www.globalfinancialdata.com.

interesting. The drivers of the investment boom in the Russian markets from 1914 through 1917 are, however, worthy of investigation.

Specifically, in studying contemporary sources, three broad factors can be identified as contributing to the Western investment boom in the Russian markets from 1914 through late 1917. First, in contrast to later observers, many contemporary foreign investors did not perceive Russia as suffering from an economic crisis—even as late as 1917. Second, a remarkably high degree of risk appetite shaped investor decision making and was in turn the product of moral hazard from government guarantees and competitive pressures. Third, geopolitics and feelings of patriotism within the context of the First World War pushed investors to engage the Russian market in the hopes of advancing home-country interests. Finally, contemporary investors felt that by investing in Russia they were participating in the transformation of a society—a belief that would enable them to overlook much of the political instability and violence of the revolutionary events of 1917.

The Wartime Economic Crisis

In Russia, seven per cent had everything, and ninety per cent had nothing. One per cent of the seven per cent was German and represented efficiency. When the war broke out this one per cent was lost and Russia was lost.

—WILLIAM BOYCE THOMPSON, DIRECTOR, FEDERAL
RESERVE BANK, NEW YORK, 20 DECEMBER 1918

In light of subsequent events, the notion that the First World War devastated the Russian economy and society appealed to many observers of the Bolshevik regime and has since influenced the historiography. The crisis of wartime Russia is and was evident to various observers, ranging from historians to Bolshevik technocrats.

One manifestation of the crisis was directly related to military losses Russia suffered early in the war. As Peter Gatrell notes, Russia lost major sites of prewar industrial production and transport early in the conflict. The Ottoman entry into the war on the side of the Central Powers in October 1914 choked Russia's key Black Sea export route, while Russia's loss of Łódź by the end of 1914 resulted in disruptive mass population displacements.[4] Vilna fell in September, and plans were already drawn up by as early as August for the movement of gold reserves from Petrograd to Vologda.[5] By late 1915, Russia had lost 14 provinces, representing a prewar population in excess of 35 million.[6]

Nevertheless, the Tsarist economy actually absorbed this initial shock remarkably well. As Gatrell and Harrison note, in spite of the loss of major industrial centers in Poland and a general enemy threat to at least 20 percent of prewar industrial capacity overall, the Tsarist economy surprisingly achieved some growth in the first two years of the war.[7] They suggest that armament output in Russia actually increased by a compound annual growth rate of almost 25 percent between year-end 1914 and 1917.[8] More recent scholarship by Markevich and Harrison confirms the view of a pickup in some sectors during the early years of the war, notably in military services, the constant-ruble output of which increased by a factor of six between 1913 and 1916.[9] Still, even after accounting for this initial continuation and increase of production, Gatrell, Harrison, and Markevich agree in various studies that two years after the war began, Russian real economic output had started to wane, with a particularly marked downturn occurring by 1917.[10]

While some scholars allow for a stronger performance than previously thought in the aggregate level, another view stresses the crisis in the consumer sector of the economy amid wartime depravations. Production disruptions were a major driver of the consumer crisis. Grain production, for example, had fallen to 10 to 15 percent of prewar levels in 1916, and in 1917 remained at about 15 percent of prewar production levels.[11] By 1917, according to Gatrell and Harrison, consumer goods availability had dropped to catastrophically low levels due to "a lack of government intervention in the consumer market."[12]

Logistical issues were a second driver of the consumer crisis. Figes cites wartime disruptions of transportation networks as having a pernicious impact on domestic distribution of basic consumption items like grain, creating shortages in cities.[13] In contrast to Gatrell and Harrison, Figes claims that overly zealous government interference in food markets, combined with a failure of distribution channels drove farmers to cut production or reorient themselves along autarkic lines as early as 1915.[14] Subsequent scholarship underscored this point, noting a nearly 20 percent per capita drop in food output between 1913 and 1916, which was exacerbated by distributional distortions that resulted in "highly uneven" waves of famine hitting both town and country.[15] Regardless of the cause, then, Figes, Gatrell, Harrison, and Markevich note a serious real economic—and specifically a consumption—crisis as occurring as early as 1915 and certainly by 1917 in Russia. As Figes writes, "On the eve of 1917 the average working woman in Petrograd was probably spending around forty hours per week in various queues for provisions."[16]

Others focused on monetary phenomena in pointing to Russia's wartime economic crisis. Grigorii Sokol'nikov, the Bolshevik placed in charge of the newly nationalized banks, in a 25 May 1918 report to the All-Russian Congress of Soviets for the National Economy, pointed to an exodus of gold from Russia at a time when British gold reserves had doubled, French reserves increased by a third, and even German reserves rose from 1.4 million to 2.3 million marks.[17] Sokol'nikov blamed parasitic capitalist financiers and a derelict pre-revolutionary Russian government for the perpetuation of trade patterns along lines unfavorable to the Russian balance of payments and for deepening Russia's dependence on foreign loans, which further drained its gold reserves.[18] Sokol'nikov's claim that future Bolshevik policies would protect and bolster Russia's gold reserves would, incidentally, prove in time to be completely hollow.[19] As Sean McMeekin shows in his study of Bolshevik money laundering and foreign trade, by early 1922 the Bolsheviks had spent most of Tsarist Russia's gold reserves—once the largest in the world.[20]

Other accounts suggest a more ambiguous picture of the wartime Tsarist economy. Norman Stone, for example, notes that "the Russian Stock-Exchanges went through something of a boom in the First World War, a process observed elsewhere only in the United States."[21] He acknowledges the bottlenecks and supply disruptions that other historians and contemporaries point out, but argues that far from being the symptoms of a looming collapse they were "crises of growth."[22] Citing figures by Soviet historian A. L. Sidorov, Stone notes that the "overall growth-rate of the Russian economy" increased by almost 19 percent between 1914 and 1916, implying an annualized growth rate of almost 10 percent—extremely high for any country under normal circumstances, let alone during a major war that it was losing.[23] Still, the same figures show a decline in output of more than 36 percent from 1916 to 1917, and Stone suggests that by 1917 the evidence indicated the boom was over, with the "gigantic industrial" effort of the boom years bringing "its own social consequences."[24] Thus, while there may be disagreement on details as to the starting point and duration—notably from the most recent scholarship of Markevich and Harrison—there is widespread agreement regarding the idea that a severe economic crisis had affected late Tsarist Russia, especially by late 1916 or early 1917.

Crisis? What Crisis?

While contemporary Russian Leninists and future historians saw a severe economic crisis in Russia in 1917, the foreign financial community held a more sanguine view of the late pre-Bolshevik economy. In early 1915, Morgan Grenfell—the British outpost of the House of Morgan—cabled New York that while the 4 percent Russian bond of 1869 was trading at a sharp discount, and could well fall further, they saw it as "intrinsically sound after [the] War."[25] More than a year into the war, the financier Sir Ernest Cassel revealed to his frequent deal partner, Lord Revelstoke, that he had 1.2 million rubles in Russia, and that he intended to keep his funds there until the end of the war, or at least until exchange rates improved.[26] Asked by Cassel to manage his Russian funds for him, Revelstoke did not dissuade him, offering to invest them in Russian Treasury bills, before the men agreed that it was probably best to keep them where they were, in a current account at a private commercial bank in Moscow.[27]

In mid-1916, National City issued a pamphlet with a constructive view of the situation in Russia. The document focused unabashedly on the big picture—citing a population "surpassed only by China and India" and vast natural resources, arguing, "Considered in relation to its undeveloped natural resources, Russia's debt and current taxation, including the additional burden of the war, is the lowest of the belligerent countries."[28] Touching on the foreign exchange volatility that Cassel and Revelstoke sought to navigate, the pamphlet argued that while the ruble had dropped 40 percent relative to its prewar value, "its purchasing power in Russia is holding its own quite well, advances and decreases in the prices of various commodities being due chiefly to changes in supply and demand. The country's internal financial condition is reported to be satisfactory."[29]

Upon his arrival in wartime Petrograd in early 1917 in an official capacity as a member of the British delegation to inter-Allied financial talks, Revelstoke was himself taken aback by the scenes of opulence he saw: "It is interesting to note the evident 'war prosperity' of the town. The shops are brilliantly illuminated, the florists' windows full of colour, and the jewelers are doing a tremendous trade. Prices have risen to a phenomenal degree; both those of commodities, and also, owing no doubt to the inflation of the currency and consequent depreciation of the Rouble, those of Bank shares and of local industrial companies. Money is being freely spent, they say, by a new class who have recently acquired fortunes."[30] As his comments suggested, Revelstoke—a

patrician Englishman no doubt horrified by the wartime nouveaux riches—
questioned the underlying substance to the "war prosperity" going on to
remark that "throughout the Empire the want of organization and the lack of
transport facilities are leading to a crisis the gravity of which cannot be overestimated. Very possible Food Riots [sic] are a startling contrast to this newly
begotten wealth and careless expenditure."[31] The same comments, however,
also underscored his view that the crisis was not necessarily in the present, and
that Russia in early 1917 was still in a boom phase.

As late as 17 March 1917—that is, after the February Revolution and the
abdication of the Tsar—London's congenitally Russophobic *Economist*
painted a rosy picture of prerevolutionary Russian public finances in 1916 along
with a very optimistic prognosis for Russian finances in 1917. In a marked contrast to its decades of critical and biting commentaries on the Russian government's financial position, the magazine noted that pre-1917 figures show "an
unexpectedly cheerful picture." Brushing aside the loss of nearly £90 million,
or one-third of central government revenues due to the government's temperance policies, the magazine reported that "the recovery in general revenue, in
spite of the devastation of some western areas by the enemy, has been satisfactory beyond expectation."[32]

Reports by National City Bank's representative in Petrograd, H. Fessenden
Meserve, describe an even more optimistic picture of wartime Russia. National
City's senior management sent Meserve—an American, Harvard-educated,
Baltimore banker who had earlier spent time in Korea—to Petrograd in late
August 1915 as the bank's representative in Russia.[33] While in Russia, from 1915
through 1917, Meserve met with local and foreign businessmen, Russian government officials, and other such individuals to stay abreast of developments
in the Russian markets and to explore business opportunities for National City
in Russia. He would eventually play the leading role in establishing National
City's physical branch network in Russia, which, by the end of 1919, included
offices in Petrograd, Moscow, and Vladivostok.[34]

Meserve was not the only representative of a major Western bank sent to
Russia, however. The London City and Midland Bank—at the time one of the
largest in the world and National City's archrival—deputed an employee to
the Banque de Commerce de l'Azoff Don in Saint Petersburg two years before
Meserve arrived in Petrograd.[35] The employee—a Russian-speaking Englishman named John Frederick Bunker—was eventually put in charge of opening
a stand-alone office for Midland in Saint Petersburg.[36] Bunker married a local
Anglo-Russian woman and quickly integrated himself into local business circles, passing on political and economic intelligence in regular letters to the
chairman of Midland, Sir Edward Holden, who, as seen in Chapter 3, took a
heightened interest in Russian affairs as early as 1907.[37]

Observers from institutions with longer ties to Russia also left observations from their time in Petrograd in 1916 and 1917. Revelstoke's diary from his trip in early 1917 is fascinating, and a reminder of the utility of banking archives for political and even social history. Recounting dinner at the British embassy upon his arrival, he relayed a dining companion's concern over the rumors, gossip about Rasputin, and "the unrestrained manner in which the probability of future tragic developments was freely canvassed in all circles here."[38] His character portraits were at times withering: Paléologue, the French ambassador, whose memoirs would be much cited by subsequent historians, was, in the opinion of the financial baron, "amiable, wordy, tiresome, and second-rate."[39]

Meserve's letters to National City's president, Frank A. Vanderlip, preserved at the Russian State Historical Archive (RGIA), as well as Bunker's letters to Holden, held at the HSBC Group Archives, are a rich and little-studied set of sources that provide important insights into how two of the most influential financial institutions in the world approached Russia and emerging markets more generally at a particularly turbulent time in the history of Russia and the world. Both firms were also representative of a shift in global finance that saw joint-stock banks play an increasingly large role in international finance, and British and American capital play a more prominent role in Russia in particular.[40] In this sense, the Meserve and Bunker accounts offer a very different perspective from that of old Russia hands such as Revelstoke and even Jack Morgan.

Meserve's letters in 1917 suggest little concern about an economic crisis. In his letter of 10/23 February 1917—his first substantive letter since having opened the bank's first Russian branch in Petrograd—Meserve noted that, in less than a month since opening, the branch was already breaking even. He went on to forecast that the Petrograd branch will "double our present earnings within three months."[41] Meserve proceeded to argue strongly in favor of opening a second branch in Moscow before closing with the observation, "I have not changed my views in the slightest as regards the great future for our bank here if we continue to work hard, fair and intelligently."[42]

Back in New York, National City was in the process of training a generation of young bankers to do deals in Russia. The bank had been a pioneer in establishing training programs to educate freshly minted college graduates in the ways of international banking, including through formal coursework in finance and foreign languages. That National City began by introducing courses in Spanish, Portuguese, and French was hardly surprising. The former reflected the bank's growing presence in Latin America, and the latter the continued importance of Paris in global finance. By 1916, however, the bank introduced Russian as its fourth language offering, reflecting the prominence of Russia in the bank's international expansion plans.[43] At the time of its opening, the

National City Petrograd branch had no fewer than 16 employees, of whom 15 were expatriates, many of whom had been taking intensive Russian classes for weeks prior to their arrival.[44]

National City's investment in Russia was evident beyond their opulent choice of headquarters, which were in any case partly a function of the dearth of space in the central business district around Nevsky Prospekt, given wartime requisitioning of commercial buildings for use as military hospitals.[45] The bank had secured a boarding house for the bachelors on the staff on the opposite—and cheaper—side of the Neva from the bank branch. Meserve had also poached two key clerks from the staff of the American embassy in Russia, as well as a senior staffer from the embassy in Stockholm.[46] The Swedish capital had been a key staging area for the organizers of the branch opening, who had bought the original consignment of safes and furniture for the branch there, only to lose it to a German torpedo en route to Petrograd.[47]

The bank's internal employee magazine attested to the ambitious Russian expansion the company was planning. In early 1916, the bank was complimentary about Russian public finances in its publications, making favorable comparisons between Russia's debt levels and immense natural resources and taxation potential—an argument it would repeat in various forms over the course of the year.[48] In an article scheduled for release around the time of the Petrograd branch opening, Citibank vice president Samuel McRoberts laid out the bank's rationale for expanding into the Russian Empire in the midst of the Great War. McRoberts had been instrumental in the prep work behind the Petrograd initiative, having traveled to Russia in the summer of 1916 and arranged financing to the tune of $75 million for the Russian government in an attempt to build goodwill.[49] He noted above all changing circumstances in the United States, where the war had made American banks flush with liquidity.[50] Acknowledging that for the American bank Mexico was "probably the greatest field" of immediate interest, he cited the enormous economic potential of Russia, not least in emerging areas such as the oil industry, as factors attracting New York's attention to the market.[51] Reflecting the prejudices of the time, McRoberts spoke also of the Russians as "a far-north people, with the physical vigor and energy characteristic of the Northern races."[52] In a telling—and ominous—remark he went on to speak of Russians as "a democratic people" and lament over how "this democratic spirit of the Russian people does not seem to be understood."[53]

Back in revolutionary Petrograd, Meserve maintained his optimistic tone on the Russian economy in his letter of 16/29 March 1917. While acknowledging the impact of revolutionary upheaval on daily life and trade to a greater extent than the *Economist*, Meserve's letter is still striking for its optimism and deserves to be quoted at length:

Before this letter reaches you, you will have been thoroughly informed regarding recent events here. Naturally at the time it was nerve racking, especially for the ladies, but as I look back on it all now I can only say, all things considered, that there was more self-restraint showed here by the Russians than would under similar circumstances have been exhibited by any other nationality in the world. I am very proud of the Russians for their wonderful self-restraint, and although matters here are still, of course, nervous for the individual, I feel more certain than ever that Russia itself will come out in the end stronger than ever. I still consider all foreign investments here advisable and safe, and I sincerely hope that the United States will now be willing to help Russia more in every way.[54]

Meserve's glowing reports to New York in the spring of 1917 should, of course, be read with care. Having just opened the bank's first Russian branch and tied his career to the bank's expansion in Russia more generally over the course of nearly two years, and no doubt cognizant of the investments the bank had already made toward building its Russian capacity on his recommendation, he had every incentive to highlight successes and opportunities and downplay risks in Russia at this critical turning point in the bank's involvement in the country.

Meserve's optimistic assessment of Russia's prospects was not unique among American bankers, however. In April 1917, a contact at the Seattle National Bank wrote to him, reporting that a series of 5.5 percent internal Russian notes "have been bought by more people than any other foreign issue."[55] Echoing McRoberts's commentary, the correspondent proceeded to say that "the feeling is general throughout this country [the United States] that Russia is in for a great development and that all previous relations between that country and ours have laid the way for eminently satisfactory relations hereafter."[56]

More striking is a rare direct letter dated 28 April 1917 from National City president Frank A. Vanderlip himself to Meserve. Vanderlip went beyond the expected praise for Meserve's handling of Petrograd operations to paint an optimistic picture of the situation in Russia: "I do not need to tell you that my own view has been for many years that we should see the time when Russia would offer perhaps the most attractive field in all the world outside of the United States for the employment of some of our surplus resources. The present tremendous current of events is undoubtedly hastening that time."[57] Whereas Vanderlip's earlier comments were prefaced with a remark about Russia's potential as a market being fully reached "when the times become more composed," his closing comment about being in agreement with Meserve's "views in regard to Moscow" is perhaps the greatest testament to his bullishness on the Russian market, since Meserve's views vis-à-vis Moscow were extremely strong and positive. That the Provisional Government was making explicit its intention to honor all Tsarist debts and obligations as early as March, and that the US government was the first to recognize the Provisional Government, of course, only gave New York more comfort.[58] In mid-May, headquarters in New York sent out yet another batch of men to continue to build the bank's Russian presence.[59]

By June, National City had decided to send 32-year-old Harold J. Dreher to Russia, ultimately to run the bank's Moscow branch.[60] Having joined the banking world at the tender age of 19 at the First National Bank of Milwaukee, Dreher had made waves in National City's New Business Department, after joining the larger New York bank as an assistant cashier.[61] He was joined by a handful of other National City veterans tapped to form the core personnel of the Moscow branch and set off on the journey to Moscow via China—where they nearly perished in a train accident—due to disruption of European travel routes during the war.[62] As late as September, the steady stream of National City employees to Russia was continuing, with the new arrivals carrying supplies of tobacco, chocolate, and even soap in a testament to the dire situation in which their colleagues in Russia found themselves.[63] But the desperation of the bankers should not be overstated. As late as October 1917, one National City employee wrote to New York reporting that he "found the social life of Petrograd so strenuous that he [was] already in need of another suit of evening clothes."[64] By 14 November—several days *after* the Bolshevik coup—National City opened its Moscow branch.[65] It would be the bank's thirteenth overseas branch and its third in Europe.[66]

Meserve and company's bullishness at National City was by no means an outlier. Bunker's spring 1917 letters to his Midland bosses in London similarly suggest genuine grounds for optimism. In a letter dated 5 April 1917, Bunker talked of "quiet" prevailing after the revolutionary upheavals of previous weeks, and commented that "a period of solid spade work by the temporary Government is now being entered upon."[67] Acknowledging the slump in industrial production, Bunker was nonetheless optimistic about the gradual resumption of factory work, pointing out that such setbacks were to be expected in the context of the rapid development and industrialization of early twentieth-century Russia.[68]

Of course, perceptions of Russia's prosperity and potential in Western financial circles were not universal or even necessarily accurate. Jack Morgan, approached by the American-Russian Chamber of Commerce to join its board and thereby further a deepening of American economic ties with newly republican Russia in April 1917, declined the invitation.[69] His claim that he would be of more help to the organization if he "were not identified with it in any official capacity" left little doubt as to his concern over reputational issues.[70] Inflation worried many, due to a significant increase in note issuance by the State Bank to cover budget deficits. An editorial in *Russkiie Vedomosti* estimated that the amount of currency in circulation had increased by 40 percent between March and August 1917.[71] Bunker repeatedly discussed the disruptive effects of inflation in his dispatches, noting at one point that the wartime rate of inflation in Russia was four times that in Britain, and complaining regularly about the rising cost of living.[72]

Still, the impact of such moves was not necessarily as unequivocally and disruptively inflationary as some feared. A Foreign Ministry communiqué noted a drop in the velocity of money, saying "bank notes accumulate for the most part in the hands of peasants and workers. And to extricate the bank notes from their owners is very difficult."[73] Bunker similarly observed this hoarding of paper money "in stockings and mattresses."[74] Moreover, plans to implement new taxes to plug budget gaps held forth the prospect for a reduced dependence on currency issuance to finance the state budget deficit.[75] Bunker observed that the inflationary situation was generally supportive of the prices of securities in domestic financial markets, even going so far as to say, "there is only one circumstance which should to some extent mitigate the fall of industrials—that is the continual watering of the rouble—during last month a further milliard of notes was pumped out by the State Bank."[76]

Indeed, even if the currency was being manipulated to the degree feared by some, it was not necessarily a bad thing for Western bankers. As the US consul in Petrograd remarked in a report: "Speculation made possible by the differences between the official Russian rate of exchange and the open commercial foreign rate has run riot. As soon as it became publicly known that the National City Bank in New York was responsible for deposits made in its Petrograd branch, its deposits grew by leaps and bounds. American businessmen now in Petrograd are constantly approached by Russians who are anxious to sell securities, concessions, and personal property on very liberal terms on the condition that payment be made in dollars in America."[77] In pointing out the exchange rate risk banks like National City assumed when engaging in such operations, Bunker acknowledged that the business could be very profitable if such risks were contained.[78]

Revelstoke, of course, was less gushing than Meserve or Bunker when he arrived in early 1917 as part of the British delegation to the inter-Allied conference. But he too was increasingly receptive to the bullish argument. In large part, this turn in perspective appears to have taken place after he saw his "old friend" and ex–finance minister Kokovtsov, with whom he had shared so many ups and downs during the 1906 loan episode discussed in Chapter 2.[79] Finding Kokovtsov to be tight-lipped about the situation at official functions, Revelstoke finally managed to discuss things openly with his old comrade over a

more intimate dinner.[80] The British financier found his Russian friend sanguine over the forthcoming Duma session—"they will not make real trouble:
. . . the whole country is too 'fatigué' to justify any prospect of serious demonstration."[81] True, Kokovtsov shared Revelstoke's apprehensions that "the greatest evil at present is not so much political as economical—'alimentation,' or
rather the want of it" and the "danger of famine."[82] However, he concluded in
Revelstoke's words, that there was not "any active revolutionary or subversive
action probable in the immediate future."[83] Clearly impressed, Revelstoke
ended his diary entry with the remark that the arrival of the Allied mission in
Petrograd and the news of souring German-American relations "have certainly
led to a 'détente' here. People have something fresh about which to think and
to talk, and are therefore less absorbed in their domestic differences of opinion."[84] But hedging his optimism, he added a caveat drawing attention to the
"urgent" nature of the "food and transport question."[85]

Crucially, however, from Revelstoke's standpoint, these economic issues
were not insoluble. Meeting with Kokovtsov the next day, for example, Revelstoke underscored the former finance minister's criticisms of contemporary
government policy.[86] Taxation in particular was an avenue that was "little
developed," with barely anything having been done to explore alternative tax
streams to replace lost revenues from the alcohol monopoly.[87] Revelstoke himself focused much of his efforts in Petrograd in trying to get the Russians to
address their trade deficit, principally through restrictions on imports, thus
reducing pressure on the ruble exchange rate and their dependency on British
transfers.[88] Speaking to his British military colleagues returned from the northern front, he found their take "more satisfactory than had been expected."[89]

It was shortly after Revelstoke's return from Russia that the February Revolution occurred. Writing from London to an associate in Egypt, he painted
a hopeful picture two days after the Provisional Government had issued a
formal declaration confirming its intent to honor all Tsarist debts and obligations, and highlighting plans for tax reforms that had been a focus of his
discussions with Kokovtsov.[90] As he said, "The convulsion in Petrograd seems
to have been of a sudden character, but the individuals who are responsible
for the direction of the Government are said to be honest and upright, and I
trust therefore that the risk of disorganisation and disorder which would be
the consequence of the direction of affairs by extremists, may be avoided."[91]
It is thus perhaps unsurprising that he had his secretary pay the back subscrip-
tion for a membership in the British Club of Moscow, which he had been
invited to join by James Wishaw, the Barings agent in Petrograd.[92] By July he
was responding to questions about Russia's willingness to honor its debts by
saying, "the reply would seem to be that these obligations are being punctually
discharged to date."[93]

If Revelstoke stood apart from Meserve or Bunker, it may have been a question of personality rather than sharply divergent views on Russian macro-economic fundamentals. These two worlds—that of the aristocratic English partner of a genteel merchant bank and that of the salaried expatriate employee of a joint-stock bank—collided in Revelstoke's meeting with Meserve in February 1917. Meserve called on Revelstoke, seeking to interest the Barings partner in Russian railroad and steel deals. The latter coolly reminded him that while he "looked favourably on prospects [of] co-operation" he could of course not engage on private business while on an official government trip.[94] Not getting the hint, Meserve proceeded to say that "he noticed with plea-sure that as regards credit, reputation and consideration on the part of the Russian Government, B.B. & Co. 'occupy the same position in Europe as the National City Bank does in America.'"[95] Revelstoke icily ended his account of the meeting with the remark that "his Bank has been established here some two months."[96]

In surveying foreign financiers' discussions about Russia, it is apparent that few among them saw a crisis that appeared obvious to later observers with the benefit of hindsight. Rather than seeing the budget deficits, inflation, and plummeting industrial production historians point to, key investors and financial middlemen foresaw opportunity in Russia. Even Revelstoke's more skeptical view and warnings of potential future problems allowed that in early 1917 the country was still experiencing "war prosperity." That National City were so optimistic on Russia is of particular interest since their "man on the spot" in Petrograd was supposed to give them an accurate view of the situation in Russia. That his views diverged so sharply from the subsequent consensus view of "crisis" in 1917 Russia suggests that either such a view is inaccurate or that the value of having a local agent in an emerging market can be a hindrance as much as a help. Bunker himself voiced this concern in one letter, wondering if "the centre of the burning house is naturally not the best place from which to observe the progress of the fire."[97]

Risk and Moral Hazard

Beyond merely not recognizing what may with hindsight appear to be objec-tive truths about the real state and direction of the Russian economy and public finances, foreign financiers were influenced by a high degree of risk appetite and moral hazard.

Meserve's business proposals suggest substantial risk appetite on the part of National City. In a lengthy 12 October 1915 letter to New York outlining his views on the markets, Meserve highlighted the debt of the Moscow-Kazan Railroad as a potentially attractive investment. While noting the appeal of the route and the guarantee of the Russian government on the debt, the financial picture he painted of the line and other railroads is shocking. The banker noted, for example, that the interest coverage (the ratio of operating income to interest charges) of the Moscow-Kazan railroad was just 0.25—an exceedingly low margin of safety for a business with such high operating leverage.[98] Meserve went on, pointing out that most Russian railroads had highly leveraged capital structures, with debt-to-equity ratios as high as 9x.[99] By contrast, in 1915, the Union Pacific railroad in the United States boasted interest coverage of 2x and a debt-to-equity ratio of 1.03x, conservatively calculated.[100]

The difference in financial margin of safety between the debt of Russian and American railroads is even starker when one accounts for the disparity in operational efficiencies. While detailed comparisons would be difficult due to a paucity of data and differences in measurement practices across countries, the frequent citation of distribution problems as a major contributor to wartime shortages suggests asset utilization on Russian rail networks was probably less effective than on comparable railroads in the West. These operational considerations then suggest that investors would demand a higher, not lower, margin of safety on Russian railroad debt, all else equal.

Of course, most of the railroad debt that Meserve was studying did enjoy a guarantee by the Russian government.[101] Such guarantees, however, were themselves highly questionable when considering the broader state of Russian public finances. The decision to sharply curb the sale of vodka to address social problems had large implications for the central government budget, which relied on the spirits monopoly for at least one-third of its ordinary revenues.[102] By the time Meserve was writing his letters pushing Russian railroad bonds, the impact of the temperance campaign was already visible in Russian budget figures. Indeed, in 1915 the *Economist* painted a rather bleak picture of the Russian budget, noting that the government was itself forecasting vodka receipts to fall from 26.2 percent of the total budget to just 4.7 percent, representing a loss of £79,185,000 in 1915 due to the temperance campaign. The magazine remained skeptical about the government's chances of being able to finance the deficit via the French and British wartime credit markets.[103] Ironically, in view of future events, the forecast for vodka revenues for the 1915 budget proved to be overly pessimistic (the government still earned more than £3 million in 1915 from the spirits monopoly—see Table 4.1), perhaps explaining the strong optimism vis-à-vis the temperance policy in subsequent years.[104] While better than nothing, then, the Russian government's guarantee of railroad debt was hardly credible.

Another, less explicit set of government guarantees, which very clearly did attract investor attention, was that by Western governments, especially the British and French. These took two forms. The first were explicit signs of

TABLE 4.1. Budget revenues from the state spirit monopoly

	1913	1914	1915	1916E	1917E
Revenues (£)	89,930,000	50,390,000	3,072,000	5,136,000	4,960,000

Source: "The Russian Revolution and Russian War Finance," *Economist*, 17 March 1917.
Note: Figures for 1916 and 1917 were estimates at the time of the article's original publication in March 1917.

Western government support for Russian securities and deals. In the initial phase of the war in 1914, creditors to both Russian and French counterparties experienced difficulties in receiving scheduled payments.[105] However, official Allied policy ultimately called for sharing the financial burden. The degree of burden sharing and mechanics were complicated, and raised sensitivities on the Russian side of being seen to depend on British credit.[106] Nevertheless by the end of 1914, Russia was already receiving British and French support to remain current on debt traded in London and Paris.[107] The degree of financial assistance to Russia was not without its critics. By late 1916, John Maynard Keynes, then serving as an advisor to the British Treasury, wrote a memo showing how much more lenient British terms were for credit lines extended to Russia versus France.[108] Still, Revelstoke himself declared in Petrograd in 1917 that "we have an interest in the prosperity of our Ally," and the degree to which the Russian government enjoyed the backing of British and French credit was apparent to all, bankers included.[109] By late 1917, the Russian government was enjoying direct financial support from the US government as well, and Vanderlip was writing Benjamin Strong, governor of the Federal Reserve Bank of New York, that a repudiation of Russian debts was inconceivable.[110]

A second form of moral hazard was more indirect, and stemmed from implied or perceived Anglo-French guarantees. The influence of moral hazard on decision making is apparent in Meserve's letter of 12 October 1915, in his discussion about a loan proposed by the Banque de Commerce de Sibérie. He opened the discussion by stating, "I would probably recommend this loan, even in these times, if I were to consider nothing here but this loan," but he went on, pointing out that considerations beyond the strict financial parameters of the loan make him even more enthusiastic: "I would surely strongly recommend the proposition for large amounts if it could be arranged that all drafts drawn by the Banque de Commerce de Siberia or other strong banks here could be also accepted or guaranteed by strong English or French banks like the London City & Midland, Lloyd's Bank, or the Credit Lyonnais: that is, banks with say 1,000 branches scattered throughout England or France."[111] Meserve continued, elaborating on the "guarantee" of "strong English and

French banks," stating that "the French Government, and in turn the English Government" would "wish to protect" the interests of a bank like Crédit Lyonnais, with "its thousand odd branches scattered all through France."[112] Thus, Meserve's willingness to increase the bank's exposure to the proposed loan beyond the level he would advise from a strictly narrow financial analysis was tied to what he believed to be the implicit guarantees of Entente governments on the issue. Whether or not National City ended up partaking in the loan in question, the reasoning outlined in Meserve's letter demonstrates the influence of moral hazard in shaping investment decisions and risk appetite within a key US financial institution operating in the Russian market.

Moreover, from the standpoint of banks—as opposed to retail or purely portfolio institutional investors—competitive and market pressures strongly influenced risk management and risk appetite. Senior National City officials openly acknowledged that wartime business made American banks flush with liquidity, and that the United States had "an abnormal proportion of the world's gold" that they were looking to deploy internationally.[113] Global relationships with Western firms also pressured Western banks to increase exposure to the Russian market. For example, on 23 September, J. Block, a Moscow-based entrepreneur representing several American firms in Russia, including the Remington Typewriter Company, Fairbanks Company, and Burroughs Adding Machines, wrote to Meserve lobbying National City to open a branch in Russia to service the growing needs of his client firms in Russia.[114] Internal National City correspondence in August 1916 testifies to the problems that American multinational corporations (MNCs) with global relations had in managing cash flows in Russia due to the lack of a National City presence in the country.[115] A report of 17 August 1916 in the Russian financial daily *Birzheviye Vedomosti* on the proposed opening of a National City branch in Russia noted, "the largest American financial and industrial institutions are grouping themselves about the American bank."[116] Meserve also pointed out that a physical branch in Russia would also serve as a key source of commercial intelligence on Russian affairs for National City's clients globally.[117] This comment reflected a broader National City strategy of leveraging its scale to build out an international branch network that would allow it to deliver a higher standard of service to corporate clients than competitor banks could offer.[118]

The importance of MNC business as a driver of National City's decision making is perhaps best shown through the case of General Electric (GE). On 13 February 1916, Meserve wrote New York informing management that GE's Petrograd office had opened a small account with National City's main New York office.[119] Meserve revealed that he had been working on the deal for several months: "The General Electric Co. of Russia is now doing the most of its business through the General Electric Company of America and having been told by Mr. Dean that the General Electric Co. of America had no account with the National City Bank, I thought that this Russia account with you might prove an opening wedge to at least help you secure a part of the General Electric Co.'s growing business in South America and the Orient."[120] He went on to acknowledge, "I rather expect that the account of the General Electric Co. of Russia with the N'l City Bank will prove a nuisance rather than a profit," but noted that the prospect of a global relationship with the industrial behemoth was worth the short-term trouble.[121] The desire for Western corporations to work with established banks that they knew well thus served as an important driver of National City's decision to commit to the Russian market.

Of course, National City was not the only American bank exploring opportunities overseas. While Meserve's letters generally show him to be on friendly terms with representatives of other Russian and Western banks, they also reveal concerns about not yielding opportunities and market share to National City's Western and particularly American competitors. The bank that most concerned National City as a competitor in Russia was Guaranty Trust.[122] Meserve's worry about competitor moves in the Russian market was apparent as early as November 1915, when he noted that a contact had "remarked 'I hope the National City Bank opens up here soon, because if they do not I am afraid the Guaranty Trust Company will.'"[123] He went on: "I was told unofficially by a Petrograd banker that he thought the London City & Midland intended to open a branch in Petrograd."[124]

The banks competed along two broad lines. First, they fought for the banking business of major Western and (in Russia) local corporations—business that included activities like cash management and short-term financing. In his note to New York on the GE Petrograd account, for example, Meserve notes, "They told me that the Guarantee [sic] Trust Co. of New York had done some business for them but in an unsatisfactory way."[125] The rivalry with Guaranty Trust even manifested itself in seemingly trivial matters, such as donations to local charities during Christmas 1915.[126]

Second, within the context of an emerging market like Russia, the banks competed for relationships with large Russian financial institutions. These relationships would involve cooperation in loan syndication for domestic loans, as well as the provision of correspondent banking services to the Russian institutions. Thus, Meserve lobbied hard to try to win "the bulk" of the business of the Russo-Asiatic Bank, at the expense of Guaranty Trust.[127] Finally, National City, at least by early 1916, was the depository bank for the Russian government in the United States—a relationship that brought not only a large deposit base and active payments business, but also a great deal of prestige to the bank in Russia and globally.[128] Maintaining a branch in Russia would only help secure these vital relationships in Russian high finance.

Incidentally, many private Russian banks, while willing to engage Western banks for correspondence purposes and occasionally for helping with loans, were less keen for them to maintain a presence in Russia as deposit-taking institutions. As early as November 1915, the Credit Chancellery of the Russian Ministry of Finance was sounding out Meserve on his willingness to agree to a cap of 3 to 4 percent on its payments on deposits.[129] Such restrictions would prove to be moot as the entry of Western banks and deposit-taking institutions fragmented the deposit market. Banks like National City attracted a large share of deposits at low rates, presumably due to their brand reputations and depositor perception of greater safety. Still, at the time, Meserve was careful to agree to the conditions only as an unwritten understanding that would not be included in the bank's proposed charter.[130]

A third form of competitive pressure influencing National City's decision making took on a more nationalistic tone. In particular, Meserve's letters reflect a widespread fear of "losing" entire countries to the banks and businesses of other states in the postwar era. On 19 April 1916, for example, Meserve noted: "After the war, I do not think that legislation of any sort can keep the German avalanche from creeping back steadily into this country, and if America and England have not secured the cream of the railways, mines, etc., etc., before the end of the war, I believe that America will have lost her present wonderful opportunity forever."[131] He went on to "strongly advise that the Russian coloring should be given all American business done here by having an operating company with a Russian name and strong Russian associations."[132]

As much as they show a rather aggressive stance toward risk management and the evaluation of opportunities in the Russian market, Meserve's letters to New York exhibit sufficient restraint and warrant being read as an experienced observer's impressions regarding the risks and opportunities for the bank in Russia. When confronted with local objections to bank policies, Meserve was not always accommodating. In recounting an interview with finance minister P. L. Bark, Meserve noted, for example, that "some of the Minister's objections the Minister himself knew were silly, and I knew they were silly; and nine times out of ten I had carefully explained away his objections at our interview."[133] In his report on the advisability of opening a branch in Russia, Meserve did devote significant attention to the risks of such a move, highlighting, among other things, the high liquidity in the banking system, attendant competition for loan businesses between banks, and the seemingly contradictory situation of a high cost of deposit funding that resulted in thin net interest margins.[134]

Indeed, Meserve's letters testify to his willingness to completely reject various proposals that he felt did not meet the bank's needs or standards. In November 1915, he wrote New York saying, "The importance of obtaining the right kind of security for the big Russian loan has been day by day revealing itself to me. . . . I have already started in trying to drive home this truth here, and I think it would be wise for you to make the same point clear to the Russians at your end."[135] In the same month he himself indicated more caution than his New York correspondents on proposals to open the Petrograd branch.[136] In a 3 November 1915 letter, he counseled the outright rejection of a business proposal for National City to coinvest in a new Petrograd bank, which he was obligated to pass on to New York as a formality.[137] Perhaps the greatest testament to the genuine nature of Meserve's commentary and the degree to which senior management valued it is that on 12 September 1916 New York took the extraordinary step of doubling his salary retroactively from the start of his service.[138]

———

When considering the commentary of foreign financiers in the midst of the Russian Revolution, it is tempting to see in Midland's Bunker an exceptionally clairvoyant figure. The reports of Bunker and Meserve are striking in the direct comparisons Bunker draws with Meserve and other foreign decision makers and observers, the alarm with which he regards some of National City's activities on multiple levels, and his own apparent relative conservatism and realism.

First, Bunker portrayed the manner in which National City sourced new business ideas as haphazard and potentially reckless. Thus, Bunker noted that—working not just for National City, but for a broader American investment group associated with the bank—Meserve was considering projects in technical fields such as mining and heavy industry without himself having an engineering background.[139] Bunker suggested that such an approach not only was wasteful in terms of time and effort devoted to technically hopeless projects, but also tended to lead to the short-listing of those projects that other groups with greater technical expertise had previously rejected.[140] The importance of technical expertise in evaluating projects at even a very preliminary stage is something that Bunker continuously returned to in his correspondence.

Second, beyond brazen laxness in the technical standards in which they sourced projects, Bunker explicitly stated his belief that National City and other American firms had exceedingly high risk appetites and lax lending standards. Recounting a conversation with a fellow banker in June 1917, he noted, for example, that National City and its closely related American International Corporation stole business from competitors by agreeing to do some transactions "at half the cost and without security."[141] Bunker went on to note that National City's aforementioned willingness to take deposits in local currency in Russia and credit dollar accounts overseas in New York exposed it to major currency risks.[142]

Finally, Bunker suggested that he was simply more sober-minded and realistic than his American counterparts in his assessment of both risks and possibilities. He noted that amid the turmoil of the summer of 1917, "Americans are even now acting with great boldness and confidence" vis-à-vis Russian business, even amid open threats to private property and with a less-than-favorable outlook for the success of the Provisional Government's "Liberty Loan."[143] Bunker pointedly attacked Meserve's competence, saying in one letter that "the [National City] Bank and Corporation appear to have no Manager really experienced in Russian affairs, and will therefore probably have to pay for inevitable mistakes."[144] Bunker continued this line of argument in later letters in the fall of 1917, when he argued that his Russia-specific knowledge and experience warranted more consideration than it was being given, and that people with little to no knowledge of Russia or its language and culture were playing too large and dangerous a role in shaping policy.[145]

Indeed, Bunker made repeated attacks on what he called the "long view argument," noting, like Keynes, that the long run can be impossibly far off.[146] In a later dispatch, Bunker was more directly contemptuous of those who remained optimistic on Russia: "I must say that the ostrich policy in connection with Russia has been, all through, a great mistake: it is much better to face facts and the inherent probabilities of the case than to cling to unreasonable hopes at all costs merely because one has not the courage to meet their disappointment."[147]

However, the notion of Bunker being a somehow exceptional figure who demonstrated a superior ability to foresee events is a false one. As much as his knowledge of Russian and apparently deeper social connections in Petrograd financial circles may have made him more connected than Meserve, his dispatches still reveal at best a conflicted, if not confused, view of Russia, alternating between extremes of optimism and pessimism. He eventually admitted on 1 November 1917, "To attempt any analysis of the position or forecast of the near future is useless," before suggesting—in the same letter—that the bank may actually do well to increase its exposure to Russia.[148] This letter drew a curt reply from the overseas manager in London, who said, "It is not reasonable to expect England to put more money into Russia."[149] Bunker showed a further willingness to believe the most fantastic scenarios in February 1918—well after the Bolshevik takeover and, crucially, after the nationalization of the banks and the default—when he went so far as to imagine that the Bolshevik "policy of casting everything into confusion will inevitably give a unique opportunity, when the right time arrives, for an outsider to step in and buy up the 'bankrupt stock.'"[150] In this thinking, he echoed the behavior of his colleagues at Midland sniffing for deals in the years before the war (see Chapter 3).

The case of Bunker shows that many of the competitive pressures—whether on the corporate or national level—that drove decision making on the part of American financiers also influenced British circles. Thus, Bunker both received and closely studied numerous letters from William Higgs & Co., a Moscow-based group of British expatriates with long histories in Russia who actively sought to secure a foothold in postwar Russia, at the expense of potential great power rivals like Germany and the United States, and who came highly recommended by the British consul in Moscow.[151]

The Higgs group made appeals to Bunker and Midland on two levels. They first appealed on nationalistic grounds, claiming that by financing their activities, Midland would secure postwar Russia as a British market, denying it to Germany and other powers.[152] Bunker certainly did sympathize with such arguments, as is evident from his later dispatches to London, with his talk of a "Teutonic flood" sweeping Russia, and his belief that "we must penetrate Russia thoroughly, or we may as well clear out altogether" lest Germany "walk in" and capture Russia's markets.[153]

Their second manner of appeal to Midland was by stressing the competitive threats other, American, banks posed in Russia. In this regard, their letters mentioning activities of National City and specifically its rapid expansion in Russia are of particular note. While Midland and Bunker do not appear to have reacted directly to such updates on the competition, Bunker's dispatches to London on the affairs of National City, as well as of local Russian banks, suggest an appreciation of the need to take certain forward steps—including applying for a branch license—to maintain a competitive position. In this sense, nationalistic and corporate competitive pressures certainly did enter the decision-making process of banks like Midland vis-à-vis Russia.

Bunker's correspondence over the course of 1917 and 1918 thus shows him to be perhaps more nuanced and fickle in his assessments of the situation in Russia than Meserve was, and at times more restrained in his recommendations to his bank, but still prone to many of the factors that influenced the assessments and decision making of Meserve and National City.

In considering the correspondence of both Midland and National City, then, it is apparent that a remarkably high degree of risk tolerance heavily influenced the decision making of Western financiers vis-à-vis Russia from 1914 through 1917. Moral hazard from Russian and Entente government guarantees, which were in turn driven by geopolitical considerations, as well as by the already high exposure of British and French banking systems to Russia, drove this increase in risk tolerance. Furthermore, competitive pressures within the global financial industry served to push risk frontiers as firms sought to win global relationships by expanding their role in Russia and to secure first-mover advantages over their competitors. By contrast, to the degree that the cases of Bunker and Meserve can be generalized, the principal-agent problems that one would expect to see in the case of a joint-stock (as opposed to partnership) multinational bank were not apparent and do not appear to have driven the increase in risk appetite. Indeed, if anything, Meserve appears to have often acted as a restraining force on his bank in its early exploration of the Russian market, while Bunker repeatedly took positions that—based on his defensive comments—appeared to be seen as too conservative by the head office.

Geopolitics

While the lack of a sense of crisis and a high risk appetite explain the weakness of deterrents to investment in the Russian markets, several very strong qualitative factors served to motivate investors to actively seek opportunities in Russia. In particular, geopolitical factors and trade politics acted as a powerful driver of financiers' decision making regarding Russia through 1917. The context of the war only accentuated these considerations by playing on bankers' insecurities and nationalism.

Home government geopolitical sympathies and personal patriotism very clearly influenced the propensity of National City—a privately owned joint-stock company with no formal connection to the US government—to invest in the Russian market. Many of Meserve's reports to New York are striking not just because of their focus on narrow themes related to National City's growing business in Russia, but because of their almost mercantilist analysis of international trade and markets at a national level. In an April 1916 report, "How Can America Best Secure Big Business in Russia?," for example, he declared, "I have absolutely made up my mind that the best way for America to secure big business in Russia is to cooperate at once with the best possible English financial groups."[154] He went on to portray international trade as a zero-sum game fought along national lines, predicting that "with America and England working together here today they can do big things easily. If America and England do not play together, everything will be very slow and very difficult, and in the end Germany will probably beat them both out."[155]

National City's senior management very clearly shared such sentiments, as evidenced by its correspondence with the British firm of Baring Brothers. Within months of Meserve's above-cited report, National City sent a team of experts from the closely allied American International Corporation (AIC) to conduct a yearlong, in-country analysis of business opportunities in Russia. The AIC was a brainchild of Vanderlip, whose rise at National City bank, by 1915, had been checked by his mentor and National City's CEO and controlling shareholder, James Stillman.[156] In Vanderlip's conception, the AIC—in which he would play the leading role—would complement National City's ambitious international expansion plans, but go a step further by actually investing directly in debt and equity stakes in overseas businesses, in the vein of a modern-day private equity fund.[157] The AIC, capitalized in 1915 and launched operationally in 1916, was notionally independent, and while Vanderlip approached other leading international financiers to join, there was little doubt as to its close ties to National City.[158] In Petrograd, the AIC office would in fact occupy the entire first floor of the National City building on the south bank of the Neva.[159] But the location near the Winter Palace and in the former home of the Ottoman embassy was perhaps appropriate, given the firm's imperial ambitions: AIC men openly spoke of their company as a successor to the British East India Company.[160] Indeed, Vanderlip's Russian expansion plans had the active encouragement of the US ambassador, David R. Francis, who was keen to see American banks open operations in Russia.[161]

Vanderlip personally wrote to Lord Revelstoke to arrange for the leader of the AIC team, F. Holbrook, to see him in London on the way to Russia.[162] The notes from the meeting made almost no mention of individual firms' interests, but rather mentioned "Russian, British, and American interests"—that is, national interests—and generally suggested a parallel, extra-governmental diplomacy between businesses along national lines.[163] This focus on national interests was itself at the core of Vanderlip's conception of the AIC outlined in his 1915 memorandum setting forth his vision. His pitch letter to would-be AIC investors and board members spoke of how "we must, as a nation, begin to think internationally," and of how "financially, we have been a provincial people."[164]

After having met with Holbrook, on 10 October 1916, Baring sent a message through Count Alexander Benckendorff to the British embassy in Petrograd, alerting it to the presence of the Holbrook team and suggesting cooperation, as "English financial circles are of the opinion that Mr. Holbrook represents a very influential American group, that they are in no way opposed to his present mission of investigation, and that they view with favor the idea of eventual cooperation with Russian and American interests."[165] In this regard, the active promotion of William Higgs & Co. by the British consul in Moscow showed a similar cooperation between British business and diplomatic circles.[166]

The influence of business and financial interests on government policy is the subject of intense debate. However, the case of National City, Barings, and AIC in the fall of 1916 suggests that, at least during the First World War, two of the most influential Western financial firms evaluated foreign involvement not solely in terms of their narrow business interests, but also within the context of the interests of their home countries. In the case of Russia, considerations of national economic interests served to encourage such firms to engage in Russian business.

Buying the Revolution

Other factors also served to draw individual firms and investors into the Russian markets. In particular, paternalistic notions of "improving" Russia served as a powerful social and even emotional influence on the decision making of financiers.

Meserve's letters and contemporary financial press reports reveal a very strong sense of paternalism as driving investment decisions vis-à-vis the Russian markets. In the report "Will Russia Have a Stable Government after the War?" Meserve argued that "a very important factor here is the deep-rooted reverence of the great peasant class toward the head of the Government. The strength and simplicity of this reverence cannot be understood by anyone who has not been in Russia."[167] He went on to paint a simplistic picture of the Russian population: "Another important factor is that the Russian people have never been stirred up and worried like the people of other nations as to the causes and rights and wrongs of this terrible war. To them this war resolves itself down to the simplest possible matter. Their country has been invaded and, consequently, they are all following the Government blindly."[168] Meserve thus described a population that was innocent, law-abiding, and almost incapable of rash, revolutionary actions.

In an earlier letter dated 1 December 1915, Meserve touched on another important social factor influencing his thinking on Russia: "A change that I consider of vital importance is now taking place in Russia. This change is the introduction of the spirit of saving, or thrift. Formerly, nearly 1,000,000,000 roubles a year went to the Russian Government as revenue from the sale of vodka. Now, the entire population of Russia, 175,000,000 people, have accepted prohibition at one stroke, with practically no opposition, and I think it is the money which formerly went to buy vodka which is being saved."[169] Meserve went on to repeat the sentiment that "Russian peasants are, like farmers the world over, honest as a class, and this class, the backbone of Russia, is growing at a rate of 2,500,000 people a year."[170]

The prohibition theme also caught the attention of financial journalists in the West. In a 3 April 1915 article, the *Economist* wrote in glowing terms about the temperance campaign in Russia. After prefacing its article with the axiom that "generally speaking, war and intoxication have been close allies," the magazine observed that "considering the conditions of Russia and the hold which vodka had taken upon the people, the suppression of drink shops in Russia must be regarded not only as a military measure, but also as a most courageous stroke of social policy."[171]

A letter to the editor forwarding an account by an Englishman in southern Russia shows further interest in the prohibition:

As regards the vodka prohibition, I consider it as one of the most remark-able things which has taken place in modern social and economic history. The prohibition is really a root and branch one, not only as regards vodka and other spirits, but also in most parts as regards wine, which is the ordi-nary beverage of the better-paid classes. It is not possible to procure vodka by any means, the sale being absolutely prohibited. It has absolutely dis-appeared from the tables of the rich, and cannot be obtained even surrep-titiously by the poor. . . . It is indeed the nearest approach to a miracle or Utopia that one can have in these days of liberty of the subject to do what he likes.[172]

This passage is particularly interesting in that it reflected positively on Tsarist state capacity in wartime to impose such a broadly sweeping ban so rapidly and effectively. The author proceeded in his gushing tone: "The result has been equal to a revolution. Drunkenness, the curse of the Russian peasant and workman has been absolutely stamped out. Workmen work regularly, and their wives and families reap the benefit, the increased expenditure in food and clothing being remarkable. All the food and clothing shops are doing a full business, notwithstanding the war, and one hardly sees a poorly dressed person, and very few beggars, which were formerly legion in the vicinity of the Government vodka shops for retail sale."[173] The observer concluded, noting as had others, the increase in deposits at the Post Office Savings Bank and arguing that while he was initially skeptical of the government's ability to com-pensate for the loss of revenues from the spirits monopoly, the productivity gains from prohibition would stimulate so much growth as to outweigh the loss in vodka tax revenues.[174]

The sometimes paternalistic comments on the character of the peasantry and the comments on the vodka ban in the National City correspondence and in the *Economist* suggest the strong influence of "soft," almost moralistic, factors in shaping foreign investor sentiment vis-à-vis the Russian market. Meserve's characterization of the peasantry as "honest as a class" and his emphasis on the "introduction of the spirit of saving" suggest that, in his view, Russia was undergoing a profound societal transformation at the time that would directly and positively affect economic growth. This connection between the supposed improvement of the moral character of the Russian peasantry, the broader social transformation such a process represented, and economic growth was made even more explicitly in the *Economist*. Indeed, to the extent that "emerging market" countries are defined not simply by high growth, cheap valuations, and above-average returns, but also by profound societal transformations that are driving a convergence of a given society to some level of "development" or "modernity," the above-cited remarks on the peasantry and the vodka ban certainly reflect investor perceptions of Russia as a particularly special market undergoing such a revolutionary—and potentially profitable—transformation. Thus, Russia was attractive not only because it was a market in which investors could achieve above-average returns, but also because on a moral level it appeared to many Westerners as a society undergoing a profound social change, which they thought would in turn boost economic growth, in a virtuous circle.

With this understanding of the moral appeal of the Russian market and attempts at Russian reform, investor perceptions and actions during the revolutionary events of 1917 become more intelligible. At first glance, such behavior would seem to conform with the model of strong institutions attracting investors as described by North and Weingast's seminal article on institutional change during the Glorious Revolution in England.[175] The moral dimension to investor thinking in 1917, however, is distinct from the institutional model of North and Weingast. Investor commentaries were at best vague about the specifics of the changes the Tsarist reformers or, later, a new government would implement. More importantly, the North and Weingast model of investor decision making does not account for the strongly paternalistic cultural overtones of foreign financiers' commentaries about how "proud" they were of the Russians, about their honesty and thrift, or about the moral dimensions of the temperance policy. Such features of financiers' thinking about Russia are simply not accounted for in institutional explanations.

Moreover, that such stereotypes were being deployed in a positive sense contrasts strongly with more traditional negative stereotypes of Russia. For example, in attributing to Russians the characteristic of being passive, Meserve was not arguing that this passivity stifled creativity or predisposed them to oppressive political systems—two popular negative stereotypes—but rather casting such passivity as a characteristic that made Russians more law-abiding. Both stereotypes were paternalistic, and the more positive version has its parallels in myriad colonial and Orientalist tropes, but the constructive framing of the latter within an investment context made the difference significant. This cultural dimension proved particularly powerful at a time when factors that economists have traditionally flagged as important drivers of investor decision making—monetary architecture or exports, for example—reflected the dislocations of war and revolution.[176]

———

Geopolitical upheaval, of course, is frequently discussed in the literature relating to investment in emerging markets. The idea that bond markets dislike uncertainty pervades much theory on finance, with political instability often being cited as a particularly pernicious shock to market confidence that frequently drives investors to flee to low-risk assets.

In an influential work, economists Paulo Mauro, Nathan Sussman, and Yishay Yafeh reach the counterintuitive conclusion that bond investors often overlook institutional factors (e.g., adherence to the gold standard), sound macroeconomic policies, and even default histories in making investment decisions with respect to emerging market bonds.[177] Instead, the authors argue that the primary determinant of emerging market bond spreads is the prevalence of "other types of events—especially wars and episodes of politically motivated violence."[178] While the study challenges some conventional theories about the determinants of bond market behavior, it largely supports the notion that political violence has a detrimental impact on sovereign bond prices.

In the context of the Russian experience, however, the study's findings are puzzling. Indeed, during much of the period that Russia was fighting the war, the spread of Russian sovereign debt yields over equivalent British consols was at multiyear lows, bottoming in late 1916. Even in September 1917—the eve of the Bolshevik takeover—yield spreads were still below levels seen in 1906. Such spread movement would seem to contradict the Mauro, Sussman, and Yafeh thesis about wars having a negative influence on emerging market spreads, not least since Russia suffered repeated defeats over the course of the First World War.

Contemporary analyses of the revolution actually show that far from fleeing it, investors—at least initially—may have actually welcomed revolution. Thus the *Economist* in its earliest story on the February Revolution said, "the reactionary Government has fallen; the Duma has asserted its power," and cited "early indications" pointing toward "the establishment of a progressive and stable Government, based upon the popular will."[179] A week later, on 24 March 1917, the same magazine noted matter-of-factly in a review of activity in the French markets: "The Bourse has been quiet, despite such events such as . . . the revolution in Russia. There have been no great movements in Russian stocks, though these were somewhat affected by the vague rumors that reached Paris in the early days of the week as to disorder in Russia. As a result of the reassuring messages on Friday, the Bourse reflected the general opinion of the country, and Russian stocks have generally recovered, and even rose in certain cases above their previous level."[180] Tellingly, the article referred to "the liberal reforms that are being carried into effect in Russia."[181] A few weeks later, Bunker forwarded to London an article by a Russian economist he liked, in which the latter argued that Russia had actually maintained a surprising degree of stability in its fiscal apparatus in spite of the upheavals of world war and revolution, that this proved that "our fiscal resources are by no means exhausted," and that reforms would enable Russia's budget in the immediate future to "exceed all expectations," easily providing revenues to service the Provisional Government's new war loans.[182]

Rowland Smith, writing to Baring Brothers from the embassy in Petrograd on 7 May 1917, was somewhat more grudging in his assessment, describing the situation as "peaceful anarchy."[183] Smith went on to say, "The people themselves have kept order[,] and excesses of any kind have been checked by weight of public opinion. How long this will last is difficult to say. No one dreams of paying taxes."[184] He proceeded to note an improving situation in the Russian rear and then excoriate the response of aristocratic British officialdom to the revolution, before saying: "If the English newspapers would stop giving advice to Russia and Russians; would content themselves with reporting facts; and would understand that the revolution was so swift and bloodless because the *whole nation* was heartily sick of the corruption and inefficiency of the old Imperialistic regime and consequently, the revolutionaries are not a ragged mob of long-haired, more or less seedy ne'er do wells and flat-chested bespectacled students, but consist of all that is best in the country—then we should become more popular."[185] Smith closed by observing the inflationary situation and shortages, but ended on a positive note hoping for a reconciliation of Britain and Russia.[186]

Even after several months, Western investors remained relatively upbeat on the situation in Russia. The *Economist* observed, "Russia has been something of a wet blanket for [London] Stock Exchange markets and business . . . Russian issues generally are less affected than might have been supposed; and Russian Oil shares, with those also of the mining companies, are not much down, having regard to the nature of the news from Petrograd."[187] As late as 4 August 1917, the *Economist* claimed, "the Russian revolution has removed the one autocratic blot from the great army of free peoples that is fighting for freedom against ruthlessness."[188]

In New York, the *Wall Street Journal* was somewhat more ambiguous about its support for the Provisional Government, but nonetheless generally sanguine in reporting on the trajectory of political developments in Russia. On 3 November 1917, it wrote a scathing portrait of the premier, Alexander Kerensky, accusing him of "crawling under the bed" and ignoring the true wishes of his "agrarian" majority population.[189] Ominously, the paper called for change, saying, "another leader must be created, for countries even in revolution cannot be governed by debating societies."[190] Even amid reports of serious shocks to the stock markets in the aftermath of the Bolshevik Revolution, the *Wall Street Journal* maintained an optimistic stance in an article of 10 November 1917, appealing to readers to maintain "a long perspective" and calling for "courage and patience."[191] A 17 November 1917 article referred to senior J. P. Morgan & Co. partners Thomas Lamont and Henry Davison as maintaining bullish views on Russia and suggesting that the political situation was in the process of reaching "a stable government."[192]

Until the very end, Meserve maintained his optimistic stance on Russia. In one of his last letters from Petrograd to New York, on 15 September 1917, he said, "I feel that there is a tremendous future in Russia for the National City Bank, as it does not seem to me that we have really gotten well started here," before leaving for Moscow to start the bank's operations there on the eve of the Bolshevik Revolution.[193] That the bank would open its Moscow branch several days *after* Lenin's coup only underscored Meserve's point.

A review of commentary on Russia by the foreign financial press and financiers in late 1917 shows a strikingly indifferent to optimistic attitude vis-à-vis political events in Russia. Foreign financiers not only were willing to overlook revolutionary political upheavals and violence, but actually embraced the revolution as a transformative experience for Russia, even going so far as to cite the French Revolution in support of their optimistic views.[194] By 1917, foreign financiers had been participating in the transformation of Russia for years— investing in the revolution by maintaining, even growing, their presence in the Russian markets was only a logical continuation of their earlier behavior.

The French Connection

The experiences of Meserve and Bunker are significant in that both men represented not only the largest banks and most important financial centers in the world, but also an important new wave of Anglo-American capital moving into Russia in the early twentieth century. This Anglo-American dimension to the Russian boom has been relatively ignored by previous scholarship.[195] Nevertheless, in spite of both having spent years in Russia and despite the importance of the Anglo-American dimension to the financial backstory of the Russian Revolution, the views of Meserve and Bunker were also those of relative newcomers. In this sense, the French perspective is particularly important and interesting, given the long-running financial ties between France and Russia.

Perhaps the most seasoned French observer of the contemporary Russian financial scene was Maurice Verstraete of the Russo-Asiatic Bank. Born into a wealthy family, Verstraete had joined the French foreign service in 1888.[196] After having served as French consul in Chicago, he was posted to the consulate in Moscow, and eventually the embassy in Saint Petersburg.[197] A close observer of financial developments, he was one of the French government's appointees to the board of the Russo-Chinese Bank in October 1899.[198] He later joined the board of the Banque du Nord in 1901.[199] Verstraete eventually left the diplomatic service for banking full-time, and became one of the architects of the merger between the Russo-Chinese and the Banque du Nord that resulted in the creation of the Russo Asiatic Bank, where he continued to work.[200] Given this background and his position as one of the most senior and well-connected foreign financiers in Russia, Verstraete's views are of particular interest in the context of a discussion of foreign investors' assessments of Russia during the revolution.

In 1920, Verstraete published his diaries from the time of war and revolution, covering the period from May 1915 through his departure in late 1918. At first glance, his account appears to be considerably more negative than the narratives in the correspondence of Meserve and Bunker. His portrayal of the liberals in the Duma in the immediate aftermath of the February Revolution is that of a group of politicians hopelessly outpaced by events and by the socialist parties, whom he saw as the real winners of February.[201] His references to a "somber" and dark future were numerous in his commentary on 1917.[202] Verstraete repeatedly made reference to the infamously mercurial personality of Kerensky, as well as characterizing Russians in general in a negative light, saying, "Le Slave n'est ni exact ni logique," among other things.[203] Most importantly, he highlighted the threat of a Bolshevik coup, ending his last entry before Lenin's putsch with the ominous warning, "The Bolsheviks are a minority in the socialist camp, and because of the attitude they have taken they are now condemned to use extra-legal means to take to the streets, but they are an active minority and the street is a field of battle they know all too well."[204]

However, there are reasons to discount Verstraete's superficially negative and cautious view. At a basic level, given that the diaries were published well after the Bolshevik nationalizations, repudiations, and violence, some degree of self-serving selectivity in the editing process should not be ruled out. Yet even in spite of any favorable spin Verstraete may have put on his narrative after the fact, his diary entries from late 1916 and 1917 betray a considerable degree of confusion and even optimism in ways that strikingly parallel the narratives that emerge from the correspondence of Bunker and Meserve.

Thus, in marked similarity to his British and American counterparts, Verstraete was scathing in his treatment of the ancien régime, painting the picture in early 1917 of an incorrigibly reactionary and obstinate regime moving "neither to the right, nor the left," but backward.[205] He spoke of the last days of Tsarism as "le chaos, l'anarchie, le sauve-qui-peut de tous ceux qui sont honnêtes," of the waste and suppression of talents and positive initiative, and of the plummeting morale of the army and the pernicious influence of the German Tsarina both on the Tsar's policies and on public opinion.[206] Ominously, he quoted a journalist contact in early February: "what is wrong in Russia is the top."[207]

In this context, it is not surprising that Verstraete betrayed signs of optimism after the February Revolution. In the same entry where he claimed the liberals were losing ground to the socialists, he acknowledged the fluidity of the situation and suggested that he was optimistic in the early days after the February Revolution. In speaking of the Tsar's abdication, he admitted to having thought that events were moving in the direction that favored the liberal outcome of a constitutional monarchy, and not the desired outcome of the socialist parties.[208] He went on to talk of the socialist camp as being fragmented, of the Bolsheviks being a minority, and of terror being "not an end in itself, but a means for achieving political revolution."[209] Crucially, he ended his first post-February entry arguing that the liberal parties could create a liberal constitutional order by creating "a population of rural proprietors as in France."[210] Even as late as March, then, Verstraete saw plenty of signs for hope in Russia.

This sanguine view is evident in his entries later through 1917. In April, he wrote that "rightly or wrongly, I am under the impression that a certain calm is returning slowly," pointing to the "dual power" between the Provisional Government and Soviet as resulting in a de facto system of checks and balances, in the context of which each body also contributed tangible concessions.[211] He framed his discussion of the crisis in agriculture later the same month with a comment about various factors showing signs for optimism, while others pointed to trouble.[212]

In continuing this conflicted narrative through 1917, Verstraete echoed many of the themes found in the Meserve and Bunker letters. The Germanophobia evident in his comments about the Tsarina is thus mirrored in his mid-1917 comments about the Bolsheviks being artificially supported by the Germans.[213] In an analogous manner Verstraete echoed the Anglo-American narrative of the February Revolution inaugurating reforms and being a force for positive change. Thus, even amid his negative commentary in June, Verstraete spoke of the need to not lose heart, and to focus on the "constructive forces of the Revolution" even as it showed its destructive capabilities.[214] He continued this line on the eve of the July days by saying that while he recognized Russia was going through an existential crisis, he still believed that in the end, a happy outcome would emerge.[215] He attributed this view to his belief that "the life and conservation instinct" would prevent "a great people to resist their collective suicide."[216] In a chilling line that was both ominous and appropriate for a child of the French Revolution, Verstraete went on to acknowledge that "we must expect further bloodshed" for the improvement to take hold.[217]

In considering the (likely favorably) edited diaries of Verstraete, then, it is evident that—even if he more closely followed the politics and expressed a sometimes more negative view of the evolving situation in Russia—one of the most prominent French financiers in Russia at the time held views largely congruent with those of Bunker and Meserve. Like his British and American counterparts, he had grown to despise the Tsarist regime and saw in the February Revolution a chance for positive change. He acknowledged the extremism embodied in Bolshevism, but initially saw it as a low-probability outcome artificially supported by the Germans, and eventually even grew to see in the radicalization of the revolution a catalyst for positive change in the long run. At the same time he grew increasingly alarmed at the prospect of postwar Russia being a German sphere of influence.[218] This emphasis on the long-run potential for Russia to emerge from the cataclysms of 1917 in a better state, as well as the concern over German competition for influence in the country, mirrored the narratives of Bunker and Meserve. Indeed, Verstraete was arguably more bullish on Russia than even the Americans and British—he certainly stayed in Russia longer than Bunker did, and in the words of one historian, even "fell under the spell of Lenin's ideas to some extent."[219] Indeed, in 1918 he would pitch commercial ideas to the Bolshevik leader through Feliks Dzerzhinskii, the dreaded founder of the Cheka—the predecessor to the KGB.[220] The case of one of the most prominent French financiers in the country, thus, also shows a remarkable degree of optimism about Russia.

Conclusion

The Bolshevik default of January 1918 was the largest in modern financial history.[221] The default was itself accompanied by waves of wholesale nationalization and expropriations of private property and businesses, including of banks. In their recent and comprehensive study, *This Time Is Different*, economists Carmen Reinhart and Kenneth Rogoff further point to the default, which, by their count, continued 69 years, as the longest lasting in their 800-year global dataset.[222] In light of future events, it is tempting to write off the financiers who increased their exposure to Russia on the eve of the Bolshevik Revolution as being caught in an emotionally driven speculative mania that prevented them from seeing the rapidly approaching financial catastrophe that awaited them.

In fact, a close reading of contemporary accounts offered in the financial press and business correspondence suggests a more complex, rationalized dynamic at play in driving investor decision making in the lead-up to the Bolshevik default of 1918. Contemporary financiers shared a particularly upbeat analysis of the health of the Russian economy through late 1917. A combination of competitive pressures and implicit and explicit government guarantees pushed them to lower standards and take on more risk than they perhaps would have under different circumstances. A desire to advance home-country political interests and a fear of German economic domination of postwar

Russia served as an added incentive to invest in Russia. Finally, the notion of Russia as a country undergoing a profound transformation to a higher level of social development was a singularly attractive force that not only drew in foreign investors before the revolutionary events but pushed many investors to see revolution as a good thing in the Russian context. Only after considering these complex, interrelated, and mutually reinforcing phenomena can the international financial history of Russia in 1917 be understood not so much as a failure of foreign investors to anticipate the revolution, but rather as a failure to accurately forecast the nature of the revolution in which they were consciously investing.

5

Revolutionary Default

AS THE RED GUARD gruffly shoved him through the door and into the biting morning cold of Petrograd, Verstraete must have reflected on his career change. Banking certainly had its advantages, but this day would have been a good one to be in his old job, as a diplomat. It was New Year's Eve 1917, and while his former colleagues at the French embassy—whom even these thugs would not dare to touch—were no doubt preparing to celebrate the end of a truly bizarre year with champagne and other delicacies that had long since become all too rare in revolutionary Petrograd, Verstraete would be ringing in 1918 in the company of Bolshevik goons.[1] With any luck, they would be some of the more refined ones. Sokol'nikov, their financial point man, seemed a more or less reasonable, if cocksure, chap—he had even studied law at the Sorbonne.[2] Anyone would be better than his current unwashed companion—the sailors seemed to be particularly uncivilized.[3]

Walking out of jail five days later on temporary release, Verstraete reflected on the heady events he had witnessed and indeed on the characters he had been dealing with ever since the Bolshevik coup. As a banker, he could not help but wonder what these radicals would ultimately do with the property of foreigners and especially all the debt Russia owed the Allied countries, not least France. Sokol'nikov had assured him that he personally was not in favor of confiscation—that he wanted to keep the interests of shareholders and creditors in mind. Verstraete, however, had his doubts about this oddball Bolshevik technocrat managing to convince the burly sailors. The nationalization of the banks struck him as being carried out in a way that was more military than financial. "When it comes to destruction, you can count on the Bolsheviks," he surmised.[4]

Verstraete would receive the answer to his questions less than a month later, when the All-Russia Central Executive Committee's (Vserossiiskii Tsentral'nyi Ispolnitel'nyi Komitet, or VTsIK) would issue its decree of 3 February 1918 annulling the state debt. This act was branded by one financial historian as "an event without historical precedent both in scale and deliberation."[5] To this day, it is arguably the largest default in history.[6] And yet the event has received little attention from specialized scholars. Compared to the Weimar hyperinflation, which is not only the subject of vast quantities of monographs and articles, but also seared into the popular imagination as one of the greatest financial catastrophes of modern times, the revolutionary default in Bolshevik Russia is all but ignored. This book is an attempt to rectify the oversight.

In exploring the drivers of the Bolshevik decision to default, it is evident that the decision was rooted partly in Bolshevik ideology but also shaped by practicalities. Considering the very possible counterfactual scenario that the Bolshevik coup in early November 1917 had failed, it is difficult to imagine a situation whereby the Provisional Government or any successor would have been able to avoid at least a fairly significant default. In this sense, investors holding on to Russian debt before, during, and after the Bolshevik Revolution not only failed to account for political factors, but also failed to remain true to the narrow financial analysis that would have dictated caution even in the absence of a Bolshevik takeover. On the Bolshevik side, the decision to default was not just consistent with the Bolsheviks' previously articulated policies, but—from both a political and economic standpoint—rational.

The Politics of Default

In his reputational theory of sovereign debt, Michael Tomz offers a schema of three types of debtors: stalwarts, who pay in good times and bad; fair-weathers, who pay only during good times; and lemons, who default even when times are good. According to Tomz's theory, countries develop reputations over time, as markets learn how they behave in different economic and financial contexts.[7] The Bolshevik default in 1918 confounds this categorization. Lindert and Morton's cross-country study of sovereign debt notes that countries in their sample such as Mexico and Turkey were repeat defaulters whose records should have served as a warning to investors, but Lindert and Morton go on to recognize that "Russia is the exception here" given that it had an exemplary payment record until its 1918 default that destroyed investors' returns in a single event.[8]

Under Tomz's theory, a default by the Bolsheviks in the context of war and revolution could have signaled to markets that they were merely unable or unwilling to pay in difficult economic times—the behavior of a classic fair-weather borrower. Yet the language and terms of the repudiation decree are so charged and categorical that they could be read as an attempt by the Bolsheviks to avoid being labeled as fair-weathers and to actively seek out the lemon designation instead. Tomz acknowledges this bizarre—within his theoretical framework—behavior, but does not try to explain it, merely saying, "the Soviet leaders squandered their reputational patrimony" through the repudiation.[9]

The question of why the Bolsheviks not only defaulted but repudiated in 1918 is important. It goes to the heart of one of the most significant events in the history of international finance, and—unless the act is to be written off as an instance of deranged irrationality—the question is political. In the case of the Bolshevik political calculus, both Bolshevik ideology and tactical political considerations combined to create a strong political impetus not only for default, but also for outright repudiation.

Ideological Drivers of Default

Not just the Bolsheviks, but a large part of the radical and liberal opposition in Russia as well had signaled at least the intention to default for some time. The 1905 Financial Manifesto of the Saint Petersburg Soviet, discussed in Chapter 2, was but one of the most prominent articulations of this intention. Between the Saint Petersburg Soviet's Financial Manifesto and the 1918 Bolshevik default, ideological opposition to the Tsarist government's financial policies only strengthened. The Vyborg Manifesto discussed in Chapter 2 and the regular Duma debates discussed in Chapter 3 were manifestations of a continuation and arguably a hardening of the liberal opposition's position on the question of finance and foreign loans. The Bolsheviks, too, maintained their opposition to government policy through this period, and did so vocally.

While the war notoriously changed the equation for many socialists and liberals on both sides of the conflict, the Bolsheviks left little doubt as to their view of the Allied cause. In his "Open Letter to Boris Souvarine," written in late 1916, Lenin railed against "bourgeois France, reactionary France, that ally and friend of tsarism, the 'world usurer' . . . who is defending his booty, his 'sacred right' to possess colonies, his 'freedom' to exploit the entire world with the help of millions loaned to weaker or poorer nations."[10]

In a lecture in late March 1917, after the February Revolution which brought the Provisional Government to power, Lenin made it clear that he did not think Russia had escaped from the ranks of the "weaker or poorer nations" that he referred to in his letter to Souvarine. Making specific reference to "Anglo-French finance capital," Lenin recalled the Provisional Government's role in opposing the 1905 Revolution, and singled out the 1906 loan (see Chapter 2) as an instance of its pernicious influence.[11] He went on to accuse the new Provisional Government of being a puppet of the bankers. An observer of the speech summarized Lenin's views on the subject: "from the standpoint of world politics and international finance capital, the Guchkov-Milyukov government is no more than an agent of the banking firm 'England and France,' an instrument for continuing the imperialist slaughter."[12]

In case there was any doubt as to the policy implications of this hostility toward foreign bankers, Lenin eliminated it in the fourth of his "Letters from Afar," sent to Alexandra Kollontai, on the eve of his departure from Zurich, for forwarding to and publication in *Pravda*.[13] In the letter, Lenin posed and then answered the question of what a pro-Bolshevik government would do if it were to come to power. In responding, Lenin laid out six points of policy. According to the first two, the new government would at once renounce all treaties signed by either the Tsarist or Provisional Government and publish said documents for the world to see.[14] The next three points dealt with the declaration of peace and the export of revolution. Crucially, Lenin devoted the last and longest point to the question of finance: "[The government] would declare that the *capitalist gentry themselves* can repay the billions of debts contracted by the bourgeois governments to wage this criminal, predatory war and that the workers and peasants *refuse to recognize* these debts. To pay the interest on these loans would mean paying the capitalists *tribute* for many years for having graciously allowed the workers to kill one another in order that the capitalists might divide the spoils."[15] As if this declaration was not sufficiently categorical, he closed by asking the workers and peasants of Russia, in the name of the future Soviet government, "are you willing to pay these gentry, the capitalists, *hundreds of millions* of rubles *every year* for a war waged for the division of the African colonies, Turkey, etc.?"[16] Although this Fourth Letter was not published until 1924, a summary of it, including the six points and declaration of the intention to default, did see publication in *Volksrecht* on 31 March and 2 April 1917.[17] By the early days of the Provisional Government, then, Lenin's ideological line was clearly set in favor of default and was circulating in the public domain. Of course *Volksrecht* was not the *Economist*, but that was the point: the Leninist line on default was a surprise only to those who had so narrowly focused their research on Russia as to have overlooked these unequivocal and publicly available signals of Bolshevik intentions vis-à-vis the debt.

As 1917 progressed, Lenin devoted increasing amounts of attention to questions of finance and to foreign debts in particular. His position on the loan also became more visible to the financial community when, for example, it was discussed in a 30 April 1917 article in the *Finansovaia Gazeta* (Financial Newspaper) about leftist positions on Provisional Government borrowing.[18] Internal documents, too, showed Lenin's continued focus on waging the revolutionary war along the financial front.

In his instructions to Bolshevik deputies elected at factory and regimental Soviets, Lenin was clear in stating that financial questions were to be a central point of Bolshevik opposition to the government. As in his Fourth Letter from

Afar, these instructions were expressed in six points. After first making clear his total opposition to the war, Lenin linked the war to finance in declaring that deputies must not allow "a single kopek" to be spent on the war.[19] Again, as in the Fourth Letter, the sixth point focused on the loan question, with Lenin declaring that the deputies should withhold funds from any government that continued the war and refused to publish secret treaties.[20] Although these instructions were ostensibly focused on the issue of the war, by the linking of issues to loans, Lenin maintained the conception of finance as a political weapon that stretched back at least to the Vyborg Manifesto of 1906 and the Financial Manifesto of 1905.

In the resolution on the war, drafted after the 20 April 1917 vote of the Petrograd Soviet in favor of the so-called *Zaem Svobody*, or "Liberty Loan"—Lenin remained focused on foreign finance as it related to the revolution.[21] Bristling at the way in which the belligerent powers played on nationalist sentiment to rope in their erstwhile socialist opponents and to convince citizens to invest their savings in war bonds, Lenin sought to refocus attention on the ultimately destructive and anti-Socialist ends that the loans supported.[22] He went on to talk about how "the thousands of threads of Russian and Anglo-French banking capital" could not renounce annexations or "the profits from the thousands of millions invested in loans, concessions, war industries."[23] The Russian, British, and French network of financial relations, in this view, formed the very core of the anti-revolution. Lenin would read the draft resolution in his speech to the All-Russia Conference of the Russian Social Democratic Party (Bolshevik) on its opening day, 7 May 1917.[24]

In continuing to fight along the financial front—now against the Provisional Government and, notably, over the issue of the Liberty Loan—Lenin continued the tradition of the Financial Manifesto of late 1905. However, whereas there is some disagreement over the effectiveness of the Financial Manifesto in 1905, the impact of the Bolshevik financial campaign against the Provisional Government was clearly devastating. By July 1917, the Ministry of Finance itself acknowledged in its publications that subscriptions reflected class divisions, with only "about two percent" of the Petrograd population subscribing, and attributing the lackluster response by workers and peasants to "Leninite" propaganda.[25]

Apostol blamed the Bolsheviks for much of the trouble in securing the loans.[26] He specifically accused them of "the dissemination of false rumors with regard to the economic situation of the country and the condition of government finances, rumors designed to create a panic and to interfere with the financing of military operations."[27] The remark is a striking echo of Kokovtsov's technocratic characterization of the opposition financial critique in Duma debates as resting on "false" data and "rumors" rather than engaging with the broader political questions the financial opposition represented. Apostol relates how the various cooperating leftist parties responded to the Bolshevik challenge on the financial front by passing the 4 July 1917 resolution of the All Russian Soviet of Workers' and Soldiers' Deputies in support of the Liberty Loan and also by ominously declaring, "in the event of its appearing very soon that subscriptions to the Liberty Loan have proved insufficient, the Provisional Government should resort to a forced loan."[28]

In a 12 July 1917 *Pravda* article, Lenin touched on the issue of financial disclosure, which would become central both to the repudiation of prerevolutionary loans, as well as to the nationalization of the banking system.[29] Lenin asserted, "unless commercial and bank secrecy is abolished . . . all phrases on control and all projects for it will be so much meaningless verbiage."[30] In his view, private firms would merely use accounting tricks to mask profits unless forced to fully disclose all confidential financial information.

Throughout 1917, Lenin also maintained a broader financial critique of the Provisional Government, in doing so taking advantage of the rapidly deteriorating financial situation. At times, these critiques suggested moderation of his position. Thus, in the section on bank nationalization in his September 1917 pamphlet "The Impending Catastrophe and How to Combat It," he spoke of nationalization of the banking system as an organizational issue meant to control the banks, rather than to expropriate investors:

> The ownership of the capital wielded by and concentrated in the banks is certified by printed and written certificates called shares, bonds, bills, receipts etc. Not a single one of these certificates would be invalidated or altered if the banks were nationalized, i.e., if all the banks were amalgamated into a single state bank. Whoever owned fifteen rubles on a savings account would continue to be the owner of fifteen rubles after the nationalization of the banks; and whoever had fifteen million rubles would continue after the nationalization of the banks to have fifteen million rubles in the form of shares, bonds bills, commercial certificates and so on.[31]

In light of future events, this claim would appear to be a cynical and barefaced lie. In the very same article, however, Lenin showed that "control" was not necessarily as benign as he first made it seem. His assertion, "it would be enough to decree confiscation of property and imprisonment as the penalty for managers, board members and big shareholders for the slightest delay or for attempting to conceal documents and accounts," left little doubt about the implications of the nationalization or Lenin's aims.[32]

The signals of ideological motivation for defaulting and for upending previously existing financial relations more generally continued until the very eve of the October coup. Thus, in his pamphlet on the "Revision of the Party

Programme," written from 19 to 21 October 1917, and published the same month—just days before the coup—Lenin specifically took up the issue of loan repudiation:

> Concerning the financial and economic part of the programme, Comrade Larin writes that "it is almost a blank, no mention is made, even of the annulment of war loans contracted by tsarism [Lenin: only tsarism?] or of the struggle against the fiscal utilization of state monopolies, etc." It is extremely desirable for Comrade Larin not to postpone his practical proposals in anticipation of the congress. He should bring them up immediately, or we shall not be well prepared for the congress. On the question of the annulment of state debts (and of course, not of tsarism alone, but also of the bourgeoisie) we must give considerable thought to the question of small bondholders. . . . I repeat: in order to prepare our programme seriously, to ensure the actual co-operation of the entire Party, all those interested must *immediately* get busy and *publish* their suggestions as well as *precise drafts* of points already edited and which contain additions and amendments.[33]

Far from restraining talk of repudiation, Lenin encouraged it, making sure to include the debts of the Provisional Government in any repudiation. These were not the words of a man who hesitated.

Practical Political Considerations for Default

Beyond the ideological considerations, there were strong tactical and strategic reasons for making default a likely Bolshevik policy. The Bolsheviks had strong incentives to build support among the peasantry, which still formed the bulk of the population in 1918. The Stolypin reforms encouraged individual landownership, and the years leading up to the revolution saw a boom in mortgage lending to peasants through the Peasants' Land Bank. Even before the outbreak of war, contemporary observers were growing increasingly worried about the bubble in agricultural land that was being fed by abundant credit to increasingly indebted peasants (see Chapter 3).

Lenin's awareness of the practical incentives for default vis-à-vis the peasantry is evident in his writings leading up to and indeed following the October Revolution. Conscious of the support the Socialist Revolutionaries enjoyed in the countryside, Lenin attacked their positions throughout 1917. In a 14 July 1917 article in *Pravda*, for instance, he quoted the Cadet newspaper *Rech'* to show how Rodzianko, the former head of the Duma, was worrying about a mass of rural defaults that would ruin landowners' credit, as well as about how it was the mass of mortgage loans that were the cornerstone of rural landownership dynamics.[34] In an 11 September 1917 article, he continued to use the land and mortgage issue to win points with the peasants. Having enumerated the various peasant demands, he pilloried what he branded a reformist program of the Socialist Revolutionaries, arguing, "you do not have to give these demands a lot of thought to see that it is absolutely impossible to realize them *in alliance* with the capitalists, without breaking completely with them."[35] Showing specifically what he meant by this, Lenin noted, "confiscation of all private land means the confiscation of hundreds of millions in capital belonging to the banks to which the greater part of this land is mortgaged."[36] Lenin's sales pitch to the peasants over the mortgage issue continued after the October Revolution. In his speech on the agrarian question in late November, he again emphasized that for the peasants to gain their land, they would have to overturn capitalist financial relations. Drawing a distinction between the Socialist Revolutionaries and Bolsheviks, Lenin said, "You want land ... but the land is mortgaged and belongs to Russian and world capital."[37]

Well before the October coup—and certainly before the decisions to nationalize the banks, suspend dividend and interest payments, and eventually repudiate state loans and guarantees—strong ideological imperatives existed for these measures. At the same time, Lenin was acutely aware of the political points to be gained by these policies—especially among valuable constituencies such as the peasantry. Practicality and ideology overlapped in the political realm, just as they would in the economic sphere.

The Economics of Default

In his discussion of the Bolshevik takeover in 1917 and Lenin's subsequent policies, Sean McMeekin suggests that it was the Bolsheviks' inept financial policies that drove the Russian economy into the ground in 1917–18. He refers to Norman Stone's compelling discussion of the Russian wartime economy in his *Eastern Front*, pointing to the wartime armament industry's stimulative effect on the economy.[38] He further claims, "the economic crisis of 1917 was not, therefore, one of insufficient growth," arguing that if anything, the economy was "overheating."[39] Acknowledging Stone's argument, that inflation, "not stagnation," drove the bread riots of 1917, McMeekin proceeds to argue that because of the glut of liquidity, "by 1917, the Russian war economy exhibited symptoms of a dangerous market bubble, with too many speculators chasing lofty wartime returns that could not possibly last forever."[40]

In McMeekin's view, "if harnessed properly, Russia's gold and cash reserves, her thriving bond and equity markets, and the whole international network of overlapping obligations tying her to Entente creditors, investors, and military suppliers could help her win the war with the Central

Powers and secure a prosperous postwar future for her people."[41] He notes, "if, however, the country's precariously balanced financial system fell apart, the consequences for Russia, her creditors, and the entire world economy would be devastating."[42]

In the end, of course, the latter scenario took form. McMeekin leaves little doubt as to whom to blame: "It was Russia's grave misfortune that a ruthless gang of Marxist ideologues appeared on the scene in 1917, just as the wartime boom had turned her capital cities into vast arsenals of weaponry, backed by a thousand tons of gold bullion in bank vaults and billions more rubles on deposit, with the entire stupendous edifice financed by 'capitalist' governments, banks, and corporations the Bolsheviks had expressly targeted for destruction. The casino was loaded and wired to the hilt. All it took was a spark to burn the whole building down."[43] In McMeekin's view, then, but for the Bolsheviks and their confiscations and nationalizations, Russia would have continued to fight and win and, crucially, would not have defaulted.

In this narrative, policies enacted by the Bolsheviks upon their assumption of power drove the Russian economy into a tailspin. Declaring, "the Bolshevik nationalization of Russia's banks in 1917 came right out of the playbook of the *Communist Manifesto*," McMeekin recounts how, after overcoming initial resistance on the part of the banking system's employees, the Bolsheviks "opened a Pandora's box with their war on the banks."[44] The Bolshevik nationalization froze the country's payments system, made industrial investment impossible, and led to a strangling of foreign trade, as the nationalization of bank assets and repudiation of debts precipitated retaliatory measures by Western powers.[45] McMeekin surmises, "the cumulative economic impact of the nationalization drive was catastrophic."[46] Acknowledging that "nearly a year of revolutionary upheaval" had disrupted the economy already, he posits that the Bolsheviks caused it to implode.[47]

In his work on sovereign debt, Michael Tomz observes that sovereign debt payments are contingent on two variables: the ability of a government to pay and its willingness to pay. Ideological explanations of the Bolshevik default stress the latter. While there is little doubt that the Bolsheviks' ideological predilection was for default, the McMeekin narrative understates the economic factors that made default almost entirely unavoidable. In focusing so much attention on the negative impact of Bolshevik nationalization of the banks on the economy, McMeekin overstates the significance of the Bolsheviks' freedom of action and Russia's ability to meet its debt obligations. Indeed, in a counterfactual scenario whereby the Bolshevik coup in November 1917 did not succeed, it is difficult to see Russia escaping default. The Bolsheviks merely added an ideological element to a default that was all but inevitable, accelerating rather than triggering an economic collapse.

The Real Economy

From an economic standpoint, by late 1917 Russia's ability to remain current on its external and internal debt was rapidly losing credibility. Although bond markets rallied until the very eve of the Bolshevik takeover, the real economy and financial system were already showing signs of significant strain.

While Stone correctly notes the stimulative effects of the war on the real economy, he himself allows that by 1917 the economy was showing cracks. Any discussion of the wartime economy is complicated by poor data on two counts. First, the convulsions and governmental changes of 1917 resulted in breaks and inconsistencies in record keeping. Second, the territory of the Russian Empire and its successor states was in flux due to the ebbs and flows of military operations during the Great War and subsequent Russian Civil War. Nevertheless, scholars have attempted to reconstruct national output data series during this turbulent period.

According to Markevich and Harrison's index of estimated wartime national income (see Table 5.1), overall wartime output peaked in 1915 before falling by between 8 and 10 percent in 1916 and by a further 11 to 13 percent in 1917, depending on the territorial footprint considered.[48] The allocation of manufacturing output, as estimated by Gatrell, reveals further strains. In Gatrell's telling, the portion of overall output in the Russian economy devoted to consumer goods plummeted by nearly 20 percentage points between 1914 and 1917 (see Table 5.2).[49] Markevich and Harrison paint a somewhat better picture than Gatrell for overall output through 1918, but this is largely due to an incorporation of military services in their figures.[50] In other areas, notably in per capita agricultural output, they paint a damning picture. According to their estimates, availability of agricultural goods per capita—an indicator of baseline consumer welfare—fell by more than 40 percent between 1913 and 1918, dropping to a paltry 44 percent of 1913 levels by 1921.[51]

While it is not surprising to have seen the share of output devoted to defense increase at the expense of household consumption in wartime, the shift was dramatic and coincided with a financial squeeze of consumers in the form of new taxes, including the inflation tax. Pasvolsky notes that after running a huge deficit in the so-called "ordinary" budget after the vodka ban was introduced in 1914, the government finally managed to balance the ordinary budget by late 1916 through a range of taxes, including the introduction of new income and war profits taxes, and higher indirect taxes on consumer items.[52] Indeed, the income tax's favorable effect on the government's fiscal balance notwithstanding, its hit to their personal incomes grated on bankers, including Midland's Bunker.[53]

TABLE 5.1. Russian national income, 1913–22

| | | Industry | | | | | | |
	Agriculture	Large-scale	Small-scale	Construction	Transport	Other civilian	Military services	Total
Russian Empire excluding Finland and Poland								
1913	100.0	100.0	100.0	100.0	100.0	100.0	100.0	100.0
1914	92.2	106.3	98.0	101.6	106.3	97.1	168.7	98.0
1915	94.1	111.0	78.4	74.7	127.9	97.0	450.6	101.6
1916	80.9	94.2	88.2	58.3	136.7	86.5	639.1	93.6
1917	79.3	73.3	78.4	41.8	79.8	75.6	560.5	81.9
1918	61.9	31.4	73.5	14.3				
1919	53.9	16.6	49.0	10.9				
Russian Empire (excluding Finland and Poland) under government control								
1913	100.0	100.0	100.0	100.0	100.0	100.0	100.0	100.0
1914	92.2	106.3	98.0	101.6	106.3	97.1	168.7	98.0
1915	88.1	111.0	78.4	74.7	127.9	93.6	450.6	98.2
1916	74.8	94.2	88.2	58.3	136.7	82.9	639.1	90.1
1917	73.0	73.3	78.4	41.8	79.8	71.9	560.5	78.2
Soviet interwar territory								
1913	100.0	100.0	100.0	100.0	100.0	100.0	100.0	100.0
1914	92.0	106.3	98.1	101.5	103.1	96.7	169.4	97.6
1915	95.0	110.9	78.4	74.6	130.6	97.8	452.2	102.3
1916	78.5	94.2	88.3	58.3	143.8	85.3	641.2	92.5
1917	80.1	73.3	78.4	41.8	79.0	75.8	562.8	82.1
1918	61.2	31.4	73.5	14.4	21.0	50.4	29.4	50.1
1919	53.2	16.6	49.0	10.9	26.7	41.0	175.1	42.7
1920	50.1	17.5	44.1	7.1	17.4	38.0	340.7	42.0
1921	45.0	15.9	49.0	6.8	21.4	35.4	251.8	38.2
1922	53.9	22.1	53.9	12.9	27.5	43.0	128.5	44.1

Source: Derived from Table 5 in Markevich and Harrison, "Great War, Civil War, and Recovery," 680.
Note: base year 1913 = 100.

In spite of the increased taxation, however, the government still relied heavily on the printing of money to finance its overall budget deficit, and inflation—which can itself be seen as a tax, insofar as it confiscates savings by depreciating their purchasing power—continued to accelerate through the war.[54] Estimates of inflation rates vary, and different areas of the economy experienced varying degrees of inflation; but the data point to a trend of generally accelerating money printing and associated inflation over the course of the war. In the first two months of the war alone, the number of notes in circulation increased by 62 percent.[55] On the eve of the Bolshevik Revolution, the stock of currency in circulation had increased nearly twelvefold (see

REVOLUTIONARY DEFAULT 173

TABLE 5.2. Manufacturing output to final demand, 1913–18 (percentages)

Year	Investment goods	Construction goods	Household consumption	Defense
1913	9.1	3.7	81.8	5.4
1914	9.7	3.6	79.0	7.7
1915	7.3	3.9	68.1	20.7
1916	5.4	3.9	61.9	28.8
1917	4.5	3.6	59.8	32.6
1H1918	5.7	1.9	85.6	6.7

Source: Gatrell, *Russia's First World War*, 250.

TABLE 5.3. Notes in circulation

	Notes in circulation (rubles, millions)	Percentage increase from preceding date
29 July 1914	1,633.3	
14 January 1915	2,946.5	80
14 January 1916	5,617.0	91
14 January 1917	9,097.3	62
14 March 1917	9,949.6	9
5 November 1917[a]	18,917.0	90

Source: Michelson, Apostol, and Bernatzky, *Russian Public Finance during the War*, 379.
a. Last return of the State Bank; the Bolshevik Revolution took place on 7 November 1917.

Table 5.3).[56] Moreover, as Bernatzky noted, "the Provisional Government was forced to issue almost as large an amount of notes during the *eight months* of its existence as the Imperial Government did during more than *thirty months* from the outbreak of war."[57]

An extremely conservative statutory limit on the issuing of currency by the State Bank was one of the foundational elements of Witte's financial reforms, in which the Russian financial establishment took great pride. At the outbreak of war, the limit was fixed at 300 million rubles.[58] Over the course of the war, the government raised this limit no fewer than ten times.[59] Moreover, each individual increase was—by prewar standards—massive in scale. The smallest increase in the limit was by 1 billion rubles—more than three times the prewar limit—and the largest and most frequent increase was for 2 billion rubles, bringing the aggregate increase of the limit to 16.2 billion rubles, or 54 times the original limit of 300 million.[60] It is particularly noteworthy that of the ten increases in the limit between the outbreak of war and the Bolshevik Revolution, six of them—totaling 11 billion rubles—took place in 1917 alone.[61]

The combination of flagging output and rapid increases in the monetary base contributed to skyrocketing inflation by late 1916 and through the course

TABLE 5.4. Semiannual retail and wholesale price indices

	Wholesale prices (Sidorov 1960)	Retail prices, USSR territory
1H1914	100	100
2H1914	101	101
1H1915	115	119
2H1915	141	139
1H1916	238	164
2H1916	398	238
1H1917	702	361
2H1917	1,171	972

Source: Gatrell, *Russia's First World War*, 146; Sidorov, *Finansovoe Polozhenie Rossii v Gody Pervoi Mirovoi Voiny*, 147.
Note: 1H1914 = 100. The base year for the retail price index has been reset to 1H1914 versus Gatrell's use of a full-year 1913 base.

TABLE 5.5. Annual price indices

	Retail prices, Moscow	Wholesale prices (wood, foodstuffs, mineral, leather, and textiles)	Wholesale prices (other industrial)
1913	100	100	100
1914	101	106	110
1915	130	117	153
1916	206	208	219
1917	775	327	434
1918	5,680	639	953

Source: Gatrell, *Russia's First World War*, 146.
Note: 1913 = 100.

of 1917. Inflation of course varied by economic sectors and regions. Estimates vary, but the trend was clearly that of accelerating inflation over the course of the war, and particularly in 1916 and 1917 (see Tables 5.4 and 5.5).

Keynes noted in his *Tract on Monetary Reform*—written shortly after completing his work at the British Treasury on the North Russian Currency Board, and after having devoted considerable attention to the Soviet monetary reforms of the early 1920s—that societies had a surprisingly high tolerance for inflation. He specifically showed how a relatively elevated rate of inflation, whereby prices doubled over the course of a given year, would equate to a relatively light "turnover tax" on everyday transactions, under reasonable assumptions of the velocity of money.[62] This phenomenon broadly appears to have played out during the first years of the war; and, as Keynes noted, the Russian

TABLE 5.6. Output and procurement of selected products, January to December 1917 (output in thousands of tons)

Month	Coal	Oil	Cotton yarn	Grain	Percentage of stipulated amount
1916 monthly average	2,390.1	*N/A*	24.8	*665*	
1917					
January	2,555.3	406.2	26.8	934	77
February	2,349.0	366.9	23.5	672	62
March	2,529.1	378.4	22.7	1,130	98
April	1,965.7	380.0	13.9	491	38
May	2,185.2	394.8	21.1	1,261	88
June	2,152.4	373.5	19.6	1,106	112
July	1,967.3	381.7	14.2	459	57
August	1,887.0	370.2	15.9	324	17
September	1,801.8	288.3	16.7	765	31
October	1,883.7	309.6	15.8	449	19
November	1,867.0	334.2	14.3	640	38
December	1,280.9	327.6	14.4	136	7

Source: Gatrell, *Russia's First World War*, 207.

TABLE 5.7. Strikes and economic demands made by workers during 1917

	Minimum estimated number of strikers	Percentage making economic demands
March 1917	41,460	38
April 1917	17,700	92
May 1917	91,140	96
June 1917	114,270	91
July 1917	384,560	26
August 1917	379,480	57
September 1917	965,000	83
October 1917	441,450	97

Source: Koenker and Rosenberg, *Strikes and Revolution in Russia*, 167, 272.

population continued to use even the sharply depreciating currency.[63] By late 1916, and especially by 1917, however, the combination of falling output (see Table 5.6), consumer shortages, and accelerating inflation had taken its toll. Data on strikes show a steady rise in participants over the course of 1917 (see Table 5.7). As Figure 5.1 shows, to say that inflation alone caused the strikes would be an overstatement. Rather, scholars of the strikes cite the overall economic crisis, of which rocketing inflation was a major aspect, as an integral part of the strikers' demands (see Table 5.7).[64]

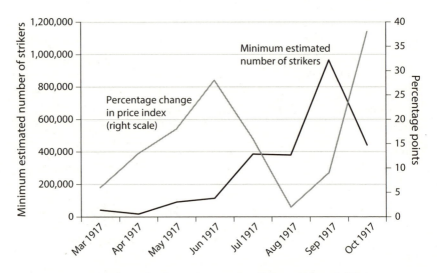

FIGURE 5.1. Strikes and inflation. Sources: Gatrell, *Russia's First World War*, 213; Koenker and Rosenberg, *Strikes and Revolution*, 167, 272.

The increase in inflation, however, raises questions about the government's borrowing policies, given that the alternative to monetizing the fiscal deficit was to cover it with borrowed funds, absent fiscal reserves. Indeed, one of the central premises of McMeekin's counterfactual is that "the whole international network of overlapping obligations tying [Russia] to Entente creditors, investors, and military suppliers" would help finance her war effort.[65] While the Bolshevik decision to sue for peace with Germany notoriously soured relations between the regime and the Allied powers, both the Tsarist and Provisional governments dutifully continued to fight the war. Surely, in this view, the Allies would have supported the regime financially.

Financing the War

Any discussion of Russian wartime finance is complicated by the paucity of reliable data. The last accounts issued by the State Audit Department were for 1914.[66] The wartime conscription of staff meant that accounts of comparable quality for 1915 and 1916 were not produced.[67] The records for 1917 are of even poorer quality up to the Bolshevik Revolution, at which point, in the words of Apostol, "bookkeeping of every description was discontinued."[68]

In principle, government spending is financed through four sources: government income from taxes, monopolies, and asset sales; utilization of fiscal reserves; debt issuance; and issuance of currency. Any discussion of Russia's debt and monetary policy during the war must be considered in this context.

TAXATION

When the war began in 1914, the Russian government did not expect a lengthy conflict, and this was reflected in budgetary policy and finance ministry projections.[69] As discussed in Chapters 1 and 2, Russia's tax regime relied heavily on indirect taxes, including through the spirits monopoly. While there had been long-standing plans dating to at least 1905 to increase the share of direct taxes—notably an income tax—the war brought new urgency to these efforts, as well as to efforts to increase the contribution from indirect taxes.[70] That the government had just embarked on a campaign to wind down the spirits monopoly which accounted for more than a quarter of so-called ordinary revenue in 1913 only added to the importance of additional revenue raising measures.[71] This urgency was not lost on contemporaries, as evidenced in Lord Revelstoke's conversations with Bark, recounted in Chapter 4, and in Kokovtsov's calls for "merciless taxation."[72] The government responded to the challenge of wartime by raising rates of existing—largely indirect and thus regressive—taxes and eventually introducing new direct and indirect taxes. As seen above, such moves did hit consumers. However, taken in aggregate, the government's attempts to raise tax revenue were stymied and proved inadequate.

First, the move to introduce direct taxation was too little, too late. The income and war profits taxes were approved only in April and May 1916, and would not take effect until 1917.[73] The income tax in particular had a top band of only 12.5 percent.[74] Collecting the tax was itself highly problematic. The system depended on honest taxpayer declaration in a country with no established tradition of income tax and widespread illiteracy.[75] Moreover, the sheer increase in the number of taxpayers placed a major burden on the bureaucracy.[76] This problem would be magnified when the income tax ultimately came into effect because high levels of inflation brought a much larger portion of the population under the tax net, making it impossible to enforce and collect the tax from an administrative standpoint.[77]

Second, political imperatives and developments interfered with the government's ability to raise tax revenue. Efforts to replace the evaporated revenues of the spirits monopoly with higher indirect taxes on textiles met with howls of protests for the regressive nature of the tax, for example.[78] After the February Revolution, the Provisional Government in theory had greater legitimacy in raising revenues, but its progressive character served as a break on attempts to raise indirect tax rates.[79] Of course, the revolution also had the proximate impact of at once disrupting the tax-collecting machinery of the government while simultaneously raising expectations of government salary increases, notably in military circles.[80] Efforts to introduce new monopoly revenue streams floundered in the face of the aforementioned political concerns, as well as the realities of wartime Russia, making it impossible to build the productive capacity of such monopolies. In the end, after much talk of new monopolies, only a sugar monopoly was created before the Bolshevik coup.[81] At a time when Russia was rapidly losing territory due to military losses, any plans for generating revenues through privatization would have been fanciful. If anything, the government was acquiring rather than disposing of assets— notably by confiscating Crown lands.[82] While Apostol's argument that other belligerent powers experienced fiscal pressures similar to those Russia experienced through early 1917 has some merit, few shared the peculiar political and bureaucratic challenges Russia did as it sought to introduce taxes already in place in other belligerent states.

The net result of all these issues was that the tax system was unable to cope with the increased demands of the war, even before considering the losses of key territory that narrowed the tax base. In Apostol's telling, when normalized for double counting, "the permanent revenue of the Government" projected in current rubles for 1917 was the same as it had been in 1913.[83] Four years of wartime inflation, of course, meant the real value of those projected revenues would be considerably lower. As he concluded, "The entire war expenditure and the deficit of the ordinary budgets of the preceding three years had had [*sic*] to be covered by loans and Treasury bills."[84] In other words, the war was financed entirely through means other than taxation.

FOREIGN DEBT

The pre-Bolshevik war finance data show that while foreign loans were an important source of funds for the government, the propensity of Western governments and investors to lend to Russia revealed its limits over time. Notwithstanding all the talk about inter-Allied war debts, foreign funding represented only a minority of the funding for the overall war effort. From the outbreak of hostilities in 1914 through 1 September 1917, the government funded roughly 62 percent of its war expenditure through borrowing.[85] Foreign loans paid for only about 21 percent of war expenditure during this period, and the share of foreign loans in total war loans was 33.8 percent, with domestic loans accounting for nearly two-thirds of all loans (see Table 5.8).[86] More importantly, foreign finance became less, not more, pronounced through the course of the war. Setting aside the figures for 1914—a lag between the opening of hostilities and the flotation of loans is to be expected—the contribution of foreign loans to total war expenditure dropped sharply in 1917, to just 16 percent.[87]

This picture of limits to Russian borrowing in foreign money markets may at first appear to contradict that of foreign optimism about Russia, and the

TABLE 5.8. Apostol's estimates of Russian war expenses and their financing, 1914–1 September 1917

Rubles, millions	War expenditure	Domestic loans and Treasury bills (in Russia)	Foreign loans	Total borrowing	Apostol estimate of fiscal reserve spending	Apostol estimate of currency issue
Year						
1914	1,655	857	82	939		
1915	8,818	3,480	2,088	5,568		
1916	14,573	6,150	3,665	9,815		
1917 through September	13,603	5,351	2,236	7,587		
Duration of war through September 1917	38,650	15,837	8,071	23,908	2,600	12,000
As percentage of total war expenditure						
Year						
1914		52	5	57		
1915		39	24	63		
1916		42	25	67		
1917 through September		39	16	56		
Duration of war through September 1917		41	21	62	7	31

Source: Derived from Michelson, Apostol, and Bernatzky, *Russian Public Finance during the War*, 220.

Note: As Apostol notes, the last fully audited figures produced by the Russian State Audit Department are for 1914. Figures for 1915, 1916, and especially 1917 are less reliable. Tsarist public accounting practices often arbitrarily assigned revenue and expenditure between the "ordinary" and "extraordinary" budgets. During the war, use of the "war fund" further clouded the picture. The figures presented in this table are Apostol's estimates. They reflect his assertion that tax revenues did not contribute to war-related spending, having fallen short of core non-war needs. Dates are in accordance with the Julian calendar.

desire of foreign financiers to engage the Russian market discussed in Chapter 4. However, seen another way, the relatively small portion of war expenditure covered by foreign borrowing only underscores the immense sums involved in the Russian war effort. As Strachan notes, Russia was the beneficiary of fully 58 percent of all Entente borrowing through April 1917.[88] While falling Russian yield spreads in the months leading up to the Bolshevik Revolution were a function of rising British and French rather than any drop in Russian absolute yields, the relative ease with which Russia was able to borrow in light of the dynamics of its public finances remains striking.

At the same time, others have overstated the extent of Russian borrowing. McMeekin, for example, erroneously claims, "nearly 11.5 billion rubles worth of fifty-year Russian war bonds . . . were sold between 1914 and 1917, mostly in London and Paris, with an assist from Wall Street buyers beginning in 1916."[89] He cites Strachan's work on war finance, but draws the 11.5 billion ruble figure from the latter's chapter and figures on *domestic*, not foreign, debt.[90] Foreign money markets were thus an important cornerstone of Russian war finance, but their importance in the overall effort was dwarfed by domestic finance.

DOMESTIC BONDS

The growing reluctance of debt markets—both foreign and domestic—to finance the government is evident in the primary market transaction data. At first glance, the terms by which Russia was raising debt were generous (see Figure 5.2). The data, however, show a steady increase in effective rates paid by the government over time, from a current yield of 5.3 percent to the investor at the time of issue in 1914 to 5.9 percent at the time of the Liberty Loan of 1917.[91] At first glance, even the rates the government was paying in 1917 seem incredibly low—representing an increase of only about 60 basis points. Moreover, these rates compared favorably with those of Germany, which was issuing debt at yields of just over 5 percent, and France, which, by the end of 1917, was issuing debt at 5.88 percent.[92] However, to focus purely on the headline figures of the yield to investors at the time of issue would be to miss important signs of trouble even in the domestic debt markets.

First, domestic bond sales did not reflect organic demand for war bonds by investors, insofar as they were a mechanism by which the government sterilized its expansion of the monetary base. Apostol bristled at accusations of this, but even he acknowledged that the government's expansion of the monetary base, coupled with the profits from the defense industry, in part drove the large increase in short-term deposits in the banking system. The government's bond issues absorbed these savings and were recycled back in the form of payments for further war orders. Seen another way, by recycling these funds through the domestic loan market, the government was able to expand the monetary base at a lower rate than would have been necessary otherwise. Cheap liquidity also helped feed the private sector, which saw a boom, although volatility in sentiment and the ease of capital raising for the private sector did increase from 1916 onward.[93]

Second, the state itself directed the investment funds of the state savings banks to bond purchases. This sort of transaction was particularly notable with respect to the Liberty Loan of 1917, whereby more than 23 percent of the funds raised by the loan came from these investment funds.[94] That the state was able

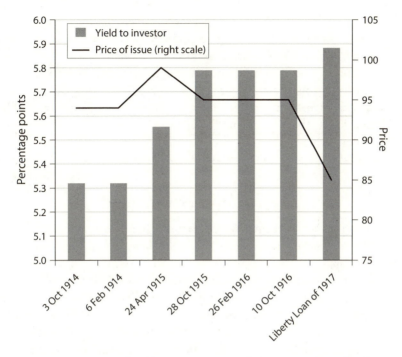

FIGURE 5.2. Price and yield to investor at issue of Russian government bonds.
Source: Calculated from Michelson, Apostol, and Bernatzky, *Russian Public
Finance*, 254. Note: Dates are in accordance with the Julian calendar.

to get only 77 percent of the loan funds from the private sector in an environment of high liquidity shows the extent to which private-sector willingness to lend to the government had flagged.

Third, the statistics on loan issuance should be evaluated in the context of the state's massive expansion of the issuance infrastructure. Over the course of the war, the state greatly increased the points of sale for the loans with the law of 5 November 1915, for example, authorizing the creation of 4,971 post offices with deposit-taking functions in rural areas.[95] The church, Bank of the Nobility, and Peasants' Land Bank were also enlisted in the war bond drive. Between July 1914 and October 1917, the total number of savings institutions increased by 73 percent.[96] As Apostol put it, "in the thirty-nine months of the war there were thus opened in Russia almost as many savings banks as in the seventy-five years that had elapsed since they were first established."[97] The government intended most of this new financial infrastructure to be able to tap the savings of poorer retail savers, particularly in the countryside, who were less sophisticated and less experienced than their urban counterparts.[98] Yet even they appear to have become increasingly skeptical about war loans.

Last, the issuance data do not reflect the considerable and—over time—increasing concessions, other than price, that the government made to buyers of war bonds. Maturities fell over time as inflation rates rose, while hefty commissions ate away at the net proceeds to the government. Since the bonds could be used as collateral for loans from the State Bank, buyers of the bonds frequently reborrowed the money they had just lent to the government by purchasing loans. These considerations and the narrow spreads between government borrowing and lending rates actually created many arbitrage opportunities that banks and other private-sector entities used to their advantage.[99]

THE TREASURY BILL MARKET

As troubling as signs in the market for domestic bonds were, the most damning indictment of the government's financial policies is starkly evident in the data on the market for the short-term debt of the government. The start of the war saw an explosion of government issues of 5 percent short-term Treasury bills, which the government used to finance deficits. Initially, the Treasury presented them to the State Bank for discount. In finance, this is a system whereby the State Bank would pay cash to the Treasury in exchange for the bills at a price representing a discount to the face value of the bill—in practice, reflecting an annualized interest rate of 5 percent plus some margin. The Treasury would then be obligated to repay the State Bank the full face value of the bill at a future date—typically within twelve months. In light of the fiscal surpluses the government ran in the years leading up to the war, the Treasury bill market was largely dormant until the outbreak of hostilities, when it grew rapidly, aided by a loosening of the laws regarding both the ability of the Treasury to issue bills and the State Bank's ability to discount them.[100] In practice, when Treasury bills came due, the Treasury and State Bank would simply roll them over by issuing and discounting new bills.

The strains in the Treasury bill market are evident in the very limited success the government had in generating demand for the bills in the private sector. Even though—or perhaps because—the stock of outstanding Treasury bills increased by a staggering 670 times between the start of hostilities in 1914 and the last days of the Provisional Government in 1917, State Bank holdings represented the vast majority of holdings of outstanding bills (see Table 5.9).

The ownership trends within the private sector were equally striking. Treasury bills are usually the cornerstone of money markets; thus, financial institutions are typically major holders of such short-term instruments. In this context, diminished interest in Treasury bills from the standpoint of the private banking sector is noteworthy and can be understood by considering the yield curve for domestic debt in Russia. In finance, the yield curve plots

TABLE 5.9. Distribution of short-term Treasury bills (percentage of total)

	To official institutions		In the open market		
	State Bank	State savings banks	Private banks in Petrograd	Others	Total (rubles, millions)
16 August 1914	100.0				25.0
1 December 1914	82.1		17.8	0.2	575.0
1 January 1915	81.7		17.2	1.2	800.0
1 July 1915	83.5		14.8	1.7	1,900.0
1 December 1915	83.2		10.7	6.2	4,000.0
1 January 1916	82.4		10.4	7.2	4,000.0
1 June 1916	65.4	3.0	13.2	18.4	5,850.0
1 December 1916	68.1	4.6	12.5	14.7	9,123.0
1 January 1917	70.2	3.1	12.6	14.2	9,775.0
1 March 1917	66.8	6.4	12.5	14.3	11,775.0
1 July 1917	71.6	5.4	7.3	15.7	14,449.9
1 August 1917	73.3	5.6	6.3	14.9	15,450.0
1 September 1917	73.7	5.6	5.9	14.8	16,741.6

Source: Calculated from data in Michelson, Apostol, and Bernatzky, *Russian Public Finance during the War*, 285.

Note: Dates are according to the Julian calendar.

the interest rates a given issuer pays for different maturities of debt. In the early years of the war, the curve in Russia was largely flat—Treasury bill rates of 5 percent were not much lower than rates of long-term domestic bonds, which had effective yields that were higher by only about 0.045 percent.[101] In this case and in an inflationary context, Treasury bills were clearly a surer bet. As long-term yields began to creep higher, with issues of 5.5 percent loans at discount and the 5 percent Liberty Loan at a 15-point discount to par, the already low holdings of Treasury bills among private banks fell to even lower levels.[102] Moreover, when the data are further deconstructed to account for varying maturities of Treasury bills (see Table 5.10), the reluctance of the private sector to hold government debt becomes even clearer, as private-sector holdings were greatest for the shortest maturities, while the State Bank held longer-term bills.

As with the data on domestic bond markets, a consideration of the context in which they were issued and traded only magnifies the data trends in the market for Treasury bills. Beyond the price incentive, the government used inducements and administrative mechanisms—including what the less charitable would label "financial repression"—to encourage private-sector market participants to buy bills. As with government bonds, the regulators granted bills a privileged status as collateral, allowing holders to obtain advances

TABLE 5.10. Distribution of maturities of 5 percent Treasury bills issued through 1 September 1917

	State Bank and sub-treasuries	Private banks	Individuals
More than 90 days (%)	78.8	13.4	24.5
Less than 90 days (%)	21.2	86.6	75.5

Notes: Derived from data presented in Michelson, Apostol, and Bernatzky, *Russian Public Finance during the War*, 286. Note: Dates are according to the Julian calendar.

against bills of 95 percent of their face value at 5.5 percent.[103] All else being equal, this would make an investment in a Treasury bill more attractive than another security in that the favorable treatment of Treasury bills would allow the holder to leverage a portfolio more than by pledging other securities. Having offered a carrot, the government deployed its regulatory stick by requiring various parties to accept Treasury bills in lieu of cash as settlement for transactions involving the government. The proportion of payments that payees were required to accept rose over time, hitting 75 percent under the Provisional Government for payments in excess of 300,000 rubles.[104] The private-sector holdings of bills outside the banking sector thus included many defense contractors, among others.

That holdings of bills remained low in spite of the government having adopted such administrative mechanisms to encourage and indeed to force the private sector to hold Treasury bills only magnifies the importance of the data as an indicator of the poor state of the short-term debt market. In this sense, Apostol's claim that "the measures [the government] adopted to encourage the investment of private capital in Treasury bills met with undeniable, though insufficient, success" is a gross exaggeration, even in view of his qualification.[105] The State Bank's discounting operations still accounted for the vast majority of Treasury bill holdings in what was a mere accounting formality that underscored the monetary expansion the bank was conducting.

THE PRINTING PRESS

As foreign loans receded in importance and taxation and domestic debt markets, too, had shown their limits, the government could rely on only two other sources of financing—previous Treasury surpluses and note issuance. Previous surpluses accounted for only 7 percent of the total war expenditures shown in Table 5.8, as the costs of the war quickly grew. Indeed, Gatrell notes that the so-called "free balance of the Treasury" of more than 2.6 billion rubles—equal to more than three-quarters of 1913 revenues—evaporated almost overnight,

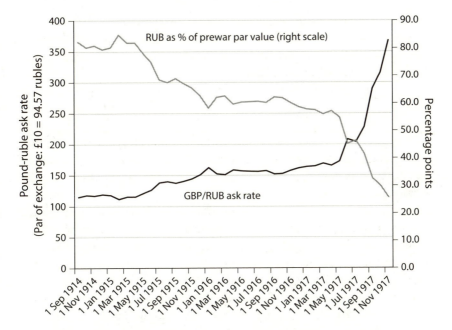

FIGURE 5.3. Rate of exchange of the ruble in London from the outbreak of the war through late 1917. Source: Michelson, Apostol, and Bernatzky, *Russian Public Finance during the War*, 398–99. Note: Dates are in accordance with the Julian calendar.

covering only the first few months of a war in which the costs of mobilization alone amounted to one-third of the total costs of fighting the Russo-Japanese War a decade earlier.[106]

Bereft of alternatives, the government relied increasingly on the printing press. Note issuance accounted for 31 percent of total war financing through 1 September 1917; but in 1917 itself, as both foreign and domestic borrowing covered less than 56 percent of expenditures, note issues rose to cover fully 44 percent of total war expenditures.[107] In the context of such a massive increase in the monetary base, the war having all but cut off Russian exports, and in the absence of any meaningful capital controls, the exchange rate collapsed (see Figure 5.3).[108]

At the same time, this drop in the ruble in international markets did not have repercussions as severe as it would superficially suggest, given the wartime context and Allied underwriting of Russian imports.[109] In a 1918 article on war finance, American economist Irving Fisher looked back at the case of Russian war finance, and argued that "one reason . . . why Russia was so easy a prey to [German] propaganda was that she financed the war on a false basis. Prices were five to eight times what they were at the beginning of the war, and naturally the Russian people were not very enthusiastic over the effect of the war on the cost of living."[110] Fisher could have been more charitable. As pernicious as inflationary war finance was, it also reflected the limited choices Russia's leaders faced by 1917.[111]

The Provisional Government as Catalyst of Economic Collapse

As data from both the real economy and the monetary realm show, Russia was in severe financial and economic stress by late 1916 and early 1917. If, to use McMeekin's phrase, Russia suffered a "grave misfortune," it was that the Provisional Government came to power at precisely this moment of extreme fragility. Apart from confronting a set of policy choices that would tax the most gifted economic policymakers, the Provisional Government addressed one of the most complex economic puzzles in generations with the added baggage of needing to satisfy the immense expectations of the various constituencies it claimed to represent.

While McMeekin extends Stone's characterization of Russia experiencing a crisis of growth into that of a period of "overheating" up to the eve of the Bolshevik takeover, the data suggest otherwise. Russia overheated in late 1916 or early 1917, at the latest. In light of the declining output and skyrocketing inflation, it is more accurate to describe Russia for much of 1917 as being—at best—in a stagflationary crisis marked by low to negative changes in output and accelerating inflation. By 1917, well before the Bolshevik takeover in November, Russia was already hurtling toward an economic collapse. Output was plummeting, inflation soaring, the basic fabric of government and the economy itself unraveling. In the entirely plausible scenario whereby Lenin did not succeed in November—if the guard who stopped him on the way to Smolny on the night of the October coup had not mistaken him for a drunk, for example[112]—it is difficult to imagine how any other government would have been able to remain current on Russia's mounting debt burden. True, what the Bolsheviks would have called a "bourgeois government" may not have repudiated the debt, and the write-down would not have been the 100 percent haircut to creditors the Bolsheviks declared, but the event would still be a default, even if dictated by economics—as in the recent cases of Greece and Argentina—and not ideology.

Pulling the Trigger: The Decision to Default

The decision making of the Bolsheviks leading up to the moment of default is the subject of some debate. In McMeekin's narrative—focused in any case on the nationalization of banks more than on foreign loans—the Bolsheviks' nationalization policy grew directly out of their ideology.[113] Pointing to the disconnect between bankers and the Bolsheviks, McMeekin specifically argues that bankers trying to reason with the Bolsheviks were "quite wrong in thinking the Bolsheviks cared about a bourgeois value such as creditworthiness."[114] Acknowledging the delay between the start of nationalization of banks and industry in late 1917 and the repudiation of debts in early 1918, McMeekin nonetheless sees them both as growing out of a common ideological frame. In his three-volume history of the revolution, E. H. Carr devotes only two pages to the default, but also casts it as a purely ideological decision.[115]

Richard Pipes paints a picture of a much more hesitant Bolshevik leadership, specifically when it came to the question of the Tsarist and Provisional governments' debts. Although his chapter on war communism places the repudiation decree in the context of decisions "inspired by an ideological belief in the need to deprive the citizens of ownership of disposable assets because they were a source of political independence," his discussion of the repudiation suggests equivocation at a time when the regime was fighting for survival.[116] In his words: "The Bolsheviks took this step with considerable trepidation: they feared that such a violation of international law, involving billions of dollars, could spark a 'capitalist crusade.' But the widespread expectation of an imminent revolution in the West overcame caution and the deed was done."[117] Equally surprising to Pipes was the calm with which Western powers took the news.[118] He quotes Iurii Larin, one of Lenin's advisors on economics, as saying that the American consul in Petrograd was prepared to accept the repudiation de facto if not "in principle."[119]

In reality, the Bolshevik decision to default is best characterized as falling in between the narratives of McMeekin and Pipes. Given the timing of the decision—in the chaotic early stages of the Soviet period, when much of the financial and economic bureaucracy was only being formed—the archival record is thin, but nevertheless suggestive of a premeditated ideological decision moderated slightly by practical considerations.

A November 1917 report to the Council of Peoples' Commissars (Sovet Narodnykh Komissarov, or Sovnarkom) coauthored by Nicholas Osinski and Vladimir Smirnov—two figures who would go on to head the Supreme Council of the National Economy (VSNKh) and the Commissariat for Trade and Industry, respectively—laid out the economic policy questions facing the regime days after the Bolshevik coup.[120] The report to what was in effect the Bolshevik cabinet opened by saying that the economic conditions of the country cried out for the building of socialism. It went on to assert—in what was euphemistically referred to as the context of the "fight against the disorganization of the economy and a fall in productive forces"—that measures differing from those being adopted for the "normal" transition to socialism would have to be taken.[121] The report stressed the need for pragmatism, literally underlining that only those measures that were absolutely necessary for organizing the country's productive forces should be adopted. In this context, nationalization of the banking system was flagged as the most pressing policy imperative in that it would allow the Bolsheviks to at once implement industrial plans and "radically eliminate the economic sabotage of the capitalists."[122]

The report then moved on to the production syndicates discussed in Chapter 3, including Produgol and Prodamet—the subject of much revolutionary vitriol. Noting that the syndicates themselves were associations with limited powers, the report suggested that nationalizing them would be a waste of valuable time under the circumstances. Heavy industry was the next focus of the document, which argued for their being placed under state control, along with the sugar industry.[123] The report pushed for other industrial production to be brought under heavy state regulation whereby a state monopoly would set prices. To aid in this, the document laid out its suggestions for agencies to manage this new Bolshevik economy.[124]

While all of these policy prescriptions conformed to Bolshevik ideology, some curious exceptions were notable. The report stated that shareholders of industrial firms should retain the right to receive dividends, and went on to stipulate that even firms taken over by the state maintain their original legal structure, their status being that of private companies requisitioned by the state. Concessions to small businesses were also apparent insofar as they were to be united into production unions under state supervision, but not taken over wholesale. Workers' interests were protected, but in a framework still reminiscent of capitalism, in that provision was made to support them in the event of layoffs.[125]

The report is striking for several reasons. First, it frankly acknowledges in principle and at a very early stage in the revolution that the Bolsheviks would have to potentially subordinate ideological aims to practical realities. Second, while remaining silent on the question of foreign and domestic debts, the report prioritizes nationalization of the banks, and a broad, but not total, nationalization of industry. In this sense, the document qualifies the notion of Bolshevik policies—even in the earliest stages of their revolution—as growing purely out of ideological considerations.

The report is of particular interest in the context of Robert Service's discussion of the relations between Lenin and his commissars in his biography of the Bolshevik leader. In Service's narrative, in the immediate aftermath of the coup, Lenin was being overrun by all manner of ideology-inspired but impractical schemes from people including Osinski, who "spent days [after the coup] elaborating charts and statistics for the perfection of the structures of industry and agriculture while the economy itself went to rack and ruin."[126]

Service proceeds to demonstrate that after Brest-Litovsk, Osinski was one of the Bolsheviks critiquing Lenin for not having been aggressive enough in moving the economy to socialism.[127] Yet in his discussion of Lenin's position, Service shows him to be following almost exactly the path outlined in the Smirnov-Osinski report. He notes that Lenin spoke of a "transition to Socialism," and emphasized the need to be selective in nationalizations—to focus on heavy industry and the banks, while leaving smaller enterprises to be more loosely organized by the state.[128] Such an approach was exactly what Osinski called for. Thus, while he may indeed have been perturbed by Brest-Litovsk and other factors by 1918, to characterize him as being totally impractical in late 1917 is to grossly overstate the case—the archival record indicates that he was one of the leading voices for a hard-nosed approach to economic policymaking in the earliest days of Bolshevik power. Indeed, when compared against future Bolshevik policy, the report can be said to be the blueprint for Lenin's early policies.

The nationalization process itself demonstrated the degree to which the Bolsheviks framed their economic decisions in an extra-ideological vein. The first wave of nationalizations occurred on a case-by-case basis within the framework laid out by the Smirnov-Osinski report. Thus, for example, on 28 December 1917, Sovnarkom approved a decision to nationalize the assets of the Russo-Belgian Metallurgical Company.[129] The decision is interesting—and typical—in that it justifies itself by referring to the refusal of the company to obey Sovnarkom decrees, including those on the "introduction of workers' control on production."[130] The language of the decree implicitly allowed, in theory at least, for the continued existence of private firms, as long as they obeyed Sovnarkom decrees. The latter, of course, were burdensome, but the theoretical right is nonetheless notable.

The protocols of the meetings of Sovnarkom offer some insight into the decision making of the Bolshevik high command. The first recorded protocol, of 28 November 1917, notes a discussion on no fewer than 20 different items ranging from the establishment of the Council of the National Economy (Sovnarkhoz) to military matters and revolutionary courts. There was no discussion of foreign loans.[131] The next day, the Bolshevik cabinet decided to pay compensation to holders of Liberty Bonds who had been defrauded of payments if they were on salaries of less than 300 rubles.[132] It proceeded to discuss several issues related to dissatisfied postal and telegraph workers.[133] The latter discussion was but an early manifestation of what the Bolshevik cabinet would have to deal with. Indeed, for much of the remainder of 1917, Sovnarkom would be oscillating in its discussions between trying to implement economic—including sundry individual nationalizations and confiscations—and other policies and rushing to put out various fires.

The Sovnarkom files underscore the degree to which striking workers in key sectors were a huge and unexpected headache for Lenin in his first months of power. Taking control of the Winter Palace had been easy—actually seizing control of the infrastructure of power in a land the size of Russia was immensely more difficult. As one observer noted dryly:

> The Government departments are empty. Officials remain grimly on strike. The much maligned Russian official is displaying heroic qualities. The councils of the People's Commissaries [*sic*] are distinctly embarrassed. Lenine [*sic*] tries to ignore the boycott and issues tonight a proclamation to peasants and workers saying the Government is in their own hands. . . . But decrees are one thing and government is another. The Council of Commissaries [*sic*] is confronted with the problem of finance. It seems simple, since they have possession of the State Bank, but no one will hand over money.[134]

Indeed, the Bolshevik attempts to take over the banking infrastructure of the country were particularly comical. Most private banks closed immediately after the coup, while the State Bank remained especially uncooperative.[135] Ordered to sign over 15 million rubles, Shipov, the director of the State Bank, simply refused.[136] Asked to open a bank account for Sovnarkom, he refused again, saying that it was not a body with which he could legally do business.[137] Next, the Bolsheviks tried brute force, threatening to use dynamite to blow open the vaults, but demurred for fear of burning paper money.[138] Meanwhile, government employees around Russia became increasingly irate at not being paid salaries on time.[139]

It was in this context that Sovnarkom devoted so much attention to breaking the resistance of government workers. Placating the post and telegraph workers was key in a country as vast as Russia if the revolution was to take hold, and this issue took up considerable time. On 29 November 1917, Sovnarkom discussed the conflict with the post and telegraph workers and approved overtime payments.[140] Three days later, the discussions over state employees continued; Sovnarkom heard a report about the urgent need to improve the material situation of the workers, and approved increases in salaries for telegraph workers.[141] Bogolepov had presented his report on the suspension of interest and dividend payments to Sovnarkom on 4 December, and the cabinet had decided to defer discussion till the following day.[142] In fact, the cabinet would not approve the associated decree until 5 January 1918.[143] Talk of suspending dividend payments and repudiating debts was totally academic when the government's control of basic infrastructure was in question.

Notwithstanding Osinski's report of 23 November on the urgent need to nationalize the banks, it was thus not until 8 December that Sovnarkom closed the Nobles' and Peasants' Land Banks, and not until the evening of 27

December that it finally approved the nationalization of the banks.[144] Only on 5 January 1918 did Sovnarkom adopt a decree suspending interest and dividend payments.[145] Sovnarkom did not discuss and approve in principle the decree annulling prerevolutionary debt until 14 January 1918—more than two months after the Bolshevik takeover.[146] The very next day, Iakov Shenkman wrote Sovnarkom asking that allowances be made for holders of small-denomination Liberty Bonds, as the Bolsheviks risked aggravating small holders to whom they should have been appealing.[147] The final decree included provisions to exempt small holders. Indeed, by 14 February 1918, Sovnarkom went further, and declared that anyone found refusing to accept Liberty Loan bonds at face value as currency would be punished with "the full vigor of revolutionary laws."[148]

Other sources also speak to a strong ideological intent to default, blunted less by fear of the Allied response than by more prosaic concerns. The testimony in the US Senate of Raymond Robins is interesting in this regard. Robins, a self-described social worker, was one of 13 Red Cross majors sent to Russia as part of an aid mission in 1917.[149] After serving in that capacity for three months, he was promoted to the head of the American Red Cross mission in Russia with the rank of colonel.[150] His tour, lasting from July 1917 through 1 June 1918, overlapped with the Bolshevik rise to power, and saw him spend much of this time in Petrograd, including during the October Revolution.[151] In his capacity, he was in close and frequent contact with both Kerensky and the top Bolsheviks.[152] Even though not a communist himself, he grew to become one of the most vocal American cheerleaders for normalization of ties with the Bolsheviks.[153]

In his Senate testimony, Robins dated the Bolshevik moves to repudiate the debts at a very early stage, and credits himself with talking the Bolsheviks out of what would have been a default in 1917. Specifically, he claims that the All-Russia Central Executive Committee (VTsIK) first discussed an annulment on 28 November 1917, at which point he spoke with Trotsky, who talked the leadership out of passing the decree.[154] According to Robins, the matter was revived while Trotsky was at Brest-Litovsk negotiating the peace treaty with the Germans, at which point Robins approached Lenin, who would not yield. When Robins reminded him of the promise of American economic assistance, Lenin allowed that the Bolsheviks would be willing to work out a deal with British and American creditors, but he was adamant that they would not do so for the French.[155] Pushed by Robins on the latter point, Lenin admitted that the greater size of French loans was one consideration, but also went on to say, as quoted by Robins: "That debt comes out of the loan of the French bourgeois bankers to the autocracy, which has kept that autocracy alive 30 years longer than it would have lived without financial support from France.

What you are really asking me to do is to pay back the money loaned by the French bourgeois to keep the Cossack whip and sword over our people for 30 years, and the workmen and the peasants are not willing."[156] In this view, repudiation was not just a matter of the ability to pay, but one of political principle. Robins went on to explain that while the debt was ultimately bought by masses of French workers and peasants, it was the focus of Bolshevik vitriol because it was contracted initially by the bankers who underwrote the deals.[157]

Robins's account is interesting in that it tells of a direct conversation with Lenin over the issue of repudiation, while addressing matters of timing. On the latter point, his narrative overstates the case. The protocols of VTsIK indeed show that Russia's debt was mentioned, but only in passing. Lozovsky quoted the French Marxist Paul Lafargue as saying, "The revolution will break out in France once Russia refuses to pay her debts."[158] Lozovsky went on to argue, "the bourgeois are weakest in their pockets: to make them dance, one has to hit them there. We can say to them: 'If you do anything against the Russian Revolution, your milliards in Russia will be finished.'"[159]

This brief remark is fascinating in that it underscores the two-sided nature of the debt question. Pipes's account of the default speaks of the hesitation of the Bolsheviks to risk provoking intervention, saying that ultimately their expectations of an imminent revolution in the West overrode these hesitations.[160] The Lozovsky speech suggests that the Bolsheviks recognized that the debt repudiation could in fact help to hasten the revolution in Western Europe. Indeed, his remarks would prove to be a prescient foreshadowing of the Bolshevik negotiating position on the question of debts in the 1920s.

Nevertheless, Lozovsky's remark, tacked as it was at the end of his speech toward the end of the VTsIK session, was hardly a formal proposal indicating an imminent repudiation. Indeed, in a testament to the often chaotic nature of these sessions of this Soviet legislature, Lozovsky's remarks about the debt were followed by a series of totally unrelated comments by assorted speakers.[161]

The VTsIK protocols suggest that the next mention of the repudiation to which Robins referred took place on 4 January 1918. In this instance, Trutovsky moved to tack on an annulment of debts to an almost totally unrelated resolution proposed by Zinoviev on the convocation of the Constituent Assembly.[162] The amendment drew swift opposition and was rejected. Moiseyev questioned in particular both the cavalier manner in which Trutovsky proposed to pass the decision, as well as—here conforming to Pipes's theory— the advisability of antagonizing the Western powers. At the same time, he voiced the concern that repudiating French debts would strike a severe blow to French workers and peasants.[163] That Sovnarkom passed the decree suspending interest payments the very next day suggests that Trutovsky's outburst may well have nudged the Bolshevik high command into acting on a proposal that lay otherwise unexamined for a month.[164]

Trutovsky would soon have his wish granted, however, when on 16 January VTsIK formally discussed a repudiation decree.[165] This formal debate, of course, took place only in the context of Sovnarkom—the real center of political power in the Leninist system—having decided to send a decree to VTsIK for approval two days prior. Still, Trutovsky was not going to merely serve as a rubber stamp, and would have his say:

> It is time to implement the resolutions of Zimmerwald and Kienthal. We are the first [country] to fulfill our obligations in this regard. We understand full well that this decree administers a sharp blow to the capitalist system. There is a difference between a state declaring itself bankrupt and a state annulling its debts. In the first case it recognizes that it cannot pay what it owes; in the second case it says that it will not pay, so challenging the bourgeois order. Of course there will be difficulties. The bourgeoisie of all countries will rally all the more solidly against us, but despite this we of the new world throw down the gauntlet to the old.[166]

As expected by the Bolshevik leadership, which was orchestrating the entire process, the assembly unanimously agreed to adopt and forward the decree to the Presidium of VTsIK for final editing. At the same time, the Trutovsky incident suggests that the chaotic VTsIK could at times create ideological pressure on the revolutionaries-turned-rulers in Sovnarkom, and that this pressure did nudge Sovnarkom further toward revolutionary default.

In surveying the documentary evidence of the decision making leading up to Sovnarkom's decision to repudiate prerevolutionary loans, then, it is apparent that both ideology and pragmatism were at play. The idea of defaulting stretched back to at least 1905, and was telegraphed by Lenin throughout the period leading up to the Bolshevik coup in late 1917. Nevertheless, the records of Sovnarkom show the Bolsheviks, once in power, to have been conscious of pragmatic realities. In the context of trying to restart the stalled machinery of the most basic parts of the Russian state and economy, Sovnarkom simply did not discuss issues such as the repudiation. In the crisis-ridden context of November 1917, such issues were academic. In this sense the caricatures of ideologues operating without any sense of practical circumstances are overstated. The Bolsheviks were, as Pipes notes, conscious of the negative reaction a repudiation would draw from Western governments. However, their decision to proceed anyway was not just—as Pipes suggests—a matter of "the widespread expectation of an imminent revolution in the West [overcoming] caution."[167] On the contrary, the processes were intimately linked in the minds of the Bolsheviks and other radicals. It was precisely by defaulting that the

Bolsheviks could promote and speed the arrival of the revolution in Western Europe. The Bolshevik negotiating positions in the early 1920s would echo this conception of finance as a revolutionary weapon.

Investor Attitudes on the Eve of Default: This Time *Was* Different

By late 1917, even outside the halls of the Smolny Institute, the signs of an impending Bolshevik default were evident for those who cared to look. For more than a decade, the Bolsheviks had vocally articulated their belief that the debts incurred by the Tsarist government were illegitimate. They maintained this line throughout 1917, and indeed Lenin's attacks on government finance and debt issuance arguably became more frequent than ever before during this crucial year. Moreover, there were strong reasons independent of ideology for the Bolsheviks—or any other government—to make good on these pre-revolutionary threats of default. The peasantry was carrying a heavy, and likely unsustainable, debt burden. Even independent of the ideological desire to use finance as a weapon against their class enemies, the annulment of debts was an easy way to help win the support of a large and politically important portion of the Russian population. Economic realities also made Russia's ability to continue to service its debts highly questionable, even before the Bolshevik coup.

And yet, as the story of National City and Midland Bank in 1917 showed, some of the most prominent foreign financiers involved with Russia remained extremely optimistic about the future course of events up to the very eve of the Bolshevik Revolution in early November. Remarkably, many financiers and other foreign observers maintained this optimism even after the Bolshevik takeover. Why they did so is one of the greatest puzzles of modern financial history. In reviewing the evidence, it is apparent that investors continued to believe in Russia's ability to grow out of its difficulties, that Russia was a stalwart debtor that would pay even in extreme difficulty, and/or that the Bolshevik regime would be defeated or moderate. Moreover, they maintained this optimistic assessment while in many cases explicitly downplaying or ruling out the potential for a default.

Ex-Ante: Discounting Signs and Talk of Default

One of the most remarkable aspects of the foreign investment community's risk assessments with regard to Russia in late 1917 and early 1918 was the degree to which a Russian default was a known unknown. The default was not a bolt from the blue insofar as rumors had circulated about it being a possibility.

Instead, the default was an event that people in financial circles simply did not think possible, and to which they assigned an exceedingly low probability—even months after the Bolshevik takeover.

Evidence that the talk of the default was dismissed is plentiful in both the press and the archival record. The local Petrograd financial press explicitly acknowledged the Bolshevik position on loans as early as April 1917. A case in point occurred during the Provisional Government's attempt to float the Liberty Loan. In a 30 April 1917 article, *Finansovaia Gazeta* (Financial Gazette) discussed the stances of various leftist parties on the loan, noting that the left was divided over the question of whether or not to support the loan and explicitly mentioning Lenin and *Pravda* as being categorically opposed.[168]

Having acknowledged the leftist opposition, the paper then launched into a scathing analysis of it, in the process providing fascinating insights into how even those financial market observers who acknowledged leftist critiques of the loan at once dismissed them. The article declared that the leftist attitude was "puzzling" and went on to express frustration that the leftists were opposing the Provisional Government for the sake of opposition, rather than because of it "having done [anything] to shirk the obligations it has assumed."[169] It went on, saying, "if . . . they cannot blame the Provisional Government for anything that it has done up to now, then naturally, they have no right to wait for its future statements and should give it their full support."[170] The paper ended by venting further frustration, noting, "straightforwardness has always been a primary virtue of socialist trends" that "the central groups of Russian socialism have abandoned these traditional principles of theirs and taken to the path of Octoberist pussyfooting."[171] The article closed with the following declaration: "Public opinion has a right to ask that they make their attitude on the question of the Loan perfectly clear, that they honestly and openly declare their participation or non-participation in it and thus fulfill their moral obligation to the Provisional Government, which means, either to give it the backing of the Left groups or to make known their disagreement with it."[172] The paper's comments are very revealing in that they betray a view of the left as a monolith, even as the article acknowledged fissures. More importantly, the talk of "moral obligation" to the government and the declarations that the government had done nothing to justify the opposition of the Bolsheviks and other uncooperative parties show that—in the eyes of an important local financial paper at least—the Bolsheviks were simply being unfair and childish.

The paper excluded the possibility that the Bolsheviks did not care about bourgeois notions of fair play or morality, that the Bolsheviks were not interested in giving the Provisional Government a chance, and that they would do everything possible to see it and its foreign backers fail. Such behavior on the part of a political party in Russia was simply out of the realm of possibility as far as the paper was concerned. In his comment on the article, Lenin noted, "The bank bosses are men of business. They take a sane view of politics: once you've promised to support the capitalist government (which is conducting an imperialist war) then come across with a Loan."[173] The bankers' mistake was to expect the same from the Bolsheviks, who in any case did not "promise" their support to the government.

The US government was particularly notable for its complacency. In early January 1918, just weeks before the largest default in history, the *Economist*, in a report on US government financing of the Allied war effort, wrote, "The report that the Bolsheviki [*sic*] Government of Russia might repudiate the country's external loans was not regarded seriously, and was promptly contradicted by the Petrograd Telegraph Agency. The U.S. Government was not greatly concerned over this statement."[174] The same article mentioned that the private sector was slightly more concerned, stating, "Perhaps the most drastic effect was upon the quotation of the 5 1/2 and 6 1/2 per cent. Dollar Credits, which, in spite of the prompt payment of interest, sold down in the open market to a 28 and 34 per cent. yield[,] respectively."[175]

The material evidence of Bolshevik willingness to seize foreign investors' property was also clear for all to see well before the default. The French industrial firm Schneider had increased its activity in Russia in 1911 in connection with the rise in Tsarist defense spending discussed in Chapter 3. Specifically, Schneider began to cooperate with Putilov's armaments firms, along with the Société Générale—through its Russo-Asiatic subsidiary—and the BUP to engage in naval and other defense work for the Tsarist government.[176] Schneider initially intended to obey the "golden rule," according to which its Russian activities should be financed from retained earnings generated in Russia; but by 1913, the company found itself working with French and Russian banks to extend a financial lifeline to Putilov.[177] By January 1915, with Schneider's activities in Russia having only broadened in what was now an active war effort, the company sent a representative, Saint-Sauveur, to Petrograd to maintain a tight watch over its operations in the Russian capital.[178] Saint-Sauveur remained in Petrograd through the Bolshevik coup, and his regular dispatches to Paris provide a blow-by-blow account of the revolution from a well-placed businessman on the ground.

Saint-Sauveur's first dispatch of 1918 underscored the breakdown of the economy, noting how the Putilov plants were working only two days per week, and had recently been totally closed for three days of holidays.[179] The Baranovsky factories were in an even worse shape, not having operated at all, but still paying workers two-thirds wages; 3,000 laid-off workers had been paid six months' severance in an environment where employee control of the factory hung over managers' heads.[180] The same day, Paris received a delayed telegram from 31 December 1917 informing headquarters that the Société Russo-Belge was now under worker control, and that Sovnarkom had published a decree confiscating all the firm's assets and declaring it property of the Russian government.[181] In what must have thrown the bankers in Paris off their chairs, Saint-Sauveur also reported the news of the arrest of Verstraete and Boutry at the Russo-Asiatic.[182] One can only imagine the embarrassment and frustration Verstraete must have felt, entering his prison cell, at having misread the situation so badly as to have been caught a sitting duck. After all, he had been a celebrated former diplomat and architect of the Société Générale's Russia strategy and had studied Russia and lived there for so many years. Learning a few days later, after he had been released temporarily on bond, that his close associate, the industrialist Putilov, had dodged arrest and remained at large would have only added insult to injury.[183]

On 13 January, Saint-Sauveur reported a Sovnarkom decree suspending payments on coupons and banning all purchase or sale of securities, on pain of confiscation and dispatch to the Revolutionary Tribunal.[184] Ominously, he reported further that the decree would remain in force until "the elaboration of a special law."[185]

Press coverage on this issue was conflicting. Before the decree was made public, some press outlets, including the *Frankfurter Zeitung* and the *Manchester Guardian*, played on rumors to express fears of annulment of domestic debt.[186] At the same time, the American *Financial Chronicle* in its coverage noted the payment of coupons on Russian debt through the cooperation of major American banks like National City and J. P. Morgan and what it referred to as "the Russian Government," making no mention of the Bolsheviks.[187]

On 14 January 1918, Saint-Sauveur confirmed to Schneider and, via the company, to BUP and Société Générale that the Supreme Council of the National Economy (VSNKh) had indeed prepared a repudiation decree.[188] VTsIK issued the decree on 3 February 1918.[189]

Ex-Post: Reactions to the Default

Even more surprising than the dismissal of numerous signs of impending default was the reaction of many in the financial community to the actual declaration of default. The French reaction in particular was remarkable, given that they had been most active in both issuing and investing in Russian debt for decades, and given the widespread nature of Russian debt ownership in France. The *Economist*'s Paris correspondent reported that the news of the default was "received here without panic."[190] The report went on to quote an influential commentator on financial affairs, Emmanuel Vidal: "The Bolsheviks can no more suppress the loss of credit than they can suppress physical laws. The State that would carry on business must enjoy credit, and it is impossible for it to get credit without satisfying its creditors. There is no case in which the State has been able to remain bankrupt, and the Bolsheviks will find this law must apply to them."[191] The *Revue de la Bourse & de la Banque* had similarly written to Paribas on 22 January to ask for its assistance in a "campaign of truth" to "prevent undesirable panics and ruinous errors."[192] Although allowing for the possibility that Paribas might end up furnishing information that would give cause for concern, the paper clearly found talk of the default to be overblown. Partly because of this sort of thinking, the market reaction was relatively muted—the price of the Russian 5 Percent Loan of 1906 fell from 55.50 to 51, a drop of 8 percent, but the 4 percent of 1893 fell by only 2.5 percent, and the 3 percent of 1891 by only 1.4 percent.[193] Indeed, that the 1906 loan was trading at 51 suggests considerable optimism on the part of holders in the face of an explicit repudiation—a 5 percent coupon on a price of 51 equaled a current yield of only 9.8 percent. True, the yield had risen from 6.25 percent at the end of 1916, but given the developments in Russia in 1917, this was still a small move (see Table 5.11). By contrast, Argentinean and Greek debt traded at yields of more than 16 percent during their defaults in the 1890s (see Figure 5.4).

A week later, the *Economist* cited the opinions of noted economist, Edmond Théry. Like Vidal, Théry thought Russia would quickly renege on the default because the consequences would be so disruptive for Russia as to make any sort of recovery to economic normality out of the question. The article ended by saying, "Monsieur Théry, in conclusion, urges the French public to receive the Bolshevik proposals with absolute calmness, as France will certainly take steps to see that the interests of French citizens are not jeopardized."[194]

For his part, Arthur Raffalovich—the principal pitchman of Russian debt in European markets for more than two decades—continued the familiar refrain (detailed in Chapter 4) about Russia's bounty that helped investors overlook so much turmoil from 1914 through the February Revolution. In a letter of late January, he closed by writing, "at any rate, the Russian resources, as far as increase of population, as fertility of the soil, as timber, as mineral wealth, cannot be destroyed."[195] Ever the salesman, even after a repudiation, Raffalovich could find a silver lining in the clouds hanging over the markets for Russian debt.

Reaction to the repudiation in British financial circles was also muted in London, the other major center for prerevolutionary Russian bond issues. On 17 January—just three days after the Sovnarkom decree, news of which was leaking out—the British chancellor of the Exchequer declared in Parliament that the British government would guarantee payment of £10 million in Russian Treasury bills that had been floated by the Bank of England in 1917, and

TABLE 5.11. Russian bond prices, 1916–17

	Prices of 1917		Implied current yields, 1917 (%)		Price end of 1916	Price end of 1917	Percentage change in price	Yield end of 1916	Yield end of 1917	Rise in Yield (bps)
	High	Low	High	Low						
Russian Government 5%, 1906	84	50.5	5.95	9.90	80	52.5	–34	6.25%	9.52%	327
Russian Government 4.5%, 1909	77	42.25	5.84	10.65	75	45	–40	6.00%	10.00%	400
Petrograd 4.5%, 1913	72.75	47.5	6.19	9.47	72	50	–31	6.25%	9.00%	275
Armavir-Touapsé Railway 4.5% bonds	72.25	41	6.23	10.98	70	43	–39	6.43%	10.47%	404
Black Sea Kuban Railway 4.5% bonds	73	41.5	6.16	10.84	73	43	–41	6.16%	10.47%	430
Grand Russian Railway 4.5% bonds	65.25	42.5	6.90	10.59	65.5	42.5	–35	6.87%	10.59%	372
Kahetian Railway 4.5% bonds	74	43	6.08	10.47	74	43	–42	6.08%	10.47%	438
Russian South-Eastern Railway 4.5% bonds	77.5	48.25	5.81	9.33	77.5	49.5	–36	5.81%	9.09%	328
Troitzk Railway 4.5% bonds	73.5	43	6.12	10.47	73.5	44	–40	6.12%	10.23%	410

Source: Computed from data in "Russia's Economic Position," *Economist*, 5 January 1918.

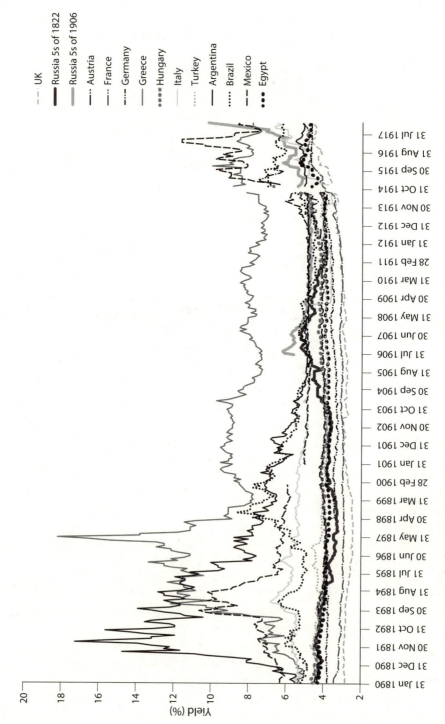

FIGURE 5.4. Absolute yields for sovereign debt, 1890–1918. Source: "GFD Database" (2012), www.globalfinancialdata.com.

which were maturing in ten days' time, as well as £7.5 million in commercial bills drawn on Russian financial institutions that were part of a revolving credit facility secured by Russian Treasury bills set to expire a year after the end of hostilities.[196] The Treasury's reasoning behind this was that since the prospectus of the Russian Treasury bill issue declared that the Bank of England was acting for the Russian government, "with the approval of H.M. Government," to solicit investments, the investors in the Treasury bills did have, in the *Economist*'s words, a "moral claim" on the British government.[197] Still, the Treasury did not offer a full bailout: it instead paid investors holding the Russian debt with 3 percent, 12-year Exchequer bonds trading in the market at the time at 82 percent of par.[198]

Even though the *Economist* thought the deal relatively fair, it acknowledged that there was resentment among some whereby if the Treasury was accepting "a moral liability," it should have paid out bondholders in full.[199] The magazine also found the case for financial institutions holding commercial bills to be stronger: the latter were reportedly reluctant creditors, accepting a larger amount of bills than they would have otherwise because they felt government pressure to help finance the Russian war effort. They were also being given the same 3 percent bonds at 82, and so stood to "suffer a considerable loss as a reward for undertaking business that some of them only entered into under semi-official pressure."[200]

On the same day as the chancellor's speech in Parliament, E. C. Grenfell, the head of the Morgan outpost in London, wrote to Jack Morgan in New York with his reflections on the whole affair.[201] He recalled how the government—and Lord Cunliffe as governor of the Bank of England—had pushed the banks to extend credit to Russia, and how the banks had reluctantly agreed to do so "in the public interest."[202] It was thus understandable, in his view, that while the 17 January deal was "satisfactory to us," the bankers "feel somewhat sore, partly with the Government and especially with Lord Cunliffe."[203]

Even if the *Economist* excoriated the British government for financing the Allied war effort with "devious credit-making devices" and for "too much 'raising the wind' and too little straightforwardness in laying on the shoulders of the nation the burden which no such devices can lighten," the admission of moral responsibility by the Treasury was significant.[204] It was certainly a step back from the initial line the Treasury took that, in Grenfell's words, the banks "had taken the business with their eyes open."[205] If the British government was willing to accept liability for short-term Russian government liabilities issued without an explicit British guarantee, optimists would look for similar payouts in other series of Russian debt. A week later, the *Economist* was much more generous in its treatment, saying that Bonar Law, the chancellor of the Exchequer, "made a most favourable impression" with his support for holders of the Russian Treasury and commercial bills.[206] The magazine went even further, saying, "it is felt to be an instance of a generous and far-sighted action that will have its effect in increasing the stability of the credit of the British Government."[207]

This mention of generosity and "moral" duties within the context of discussions of the partial British government bailout of creditors of the Tsarist government was echoed in other comments on the defaults, and underscores another way in which financial markets framed the Bolshevik default. Indeed, it is evident from these comments that financial market participants discounted the default announcement not only because they saw it as unlikely from the standpoint of the self-interest of the Russian government or because they were expecting bailouts from Allied governments. Beyond these considerations of hard-nosed self-interest, investors at the time placed great stock on morality as a guiding force of government financial policy. In this view, the Russian government would not actually follow through on its repudiation, even under the Bolsheviks, because to do so would be dishonorable.

In France, *Le Temps* on 14 January argued that a Bolshevik default would be a blow against the masses of peasants and workers in France who had invested their savings in Russian bonds. It further made the point that a default would be a poor reward indeed for what the *Economist* called "the services of French thrift to Russia."[208] Either blissfully unaware of or—more likely—conveniently ignoring the Russian opposition's vehement disapproval of the Tsarist government's financial policy, the paper recounted how it was French investors' willingness to buy Russian bonds that allowed the country to expand its railroad network, which in its view reduced the prevalence of famine in Russia. Moreover, the Russian peasantry owed its ability to purchase land at low mortgage rates—down by 150 basis points in 1911, according to the paper—to the goodwill of French investors. In this view, the French investor similarly allowed the growth of Russian industry. *Le Temps* thus concluded that any successor state or states to Tsarist Russia were thereby responsible for a proportionate share of the debt of the prerevolutionary state.[209]

To be fair, absent a full appreciation of what Bolshevism entailed, investors could be forgiven for thinking morality would guide Russian efforts. The British press noted that the Russian government had never engaged in an outright default.[210] After the February Revolution, Russia remained in the war and current on its debts. As evidence of the lengths to which the government would go to uphold its contractual obligations, observers pointed to Russia having remained current on its debts to British bondholders throughout the course of the Crimean War, in which it was fighting their government.[211]

This moralistic and cultural dimension to investors' perceptions in 1918 of risk in the Russian context of course carried over from the pre-Bolshevik period. The comments indicating Russia's moral duty to the Allied cause are congruent with the talk of Western bankers like Meserve about the "noble" Russian people, for example.

Meserve and his colleagues would in fact make what in hindsight surely rates as one of the most bizarre business decisions in American banking history. On 27 November 1917—nearly three weeks *after* the Bolshevik takeover—the First National City Bank of New York opened its Moscow branch at the National Hotel, directly opposite the Kremlin and within sight of Red Square.[212] The location was especially ironic, as the luxury hotel served as a key Bolshevik outpost in the city. Lenin, Stalin, and the American communist John Reed all stayed at the National in the early days of the revolution, and would have rubbed shoulders with the American bankers passing through the small lobby. Even the bank's official internal history—prepared for the benefit of its lawyers during postrevolution litigation and negotiations—remarked that "there is some confusion as to why the Moscow Branch was opened in view of the unsettled conditions. The records do not show clearly who authorized the opening of this Branch."[213] The bank's internal account suggests that Dreher— a forceful personality apparently recalled to New York in February 1918 due to "friction with other employees"—pushed for the opening to continue to prevent a loss of face for the bank.[214]

H. A. Koelsch, Jr., one of the employees of the Moscow branch, was more direct in his commentary. His portrait of Dreher was of a pushy, unstable, and disagreeable man who managed to sour relations with important American counterparts in Russia—not least the head of National City client International Harvester, as well as the US ambassador—before his recall to New York and replacement by Koelsch.[215] His account also points to institutional inertia as driving the Moscow opening forward:

> I do not consider the statement "the records do not show clearly who authorized the opening of this Branch" is in any sense correct. A certain number of men were sent out there to open and run the Branch. Permission to open under the original Charter was received from the Provisional Government. Quarters were secured and fitted, and the opening was delayed on account of the Bolshevik uprising which took place very soon after. No instructions had been received from anyone to defer the opening, and in consideration of the fact that the Allies were still trying to pull Russia through, those men who were on the spot could not very well do otherwise. Mr. Meserve, who was then the Bank's Representative in Russia, was there through the Bolshevik revolution and left immediately afterwards; but before leaving he had a conference separately with both Mr. Dreher and myself, in which he made certain rulings which included the rates we would pay on deposits, fixed limits for the amounts we might carry at the various Russian banks, and so forth. No mention was ever made about deferring the opening.[216]

Once again, having men on the ground appeared to be a double-edged sword.

Still, Koelsch was nothing if not entrepreneurial: when the Bolsheviks decided they needed more space at the National, Koelsch negotiated for more time, and then arranged for the revolutionaries to annul the bank's lease. The Bolsheviks offered to requisition another property for them, but the bank moved into the International Harvester office.[217] Having opened in Moscow weeks after the Bolshevik coup, the bank continued to operate branches in Petrograd, Moscow, and Vologda through late August 1918.[218] But neither the Bolshevik default, nor the harrowing evacuation of its employees in Russia past German troops in Finland in September 1918, nor the seizure of the bank's Petrograd premises in December managed to kill the bank's interest in Russia.[219] By February 1919, National City was opening another Russian branch—under the leadership of Koelsch—in Vladivostok.[220] Others in the financial community saw hope in Russia, too, in early 1919—even in the territory under Bolshevik control. Morgan partner Thomas Lamont cabled New York arguing that even as Trotsky maintained a radical line, Lenin and the Soviets were "growing more conservative."[221]

"Do not make the geographical mistake of confusing Russia with Turkey," Kokovtsov had warned Verstraete and Lombardo in 1908.[222] Bankers took this Orientalist distinction to heart: Russia was a great power not to be pushed around by financiers, and was a responsible member of the European family of civilized nations. The great error of applying this already flawed comparison after 1918 was of course that it obscured how, from the standpoint of markets, the Bolsheviks were worse than the worst Orientalist caricature of the Ottoman Empire. This sense of cultural and diplomatic betrayal is difficult to overstate. Long after the Bolshevik default, when receiving Leonid Krasin, the Soviet foreign trade commissar—a fascinating champagne socialist, who once headed Siemens in Russia—British foreign secretary Lord Curzon refused to shake his guest's hand, so repulsed was he by Bolshevism.[223]

Continuing the Financial Fight, 1918–22

Just as the October Revolution did not mark a closure in the financial front along which the Bolsheviks were fighting, neither did the nationalization of the banks or the repudiation. Instead, the financial front took on new dimensions as the Bolshevik regime sought to consolidate power. Indeed, many of the foreigners who had invested in Russia, too, held onto their bonds as they followed the saga of Allied intervention and Civil War, hoping for bailouts or a Bolshevik defeat.[224]

Domestically, the immediate aftermath of the Bolshevik Revolution saw spiraling inflation in Russia. The inflation reflected two realities—the collapse of any meaningful tax and debt raising powers and an ambivalent

TABLE 5.12. Volume and value of note issues, 1919–23

Russia	Volume of note issues in billion paper rubles	Number of paper rubles = 1 gold ruble	Value of note issues in million gold rubles
January 1919	61	103	592
January 1920	225	1,670	135
January 1921	1,169	26,000	45
January 1922	17,539	172,000	102
March 1922	48,535	1,060,000	46
May 1922	145,635	3,800,000	38
July 1922	320,497	4,102,000	78
October 1922	815,486	6,964,000	117
January 1923	2,138,711	15,790,000	135
June 1923	8,050,000	97,690,000	82

Source: Keynes, *Tract on Monetary Reform*, 52.

Bolshevik relationship with money. In the context of the chaos of the Civil War, the Bolshevik regime's fiscal machinery was in even worse shape than that of the Provisional Government, leading it to monetize the deficit to an even greater degree. As Keynes pointed out in his *Tract on Monetary Reform*, this strategy entailed sharply diminishing returns. Already having suffered massive depreciation under the Tsarist and Provisional governments during wartime, the value of the ruble plunged further under the Bolsheviks, such that on the eve of the introduction of the New Economic Policy in 1921, the theoretical gold value of a ruble stood at less than half a percent of its early 1919 value (see Table 5.12).[225] Bolshevik Russia had entered the monetary twilight zone whereby the value of the currency was dropping faster than the central bank could print it.

At the same time, the Bolsheviks were seeking to forge a new economic order. Preobrazhensky notoriously referred to the printing presses as the "machine-gun of the People's Commissariat of Finance" with which it destroyed the value of paper assets held by the bourgeoisie as the Bolsheviks continued fighting the revolution along the financial front.[226] "Communist society will know nothing of money," he declared with Bukharin in *The ABC of Communism*.[227] However, communism had not arrived in 1918 with the revolution, and the socialist transition phase would see Lenin, Sokol'nikov, and the other theorists struggle with the "money famine."[228] The struggle to stabilize the real economy and financial realm would continue for a decade.

Just as the Bolsheviks continued the financial struggle domestically, so they continued to fight on the financial front abroad. In this latter case, Russia's foreign debt remained the weapon of choice. As the Bolsheviks established de facto and later de jure diplomatic relations with Western powers, trade and the debt issue became key points of negotiations. In August 1918, the Bolsheviks signed a financial addendum to the Brest-Litovsk treaty with Germany, but this was eventually rendered moot with the break in relations later in the year. Although after the end of Allied intervention in Russia the Soviets were able to negotiate the landmark Anglo-Soviet trade agreement in 1921, the debt issue remained a roadblock to full diplomatic ties.[229]

It was in this context that Russia's Western creditors invited the Bolsheviks to discuss debts and a final diplomatic settlement at Genoa in 1922. The Soviet delegation, headed by Chicherin, was tasked by Lenin to hold a very firm line.[230] The official Bolshevik reply of 11 May 1922 to the memorandum of the European powers underscores the degree to which the financial front remained active through the question of debts. The document speaks of the "New Russia" and of "the repudiation of the debts and obligations contracted by the former regime, abhorred as it was by the Russian people," making it very clear that the default was still very much a matter of the will to pay as much as the ability to do so.[231] Indeed, the Bolsheviks made reference to previous repudiations of debt by governments represented at the conference and, to legitimize their act further, spoke of the French revolutionary declaration: "the sovereignty of peoples is not bound by the treaties of tyrants."[232]

Far from just being an act of self-legitimization, however, the Russian reply to the Genoa Memorandum continued to use the debt issue as an offensive revolutionary tool. The Bolsheviks were quick to exploit opportunities to divide the creditor camp. This was evident in their industrial concessions policies, as well as their later signing of bilateral Rapallo Accords with Germany, which ultimately broke creditor unity in the debt negotiations. By the summer of 1918, J. P. Morgan & Co. and Baring Brothers were already trying to strike a delicate balance between showing unity with other claimants in the face of repudiation and delicately handling investor representatives such as the secretary of the British Council of Foreign Bondholders. In the view of Morgan Grenfell, the latter was an "able, pushing man but very conceited and anxious to make a name for himself," even at the expense of the issuing banks in London.[233]

At Genoa, this desire to create and exploit divisions among creditors emerged in the Bolsheviks' claiming to look out for the interests of the French small holders. Having at the stroke of a pen written off debts to hundreds of thousands of French workers and peasants, the Bolsheviks now claimed to be speaking in their interest. They accused the representatives at Genoa of "reserving all their solicitude for a small group of foreign capitalists and maintaining an inexplicable doctrinaire intransigence" and of "[sacrificing] as well the interests of a multitude of small holders of Russian bonds and small foreign proprietors whose property has been nationalized or sequestered and whom the Russian government had intended to include among those the justice and merit of whose claims she recognized."[234] Lozovsky's dreams of riling up the French masses against their government through revolutionary default had not died.

Conclusion: The Rationality of Revolutionary Default and Logic of Financial War

When the Bolsheviks defaulted in early 1918, many observers were simply reduced to disbelief. Apart from the unprecedented size of the event, orthodox economics—particularly at the time—held that default was irrational and immoral, and the behavior of the Bolsheviks flew in the face of more than a century of Russian financial history. In reality, it was the Bolsheviks who were behaving in an eminently rational way.

The Bolsheviks ultimately defaulted in early 1918 because they were neither willing nor able to pay. Their lack of willingness stemmed from a deeply held conviction that the debts that the Tsarist and Provisional governments incurred in the name of the Russian people were illegitimate. Outlandish as such a claim may have sounded to many foreigners, the Bolsheviks were not alone in their sentiment. Many in the Provisional Government itself had once opposed Tsarist policies of borrowing in the French money market—not least Shingarev, who served as finance minister in 1917, but only after having railed against Kokovtsov in the Duma for years.

Beyond any political issues was the consideration that Russia was simply unable to continue debt service absent a substantial restructuring. Years of war and revolution finally caught up with Russia by late 1917, and it is highly unlikely that in a counterfactual scenario, whereby Lenin did not succeed in taking power in November, a different regime would have been able to avoid a default—even if in the form of a restructuring.

In this sense, if anyone acted irrationally, it was the foreigners who continued to believe in the Russian investment story up to and even past the moment of default. At a very basic level, they failed to see the sorry state of the Russian economy for what it was. More profound was the failure to understand the political dimension. In the early months of the war, the New York financier Jacob Schiff had written to Jack Morgan with his concerns over the latter's involvement in the financing of one the most virulently anti-Semitic governments in the world. Echoing the attitude of countless "emerging market" investors before and since, the latter replied, "I do not think it is for us to endeavor to change the attitude of Russia by applying financial pressure. It seems to me that the question of whether or not Russia is a good and solvent debtor can hardly be mixed up with questions of internal social or policing regulations. I say this with very great respect for, and a full appreciation of, your own opinion in the matter."[235] As in 1905, financiers failed to understand the degree to which the debt issue was politicized, not realizing that the Bolsheviks were fighting a financial war as much as a political one, and that investing in Russia was an inherently political act—until it was too late. In this sense, Verstraete's remark in early 1918, that the nationalization of the banks was "more military than financial," was all too appropriate.[236]

Conclusion

AT THE HEIGHT of the revolutionary turmoil of 1905, the British foreign secretary Sir Edward Grey wrote to his chargé d'affaires at the British embassy in Saint Petersburg, Cecil Spring Rice: "I have no idea of what the outcome of the Revolution will be: the laws of the course of Revolutions are not capable of scientific analysis. The general rule is that what is on the top at the beginning is not on the top at the end. I hope the struggle won't last too long. I want to see Russia re-established in the councils of Europe, and I hope on better terms with us than she has yet been."[1] Grey's words would prove prescient, and his hopes would be dashed. The Russian Revolution developed differently from the revolutionaries' expectations at the outset. Notwithstanding Lenin's talk of the 1905 Revolution as "a dress rehearsal" for the events of 1917, as Ascher notes, "the individuals who participated in the mass movements of 1904 did not believe that they were merely preparing the way for the real event at some future date."[2] An analogous statement may be made from the standpoint of reaction—the Tsarist government's tense relations with the Duma after 1905 were just the most visible manifestation of the ancien régime's struggle with the post-1905 order.

More broadly, Grey's statement expresses the difficulty of establishing a general roadmap for revolution. In this sense, it is striking that Crane Brinton—whose *Anatomy of Revolution* offers one of the most famous such roadmaps—demarcates the Russian Revolution as having begun with the Petrograd riots of March 1917.[3] While this starting date simplifies his narrative, it also misses many potential turning points in the broader story of the Russian Revolution.

In taking the longer view, it is evident that neither the Bolshevik Revolution nor the Russian default of 1918, which was its biggest financial consequence, was inevitable. Rather, both were the products of complex historical processes with no predetermined course or outcome. Seen through the lens of financial history, several turning points are evident in this story.

Sergei Witte's tenure as finance minister witnessed a great deal of rapid economic growth, for which his predecessors laid much of the groundwork; but it also saw the Tsarist technocrat commit key strategic unforced errors. Indeed, Witte's management of Tsarist finances was characterized by the large, leveraged, and unidirectional wagers he implicitly made on the future appetite of the French investment community for Russian investments, as well as on the future of the Paris Bourse itself as a center of international finance. Witte notably failed to develop relations with the financial markets of New York and London.

This omission would subsequently haunt the regime during the crisis of 1905–6 as it fought for its financial survival in the face of attacks on its financial edifice from both domestic and foreign opponents. True, Witte did secure the so-called loan that saved Russia from Western bankers, including the British, but the troubled story of the loan after its flotation revealed the fragility of Russian credit in London in the absence of a committed investor base. The contrast between the behavior of British bondholders in 1906 and that of the more stoic French bondholders through 1918 is striking in this regard—the former had been proven to be fickle in 1906, while the latter were remarkably willing to hold onto bonds even after rumors and indeed declarations of default.

More importantly, the regime and its foreign bankers agreed on the deal without Duma approval, and in the face of vocal opposition. In doing so, the French bankers and French government in particular missed an opportunity to push the Tsarist government further down the path of reform. Their failure to do so was particularly striking given that the French had linked approval of an earlier loan to Russian promises to place defense orders with French firms and to support France diplomatically. When finally agreed, the loan only incensed and radicalized the opposition, as seen in the Kadets' adoption of a much more radical line on financial questions in the Vyborg Manifesto of the summer of 1906. The events of 1905–6 thus showed the regime to be engaged in a life-and-death struggle with its opponents not only in the streets or in the press, but also in the financial realm.

Even as the loan of 1906 and the Stolypin coup d'état of 1907 superficially indicated a reassertion of Tsarist authority, this financial front remained very much alive through the interrevolutionary period, as evidenced by the continued focus of the Kadets and other opposition figures on financial issues as a way of opposing the regime. Meanwhile, perceptions of recovery in the real economy, coupled with the attraction of distressed investment opportunities and competitive pressures, lured foreign investors into the Russian market. By 1909, foreign investors, having forgotten the events of 1905, and paying little attention to the opposition's continued protests over financial questions, were back in force in the Russian market.

Moreover, this new foreign investment boom took on a character that was different from those that preceded it. British capital was a more noticeable feature this time around, as was the participation of larger joint-stock commercial banks. The London City and Midland Bank—which was not only growing more powerful in the City of London but also making inroads into the international lending business via its Russian deals—exemplified both these trends. The Tsarist government was quick to take advantage of this growing competition by playing on the bankers' insecurities.

Not only were the identities of the foreign financiers in the Russian markets changing but so were their lending profiles. The interrevolutionary decade thus saw government-backed municipal and mortgage loans, as well as private-sector issues, grow in prominence while the proportion of central government debt in the overall stock of outstanding Russian debt declined. In one sense, this trend suggested a deepening bond market, but it also reflected a higher risk profile and growing financial and operational leverage.

In this context of increasing leverage, alarming signs of a bubble about to burst emerged in various reports from across the European provinces of the empire. Just as the signs of a looming crisis were growing—not only in the economy, but in the social and political spheres as well—the Tsarist rearmament program and, ultimately, the advent of the First World War provided a fiscal stimulus and relaxed constraints on monetary policy, which combined to boost the economy. Thus, once again, the Tsarist regime averted a potentially disastrous crisis—even if the mechanism by which it did so ultimately aggravated underlying problems.

The war indeed had a contradictory effect vis-à-vis international finance and its relationship with Russia. The early years of conflict were marked by an industrial and financial boom that only excited the interest of foreign investors, not least the newly arrived, deep-pocketed British and Americans. Both these new entrants into the Russian market, as well as their French counterparts, grew increasingly frustrated with the ineptitude of the Tsarist regime in the context of wartime challenges, and initially welcomed, rather than feared, the February Revolution. For investors, as for many who supported the revolution, February was supposed to inaugurate a period of much-needed liberal change and reform in Russia. Foreign financiers consciously invested in this revolution. The prospect of institutional change partly attracted this investment, but does not fully explain it. Rather, framed in part by wartime narratives, and in part by prewar stereotypes, foreign investment in Russia during the revolution took on a strongly cultural and moralistic dimension. The fear of losing Russia to allied competitors or to the Germans, as well as the belief that Russia was too important and too big to fail in the eyes of the French and British governments, only fueled the desire to invest in Russia. In the face of devastating military defeats and violent domestic political turmoil, Russia continued to attract the interest of the foreign investment community precisely as it was hurtling toward a financial cliff.

Indeed, by 1917 and well before the Bolshevik takeover, a default in Russia— whether in the form of an outright cancellation of debts or a "restructuring"— had become inevitable. Three years of war had seen the Russian Empire lose critical parts of its economy to the enemy, while the strategy of relying on domestic debt markets had seen diminishing returns, forcing the government to resort to the printing press. Even by employing the latter method, the government could not keep up—by the late summer of 1917, the Provisional Government began cutting corners, reducing the quality of the notes it printed to maintain the necessary output at the presses, indeed even issuing notes in uncut sheets.[4] Under such circumstances, even counterfeiters could not keep pace with the rate at which currency was being issued.

This policy of debt monetization produced predictably disastrous results. Inflation ate away at the very fabric of society and the economy. Financial woes only contributed to strikes. Keen students of the financial system, the Bolsheviks were quick to seize on the Provisional Government's economic woes— not least by undermining its attempts to raise funds through the domestic debt markets, thereby condemning it to yet more inflationary policies. Thus, like its predecessor, the Provisional Government began fighting its opponents along the financial front—only with considerably less success.

By the time the Bolsheviks succeeded in their coup, Russia's economic output had already fallen to a fraction of its prewar level, while its debts had ballooned. To be sure, the Bolsheviks—as well as more moderate liberals— telegraphed their intention to default well before the October Revolution. Nevertheless, material realities dictated some sort of restructuring—if not a 100 percent haircut, then at least one that was substantial—independent of ideological imperatives. If anything came as a surprise, it was that the Bolsheviks waited until early 1918 to repudiate Tsarist debts.

The ideological impulse driving the Bolshevik line on default, however, remained evident even after 1918, as the Bolsheviks extended their financial fight against their enemies—foreign and domestic. The continuation of this revolutionary financial struggle was apparent in the domestic sphere in the attempts alternately to use the printing press as a tool of class war and to control inflation. In the international sphere, the repudiation of prerevolutionary debts took on a new meaning as the Bolsheviks sought to use the act of repudiation as a way of legitimizing their new regime, to strike a divisive blow against Western creditors, and to instigate revolution among worker and peasant bondholders.

As historical events, then, both the Bolshevik Revolution and the subsequent default were intertwined and historically contingent. They emerged from a particular set of historical circumstances, processes, and turning points. The events and the processes that produced them were linked by the explicitly financial character of the war the Bolsheviks waged against their opponents—be they the ancien régime, the Provisional Government, domestic class enemies, or foreign powers.

Gatekeeper Finance and Global Capital Flows in a Russian Perspective

The experience of foreign investors in the narrative of Russia at the turn of the century had a dual significance. First, foreign investors emerge as actors in the story of the revolution—their actions influenced not only economic developments, but political ones too. Investment was as much a political act as an economic one in Russia in the late nineteenth and early twentieth centuries. The tragedy is that financiers at first failed to appreciate the political consequences of their actions, and then, in the context of the war, began to focus belatedly on the political dimension of their investments—increasingly to the exclusion of financial considerations and analysis.

Second, the behavior of foreign financiers confounds existing ideas about what drove international capital flows at the time. Specifically, the small but highly influential group of financiers at the center of this study showed that government interventions, competitive dynamics, and cultural factors influenced their decision making—often to a greater degree than the factors that several influential modern economic theories would suggest. Thus, expectations and signals of government bailouts and support were important influences on investor thinking and decision making at the time, as was the fear of losing out to competing banks and, indeed, countries—not least Germany. Finally, strong cultural influences—paternalism and patriotism, among others—played a major role in shaping financiers' conceptions and decisions, not least during the war.

It is particularly striking how modern economic theories fail to explain the highly significant case of the Russian investment boom on the eve of and during the First World War. The phenomenon of banks such as Midland and National City initiating and expanding their presence in Russia in 1916 and 1917 confounds explanatory frameworks stressing fixed exchange rates and sensitivity to political violence as drivers of financiers' decision making. Similarly, institutional explanations do not fully explain investors' enthusiasm after the February Revolution, nor do they account for the large capital inflows into Tsarist Russia—a reactionary state where, in spite of Witte's reforms, government was still a highly personalized enterprise revolving around the whims of the Tsar and his reactionary clique.

The experience of foreign financiers in the Russian markets thus suggests that explanations of international capital flows during the first modern age of globalization must not only devote more attention to influences at the level of financial gatekeepers, but also adopt a broader scope. Competitive dynamics and government pressures influencing individual firms emerge as important drivers of capital flows in the significant case of Russia. Crucially, so too did cultural and behavioral factors such as the nationalism and paternalism so evident in financiers' thinking about Russia during the war. Focusing through historical methods on the individuals who acted as gatekeepers in these markets allows for a consideration of this broader set of influences on capital flows.

The Personal Dimension

Proust's reference to Russian bonds in *Remembrance of Things Past* and his own unfortunate investment in such securities is an important reminder of the personal dimension to international finance. The financial history of the first modern age of globalization is the story of individuals as much as of large impersonal flows of capital sloshing around the global economic system and into the Russian market.

The social history of the ordinary French citizens who suffered so much at the hands of the Bolsheviks still awaits its author.[5] Nevertheless, the scale of the blow landed by the Bolshevik default is evident in the lasting cultural legacy of "les emprunts russes." Beyond the literary references, such as those of Proust, the countless jokes and sayings, the millions of bond certificates passed on through generations of French families, and even the Internet forums for the descendants of bondholders are testaments to the deep impact of the Bolshevik default on the French national psyche.[6] The postwar litigation to which the French banks were subject as well as the organizations of bondholders provide some sense of the deep and long-lasting hangover the French suffered after their Russian investment binge.

The fate of ordinary Russians, of course, was much worse. Apart from the wholesale expropriation of Russian bondholders under the Bolsheviks, the repudiation blocked the nascent communist regime from raising funds through debt issues and, absent a reliable tax system, pushed it to rely heavily on the printing press. The resulting inflation erased the savings of millions of Russians, and rendered meaningless any earlier Bolshevik concessions to small holders of Russian securities. The inflation's disruption of the real economy only magnified its immediate financial impact.

The story of financial gatekeepers in the case of turn-of-the-century Russia was one not just of firms but also of individuals who in many cases were direct witnesses to the events of 1905, 1917, and other turning points in Russian and indeed world history. Frederick Bunker, Midland's man in Petrograd, remained in the city after even the British embassy had shut down, escaping in a perilous run through the White and Red lines in Finland in 1918.[7] Having caught Edward Holden's eye through his Russia work, he would go on to head the overseas department of the London bank.[8] Midland would actually see a boom in Russian business related to renewed Anglo-Russian trade in the 1920s.[9] Lord Revelstoke—one of the chief architects of the 1906 loan, who found himself in Saint Petersburg at the height of the strikes in late 1905— would take a final bow on the Russian stage, advising the British government on the financial resources available to the Dowager Empress Maria as they prepared to evacuate her from Russia after the murder of her son, Nicholas II.[10] As late as 1921, Russian émigrés were trying to borrow from Barings and other British banks against prerevolutionary securities. It fell to Cecil Baring to disabuse them of any notion they might succeed.[11] Revelstoke remained at the helm of his family's firm, dying of a heart attack while in the midst of negotiating a deal in 1929.[12] In 1986, Barings would finally release $71.7 million in frozen Imperial Russian Government funds as part of the final settlement of the debt issue between the British and Soviet governments.[13]

H. F. Meserve—National City's representative in Russia—witnessed the Bolshevik Revolution, and left immediately thereafter.[14] Having made a harrowing journey to Moscow via the Far East, his associate H. J. Dreher proceeded to open the Moscow branch on 27 November 1917, apparently undeterred by the communist takeover.[15] The Moscow and Petrograd staff remained in Bolshevik Russia for more than nine months. In March, the bulk of the Petrograd staff were evacuated to Vologda for fear of falling into German hands.[16] National City's expatriate staff would eventually leave in early September 1918 through Finland, dodging the 30,000 German troops stationed there in the closing days of the war.[17] In December, the Bolshevik Fifth Army Corps requisitioned the Petrograd branch building.[18] Still seeing opportunity, Moscow branch veteran H. A. Koelsch, Jr. led a National City team to open a branch in Vladivostok in early February 1919. The branch would close by mid-March 1920.[19] Citibank, the successor to National City, would return to Russia after the fall of communism, opening a representative office in Moscow in 1992.[20] The mayor of Saint Petersburg at the time, Anatoly Sobchak, met with Meserve's successor, Bill Rhodes, in 1993, offering to return the old National City Petrograd branch building to the bank in an effort to restore the bank's presence in the old Tsarist capital.[21]

In the short time National City's Russian branches were operational, they managed to attract such a large amount of deposits that litigation after the revolution threatened to force the bank to pay depositors an amount equal to 40 percent of the bank's entire capital in dollars in New York.[22] For years, the bank's attempts to sort out postrevolutionary lawsuits were frustrated by the Russian operation's records having been left behind during the evacuation. Bank staff left the documents in the care of the Swedish consulate in Moscow, which the Cheka raided in June 1919, blowing open the safes and destroying some papers in the process. By 1920, the records were lying in a shed on Brusov Lane in central Moscow.[23] Before long, the Bolshevik commissar for foreign trade, Leonid Krasin, was using the papers as a bargaining chip with the bank to lobby for American diplomatic recognition.[24] Yet, in the end even the Bolsheviks' ability to leverage this latest twist in the financial tale of the revolution proved limited. As two veterans of the Petrograd branch recounted: "It has been reported to us that some of our books and papers which were lying in the stable adjacent to the Swedish Moscow Consulate General have been sold on the streets of Moscow, owing to the grave shortage of all kinds of paper. Paper in Moscow at the present writing is selling for Rs. 10,000 a Russian pound, and therefore, it can be readily understood the temptation placed in the way of ignorant yardsmen or guards, who know that this immense quantity of paper is lying in a wood shed and evidently not required by the Government."[25] That important papers over which one of the most powerful banks in the world and the Bolshevik government haggled lay in a shed, from which they were being pilfered daily for use as toilet paper, underscores the depths to which affairs in Russia had slipped by the early 1920s.

National City's Russia disaster prompted James Stillman to return from Paris and oust president Frank A. Vanderlip in a boardroom coup.[26] Meserve, however, only saw his star rise, taking up the post of the head of National City's European operations from early 1919 in Paris, where he kept up with many of his associates from his Russian days now living in exile.[27] Indeed, later the same year his daughter became engaged to a Russian diplomat in the Paris embassy of Admiral Kolchak's Omsk government.[28] Among others, Meserve would have seen Kokovtsov. The latter penned his memoirs in exile, giving him the last word in his long-running feud with Witte, who died before the revolution, in 1915.

Less fortunate was the fate of Peter Bark, the last finance minister of Tsarist Russia, who arrived in France in 1919.[29] As was the case with many of his compatriots, Bark fell on hard times. He struggled while living in England, his eventual home, where he was knighted, to maintain the appearances of one of the highest officials of Tsarist Russia.[30] Desperate to make ends meet, he petitioned his old colleague, Montagu Norman, the governor of the Bank of England, to take him on as a consultant and to lend him enough money to allow him to clear his earlier debts.[31] Norman's assistance led only to more requests, such that by 1935 a bank official wrote to the governor saying, "I always try to evade Sir Peter Bark" because of his habit of masking requests for financial help dressed up as offers of services, before asking in exasperation, "What is to be done about him?"[32]

Ivan Shingarev—Kokovtsov's bête noire in the Duma debates on financial questions, and later himself finance minister under the Provisional Government—suffered an even worse fate than that of the destitute Bark. A group of Red Guards murdered this well-meaning liberal doctor-turned-finance-expert while he was lying in a Petrograd hospital bed in January 1918.[33]

In the end, then, it was the individual small investors in the West, ordinary Russians stuck in the financial hell of early Bolshevik Russia, and the exiled technocrats of the Tsarist and Provisional governments who suffered most in one of the greatest investment booms and busts of modern financial history.

The bankers, by contrast, simply moved on.

Rethinking Sovereign Default Rankings

IN A SERIES OF PAPERS and monographs, several authors, most notably Carmen Reinhart and Kenneth Rogoff, and Michael Tomz and Mark Wright, have offered rankings of defaults by governments on their external debt across time and space. Even if differing on some of the details, both groups of authors offer a similar ranking of default by size. According to both, the Greek default of more than €205 billion of central government debt in 2012 was the largest in history, followed by that of Argentina of more than $90 billion in 2001. Tomz and Wright explicitly rank the Bolshevik default of 1918 as the third largest in history, while Reinhart and Rogoff do not name it as the largest, but acknowledge that it was the longest-running, lasting 69 years by their count.

The Reinhart-Rogoff and Tomz-Wright rankings are important attempts by social scientists to establish a reliable database of comparative data on sovereign debt over time, thus creating the basis for historically minded work on the subject. However, a closer consideration of their data and methodology suggests an alternate ranking that would privilege more recent experience less and instead rank the 1918 Russian default as the largest in history.

Defining Default

Scholars and financial market participants define and measure sovereign defaults through a range of different mechanisms and methods. The issue of what constitutes a default is the first relevant concern. In sovereign debt markets, a default is typically determined to have occurred when the issuer of debt fails to make a scheduled interest payment or otherwise changes the terms of its contract with creditors in a manner adverse to their interests. In the recent Eurozone debt crisis, the declaration of default became a topic of some concern to financial market participants because of the large amount of derivative instruments—largely in the form of credit default swaps (CDS)—tied to Greek sovereign bonds.

In this most recent case, even if a range of scholars, ratings agencies, and financial market participants may have made their own determination of default, it was the formal ruling of the International Swaps and Derivatives Association (ISDA) that carried the most weight insofar as most CDS contracts stipulated that the issuer of the CDS was to pay the buyer only when ISDA ruled that the sovereign debtor in question had in fact defaulted.

In ISDA's parlance, what is colloquially thought of as a default can in fact take several forms. According to ISDA's official definition, a so-called credit event can include "one or more of Bankruptcy, Failure to Pay, Obligation Acceleration, Obligation Default, Repudiation/Moratorium or Restructuring."[1] The complexity and sensitivity of the decision was reflected in the need for ISDA's EMEA (Europe, Middle East, and Africa) Credit Determinations Committee—composed of representatives of no fewer than 15 banks and investment managers, of which the bulk were in fact hedge funds—to determine whether or not a credit event had occurred in the case of Greece.[2] Beyond simply determining whether or not the Greek government's actions represented a credit event, the ISDA committee further had to determine when the event took place. Once the committee issued its formal declaration, the international financial press lost no time in declaring that Greece's default was "official," even if financial markets had largely discounted the news in their pricing of Greek assets.[3] By contrast, when the Greek government failed to make scheduled payments tied to loans with the IMF in 2015, neither ISDA nor three major credit ratings agencies declared a default.[4] For this reason, despite Greece's subsequent payment issues, 2012 remains the relevant event from the standpoint of comparative default rankings.

Even though an organization like ISDA is a relatively recent creation, its handling of the Greek default has important parallels with financial markets' engagement with sovereign default in what can be thought of as the first modern age of globalization during the late nineteenth and early twentieth centuries, when global financial markets were integrated as much as—if not more than—they are today. The participation of private-sector institutions, notably investment banks and hedge funds, mirrors the leading role private banks played in the past in addressing sovereign defaults. As in the past, today it is private financial intermediaries and investors that retain a significant role in determining whether a default has occurred or not.

Even if ISDA's default committees are a recent phenomenon in a narrow sense, definitions of what constitutes a default have been relatively consistent over time. In this sense, most market participants and scholars would agree on the Reinhart and Rogoff definition of what constitutes a sovereign default:

"The failure of a government to meet a principal or interest payment on the due date (or within the specified grace period). These episodes include instances in which rescheduled debt is ultimately extinguished in terms less favorable than the original obligation."[5] Yet broadening the definition of default to include the various restructurings and reschedulings to which both the Reinhart-Rogoff and ISDA definitions allude opens up new complexities.

Measuring the size of defaults is the most obvious such difficulty. Some analysts focus on the total face value of the debt subject to default; others focus on the principal lost through restructuring alone. Different treatments of past due interest in accounting for defaults can lead to widely varying estimates as to the size of a given default. More recent cases of default through restructuring—notably the Argentinean default of 2001—raised the issue of how to value assets that creditors suffering default gain in a restructuring. In the Argentinean case, bondholders subject to default were assigned derivate instruments in the form of GDP warrants that would trigger payments if the real economy grew faster than expected. This novel form of derivative was tied to economic growth itself rather than to a specific security. Although difficult to price and illiquid, it did in theory have some value. Similarly, past due interest could account for as much as 10 percent of various headline figures of the size of the default.[6]

The different methodologies employed in determining the size of defaults complicate any attempt at comparison. Both the Reinhart-Rogoff and Tomz-Wright studies determine the size of a default to be the face value of the debt subject to default. In this sense, they make no distinction between repudiations of 100 percent of a public debt or restructurings that see only part of the principal wiped out, or interest payments reduced or rescheduled. This academic practice is at odds with common practice in financial markets, where banks, regulators, and bond traders use the concept of "loss given default" (LGD) to distinguish between different potential and actual defaults. Indeed, different estimates of LGD motivated many so-called vulture funds like Elliott Management to snap up defaulted Argentinean bonds in the early 2000s.[7]

Using the relatively simplistic academic methodology, publishing their monograph on sovereign debt three years before the 2012 Greek default, Reinhart and Rogoff declared, "Argentina holds the record for the largest default; in 2001 it defaulted on more than $95 billion in external debt."[8] This figure generally falls in line with other estimates insofar as media reports also cited a $95 billion figure, but estimates do vary.[9] Some scholars assess the default to have been as little as $91 billion.[10] While the Congressional Budget Office placed the default at $102.6 billion, calling it "unprecedented for its size," this figure includes approximately $5 billion in past due interest.[11] Stripping out estimates of past due interest from the size of defaults becomes necessary when considering the wide variance in the maturity of debts subject to default. For example, Russia's 1918 default, cited by Reinhart and Rogoff as the longest-lasting (69 years) in their dataset, would skew any comparisons of the size of default that included past due interest.[12] Indeed, all else equal, inclusion of past due interest in default sizes would simply privilege older defaults in any dataset on sovereign defaults over time.

Of course, when Argentina engaged in "selective default" in 2014, ISDA and ratings agencies declared a credit event, raising the question of whether 2014 and not 2001 should be the reference point for Argentinean default.[13] The 2014 Argentinean default stemmed from a missed payment of $539 million on $13 billion of bonds issued as part of the post-2001 default restructuring. Even though the country was able and willing to make the payments, a US judge declared that a group of "hold-out" creditors who had not agreed to the terms of the 2001 restructuring must be paid prior to making payments on restructured bonds. At the time of default, ratings agency Standard and Poor's estimated Argentina's foreign currency debt as standing at approximately $200 billion, with $30 billion of restructured bonds.[14] Given that the 2014 act was a continuation of an event begun in 2001, it remains appropriate to use the 2001 default of Argentina as the key default event to avoid double counting.

The 2012 default by the Greek government is generally accepted to have exceeded the 2001 Argentinean default in size, yet even if this is the case, estimates as to the size of the default vary based on different accounting methodologies. Tomz and Wright rate the default as having been more than €200 billion, and explicitly refer to it as "the largest default in history (by present value) . . . followed by Argentina in 2001 and Russia in 1918."[15] Although contemporary financial press reports largely agreed with the headline figure and with the notion of the Greek default having been the largest in history, there was some variation in presentation. Thus, the *Economist* cited a figure of €100 billion, focusing on the amount of principal that was written off.[16] Adopting the more commonly used convention of focusing on the total amount of principal subject to some sort of default or restructuring, official statements by the Greek government and the European Commission imply a default size of €205.6 billion, or $271.4 billion at the then-prevailing exchange rate.[17]

These large figures would seem to fall, however, when considering the jurisdiction under which the Greek debt was issued. While such a distinction may seem arcane, it is in fact important insofar as many definitions of sovereign debt make a distinction between domestic and foreign debt. In the case of the Reinhart-Rogoff study, the distinction between external and domestic debt is rooted not in the currency in which said debt is denominated, but rather according to the legal jurisdiction under which the debt contracts were conceived.[18] Thus, the authors define external debt as the private and public debt of a country held by foreigners, usually falling under some foreign or international jurisdiction.[19] The authors by contrast define "government domestic debt" as "all debt liabilities of a government that are issued under and subject to national jurisdiction, regardless of the nationality of the creditor or the currency denomination of the debt; therefore, it includes government foreign-currency domestic debt."[20]

In the Greek case of 2012, according to the Greek finance ministry, €29 billion ($38.3 billion) of the debt was issued under foreign law, with the remaining €177 billion issued under Greek law.[21] Of course, operating within the context of a common currency and the framework of the European Union, the distinction between the two types of debt in the Greek case may seem less significant than in other cases. Nevertheless, it is arguably the case that the gold standard and formal and informal empires, which created de facto legal zones and umbrellas in historical cases, offer analogs. In this sense, estimates for the size of the Greek default could range from as little as €29 billion ($38.3 billion), if adopting the narrowest definition of external debt under foreign jurisdiction, to as much as €205.6 billion ($271.41 billion), if incorporating the full amount of debt "eligible for exchange or offer" under the terms of the restructuring.[22]

Contextualizing the 1918 Bolshevik Repudiation

Any discussion of the Bolshevik default is complicated by disagreements on the most basic details. There is, for example, substantial divergence of opinion regarding the actual date of default. In his survey on modern global financial history, James Macdonald dates the default as being "one of Lenin's first acts" in 1917, implying a default date in November 1917.[23] Economists Kim Oosterlinck and John Landon-Lane acknowledge rumors preceding the event but date the default as having taken place on 8 February 1918.[24] Pipes gives the date as being 28 January/10 February 1918.[25] This does not seem accurate insofar as the Bolsheviks published the decree before 10 February 1918. The discussion of dates in the early Bolshevik period is further confused by the Bolshevik calendar reforms, which saw Russia finally adopt the Gregorian calendar in early 1918, when 31 January 1918 was followed by 14 February 1918. The most widely quoted date for the default is 3 February 1918 (in line with the new, Gregorian style), with the formal adoption of the VTsIK "Decree on the Annulment of Foreign Debts," applied retroactively to payments from 1 December 1917 (old calendar/Julian, which corresponds to 14 December 1917 in the new style/Gregorian).[26]

The decree of 3 February, however, was not the very first declaration—even in an official sense—of default by the regime. The archival record and financial press evidence open discussions of Bolshevik "proposals" about default in December and January. The VTsIK decree in fact only followed on from and slightly modified—to include limited provisions protecting small retail bondholders in Russia—a 1/14 January decree of the Council of Peoples' Commissars (Sovet Narodnykh Komissarov, or Sovnarkom), Lenin's cabinet.[27] The February decree appeared in a Soviet bulletin on 8 February, but to use this date for the repudiation is incorrect insofar as the decree was formally adopted five days prior, and financial market participants were aware of the act of repudiation in January. That this decree was published on 8 February further brings into question Pipes's use of 28 January/10 February as the date of the default announcement. By that point, markets were well aware of the declaration of default.

The VTsIK decree consisted of just 10 articles and was categorical in its repudiation of prerevolutionary debts. Specifically, the decree annulled "all national loans concluded by the governments of Russian landowners and Russian bourgeoisie" effective 1 December 1917 (Julian calendar).[28] In addition to cancelling all Russian government guarantees for other debts, such as those of private railroad companies, the decree stated as its third point, "unconditionally and without exception, all foreign loans are annulled."[29] The decree further declared that short-term government notes remained "in force" as currency, even if they would not earn interest.[30] Small investors' interests were crucially upheld—at least in theory. Provision was made for "citizens of small means" such that their holdings of domestic debt up to 10,000 rubles would be exchanged for debt of the new Russian Socialist Federal Soviet Republic (RSFSR) in the same amount, but with new payment terms to be determined at a future date.[31] The decree, which the Bolsheviks' inflationary policies would turn into a meaningless concession, explicitly declared, "deposits in national savings banks and interest on them remain unaffected."[32] The Bolsheviks gave some vague allowances to various organizations of a charitable and democratic nature, as long as the latter acquired the securities prior to the decree's issuance, but left this all to the full discretion of the Soviet authorities. The last several clauses of the decree laid out the rules for its execution: predictably, state and soviet authorities would carry out or delegate the work, and citizens were obligated to disclose their holdings, regardless of whether or not they were subject to cancellation. In a final blow, the decree declared that the authorities had "the right to annul in entirety savings not gained by toil, even if these savings do not exceed five thousand rubles."[33]

Even before comparing the various defaults in terms of amounts, the sweeping nature of the Bolshevik default is immediately apparent. The Greek default adopted the language of "private sector involvement" (PSI), "restructuring," and "exchange." Even if it balked at IMF austerity demands, Argentina, too, acknowledged the foreign debts it had contracted. It rather framed its decisions—both at the time of default, as well as in subsequent discussions with multilateral and private-sector creditors—in the context of its inability to pay.[34] Indeed, the use of derivatives—in the form of GDP warrants—as part of Argentina's June 2005 exchange with creditors was an indication of the government's recognition of and desire to meet its obligations.[35] The Argentinean government convinced creditors to accept a large haircut because of the poor performance of the economy; if the economy improved beyond the government's projections, the GDP warrants would allow the creditors to benefit from the outperformance relative to expectations.[36]

Needless to say, the Bolshevik default, with its talk of wealth being acquired "without toil" and taking place in the midst of a communist revolution, made no offers of PSI, restructuring, or GDP warrants. The act was a clear and unequivocal repudiation of all prior debts, and especially—"absolutely and without exception"—foreign loans. These starkly differing terms of default are a reminder that even normalizing for different sizes of defaults, there is significant variation across sovereign defaults for which comparisons of the dollar values of defaulted debt do not account. The gap between financial market participants' practice of focusing on LGD and the academic convention of considering solely the face value of defaulted debt only underscores the severity of the Bolshevik default. Yet, even purely on the dollar amount of the face value of the debt, the Bolshevik default remains unmatched in its scale.

The size of the Bolshevik default and its present value today are questions open to even wider interpretation than those relating to the recent Greek and Argentinean defaults. The difficulty rests in determining both the size of the default in 1918 and the appropriate method by which to inflate the 1918 sum into contemporary terms. The question of the size of the default in 1918 is extremely complex, not least because the financial record of the last days of the Provisional Government is incomplete.

Moreover, the types of debt in question were varied. Even if one can arrive at a reasonable estimate of central government debt based on those loans that were entered into the *Gosudarstvennaia Dolgovaia Kniga* (Public Debt Book), this figure does not include some loans issued in the name of third parties but guaranteed by the government.[37] Under the political economy of the late Tsarist period, such loans to railroads, the Peasants' Land Bank, and the Land Bank of the Nobility were substantial.[38] The Public Debt Book would also not include guarantees to industry, which in any case often did not take the form of bonds, but which were nonetheless government liabilities covered by the repudiation decree.

In contrast to more recent times, the distribution of debt holdings is again very difficult to estimate. The record of transactions such as the 1906 loan shows that it would be false to assume that the geographical distribution of bond holdings corresponded to the geographical distribution of the offering of the loan. In 1906, German banks unable to participate in the offering because of official pressure bought the Russian loan in London, among other places. The purchase of Russian securities in foreign markets by Russian individuals and institutions was also a growing trend in the years leading up to 1914, and reflected the deepening base of domestic Russian savings and growth of the banking system. That all of these transactions were occurring in an environment (at least till 1914) of free capital flows and fixed exchange rates, and that the securities in question were usually bearer bonds—often kept in safe deposit boxes or under the proverbial mattress—further complicates attempts to develop even a crude metric of foreign versus domestic holdings of Russian debt.[39] It is no accident that the repudiation decree required holders of debt to declare their holdings—the Tsarist government simply never had such data in such an anonymized market, and the Bolsheviks were keen to document the distribution of wealth to facilitate its confiscation.[40] This requirement was in full accordance with Bolshevik practice and echoed the decree on the nationalization of the banks.[41]

In the face of these difficulties, scholarship on the comparative history of sovereign defaults draws on differing estimates to determine the scale of the 1918 Bolshevik repudiation (see Table A.1). Reinhart and Rogoff compiled their estimate by drawing on bond issuance data—two published works, in particular.[42] Based on a tabulation of issuance data, Reinhart and Rogoff estimate the face value of Russian debt at the time of default in 1918 to be $4,560,016,792.[43]

Tomz and Wright, by contrast, rely on the works of Moulton, Pasvolsky, and Apostol. The latter approach is better for several reasons. Leo Pasvolsky was a comparatively junior figure at the time he penned his work, which was billed "a study in investment credit analysis."[44] The Russian émigré, nevertheless, had already published another tome, *The Economics of Communism*, and drew on leading pre-Bolshevik Russian technocrats to inform his work. Harold G. Moulton was a University of Chicago economist who developed an expertise in war debts and would go on to serve as the first president of the Brookings Institution.[45] Unlike Miller, whose work was a general economic history of Russia, Moulton and Pasvolsky wrote their work in the context of the ongoing sparring between Russia and the Western powers over repudiated debts and nationalized private property.

Both the Moulton-Pasvolsky and Apostol volumes were produced by the Carnegie Endowment for International Peace, and were written in a technocratic mode shortly after the repudiation with the aim of determining the size of the default. In fact, Apostol's work is the second of three monographs combined in a single volume with contributions from leaders of the financial policy establishment of pre-Bolshevik Russia, and includes, among other useful data, previously unreleased figures on the Provisional Government's Liberty Loan of 1917. Apostol was himself the assistant to Raffalovich in Paris, and his two coauthors, Michelson and Bernatzky, were academic economists, with the latter having the unenviable task of serving as a minister of finance for the Provisional Government. Kokovtsov, the long-serving finance minister, wrote the introduction to the volume. Indeed, one of the fascinating aspects of this single volume combining three monographs is that it can be read not just as a technocratic treatise on Russian fiscal and monetary policy in the last years of pre-Bolshevik Russia, but also as a memoir of sorts of the leading figures in Russian public finance at the time.

Beyond the pedigree of the authors on whose work it draws, an approach using the Moulton-Pasvolsky and Apostol data is useful because their estimates explicitly account for the impact of the First World War on Russia. Reinhart and Rogoff's compilation of issuance data crucially omits much of the Russian war debt. The last prewar loans in their data are the 1913 Russian 4 Percent Rente (rolled over from 1894) and the City of Vilna Gold Bonds of the same year. The only subsequent issues they cite are the Russian Government Five-Year 5.5 Percent Gold Bond and the Russian Government Three-Year 6.5 Percent Credit Bond, both of 1916.[46] Crucially, in approaching the problem from the standpoint of public issues, Reinhart and Rogoff miss the very large sums that the Russian government raised through inter-Allied loans, which the Bolsheviks also repudiated in their 1918 decree.

Data on war debts are necessarily approximate, because, by Apostol's own admission, "under the circumstances in which Russia ended the war, accurate and final estimates of her war expenditure and debt are not available."[47] Nevertheless, the Moulton-Pasvolsky and Apostol volumes give some sense as to the scale of the war debts. Thus, Apostol notes that the Russian government raised a total of 12.01 billion rubles in nominal domestic debt tied to the war, yielding actual proceeds of 11.4 billion rubles.[48]

Soviet scholars—publishing in Russian, and therefore not consulted by Reinhart, Rogoff, Tomz, or Wright—built on and refined the Apostol and Moulton-Pasvolsky data. Gatrell, for example, drew also on the work of Volobuev on the debt, although the latter's figure of 11.2 billion rubles seems low insofar as it appears to account for only central government debt, narrowly defined.[49] The most interesting of the Soviet assessments of the question, however, is Gindin's 1957 work, which specifically engages the question of the size of the Bolshevik repudiation. Beyond its critical examination of the Moulton-Pasvolsky and Apostol data, Gindin's work offers a new estimate based on documentation from the Credit Chancellery of the old Tsarist and

TABLE A.1. Selected estimates for the size of the Greece, Argentina, and Russia defaults in historical and 2012 dollars (millions)

Greece 2012	€205,600	$271,413			

Argentina 2001 (principal only)		Inflation-adjusted by metric to 2012 US dollars			
	2001 USD	CPI	Unskilled wage index	March 2012 gold price	Share of GDP method
Porzecanski	91,000	118,000	112,000	535,112	139,000
Press reports, including *Bloomberg*	95,000	123,000	117,000	558,633	145,000
CBO, including Paris Club and IMF	97,600	127,000	120,000	573,922	149,000

Russia 1918	Rubles	1918 USD par rates	CPI	Unskilled wage index	March 2012 gold price	Share of GDP method
External only						
Volobuev, central government only	11,194	5,758	87,800	292,000	453,417	1,190,000
Moulton-Pasvolsky, public only	12,823	6,596	101,000	334,000	519,400	1,360,000
Gindin	13,256	6,819	104,000	346,000	536,939	1,410,000
Moulton-Pasvolsky	14,823	7,625	116,000	386,000	600,411	1,580,000

TABLE A.1. (continued)

Russia 1918	Rubles	1918 USD par rates	CPI	Inflation-adjusted by metric to 2012 US dollars		
				Unskilled wage index	March 2012 gold price	Share of GDP method
Domestic and external						
Gindin, ex-Clause 4	30,564	15,722	240,000	797,000	1,238,006	3,250,000
Apostol	39,078	20,101	306,000	1,020,000	1,582,868	4,160,000
Volobuev	49,005	25,207	384,000	1,280,000	1,984,965	5,210,000
Apostol, including State Bank T-bills	52,895	27,208	415,000	1,380,000	2,142,531	5,630,000

Sources: European Commission, "Financial Assistance to Greece"; Porzecanski, "From Rogue Creditors to Rogue Debtors"; *Bloomberg*, "Argentina to Repay IMF Debt"; Hornbeck, "Argentina's Defaulted Sovereign Debt"; Volobuev, *Ekonomicheskaia Politika Vremennogo Pravitel'stva*, 379; Moulton and Pasvolsky, *Russian Debts and Russian Reconstruction*, 17, 21; Gindin, "O Velichenii i Kharaktere Gosudarstvennogo Dolga Rossii v Kontse 1917 Goda," 169–70; Michelson, Apostol, and Bernatzky, *Russian Public Finance during the War*, 321–22.

Notes: Greek figures are represented in 2012 euros and US dollars. The Argentinean figures are represented in 2001 dollars and then inflated according to a variety of metrics for transparency into 2012 dollars. The Russian figures are taken in the first instance in rubles. Given the extreme volatility of exchange rates at the moment of default, ruble values are converted at a normalized exchange rate into US dollars, and then inflated into 2012 terms. The dollar-ruble par in this table is assumed to have been ~1.94 to be conservative. Others have indicated a stronger ruble—the rate implied by Apostol (1.86) only increases the dollar value of Russian sums. Inflation adjustments are made via www .measuringworth.com according to methodologies outlined therein. Official ECB exchange rate used for USD-EUR. "Clause 4" refers to the provision in the original Bolshevik repudiation decree declaring that short-term Treasury obligations remained in force as interest-free notes.

then Provisional Government Ministry of Finance, which was subsumed into and briefly allowed to exist as part of the Bolshevik People's Commissariat for Finance (NarKomFin).[50] This bureaucratic continuity—however brief—that survived the emigration of financial technocrats such as Apostol and Pasvolsky allowed Gindin to compile estimates for the debt at the time of default that are more conservative than the Moulton and Pasvolsky data used by Tomz and Wright, but which are significantly higher than those of Reinhart and Rogoff. Indeed, Gindin's data suggest that the actual value of the Russian default in 1918 was 50 percent higher than that used by Reinhart and Rogoff in their dataset. If the Reinhart and Rogoff data are compared to the much narrower estimate of Volobuev, which includes only central government debt, the former estimate still undervalues the scale of the default in 1918 dollars by more than 25 percent.

Incidentally, if a broader scope is applied so as to include the domestic debt the Bolsheviks simultaneously repudiated in 1918, the scale of the default balloons to more than double the size suggested by Moulton and Pasvolsky's highest estimate of foreign debt. Even Gindin's low total estimate—which does not count in the default figure the short-term debt instruments the Bolsheviks stripped of interest but allowed to circulate as currency—suggests a default of 30.6 billion rubles, or $15.72 billion in 1918 dollars at par.[51] To compare this figure to the Argentinean or Greek defaults may be a bridge too far, but it nonetheless underscores the vast scale of the Russian default of 1918.

While Reinhart and Rogoff adopt data that are too narrow in scope to fully account for the size of the Russian default in historical terms, Tomz and Wright use more comprehensive data but are overly conservative in determining the present value of the debt. In their ranking, Tomz and Wright collect the value of repudiated Russian debt in ruble terms, convert the amount to US dollars at historical exchange rates, and then use the US consumer price index (CPI) to inflate the size of the Bolshevik repudiation to present-day terms.[52] This method is problematic in that the metric they chose to put historical values in contemporary terms does not sufficiently account for the nature of the value in question. While the CPI is the most commonly used inflation adjustment tool, it is also the least useful when comparing large-scale government expenditures, which the Russian debt essentially capitalized.[53] As its name implies, the US CPI is based on the changing prices of American consumer goods over time. As such, it is useful in comparing the US prices of consumer items, such as a loaf of bread, or the workers' wages used to buy such items. If one were comparing the price of a loaf of bread in 1918 to the price today, for example, the CPI would be the ideal metric to use.

Inflating the value of repudiated government debts using the CPI, however, takes into account neither the different spending patterns nor the greater relative size of the sum in question. As McMeekin notes in his own discussion about how best to put historical prices into contemporary perspective, the Bolsheviks did not "purchase largely nonexistent 'consumer bundles' inside Russia."[54] Government spending, and especially spending by the Tsarist and Provisional governments during the First World War and by the Bolsheviks in the context of Civil War, heavily favored the defense and industrial sectors, the price dynamics of which the US CPI does not capture.

Converting based on changes in the gold price is an improvement but also has its flaws. While the war saw countries on the gold standard suspend convertibility as an emergency measure, expectations were that it would be restored upon the cessation of hostilities. As Eichengreen put it, countries sought to "maintain the appearance of the gold standard even when forced to suspend the reality."[55] In this sense, debt and other contracts had an implicit link to gold that makes conversion at prewar parities justifiable. The problem with gold lies not in the historical conversion, but rather in more recent trends in gold prices. In the context of a general commodity boom, financial crises, and unorthodox monetary policies, gold prices have been extremely volatile over the past two decades. At the time of Argentina's default, gold was trading at $276.80 per troy ounce, while just a decade later it had risen by more than six times, to $1,627.68, before falling to less than $1,200 by mid-2012, a drop of 27 percent.[56] In this context, use of an alternate real value as a gauge would be preferable. Labor price indices, for example, are an objective standard against which to measure paper money, while also showing less volatility than gold.

However, even if gold and labor values offer an improvement over the CPI as an inflation metric, such an approach does not account for the relative size of the repudiated debt—what McMeekin aptly calls "the size of a particular fish in the economic sea of that fish's time."[57] Contemporary sources almost universally agree that the size of the Russian debt in aggregate at the time of default was huge in the context of that time. The US CPI does not capture this concept of economic power, whereas a measure such as the share of GDP the sum in question represented does.

If anything, even this latter metric understates the present value of historical sums, given the degree to which holdings of Russian debt were more widely held than those of Greece or Argentina were more recently. Even allowing for the frequently mentioned involvement of retail Italian bondholders in the Argentinean case, the phenomenon of hundreds of thousands of French investors directly buying Russian bonds for decades was not mirrored in more recent debt crises, in which institutional investors dominated fixed-income markets. While this social-psychological aspect of the impact of the default is impossible to capture through economic indicators, it is nonetheless significant.

In considering the range of size estimates for Russia's prewar and wartime debts, converting these debts into dollar and sterling terms, and then inflating by measures that more properly account for the sums in question, it is evident that the Bolshevik repudiation is still the largest in history. Of the measures shown in Table A.1, only the CPI suggests that the defaults of more recent times are larger in inflation-adjusted terms than the Bolshevik default. True, adjusting by the gold price suggests Argentina's default may still be the largest in 2012 dollars, but this particular result should be discounted heavily since, in 2001, global commodity prices were near the bottom of a multidecade trough following the 1997 Asian and associated 1998 Russian crises. Adjusting by the unskilled wage rate index shows the Russian default to have been far larger than that of Argentina—a gap that would only increase if one were to substitute skilled for unskilled wages.

The largest gap is apparent when comparing the results within the framework of economic power. While the scale of the difference between the figures adjusted by share of GDP may suggest hyperbole, they in fact make intuitive sense. Russia was the largest net international debtor in the world during the period in question and held some of the largest gold reserves on Earth, which it lent as necessary to maintain global financial stability, notably to the Bank of England during the Baring Crisis of 1890.[58] Unlike "peripheral" Eurozone member Greece in 2012 or Argentina in 2002, Russia was at the very core of the global financial system during the first modern age of globalization. In this context, that the sudden and total repudiation of one of the largest debts in the world in 1918 could represent a blow equal in force to a $1.5 trillion shock today does not seem unreasonable.

Of course, the approach employed to construct Table A.1 is not perfect. The methodology is notably open to the critique that a more exact measurement would be obtained by taking into account the distribution of foreign debt holdings by country and by applying specific national inflation gauges to convert the debts in question. In this instance, that portion of Russia's debt held in France could be inflated according to French unskilled wage indices, thereby accounting for the large portion of debt placed among ordinary French savers.

While in theory such a method is ideal, it is impossible to put into practice due to the quality of the historical data. Any measures of the distribution of the debts by nation are extremely rough, and further complicated by trading across borders in 1917. In early 1918, for example, the American financial press reported German buying of Russian debt in expectation of favorable treatment should a default occur.[59] The various country-specific estimates compiled by individual Allied governments are similarly unreliable, because both the governments and individual investors had every incentive to overstate their values, and because of the lack of any central and standardized process adopted across countries, there is no accurate way to normalize figures for any double or, for that matter, triple or quadruple counting. As such, the data in Table A.1 are necessarily approximations of both the historical and contemporary value of the debt repudiated by the Bolsheviks. However, a consideration of the size of the margin between the Russian and Greco-Argentinean figures, coupled with an appreciation of the context of the Bolshevik default, which is not reflected in mere currency figures, gives strong support to the notion that the Bolshevik default is still the "largest" in modern financial history.

Conclusion

Recent events in global financial markets have led to an increased interest in the history of sovereign debt. The subject is a complicated one, and any comparisons are open to critiques over accounting methodologies. When adopting a methodology that encompasses the true nature and extent of the debt which the Tsarist and Provisional governments incurred prior to the Bolshevik Revolution of 1917, and which fairly accounts for the present value of these debts, it is evident that the Bolshevik repudiation of all such debts in 1918 was an event that not only was unprecedented in financial history, but to this day remains the single largest default in global financial history.

Of course, skeptics may write off the entire exercise of default ranking across time and space as a narrow academic exercise with little broader significance. Does size really matter? In the case of sovereign debt, it does, because rankings of sovereign default and other major financial and economic events, such as depressions and stock market crises, influence research agendas. Argentina's ranking as the largest default in history in 2001 was important because it continued to attract academic research efforts long after the financial press and investment community moved on to other topics. In this context, the Russian default and the financial turmoil that bracketed it stands out because of not only the size of the shock, but the degree to which it has been all but ignored in both the broad narrative histories of modern international finance as well as more specialist work by financial and economic historians.

NOTES

Introduction

1. Excerpt(s) from *Swann's Way: Within a Budding Grove* (*Remembrance of Things Past*, Vol. 1), by Marcel Proust, translated by C. K. Scott Moncrieff and Terence Kilmartin, translation copyright © 1981 by Penguin Random House LLC and Chatto & Windus. Used by permission of Random House, an imprint and division of Penguin Random House LLC. All rights reserved.

2. Previous scholarship places the Russian default as the third largest in history after the $271 billion Greek default of 2012 and the $98 billion Argentine default of 2001. The appendix details the evidence for the claim that Russia's 1918 default is—in current dollars—still the largest in history. All dollar amounts throughout are in US dollars.

3. William C. Carter, *Marcel Proust: A Life* (New Haven: Yale University Press, 2000), 618.

4. Ibid., 617–18; Jean-Yves Tadié, *Marcel Proust* (New York: Viking, 2000), 507–8.

5. Tadié, *Marcel Proust*, 769.

6. The revolutions of 1917 in Russia took place while the country was still officially using the Julian calendar. As such, what is known as the February Revolution in fact took place in March according to the Gregorian calendar, while the October Revolution that brought the Bolsheviks to power occurred in November.

7. Vladimir Il'ich Lenin, *Imperialism, the Highest Stage of Capitalism: A Popular Outline* (*1917*), in *V. I. Lenin: Collected Works* (Moscow: Progress Publishers, 1974), 22:183, 188.

8. Ibid., 22:195.

9. Ibid., 22:211–13.

10. Ibid., 22:218.

11. Ibid., 22:222–23, 277–78.

12. Ibid., 22:282–83.

13. See Chapter 5. The description of the October Revolution as a Bolshevik coup d'état is the subject of historiographical controversy. The term is used in this book not in a partisan or ideological sense within the framework of this debate, but neutrally and in keeping with how the Bolsheviks themselves referred to the events of October as a *perevorot*. For more on the historiographical debate, see Ronald Grigor Suny, "Revision and Retreat in the Historiography of 1917: Social History and Its Critics," *Russian Review* 53, no. 2 (April 1994): 165–82, doi:10.2307/130821.

14. Sheila Fitzpatrick, *The Russian Revolution*, 2nd ed. (Oxford: Oxford University Press, 2001), 33, 39.

15. Oleg V. Budnitskii, *Den'gi Russkoi Emigratsii: Kolchakovskoe Zoloto, 1918–1957* (Moscow: Novoe Literaturnoe Obozrenie, 2008), 21.

16. Ekaterina A. Pravilova, *Finansy Imperii: Den'gi i Vlast' v Politike Rossii na Natsional'nykh Okrainakh, 1801–1917* (Moscow: Novoe Izdatel'stvo, 2006).

17. Leon Trotsky, *My Life* (New York: Charles Scribner's Sons, 1930), 441.

18. Vladimir Il'ich Lenin, "Report on the Activities of the Council of People's Commissars, 24 January 1918," in *V. I. Lenin: Collected Works*, 26:455.

19. Crane Brinton, *The Anatomy of Revolution*, 2nd ed. (New York: Vintage, 1965). See in particular the preface to the first (1956) Vintage edition.

20. Ibid., 18.

21. Theda Skocpol, *States and Social Revolutions: A Comparative Analysis of France, Russia, and China* (Cambridge: Cambridge University Press, 1979).

22. Vladimir A. Mau and Irina Starodubrovskaya, *The Challenge of Revolution: Contemporary Russia in Historical Perspective* (New York: Oxford University Press, 2001), 25–26, 30.

23. Ibid., 2.

24. Brinton, *Anatomy of Revolution*, 19.

25. Mau and Starodubrovskaya, *Challenge of Revolution*, 99.

26. Brinton, *Anatomy of Revolution*, 29.

27. Ibid., 30.

28. Mau and Starodubrovskaya, *Challenge of Revolution*, 334.

29. Ibid.

30. Moritz Schularick, "A Tale of Two 'Globalizations': Capital Flows from Rich to Poor in Two Eras of Global Finance," *International Journal of Finance and Economics* 11 (2006): 342, doi:100.1002/ijfe.302.

31. Ibid., 343.

32. Hong Kong has itself graduated in many rankings to "developed" status. If one were to exclude Hong Kong, the highest ranking "emerging market" in Schularick's foreign investment ranking in 2001 would be China in the 11th position, with only 2.3 percent of total global foreign investment. Schularick, "Tale of Two 'Globalizations,'" 343.

33. Ibid., 346; Robert E. Lucas, "Why Doesn't Capital Flow from Rich to Poor Countries?," *American Economic Review* 80, no. 2 (May 1990): 92–96, doi:10.2307/2006549.

34. For an example of this, see Charles Robertson, Yvonne Mhango, and Michael Moran, *The Fastest Billion: The Story Behind Africa's Economic Revolution* (London: Renaissance Capital, 2012).

35. "Economics Focus: Why the Tail Wags the Dog," *Economist*, 6 August 2011, http://www.economist.com/node/21525373.

36. "MSCI Emerging Markets Index Factsheet," *MSCI*, 30 March 2018, https://www.msci.com/resources/factsheets/index_fact_sheet/msci-emerging-markets-index-usd-net.pdf; "MSCI World Index Factsheet," *MSCI*, 30 March 2018, https://www.msci.com/resources/factsheets/index_fact_sheet/msci-world-index.pdf.

37. Jim O'Neill, "Building Better Global Economic BRICs," Goldman Sachs Global Economic Papers (30 November 2001), http://www.goldmansachs.com/our-thinking/archive/archive-pdfs/build-better-brics.pdf; Gillian Tett, "The Story of the Brics," *Financial Times*, 15 January 2010.

38. Rondo E. Cameron, Valerii I. Bovykin, and Boris V. Anan'ich, eds., *International Banking, 1870–1914* (New York: Oxford University Press, 1991), 13.

39. Ibid.

40. Marc Flandreau and Frédéric Zumer, *The Making of Global Finance, 1880–1913* (Paris: Organisation for Economic Co-operation and Development, 2004), 29.

41. Michael D. Bordo and Hugh Rockoff, "The Gold Standard as a 'Good Housekeeping Seal of Approval,'" *Journal of Economic History* 56, no. 2 (June 1996): 389, doi:10.2307/2123971.

42. Ibid., 414–15.

43. Ibid., 415.

44. Maurice Obstfeld and Alan M. Taylor, "Sovereign Risk, Credibility and the Gold Standard: 1870–1913 versus 1925–31," *Economic Journal* 113, no. 487 (April 2003): 244. One basis point equals one one-hundredth of a percent.

45. Niall Ferguson and Moritz Schularick, "The 'Thin Film of Gold': Monetary Rules and Policy Credibility," *European Review of Economic History* 16 (2012): 384–407, doi:10.1093/ereh/hes006.

46. Obstfeld and Taylor, "Sovereign Risk," 265–66.

47. Ferguson and Schularick, "'Thin Film of Gold.'"

48. Douglass C. North and Barry R. Weingast, "Constitutions and Commitment: The Evolution of Institutions Governing Public Choice in Seventeenth-Century England," *Journal of Economic History* 49, no. 4 (December 1989): 803–32, doi:10.2307/2122739.

49. Ibid., 824.

50. Ibid., 831–32.

51. Flandreau and Zumer, *Making of Global Finance*, 33–34. The authors are careful to note that economic thinkers of the time did conceive of a measure of national income like GDP, but faced statistical barriers in terms of standardized data collection and reporting mechanisms.

52. Ibid., 57–58.

53. Ibid., 97. The Service des études financières was a research department of Crédit Lyonnais that conducted extensive in-house proprietary analyses of economic conditions across a range of countries.

54. Ibid., 38–39.

55. Niall Ferguson and Moritz Schularick, "The Empire Effect: The Determinants of Country Risk in the First Age of Globalization, 1880–1913," *Journal of Economic History* 66, no. 2 (June 2006): 283–312.

56. Michael Tomz, *Reputation and International Cooperation: Sovereign Debt across Three Centuries* (Princeton: Princeton University Press, 2007), 14–17.

57. Paolo Mauro, Nathan Sussman, and Yishay Yafeh, *Emerging Markets and Financial Globalization: Sovereign Bond Spreads in 1870–1913 and Today* (Oxford: Oxford University Press, 2006), 7.

58. Flandreau and Zumer, *Making of Global Finance*, 97–98.

59. Marc Flandreau, Juan H. Flores, Norbert Gaillard, and Sebastián Nieto-Parra, "The End of Gatekeeping: Underwriters and the Quality of Sovereign Bond Markets, 1815–2007," *NBER International Seminar on Macroeconomics* 6, no. 1 (2009): 53.

60. Ibid., 81.

61. The authors are right to draw the distinction between current and historical practice as related to bond markets, but in the contemporary market for equity securities investment banks still do play a de facto role as certifiers of issues. They also often play a "buyer of last

resort" role to support initial public offerings (IPOs) in the secondary market, although this has limits.

62. Flandreau et al., "End of Gatekeeping," 72.

63. Marc Flandreau and Juan H. Flores, "The Peaceful Conspiracy: Bond Markets and International Relations During the Pax Britannica," *International Organization* 66, no. 2 (2012): 211–41.

64. Flandreau et al., "End of Gatekeeping," 60.

65. Flandreau and Zumer, *Making of Global Finance*, 46.

66. Vincent Bignon and Marc Flandreau, "The Economics of Badmouthing: Libel Law and the Underworld of the Financial Press in France Before World War I," *Journal of Economic History* 71, no. 3 (2011): 616–53, doi:10.1017/S0022050711001860.

67. The classic study on Franco-Russian financial ties, researched in the 1960s and first published in 1973, is René Girault, *Emprunts Russes et Investissements Français En Russie, 1887–1914* (1973; Paris: Comité pour l'Histoire Economique et Financière de la France, 1999).

Chapter 1: Fault Lines

1. Centre des Archives Économiques et Financières (CAEF) B/0031250/1, de Montebello in Saint Petersburg to Ribot in Paris, 8 September 1892.

2. Orlando Figes, *A People's Tragedy: The Russian Revolution, 1891–1924* (New York: Penguin, 1998), 158.

3. V. L. Stepanov, "Laying the Groundwork for Sergei Witte's Monetary Reform: The Policy of Finance Minister I. A. Vyshnegradskii (1887–1892)," *Russian Studies in History* 47, no. 3 (December 2008): 64, doi:10.2753/RSH1061-1983470302.

4. "The Projected New Russian Loan," *Economist*, 15 October 1892.

5. "Germany," *Economist*, 10 September 1892.

6. CAEF/B0031250/1, de Montebello in Saint Petersburg to Ribot in Paris, 8 September 1892.

7. Richard Pipes, *The Russian Revolution* (New York: Knopf, 1990), 31.

8. CAEF/B0031250/1, de Montebello in Saint Petersburg to Ribot in Paris, 8 September 1892.

9. Fitzpatrick, *Russian Revolution*, 23.

10. Pipes, *Russian Revolution*, 77.

11. Vladimir Il'ich Lenin, "The Dying Authority and New Organs of Popular Rule, 6 October 1905," in *V. I. Lenin: Collected Works*, 10:66.

12. Daniel Yergin, *The Prize: The Epic Quest for Oil, Money, & Power* (New York: Free Press, 1993), 128.

13. Francis William Wcislo, "Sergei Witte and His Times: A Historiographical Note," *Kritika: Explorations in Russian and Eurasian History* 5, no. 4 (2004): 749–58, doi:10.1353/kri.2004.0064; B. V. Anan'ich and R. Sh. Ganelin, *Sergei Iul'evich Vitte I Ego Vremia* (Saint Petersburg: Russian Academy of Sciences, 1999), 60.

14. Anan'ich and Ganelin, *Sergei Iul'evich Vitte I Ego Vremia*, 69.

15. Sidney Harcave, *Count Sergei Witte and the Twilight of Imperial Russia: A Biography* (Armonk, NY: M.E. Sharpe, 2004), 49.

16. Ibid., 50.

17. Theodore H. Von Laue, *Sergei Witte and the Industrialization of Russia* (New York: Columbia University Press, 1963), 5.

18. Ibid., 35.

19. Ibid., 293.

20. See Francis W. Wcislo, *Tales of Imperial Russia: The Life and Times of Sergei Witte, 1849–1915* (New York: Oxford University Press, 2011), 143.

21. Anan'ich and Ganelin, *Sergei Iiul'evich Vitte I Ego Vremia*, 69.

22. Girault, *Emprunts Russes*, 36, 39–40.

23. Anan'ich and Ganelin, *Sergei Iiul'evich Vitte I Ego Vremia*, 83.

24. Wcislo, *Tales of Imperial Russia*, 121.

25. Niall Ferguson, *The House of Rothschild: The World's Banker, 1849–1999*, vol. 2 (New York: Penguin, 1998), 381.

26. Wcislo, *Tales of Imperial Russia*, 144.

27. Sergei Witte, *The Memoirs of Count Witte*, trans. and ed. Abraham Yarmolinsky (Garden City, NY: Doubleday, 1921), ix.

28. George F. Kennan, "The Curious Monsieur Cyon," *American Scholar* 55, no. 4 (September 1986): 451.

29. Ibid., 454, 464–65.

30. Ibid., 458.

31. Ibid., 460.

32. Ibid., 460–62, 468. Cyon would later be suspected of authoring an anti-Semitic text, "The Protocols of the Elders of Zion."

33. Ibid., 464.

34. Ibid. Partly because of Cyon's accusations, Vyshnegradskii was notorious for personally profiting from Russian government loans.

35. Élie de Cyon, "Où la Dictature de M. Witte Conduit la Russie" (Paris: Haar et Steinert, Eichler Successeur, 1897); Élie de Cyon, "M. Witte et Les Finances Russes d'Après des Documents Officiels et Inédits" (Paris: Chamerot et Renouard, 1895).

36. Andrey Ukhov, "Financial Innovation and Russian Government Debt Before 1918" (Yale ICF Working Paper 03-20, May 2003), 5.

37. Ibid., 6–7.

38. Olga Crisp, "Russian Financial Policy and the Gold Standard at the End of the Nineteenth Century," *Economic History Review*, n.s., 6, no. 2 (January 1953): 156, doi:10.2307/2590949.

39. Ukhov, "Financial Innovation," 8.

40. Ibid., 9; Crisp, "Russian Financial Policy," 156.

41. Calculated from data in Ukhov, "Financial Innovation," 9–10.

42. Ibid., 10.

43. "Predstavlenie v Komitet Finansov 'O Razreshenii Sdelok Na Zolotuiu Monetu,' 4 February 1895," in Sergei Witte, *S. Iu. Vitte: Sobranie Sochinenii i Dokumental'nykh Materialov* (Moscow: Nauka, 2006), 3.1:36–37. In finance, Gresham's Law is the principle that "bad money drives out good" as people would rather hoard a valuable currency when they can engage in transactions with a newly introduced and debased, inferior currency.

44. Crisp, "Russian Financial Policy," 157.

45. Ibid.

46. "Predstavlenie v Komitet Finansov," 59.

47. Ibid. The Imperial was a gold coin and unit of account equivalent to 10 rubles and used in international settlements. The 5-ruble Demi-Imperial was nearly equal to the 20-franc coin. See Crisp, "Russian Financial Policy," 158.

48. Crisp, "Russian Financial Policy," 159.

49. Quoted in ibid.

50. Ibid.

51. "Predstavlenie v Komitet Finansov," 59; Crisp, "Russian Financial Policy," 166.

52. Élie de Cyon, M. Witte et ses Projects de Faillite: Devant le Conseil de l'Empire, trans. Victor Derély (Paris: Haar & Steinert, A. Eichler, 1897), 2.

53. Crisp, "Russian Financial Policy," 167.

54. Ibid.

55. Ibid.

56. Cyon, M. Witte et ses Projects de Faillite, 2.

57. Ibid., 6–7.

58. Ibid., 19.

59. Ibid., 22–23.

60. Ibid., 23.

61. Ibid., vii, 13.

62. Ibid., 7.

63. Ibid., 5.

64. Ibid., 11.

65. In discussing foreign investment, economists draw distinctions between portfolio investment and foreign direct investment (FDI). Portfolio investment represents investment in securities and other liquid assets that can be relatively quickly converted into cash and withdrawn rapidly—often in seconds. FDI, by contrast, represents major stakes in companies, investment in physical assets, and other less liquid forms of investment that take a significantly longer period to exit. From the standpoint of a recipient economy, investment in the form of FDI is generally preferable to portfolio investment insofar as the former represents a deeper level of commitment and confidence on the part of the foreign investor and provides a more stable base of funding.

66. Girault, Emprunts Russes, 84. In finance, bonds have a face value that represents the principal amount that investors receive upon redemption by the issuer. The price at which a bond is issued or traded, however, may and frequently does diverge from the face value. It was common practice at the time to issue Russian and other foreign bonds at a discount to face value, thus increasing the rate of return to investors.

67. Ibid., 85.

68. Paul R. Gregory, Russian National Income, 1885–1913 (Cambridge: Cambridge University Press, 1982), 56–58.

69. In simplest terms, the current yield can be defined as the percentage rate that results from dividing the annual coupon payments on a bond by the price of the bond $\left(\text{yield} = \frac{\text{coupon}}{\text{price of bond}}\right)$. Thus, the current yield for a bond with annual coupons of $5 trading in the market at $96 is 5.21 percent. Spreads are typically expressed in basis points, with one basis point equaling one one-hundredth of a percent.

70. The maturity, or time until a bond is repaid, can influence the return of a bond, as can any embedded options in the bond that would allow an issuer to repay the bond early or otherwise change the payment terms or schedule. Today, investors frequently quote bond yields on a "yield to maturity" basis to normalize for different maturities in comparisons between bonds. Furthermore, investors today often adjust prices and yields to account for embedded options in bonds. For the purposes of this study—which considers bonds at a time when maturities were typically very long and when investors did not have the benefit of the yield calculators or derivative pricing models used by traders today—simple yields instead of yields to maturity and option-adjusted spreads are used. This is in keeping with what was the typical convention at the time.

71. Crisp, "Russian Financial Policy," 171.

72. Ibid., 171.

73. Calculated from data in Gregory, *Russian National Income*, 56–58.

74. Calculated from data in Arcadius Kahan, *Russian Economic History: The Nineteenth Century*, ed. Roger Weiss (Chicago: University of Chicago Press, 1989), 30.

75. Calculated from data in P. A. Khromov, *Ekonomicheskoe Razvitie Rossii v XIX–XX Vekakh, 1800–1917* (Moscow: Gosudarstvennoe Izdatel'stvo Politicheskoi Literatury, 1950), 459.

76. Marshall I. Goldman, *The Enigma of Soviet Petroleum: Half-Full or Half-Empty?* (Boston: Allen & Unwin, 1980), 19.

77. Calculated from data in Khromov, *Ekonomicheskoe Razvitie Rossii*, 456.

78. Calculated from data in Kahan, *Russian Economic History*, 15.

79. Anan'ich and Ganelin, *Sergei Iiul'evich Vitte I Ego Vremia*, 72.

80. Girault, *Emprunts Russes*, 98.

81. Ibid., 100.

82. Gregory, *Russian National Income*, 56–58.

83. Calculated from data in Khromov, *Ekonomicheskoe Razvitie Rossii*, 456.

84. Calculated from data in ibid., 459.

85. "Germany," *Economist*, 3 September 1892.

86. If one is to consider the spreads not in terms of basis points but in terms of the ratio that the spread represents over the raw yield of consols, thus controlling for changes in the yield on consols, the magnitude of the changes attributable to each period is similar, with more than 60 percent of the decline taking place before Witte's tenure.

87. Bordo and Rockoff, "Gold Standard." See also the literature review on this theme in the introduction.

88. Paul R. Gregory, "The Russian Balance of Payments, the Gold Standard, and Monetary Policy: A Historical Example of Foreign Capital Movements," *Journal of Economic History* 39, no. 2 (June 1979): 379–400, doi:10.2307/2118944.

89. Ibid., 391. In finance, the discount rate is the rate the central bank charges banks to borrow from it. While the authorities in theory change the discount rate to reflect market realities, it is in fact set by a small number of officials. The interest rates in the secondary market for sovereign debt, by contrast, reflect the daily—and typically more volatile—views of a much larger and more diverse group of domestic and foreign investors.

90. Ibid., 381.

91. Ibid., 385.

92. Ukhov, "Financial Innovation," 4.

93. Crisp, "Russian Financial Policy," 156.

94. Ibid.

95. Ibid., 159.

96. Anan'ich and Ganelin, *Sergei Iul'evich Vitte I Ego Vremia*, 70.

97. Ibid., 88; Von Laue, *Sergei Witte*, 83.

98. Anan'ich and Ganelin, *Sergei Iul'evich Vitte I Ego Vremia*, 70.

99. Ibid., 83.

100. B. V. Anan'ich and Valerii I. Bovykin, "Foreign Banks and Foreign Investment in Russia," in Cameron, Bovykin, and Anan'ich, *International Banking*, 84.

101. Anan'ich and Ganelin, *Sergei Iul'evich Vitte I Ego Vremia*, 88.

102. Harcave, *Count Sergei Witte*, 10.

103. Anan'ich and Bovykin, "Foreign Banks," 84.

104. Sergei Witte, *The Memoirs of Count Witte*, trans. and ed. Sidney Harcave (New York: Routledge, 2015), 176.

105. D. E. Sorokin, "Vvodnoe Slovo: S. Iu. Vitte i Finansy Rossii," in *S.Iu. Vitte: Sobranie Sochinenii i Dokumental'nykh Materialov*, vol. 2, bk. 1 (Moscow: Nauka, 2003), 7.

106. Stepanov, "Laying the Groundwork," 46.

107. Ibid.

108. Witte, *Memoirs of Count Witte*, trans. and ed. Abraham Yarmolinsky, 59.

109. "Arthur Raffalovich," *New York Times*, 13 January 1922.

110. For a study that makes use of this unusual source, see Kim Oosterlinck and John S. Landon-Lane, "Hope Springs Eternal—French Bondholders and the Soviet Repudiation (1915–1919)," *Review of Finance* 10, no. 4 (2006): 507–35.

111. Bignon and Flandreau, "Economics of Badmouthing."

112. In finance, speculators can bet on a downward movement in a security by "shorting" the instrument in question. In its simplest form, shorting entails borrowing the security in question and then selling it immediately for cash, betting that a decline in the price of the security will allow one to buy it back at a lower price, thus "covering" the short and pocketing the difference between the initial sale price and the repurchase price as a profit. Without hedging, however, shorting a security can be a particularly risky strategy because unlike a "long" strategy, in which one bets on an increase in a security's price and has a maximum theoretical loss of 100 percent, a short strategy's maximum potential loss is unlimited. A "short squeeze" occurs when the market in a security that speculators have heavily shorted sees a dearth of the security in question. Attempting to cover their positions, speculators with short positions scramble to buy the security to avoid massive losses—an act that generates a self-fulfilling prophecy and a violent price spike. For this reason, large speculative short positions in otherwise benighted securities are themselves seen as a positive sign.

113. CAEF/B0031250/1, de Chambres in Warsaw to Hanotaux in Paris, 31 October 1894.

114. Ibid.

115. Ibid.

116. Ibid.

117. Ibid.

118. Youssef Cassis, *Capitals of Capital: A History of International Financial Centres, 1780–2005*, trans. Jacqueline Collier (Cambridge: Cambridge University Press, 2006), 79.

119. Ibid., 98.

120. Ibid., 99.

121. Morgan Library (ML) ARC 1214 Box 35, A. Koch to J. Pierpont Morgan, 22 February 1898.

122. William Craft Brumfield, Boris V. Anan'ich, and Yuri A. Petrov, eds., *Commerce in Russian Urban Culture, 1861–1914* (Washington, DC: Baltimore: Johns Hopkins University Press, 2002), 16; ML ARC 1214 Box 35, A. Koch to J. Pierpont Morgan, 22 February 1898.

123. ML ARC 1214 Box 35, A. Koch to J. Pierpont Morgan, 22 February 1898.

124. Ibid.

125. Ibid.

126. Ibid.

127. Cameron, Bovykin, and Anan'ich, *International Banking*, 303.

128. Ibid., 303.

129. Ibid.

130. Ruth Amende Roosa, "Banking and Financial Relations between Russia and the United States," in Cameron, Bovykin, and Anan'ich, *International Banking*, 291, 293.

131. Ibid., 296.

132. Ibid.

133. Ibid., 302.

134. Ibid., 305.

135. Ibid.

136. Ibid.

137. Ibid.

138. Anan'ich and Bovykin, "Foreign Banks," 260.

139. Ibid., 260–61.

140. Ibid., 261.

141. Ibid.

142. Roosa, "Banking and Financial Relations," 305.

143. Ibid., 306.

144. Ibid.

145. Ibid.

146. Ibid., 308.

147. BAR/HC10–63(v), Barings London to Baring, Magoun New York, 2 May 1899.

148. A bond "issuer" is a government, company, or other entity issuing the bond. In doing so, the entity is taking on a loan. As such, the words "issuer," "borrower," and "debtor" are used interchangeably in discussions of sovereign debt. Conversely, "investor", "lender," and "creditor" are used interchangeably in referring to the owners of the bonds in question.

149. BAR/HC10–63(v), Barings London to Baring, Magoun in New York, 2 May 1899.

150. BAR/HC10–63(v), Baring, Magoun in New York to Barings in London, 3 May 1899.

151. BAR/HC10–63(v), Revelstoke in London to Baring, Magoun in New York, 2 May 1899.

152. BAR/HC10–63(v), Revelstoke in London to Hope & Co. in Amsterdam, 3 May 1899.

153. BAR/HC10–63(v), Barings in London to Hope & Co. in Amsterdam, 4 May 1899.

154. BAR/HC10–63(v), Hope in Amsterdam to Barings in London, 4 May 1899.

155. Ibid.

156. Ibid.

157. BAR/HC10–63(v), Hope in Amsterdam to Barings in London, 5 May 1899.

158. Ibid.

159. Ibid.

160. BAR/HC10–63(v), Barings in London to Hope in Amsterdam, 6 May 1899.

161. BAR/HC10–63(v), Barings in London to Hope in Amsterdam, 8 May 1899.

162. Ibid. Barings was a particularly active lender to the Russian government for much of the nineteenth century, engaging frequently in deals in tandem with Hope & Co.; see Anan'ich and Bovykin, "Foreign Banks," 257.

163. BAR/HC10–63(v), Hope in Amsterdam to Barings in London, 5 May 1899; Barings in London to Hope in Amsterdam, 8 May 1899.

164. BAR/HC10–63(v), Barings in London to Hope in Amsterdam, 8 May 1899; Hope in Amsterdam to Barings in London, 9 May 1899.

165. BAR/HC10–63(v), Barings London to Baring, Magoun in New York, 11 May 1899.

166. BAR/HC10–63(v), Cables between Barings London and Baring, Magoun New York, 11 to 19 May 1899.

167. BAR/HC10–63(v), Baring, Magoun, New York to Barings London, 19 May 1899.

168. ML ARC 1214 Box 12, Correspondence between J. S. Morgan & Co. and J. P. Morgan (NY), 20–21 December 1898.

169. BAR/HC10–63(v), Betzold to Barings London, 20 May 1899; Barings London to Baring, Magoun, New York, 20 May 1899.

170. BAR/HC10–63(v), Barings London to J. P. Morgan Paris, 20 May 1899; Betzold to Barings London, 22 May 1899; Revelstoke London to Betzold, 5 May 1899; Barings London to Hope & Co., 23 May 1899.

171. BAR/HC10–63(v), Barings London to Baring, Magoun, New York, 21 May 1899; Barings London to Hope & Co., 23 May 1899.

172. BAR/HC10–63(v), Barings London to Baring, Magoun, New York, 23 May 1899. Revelstoke had seen a partner of Mendelssohn the same day who said there was little chance of a deal happening in the near term; see Revelstoke to John Luden in Amsterdam, 23 May 1899.

173. BAR/HC10–63(v), Barings London to Baring, Magoun, New York, 23 May 1899.

174. BAR/HC10–63(v), Revelstoke to Stillman, 26 May 1899.

175. Ibid.

176. Ibid.

177. Ibid.

178. Ibid.

179. BAR HC10–63(v), Thomas Baring to G. F. Crane, 26 May 1899.

180. Ibid.

181. Ibid.

182. Ibid.

183. BAR HC10–63(v), Revelstoke to John Luden, Amsterdam, 29 May 1899.

184. BAR HC10–63(v), Luden to Revelstoke, 31 May 1899.

185. ML ARC 1214 Box 35, Saunders & Co. to J. S. Morgan & Co., 1 August 1899.

186. Ibid.

187. Ibid.

188. Ibid.

189. Ibid.

190. ML ARC 1214 Box 35, J. P. Morgan to J. P. "Jack" Morgan, Jr., 16 August 1899.

191. Philip Ziegler, *The Sixth Great Power: Barings 1762–1929* (London: Collins, 1988), 10.

192. Roosa, "Banking and Financial Relations," 305.

193. Ibid., 308.

194. See, for example, Russian State Historical Archive (RGIA) 560/22/188/20–25, Raffa-lovich in London to Witte in Saint Petersburg, 5 December 1894; and Sergei Iulievich Witte, *Vospominaniia: Tsarstvovanie Nikolaia II*, 2 vols. (Berlin: Slovo, 1922), 2:194.

195. Witte, *Vospominaniia*, 2:194.

196. Ferguson, *House of Rothschild*, 381.

197. Ibid., 381–82.

198. See, for example, the Rothschild Archive, London (RAL) XI/130A/2/19080603, Lon-don to Paris, 3 June 1908.

199. Anan'ich and Bovykin, "Foreign Banks," 261.

200. S. K. Lebedev, "Biudzhet i Gosudarstvennyi Dolg Rossii pri S. Iu. Vitte," in *Sobranie Sochinenii i Dokumental'nykh Materialov S. Iu. Vitte*, vol. 2, Book 2 (Moscow: Nauka, 2002), 16.

201. Ferguson, *House of Rothschild*, 383.

202. Ibid.

203. Lebedev, "Biudzhet i Gossudarstvennyi," 17.

204. BAR/HC10–63(v), Hope Amsterdam to Barings London, 5 May 1899.

205. CAEF B-0031252–2 French Ambassador in Saint Petersburg, de Montebello to French Finance Ministry with Review of 1893 Budget, 17 January 1893.

Chapter 2: The Loan That Saved Russia?

1. Witte, *Vospominaniia*, 2:202.

2. Figes, *People's Tragedy*, 200.

3. Ibid., 202.

4. Witte, *Vospominaniia*, 2:201.

5. Ibid., 2:202.

6. Pipes, *Russian Revolution*, 50. See also Witte, *Vospominaniia*, 2:217.

7. Witte, *Memoirs of Count Witte*, trans. and ed. Abraham Yarmolinsky, esp. chap 11; Harcave, *Count Sergei Witte*, chap. 19.

8. Vladimir Il'ich Lenin, *"Left-Wing" Communism—An Infantile Disorder (1920)*, in *V. I. Lenin: Collected Works*, 31:27.

9. Girault, *Emprunts Russes*, 347.

10. Gregory, *Russian National Income*, 56–58.

11. "Uncertainty in Russia: General Trend of Affairs Favorable, but Many Elements in the Political Situation May Affect Business," *New York Times*, 3 January 1904.

12. Abraham Ascher, *The Revolution of 1905: Russia in Disarray* (Stanford: Stanford Univer-sity Press, 1988).

13. "Russia Shows War's Effect: She Exports No More Grain into Germany," *New York Times*, 20 February 1904.

14. Ascher, *Revolution of 1905: Russia in Disarray,* 52–53.

15. Ibid., 1:53.

16. Ibid.

17. Ibid.

18. "The Industrial Crisis in Russia," *New York Times,* 24 January 1904; James Long, "Franco-Russian Relations during the Russo-Japanese War," *Slavonic and East European Review* 52, no. 127 (April 1974): 213–33, doi:10.2307/4206868.

19. "The Finances of Russia," *Economist,* 23 January 1904.

20. Long, "Franco-Russian Relations," 215–18.

21. Ibid., 222.

22. Ibid.

23. Ibid. Kokovtsov's plan was to raise 800 million francs in Paris, with the remainder in Berlin, Amsterdam, and Saint Petersburg.

24. Ibid., 224.

25. Witte died in 1915.

26. Whereas the original Russian edition of Witte's memoirs simply titles the chapter in question "The Loan," the abridged and edited English edition, published contemporaneously, uses the more elaborate "The Loan That Saved Russia." Girault and others, using translated versions of the memoirs or a 1913 pamphlet by Witte on the loan, have incorrectly attributed the expression to Witte, who in the original full-length Russian version of his memoirs attributes the expression to Kokovtsov, who first used it in a speech in the First Duma shortly after the loan was floated. See Witte, *Vospominaniia,* 2:219.

27. Ibid., 2:192.

28. Ibid., 2:198, 202.

29. Ibid., 2:217–18.

30. Ibid., 2:219. Witte did use the term in his 1913 pamphlet, but only after Kokovtsov introduced it.

31. Pipes, *Russian Revolution,* 50.

32. Fitzpatrick, *Russian Revolution,* 36.

33. Figes, *People's Tragedy,* 216.

34. Ibid., 217.

35. Olga Crisp, "The Russian Liberals and the 1906 Anglo-French Loan to Russia," *Slavonic and East European Review* 39, no. 93 (June 1961): 497.

36. Ibid.; Seema Jayachandran and Michael Kremer, "Odious Debt," *American Economic Review* 96, no. 1 (March 2006): 82, doi:10.2307/30034355.

37. Girault, *Emprunts Russes,* 447.

38. See in particular the reprinted memorandum addressed to the French government by Maklakov, dated 18 April 1906—two days after the loan contract was signed at the Russian embassy in Crisp, "Russian Liberals," 508–11. On Kadet distancing from repudiation, see Abraham Ascher, *The Revolution of 1905: Authority Restored* (Stanford: Stanford University Press, 1992), 2:58.

39. Long, "Franco-Russian Relations"; James W. Long, "French Attempts at Constitutional Reform in Russia," *Jahrbücher Für Geschichte Osteuropas* 23, no. 4 (January 1975): 496–503, doi:10.2307/41045104; James W. Long, "Organized Protest Against the 1906 Russian Loan,"

Cahiers Du Monde Russe et Soviétique 13, no. 1 (January 1972): 24–39. For a more recent account, focused more on the French perspective, see Suzanne Berger, "Puzzles from the First Globalization," in *Politics in the New Hard Times*, ed. Miles Kahler and David Lake (Ithaca: Cornell University Press, 2013), http://dspace.mit.edu/handle/1721.1/71702.

40. Long, "Organized Protest," 39.

41. Ibid.; James Macdonald, *A Free Nation Deep in Debt: The Financial Roots of Democracy* (Princeton: Princeton University Press, 2006), 430; Carmen M. Reinhart and Kenneth S. Rogoff, *This Time Is Different: Eight Centuries of Financial Folly*, reprint ed. (Princeton University Press, 2009), 12.

42. Girault, *Emprunts Russes*, 430.

43. Ascher, *Revolution of 1905: Authority Restored*, 58.

44. Ibid., 58.

45. Long, "Organized Protest," 39.

46. James W. Long, "Russian Manipulation of the French Press, 1904–1906," *Slavic Review* 31, no. 2 (June 1972): 354, doi:10.2307/2494338.

47. Crisp, "Russian Liberals," 498, 508.

48. Ibid., 508.

49. Long, "Franco-Russian Relations," 233.

50. Sergei Witte, "Spravka o tom, kak byl Zakliuchen Vneshnii Zaem 1906 g., Spashii Finansovoe Polozhenie Rossii," in Witte, *S. Iu. Vitte*, 2.2:436.

51. BAR/200164, Revelstoke to Landsdowne, 11 September 1905.

52. BAR/200164, Revelstoke to Baring Brothers & Co., 15 October 1905, 21 October 1905.

53. ML ARC 1214 Box 10 J. P. Morgan, Jr. to J. P. Morgan, 4 and 5 October 1905.

54. ML ARC 1216 (003) Box 4, J. P. Morgan, Jr. to Walter and E.C. Grenfell, 3 February 1905; J. P. Morgan, Jr. to E. C. Grenfell, 24 February 1905; J. P. Morgan, Jr. to Vivian Smith, 7 April 1905.

55. ML ARC 1214 Box 10, J. P. Morgan to J. P. Morgan, Jr., 5 October 1905.

56. ML ARC 1214 Box 10, J. P. Morgan Jr., to J. P. Morgan, 7 and 10 October 1905.

57. ML ARC 1214 Box 10, G. W. Perkins and J. P. Morgan, Jr. to J. P. Morgan, 12 October 1905, J. P. Morgan, Jr. to J. P. M., 17 October 1905 and BAR 200164, Revelstoke to Hardinge and Revelstoke to Noetzlin, 12 October 1905.

58. Pipes, *Russian Revolution*, 37.

59. BAR/200164, Revelstoke to Baring Brothers & Co., 21 October 1905.

60. ML ARC 1216 (017) Box 31, J. P. Morgan Jr. and G. W. Perkins to J. P. M., 21 October 1905 and ARC 1214 Box 10, Memorandum on Russia, 21 October 1905.

61. ML ARC 1216 (017) Box 31, J. P. Morgan to G. W. Perkins and J. P. Morgan, Jr., 17 October 1905.

62. ML ARC 1216 (017) Box 31, J. P. Morgan, Jr. and G. W. Perkins to J. P. Morgan, 18 October 1905.

63. ML ARC 1216 (017) Box 31, J. P. Morgan to G. W. Perkins and J. P. Morgan, Jr., 22 October 1905.

64. Ibid.

65. ML ARC 1216 (017) Box 31, G. W. Perkins and J. P. Morgan, Jr. to J. P. M., 22 October 1905.

66. Ibid.

67. ML ARC 1216 (017) Box 31, Perkins and Jack Morgan to J. P. M. in NY, 23 October 1905.

68. Ibid.

69. Ibid.

70. Ibid.

71. Ibid.

72. Ibid.

73. Ibid.

74. Ibid.

75. Ibid.

76. ML ARC 1216 (017) Box 31, J. P. Morgan to Perkins and Jack Morgan, 24 October 1905.

77. Ibid.

78. Ibid.

79. BAR/200164, Noetzlin to Kokovtsov; Kokovtsov to Noetzlin; Baring Brothers & Co. (London) to Paribas (Paris) 25 October 1905.

80. Pipes, *Russian Revolution*, 40.

81. ML ARC 1216 (017) Box 31, Perkins to J. P. Morgan, 27 October 1905.

82. ML ARC 1216 (002) Box 3, Perkins and Jack Morgan to J. P. Morgan, 31 October 1905.

83. BAR/200164, Revelstoke to Baring Brothers & Co., 31 October 1905.

84. ML ARC 1216 (002) Box 3, Jack Morgan to J. P. Morgan, 10 November 1905.

85. Ibid.

86. ML ARC 1216 (002) Box 3, Jack Morgan to G. W. Perkins, 13 November 1906.

87. Ibid.

88. BAR/200164, Spring Rice to Revelstoke, 2 December 1905.

89. George Garvy, "The Financial Manifesto of the St Petersburg Soviet, 1905," *International Review of Social History* 20, no. 1 (1975): 30, doi:10.1017/S0020859000004818.

90. Ibid., 30.

91. Ibid.

92. Ibid.

93. Ibid., 30–31.

94. Ibid., 31.

95. G. M. Dempster, "The Fiscal Background of the Russian Revolution," *European Review of Economic History* 10, no. 1 (2006): 39.

96. Olga Crisp, *Studies in the Russian Economy before 1914* (London: Macmillan, 1976), 119.

97. See, for example, "The Russian Budget," *Economist*, 20 January 1906; "Russia's Financial Position," *Economist*, 16 December 1905; "The Finances of Russia," *Economist*, 23 January 1904.

98. Garvy, "Financial Manifesto," 31.

99. Redemption payments were made by peasants for the land they received as part of the 1861 emancipation of the serfs. They were used to compensate the landowners.

100. Garvy, "Financial Manifesto," 31.

101. Ibid., 25–26.

102. Ascher, *Revolution of 1905: Russia in Disarray*, 299–300.

103. See, for example, "Russia: Count Witte and the Strikers," *Times*, 6 December 1905; "Russia: The Moscow Revolt," *Times*, 29 December 1905.

104. "Attitude of the Press," *Times*, 19 December 1905.

105. Robert Service, *Lenin: A Biography* (Cambridge, MA: Harvard University Press, 2000), 176–77.

106. "Russia: Count Witte and the Strikers," *Times*, 6 December 1905. The paper, with a circulation of some 200,000, had long been a reliably ultranationalist, Judeophobic publication read by the Tsar and, among other things, an instigator of the infamous Kishinev pogrom of 1903. See Daniel Balmuth, "Novoe Vremia's War Against the Jews," *East European Jewish Affairs* 35, no. 1 (2005): 33–54, doi:10.1080/13501670500191645; Thomas Riha, "Riech': A Portrait of a Russian Newspaper," *Slavic Review* 22, no. 4 (December 1963): 663–82, doi:10.2307/2492564.

107. Witte, *Vospominaniia*, 2:196–97.

108. "The State of Russia," *Times*, 18 December 1905.

109. A. L. Sidorov, ed., "Finansovoe Polozhenie Tsarskogo Samoderzhaviia v Period Russko-Iaponskoi Voiny i Pervoi Russkoi Revoliutsii," *Istoricheskii Arkhiv* 1955, no. 2 (January–February): 125–27.

110. Ibid., 127–28.

111. Global Financial Data database.

112. Witte, *Vospominaniia*, 2:196–97.

113. "Measures Against the Press," *Times*, 18 December 1905. The government could not remove all printed copies, however; the same story reported more than a thousand copies of a Polish paper having escaped the censor's grasp.

114. "Russia: Task of the Government," *Times*, 4 January 1906.

115. "The State of Russia: Signs of Reaction," *Times*, 12 January 1906.

116. "Russia: Budget and Financial Report," *Times*, 15 January 1906.

117. Ibid.

118. "Russia's Financial Position," *Economist*, 13 January 1906; see also "The Breakdown of the Gold Standard in Russia," *Economist*, 6 January 1906; "The Russian Currency," *Economist*, 3 February 1906.

119. "Russian Finance," *Times*, 20 January 1906.

120. Ibid.

121. Ascher, *Revolution of 1905: Authority Restored*, 7.

122. "The State of Russia: The Political Unrest," *Times*, 24 January 1906.

123. "Sentence on a Newspaper Editor," *Times*, 22 January 1906.

124. Ibid. For an example of how the newspaper and Kadets were later opposed under Stolypin, see Ascher, *Revolution of 1905: Authority Restored*, 350.

125. Shmuel Galai, "The Impact of the Vyborg Manifesto on the Fortunes of the Kadet Party," *Revolutionary Russia* 20, no. 2 (2007): 200, doi:10.1080/09546540701633486.

126. Ibid., 201–2.

127. See ibid., 198. Long, for instance, gives an incorrect date and claims there were more than 200 participants at the first meeting; Long, "Organized Protest," 36. E. H. Carr offers a particularly erroneous account in that he confuses the Financial Manifesto of the Saint Petersburg Soviet with the Vyborg Manifesto. In his narrative, the Soviet issued the Vyborg Manifesto in 1905. This is incorrect: the Soviet issued the Financial Manifesto in December 1905, and the members of the dissolved Duma signed the Vyborg Manifesto several months later, in July 1906. See Edward Hallett Carr, *The Bolshevik Revolution 1917–1923*, 3 vols. (New York: Macmillan, 1952), 2:138.

128. Galai, "Impact of the Vyborg Manifesto," 217.

129. Ascher, *Revolution of 1905: Authority Restored*, 205–6.

130. Ibid., 2:203.

131. Vladimir Nabokov, *Speak, Memory: An Autobiography Revisited* (New York: Vintage, 1989), 163.

132. Long, "Organized Protest," 37; Ascher, *Revolution of 1905: Authority Restored*, 209.

133. Ascher, *Revolution of 1905: Authority Restored*, 206.

134. Galai, "Impact of the Vyborg Manifesto," 204.

135. BAR/200169, Cecil Spring Rice, "Notes on the Russian Financial Situation," 2 January 1906. Spring Rice maintained an active dialogue with the Morgans as well. His conversations with Jack Morgan contributed to the latter's bearish outlook on Russian affairs in early 1905. See ML ARC 1216 (003) Box 4, J. P. Morgan, Jr. to Walter and E.C. Grenfell, 3 February 1905.

136. BAR/200169, Noetzlin to Revelstoke, 9 January 1906.

137. Harcave, *Count Sergei Witte*, 215; Witte, *Vospominaniia*, 2:200.

138. Harcave, *Count Sergei Witte*, 218.

139. Girault, *Emprunts Russes*, 419.

140. Ibid., 424. The discount rate was the annualized rate at which the central bank would lend funds to financial institutions. In this sense, it can be seen as a baseline rate against which banks and other lenders priced their own loans to third parties.

141. Witte, *Vospominaniia*, 2:200, 205.

142. Ibid., 2:202.

143. Ibid., 2:211.

144. The nominal yield was 5 percent. A callable bond is one that includes an embedded option allowing the issuer to redeem or "call" the bond prematurely. In the case of the 1906 loan, given that the loan was priced at a time when Russia was in distressed circumstances, the government had an interest in refinancing the loan at a lower rate if and when the situation stabilized. Bondholders, by contrast, would see a reduction in their total return if the bond were prematurely paid off or exchanged for a lower yielding bond. The restriction on callability served to protect the bondholders' interests.

145. Witte, *Vospominaniia*, 2:202.

146. Witte, "Spravka o tom"; BAR/200169, Noetzlin to Revelstoke, 31 March 1906.

147. ML ARC 1216 (017) Box 31, J. P. Morgan to Jack Morgan, 2 April 1906.

148. ML ARC 1216 (017) Box 31, Jack Morgan to J. P. Morgan, 7 April 1906.

149. ML ARC 1216 (017) Box 31, J. P. Morgan to Jack Morgan, 7 April 1906.

150. ML ARC 1216 (017) Box 31, J. P. Morgan in Paris to Jack Morgan, 7 April 1906.

151. Ibid.

152. ML ARC 1216 (017) Box 31, Perkins and Jack Morgan to JPM, 11 April 1906.

153. Ibid.

154. Ibid.

155. Ibid.

156. ML ARC 1216 (017) Box 31, J. P. Morgan Paris to C. S. Morgan, 11 April 1906.

157. Witte, *Vospominaniia*, 2:212–13.

158. BAR/200165, Revelstoke to Sir Edward Grey, 6 April 1906.

159. Harcave, *Count Sergei Witte*, 106.

160. NA/FO/800/72/0/2/16, Spring Rice to Grey, 3 January 1906.

161. Ibid.

162. Ibid.

163. BAR/200165, Spring Rice to Revelstoke, 3 April 1906.

164. Witte, *Vospominaniia*, 2:194.

165. BAR/200165, Contract for 5 Percent Russian State Loan of 1906; Noetzlin to Revelstoke, 16 April 1906.

166. Even though the key members of the syndicate signed the main documents on 16 April, the completion of the paperwork, the solicitation of orders, and the decision to actually exercise the additional allotment option did not take place until several days later—well after the California earthquake.

167. RAL/XI/130A/19060419, London to Paris, 19 April 1906.

168. RAL/XI/130A/19060528, London to Paris, 28 May 1906.

169. ML ARC 1216 (017) Box 31, Vivian H. Smith to Jack Morgan, 23 May 1906.

170. RAL/XI/130A/19060615, London to Paris, 15 June 1906.

171. BAR/200166, Kokovtsov to Revelstoke; Revelstoke to Kokovtsov, 17–18 June 1906.

172. See Chapter 1 and Bignon and Flandreau, "Economics of Badmouthing."

173. BAR/201166, Noetzlin to Revelstoke, 18 June 1906.

174. BAR/200166, Noetzlin to Revelstoke; Revelstoke to Noetzlin, 20–21 June 1906.

175. BAR/200166, Kokovtsov to Revelstoke, 20 June 1906.

176. RAL/XI/130A/0A/19060720, London to Paris, 20 July 1906.

177. Ibid.

178. Robert F. Bruner and Sean D. Carr, *The Panic of 1907: Lessons Learned from the Market's Perfect Storm* (Hoboken, NJ: John Wiley, 2007), 13–17.

179. Harcave, *Count Sergei Witte*, 149; see also RAL/XI/130A/0/19060105, London to Paris, 5 January 1906.

180. BAR/200166, Rutkovskii to Lord Rothschild, 3 November 1906; Lord Rothschild to Rutkovskii, 5 November 1906.

181. See, for example, RAL/XI/130A/0/19060123, London to Paris, 23 January 1906.

182. For a detailed discussion of the diplomatic dimensions of the Russo-French financial relationship, see Jennifer Siegel, *For Peace and Money: French and British Finance in the Service of Tsars and Commissars* (Oxford: Oxford University Press, 2014).

183. The case of Tsarist Russia in 1905–6 is distinct from that described in Mauricio Drelichman and Hans-Joachim Voth, *Lending to the Borrower from Hell: Debt, Taxes, and Default in the Age of Philip II* (Princeton: Princeton University Press, 2014), 3. Beyond the French reluctance to impose conditionality on the Tsarist regime, there was no "risk transfer mechanism" along the lines the authors describe in Philip II's Spain.

Chapter 3: The Interrevolutionary Recovery and Rally

1. Girault, *Emprunts Russes*, 500; Catherine Potier, "Witnesses to Revolution: The Archives of Foreign Banks in Russia," in *Crisis and Renewal in Twentieth Century Banking: Exploring the History and Archives of Banking at Times of Political and Social Stress*, ed. Edwin Green, John Lampe, and Franjo Štiblar (Aldershot, England: Ashgate, 2004), 40.

2. Société Générale Archive (SGA), SGA/BUP/144761, Lombardo in Saint Petersburg to Lustgarten in Paris, 28 September 1907.

3. Reinhart and Rogoff, *This Time Is Different*, 96.

4. Ibid.

5. Gregory, *Russian National Income*, 56–58, figures in 1913 rubles. A negative reading in the net foreign investment account indicates a capital inflow, while a positive reading indicates a net outflow from Russia.

6. Ibid.

7. Mauro, Sussman, and Yafeh, *Emerging Markets and Financial Globalization*. See the introduction for a detailed discussion of this and other related theories on the drivers of cross-border capital flows in a globalized world.

8. The concept of fragility in this discussion draws in part on Nassim Taleb's latest work, *Antifragile* (New York: Random House, 2012), 12. The concept is employed in a broader sense rather than in strict adherence to Taleb's definition.

9. Ascher makes the point that "lawlessness and political terror were more widespread" in 1906 and 1907 than in 1905 itself. See Ascher, *Revolution of 1905: Authority Restored*, 7.

10. Figes, *People's Tragedy*, 220.

11. "Eve of the Duma," *Times*, 5 March 1907.

12. "Attempted Outrage at Tsarskoe Selo," *Times*, 28 February 1907.

13. "Eve of the Duma," *Times*, 5 March 1907.

14. Ibid.

15. "The Second Russian Duma," *Economist*, 23 February 1907.

16. Ibid.

17. Abraham Ascher, *P.A. Stolypin: The Search for Stability in Late Imperial Russia* (Stanford: Stanford University Press, 2001), 202.

18. Ibid.

19. Ibid., 202–3.

20. SGA/BUP/144761, Lion in Saint Petersburg to Villars in Paris, 17 June 1907.

21. Ibid.

22. SGA/BUP/144761, Lion in Saint Petersburg to Villars in Paris, 16 and 17 June 1907.

23. Cassis, *Capitals of Capital*, 106–7.

24. CAEF/B/0031263/5, Protocols of Bankers' Meeting, 15 January 1907.

25. Ibid.

26. Girault, *Emprunts Russes*, 347–48.

27. Calculated from data in ibid., 349.

28. Khromov, *Ekonomicheskoe Razvitie Rossii*, 459.

29. Alexander Gerschenkron, "The Rate of Industrial Growth in Russia since 1885," *Journal of Economic History* 7 (January 1947): 151, doi:10.2307/2113273.

30. Gregory, *Russian National Income*, 56–58.

31. Peter Gatrell, *Government, Industry, and Rearmament in Russia, 1900–1914: The Last Argument of Tsarism* (Cambridge: Cambridge University Press, 1994), 108.

32. Gregory, *Russian National Income*, 56–58.

33. Ibid.

34. Ascher, *P.A. Stolypin*, 154.

35. Ibid.

36. Ibid.

37. Ibid., 154–55.

38. Ibid., 153.

39. Ibid., 155.

40. Ibid.

41. Figes, *People's Tragedy*, 235.

42. Ibid., 237–38.

43. Ibid., 206.

44. SGA/BUP/144761, Lombardo in Saint Petersburg to Lustgarten in Paris, 28 September 1907.

45. Ibid.

46. SGA/BUP/144761, Lombardo in Saint Petersburg to Lustgarten in Paris, 28 October 1907.

47. SGA/BUP/144761, Lombardo in Saint Petersburg to Lustgarten in Paris, 1 November 1907.

48. HSBC Archive (HSBC), HSBC/30/218, Extract from the 1907 Report of the Manager of the Moscow Branch of the Imperial State Bank to the Manager-in-Chief in Saint Petersburg.

49. A desiatina is equal to 2.7 acres. Margaret Stevenson Miller, *The Economic Development of Russia, 1905–1914: With Special Reference to Trade, Industry, and Finance* (London: P. S. King & Son, 1926; 2nd ed., 1967), xviii.

50. BNP Paribas Archive (BNP), BNP/5/DFOM/221/27, Davydov in Saint Petersburg to Turrettini in Paris, 13 December 1908.

51. BNP/5/DFOM/221/27, Davydov in Saint Petersburg to Turrettini in Paris, 13 February 1909.

52. Ibid.

53. Ibid.

54. Ibid.

55. Ibid.

56. Ibid.

57. "Harvest at Home and Abroad," *Economist*, 7 August 1909.

58. "The Russian Budget and the Russian Loan," *Economist*, 9 January 1909.

59. "Russia's Financial Outlook," *Economist*, 4 September 1909.

60. Ibid.

61. Ibid.

62. N. M. Dronin and E. G. Bellinger, *Climate Dependence and Food Problems in Russia, 1900–1990: The Interaction of Climate and Agricultural Policy and Their Effect on Food Problems* (Budapest: Central European University Press, 2005), 32.

63. Ibid., 35.

64. Ibid., 33.

65. Ibid., 37.

66. Ibid., 32.

67. Ibid., 36.

68. George Soros developed his theory of "reflexivity" around this notion in *The Alchemy of Finance* (Hoboken, NJ: John Wiley, 2003).

69. "Quai d'Orsay Archive," n.d. CorrPolCom-NS-Russie-57; Kokovtsov to Poincaré, 15 April 1906.

70. Vladimir Nikolaevich Kokovtsov, *Out of My Past: The Memoirs of Count Kokovtsov, Russian Minister of Finance, 1904–1914, Chairman of the Council of Ministers, 1911–1914*, trans. Harold H. Fisher and Laura Matveev (Stanford: Stanford University Press, 1935), 224.

71. Ibid., 224–25.

72. Ibid., 225.

73. Ibid.

74. Archives Diplomatiques du Ministère des Affaires Étrangères (French Foreign Ministry Archives; MAE), MAE/CPC/NSR/57, Ministry Transcript of Chamber of Deputies Session, 7 February 1907. "The Russian people are our ally, and the Tsar is an assassin!"

75. Ibid.

76. MAE/CPC/NSR/57, Kokovtsov to Pichon, 9 February 1907.

77. SGA/BUP/14788, *Berliner Tageblatt* interview with Kokovtsov, 17 August 1907.

78. Kokovtsov, *Out of My Past*, 225.

79. Ibid.

80. Jennifer Siegel, *Endgame: Britain, Russia, and the Final Struggle for Central Asia* (New York: I.B. Tauris, 2002), 21. See also Siegel, *For Peace and Money*.

81. Siegel, *Endgame*, 19–20.

82. "Foreign Government Securities—September 1907," *Investor's Monthly Manual*, September 1907, 500.

83. Ibid.

84. "Foreign Government Securities—October 1907," *Investor's Monthly Manual*, October 1907, 557.

85. Ibid., 557.

86. "The Collapse of English Petroleum Companies," *Investor's Monthly Manual*, October 1907, 554–55.

87. CLCA/98AH67, Crédit Lyonnais note on Revelstoke's visit to Paris and Russia Affairs, 4 October 1907.

88. BAR 200168, Revelstoke to Kokovtsov, 19 January 1909.

89. CAEF/B/0031251/2, Note from de Verneuil in Saint Petersburg to French foreign minister, 24 July 1913.

90. Niall Ferguson, "Political Risk and the International Bond Market between the 1848 Revolution and the Outbreak of the First World War," *Economic History Review* 59, no. 1 (1 February 2006): 70–112, doi:10.2307/3806003.

91. Niall Ferguson, *The Pity of War* (New York: Basic Books, 1999), 21.

92. Ibid., 9–10. See also Dominic Lieven, *The End of Tsarist Russia: The March to World War I and Revolution* (New York: Viking, 2015), 152.

93. Anan'ich and Ganelin, *Sergei Iul'evich Vitte I Ego Vremia*, 13.

94. Ibid.

95. Flandreau et al., "End of Gatekeeping."

96. Girault, *Emprunts Russes*, 353.

97. Ibid., 356.

98. Ibid., 358.

99. Ibid.

100. Ibid., 358–59.

101. Ibid., 359.

102. Ibid.

103. Ibid., 361–62.

104. Ibid., 363.

105. Ibid., 365.

106. Gatrell, *Government, Industry, and Rearmament*, 57.

107. Ibid.

108. Ibid.

109. Ibid., 60.

110. Ibid.

111. Girault, *Emprunts Russes*, 449.

112. Gatrell, *Government, Industry, and Rearmament*, 57.

113. B. V. Anan'ich, *Bankirskie Doma v Rossii, 1860–1914 gg.: Ocherki Istorii Chastnogo Predprinimatel'stva*, 2nd ed. (Moscow: ROSSPEN, 2006), 116–17.

114. Ibid., 117.

115. Ibid., 118.

116. Ibid., 118–20.

117. Ibid., 121.

118. Ibid.

119. Ibid., 122.

120. Ibid., 123.

121. Ibid., 124.

122. Ibid., 122, 125.

123. Ibid., 131–32.

124. SGA/BUP/14401, Lombardo in Saint Petersburg to Villars in Paris, 17 December 1905.

125. Ibid.

126. HSBC/30/225, F. W. Riches in Saint Petersburg to D. A. Miller in London, 2 July 1909.

127. HSBC/30/218, Memorandum re: The United Bank, September 1909.

128. Ibid.

129. Girault, *Emprunts Russes*, 507.

130. Ibid.

131. SGA/BUP/14390, BUP Paris to Darcy in Saint Petersburg, 20 December 1913.

132. Kokovtsov, *Out of My Past*, 365.

133. Ibid.

134. CAEF/B/0031260, Note sur la Banque Russo-Chinoise, la Banque Franco Chinoise, et l'Établissement de la Banque de l'Indo-Chine en Chine, 15 June 1898.

135. CAEF/B/0031260/1, Pichon to Caillaux, 5 February 1908.

136. CAEF/B/0031260/1, Cochery to Pichon, 25 November 1909.

137. CAEF/B/0031260/1, French foreign minister to Louis in Saint Petersburg, 3 December 1909.

138. BNP/5/DFOM/221/27, Verstraete in Saint Petersburg to Noetzlin in Paris, 14 December 1909.

139. CAEF/B/0031260/3, Décisions de l'Assemblée Générale Extraordinaire des actionnaires de la Banque Russo-Chinoise, 6 March 1910.

140. A. R. Holmes and Edwin Green, *Midland: 150 Years of Banking Business* (London: B.T. Batsford, 1986), 135.

141. Ibid.

142. Ibid., 121.

143. HSBC/30/222, Memorandum on the Proposed Anglo-Russian Bank, 1 April 1909.

144. HSBC/30/225, Miller in Saint Petersburg to Madders in London, 22 July 1909.

145. Holmes and Green, *Midland*, 137–38.

146. HSBC 30/226, Diary entry of S. B. Murray, 23 September 1909.

147. HSBC/30/226, Diary entry of S. B. Murray, 24 September 1909.

148. HSBC/30/226, Diary entry of S. B. Murray, 28 September 1909.

149. "HSBC Group Archives," n.d.30–226; Diary of S. B. Murray, 29 September 1909.

150. Holmes and Green, *Midland*, 138.

151. HSBC/30/225, E. H. Holden to Joint General Managers, Head Office, London & City Midland Bank, 26 October 1909.

152. Ibid.

153. CAEF/B/0031256/1, "Centre Des Archives Économiques et Financières," n.d. B-0031256–1; de Verneuil in to the French Minister of Finance, 13 January 1909.

154. BAR 200167, Revelstoke to Noetzlin, 29 June 1908.

155. BAR 200167, Revelstoke to Kokovtsov, 28 July 1908.

156. Ibid.

157. RGIA/560/22/309/54, Noetzlin to Kokovtsov, 11 February 1909.

158. HSBC/30/226, Diary of S. B. Murray, 3 October 1909.

159. BAR 200167, Revelstoke to Farrer, 29 August 1908.

160. BAR 200167, Noetzlin to Revelstoke, 4 January 1909.

161. BAR 200167, Revelstoke to Gaspard, 11 January 1909.

162. BAR 200168, Revelstoke to Kokovtsov, 19 January 1909.

163. RGIA/560/22/309/69, Stenogram of Budget Committee Meeting, 13 February 1909.

164. Ibid.

165. BAR 200167, Revelstoke to Kokovtsov, 8 September 1908. "A sort of bastard."

166. RGIA/560/22/309/54–57, Noetzlin to Kokovtsov, 11 February 1909.

167. RGIA/560/22/309/70, Stenogram of Budget Committee Meeting, 13 February 1909.

168. "I have done what I could, let those who can do better"; RGIA/560/22/309/73–76, Stenogram of Budget Committee Meeting, 13 February 1909.

169. HSBC/30/225, D. A. Miller in Saint Petersburg to Madders in London, 22 July 1909.

170. Ibid., emphasis original.

171. HSBC/30/225, D. A. Miller in Saint Petersburg to Midland London, July 1909 (day unknown, emphasis original).

172. Ibid.

173. BNP/5/DFOM/221/27, Victor Davydov in Saint Petersburg to Noetzlin in Paris, 13 August 1909.

174. CAEF/B/0031251/2, Cochery to Pichon, 23 August 1909.

175. Ibid.

176. CAEF/B/0031251/2, Pichon to Cochery, 27 August 1909.

177. Crédit Lyonnais–Crédit Agricole Archive (CLCA), CLCA/98AH67, Note on discussion between Bethenod and Noetzlin, 14 September 1909.

178. Ibid.

179. Ibid.

180. Ibid.

181. CAEF/B/00312521/2, French Chargé in Saint Petersburg to Minister of Finance in Paris, 18 September 1909; see also Chapter 1.

182. CAEF/B/0031257/3, French consul in Kharkov to French Ministry of Foreign Affairs, 14 April 1911.

183. Ibid.

184. Ibid.

185. Ibid.

186. BAR 200167, 2 October 1908, Revelstoke to Kokovtsov.

187. BAR 200167, 23 December 1908, Noetzlin to Farrer.

188. CAEF/B/0031257/3, Annex to report from French ambassador Saint Petersburg to Ministry of Foreign Affairs, 27 May 1911.

189. SGA/BUP/14403, Guibert in Saint Petersburg to Thalmann in Paris, 24 May 1911.

190. RAL/XI/130A/5, London to Paris, 16 October 1911.

191. CAEF/B/0031258/6, Louis to Poincaré, 24 February 1912.

192. Kokovtsov, *Out of My Past*, 196–97.

193. Figes, *People's Tragedy*, 336.

194. Kokovtsov, *Out of My Past*, 200.

195. Ibid., 225–26.

196. Ibid., 226.

197. Ibid., 226–27.

198. Leopold H. Haimson, "'The Problem of Political and Social Stability in Urban Russia on the Eve of War and Revolution' Revisited," *Slavic Review* 59, no. 4 (December 2000): 860, doi:10.2307/2697422.

199. BAR 200167, British Embassy Saint Petersburg to Revelstoke, 21 September 1908.

200. CAEF/B/0031257/3, French consul Odessa to Minister of Commerce and Industry in Paris, 3 January 1910.

201. Vladimir Il'ich Lenin, "The Cadet Duma Grants Money to the Pogrom-Mongers' Government (8 July 1906)," in *V. I. Lenin: Collected Works*, 11:60–61.

202. Vladimir Il'ich Lenin, "The Famine and the Reactionary Duma (4 January 1912)," in *V. I. Lenin: Collected Works*, 17:446.

203. CAEF/B/0031251/2, French embassy in Saint Petersburg to Ministry of Foreign Affairs Paris, 15 July 1910.

204. Ibid.

205. Ibid.

206. Ferguson, *House of Rothschild*, 416.

207. Aleksandr Mikhailovich Michelson, P. N. Apostol, and M. V. Bernatzky, *Russian Public Finance during the War* (New Haven: Yale University Press, 1928), 239. The total government debt dropped from 9.1 billion rubles on 1 January 1910 to 8.8 billion on 1 January 1914.

208. Ibid., 236.

209. Michelson, Apostol, and Bernatzky, *Russian Public Finance during the War*, 240, 243.

210. Ibid., 237.

211. Ibid.

212. Ibid.

213. Ibid.

214. Ibid., 238.

215. CAEF/B/0031250/1, French consul Odessa to Minister of Foreign Affairs in Paris, 22 May 1913.

216. Ibid.

217. Ibid.

218. Ibid.

219. Ibid.

220. Ibid.

221. Ibid.

222. CAEF/B/0031250/1, French consul Warsaw to Ministry of Foreign Affairs in Paris, 25 June 1912.

223. Ibid.

224. Figes, *People's Tragedy*, 185.

225. CAEF/B/0031250/1, French consul Warsaw to Ministry of Foreign Affairs in Paris, 25 June 1912.

226. Crisp, *Studies in the Russian Economy*, 100.

227. Peter Gatrell, *The Tsarist Economy 1850–1917* (London: Batsford, 1986), 139–40.

228. CAEF/B/0031257/3, French Foreign Minister to Minister of Finance, 27 October 1913.

229. SGA/BUP/14390, Octave Homburg to Darcy, 16 December 1913.

230. SGA/BUP/14390, Minutes of board meeting on the Banque de Union Moscou, 20 December 1913.

231. CAEF/B/0031253/2, Cours Moyens des Valeurs Russes en 1913, February 1914.

232. CAEF/B/0031253/2, Paléologue in Saint Petersburg to Doumergue in Paris, 4 April 1914.

233. CAEF/B/0031250/1, French consul Warsaw to Ministry of Foreign Affairs Paris, 25 June 1912.

234. CAEF/B/0031251/2, Russian Embassy Paris to French Foreign Ministry, 9 January 1914.

235. Gatrell, *Government, Industry, and Rearmament*, 244.

236. Ibid., 324.

237. Ibid., 163.

238. Ibid., 324–26.

239. Ibid., 300–301.

240. Leopold Haimson, "The Problem of Social Stability in Urban Russia, 1905–1917 (Part One)," *Slavic Review* 23, no. 4 (December 1964): 619–42, doi:10.2307/2492201; Leopold Haimson, "The Problem of Social Stability in Urban Russia, 1905–1917 (Part Two)," *Slavic Review* 24,

no. 1 (March 1965): 1–22, doi:10.2307/2492986; Arthur P. Mendel, "Peasant and Worker on the Eve of the First World War," *Slavic Review* 24, no. 1 (March 1965): 23–33, doi:10.2307/2492987; Theodore H. Von Laue, "The Chances for Liberal Constitutionalism," *Slavic Review* 24, no. 1 (March 1965): 34–46, doi:10.2307/2492988; Leopold Haimson, "Reply," *Slavic Review* 24, no. 1 (March 1965): 47–56, doi:10.2307/2492989. Haimson's updated views, based on archival research and continuing into the wartime period in greater depth, are available in "'Problem of Political and Social Stability.'"

241. Haimson, "Problem of Social Stability in Urban Russia, 1905–1917 (Part One)," 620.

242. Ibid.

243. Ascher, *P.A. Stolypin*, 294.

244. Haimson, "Problem of Social Stability in Urban Russia, 1905–1917 (Part One)," 624, 629.

245. Haimson, "Problem of Social Stability in Urban Russia, 1905–1917 (Part Two)," 2.

246. Ibid., 8.

247. Haimson, "Problem of Social Stability in Urban Russia, 1905–1917 (Part One)," 627–29.

248. Haimson, "'Problem of Political and Social Stability,'" 849–50.

Chapter 4: Investing in the Revolution

1. "To Open Petrograd Branch Next Monday: National City Bank Extends Its Foreign Business," *New York Tribune*, 10 January 1917.

2. V. V. Lebedev, *Russko-Amerikanskie Ekonomicheskie Otnosheniia: 1900–1917 gg.* (Moscow: Mezhdunarodnye Otnosheniia, 1964), 250. Bark had originally requested a much larger loan of $300 million, but the bank's representative said the contemporary situation in the United States made such a loan impossible.

3. "Reds Seize U.S. Bank," *Washington Post*, 29 December 1917.

4. Peter Gatrell, *A Whole Empire Walking: Refugees in Russia during World War I* (Bloomington: Indiana University Press, 2005), 17–18.

5. Ibid., 20.

6. Ibid., 31.

7. Peter Gatrell and Mark Harrison, "The Russian and Soviet Economies in Two World Wars: A Comparative View," *Economic History Review* 46, no. 3 (August 1993): 439–40, doi:10.2307/2598362.

8. Ibid., 440.

9. Andrei Markevich and Mark Harrison, "Great War, Civil War, and Recovery: Russia's National Income, 1913 to 1928," *Journal of Economic History* 71, no. 3 (2011): 680, doi:10.1017/S0022050711001884.

10. Ibid.; Gatrell and Harrison, "Russian and Soviet Economies," 440.

11. Gatrell and Harrison, "Russian and Soviet Economies," 441.

12. Ibid., 442.

13. Figes, *People's Tragedy*, 298.

14. Ibid., 299.

15. Markevich and Harrison, "Great War, Civil War, and Recovery," 684, 686.

16. Figes, *People's Tragedy*, 300.

17. G. Ia. Sokol'nikov, *Finansovaia Politika Revoliutsii*, 2 vols. (1928; Moscow: Obshchestvo Kuptsov i Promyshlennikov Rossii, 2006), 1:21.

18. Ibid., 1:20.

19. Sokol'nikov's report is also notable in that in his discussion on gold reserves and paper currency issuance, he shows a greater willingness to maintain a monetized economy than the stereotype of the early Bolsheviks as trying to demonetize the early post-1917 economy would suggest.

20. Sean McMeekin, *History's Greatest Heist: The Looting of Russia by the Bolsheviks* (New Haven: Yale University Press, 2009), 194–95.

21. Norman Stone, *Eastern Front 1914–1917*, 2nd ed. (New York: Penguin, 2004), 208.

22. Ibid., 208.

23. Ibid., 209.

24. Ibid., 209–11.

25. ML ARC 1214, Box 33, Morgan Grenfell to J. P. Morgan & Co., 9 January 1915.

26. BAR 200021, Telephone call between Revelstoke and Sir Ernest Cassel, 29 October 1915.

27. Ibid.

28. Citibank Archive (Citi), Citi RG10, "Russia and the Imperial Russian Government," 13 June 1916, 1, 4.

29. Ibid., 8.

30. BAR 200021, Revelstoke Petrograd Mission Diary, 30 January 1917.

31. Ibid.

32. "The Russian Revolution and Russian War Finance," *Economist*, 17 March 1917.

33. RGIA/624/1/5/1–2, Meserve to Vanderlip, 29 August 1915.

34. "Annual Report" (First National City Bank of New York, 4 March 1919).

35. HSBC/151/1, Employment Agreement between Bunker and Midland, 2 December 1913.

36. Ibid.

37. HSBC/151/1, Bunker to Holden, 17 August 1916. See also Holmes and Green, *Midland*, 136.

38. BAR 200021, Revelstoke Petrograd Mission Diary, 29 January 1917.

39. BAR 200021, Revelstoke Petrograd Mission Diary, 30 January 1917.

40. Cassis, *Capitals of Capital*, 91–93.

41. RGIA/624/1/5/195, Meserve to New York, 23 February 1917.

42. Ibid.

43. "The Language Classes," *No. 8*, September 1916.

44. "The National City Bank of New York in Petrograd," *No. 8*, February 1917, 29–30.

45. Ibid., 32.

46. Ibid., 30.

47. Ibid.

48. Citi RG10, Russia and the Imperial Government, 13 March 1916.

49. Citi RG 12, "History of the Operations of the Petrograd and Moscow Branches of the National City Bank of New York," 1922, 2.

50. "Russia," *No. 8*, February 1917, 3.

51. Ibid., 6.

52. Ibid., 9.

53. Ibid.

54. RGIA/624/1/5/202, Meserve to New York, 29 March 1917.

55. RGIA/624/1/5/207, Seattle National Bank to Meserve, 3 May 1917.

56. Ibid.

57. RGIA/624/1/5/208b, Vanderlip to Meserve, 28 April 1917.

58. "History of the Operations of the Petrograd and Moscow Branches of the National City Bank of New York," 5.

59. "Branch News," *No. 8*, May 1917, 50.

60. "The Moscow Branch," *No. 8*, June 1917, 47.

61. Ibid.

62. F. J. Macguire, "An Unsuccessful Calamity," *No. 8*, September 1917, 22.

63. "Branch Bank Notes," *No. 8*, October 1917, 38.

64. Ibid.

65. "Branch Bank News," *No. 8*, November 1917, 47.

66. "A Little History," *No. 8*, December 1917, 13.

67. HSBC/151/2, Bunker to Holden, 5 April 1917.

68. Ibid.

69. ML ARC 1216 (017) Box 13, J. P. Morgan, Jr. to E. C. Porter, 1 May 1917.

70. Ibid.

71. "The Flood of Paper Money," in Robert Paul Browder and Aleksandr Fyodorovich Kerensky, eds., *The Russian Provisional Government, 1917: Documents* (Stanford: Stanford University Press, 1961), 509.

72. HSBC/151/2, Bunker to Midland, 31 May 1917.

73. "The Financial Situation of Russia as of Mid-August 1917," in Browder and Kerensky, *Russian Provisional Government*, 517.

74. HSBC/151/2, Bunker to Midland, 31 May 1917.

75. "The Enactment of an Extraordinary Income Tax Levy," in Browder and Kerensky, *Russian Provisional Government*, 496.

76. HSBC/151/2, Bunker to Holden, 24 April 1917.

77. "Report of United States Consul Winship at Petrograd on the Currency Crisis," in Browder and Kerensky, *Russian Provisional Government*, 510.

78. HSBC/151/2, Bunker to Holden, 29 June 1917.

79. BAR 200021, Revelstoke Petrograd Mission Diary, 2 February 1917.

80. BAR 200021, Revelstoke Petrograd Mission Diary, 2 February 1917 and 7 February 1917.

81. BAR 200021, Revelstoke Petrograd Mission Diary, 7 February 1917.

82. Ibid.

83. Ibid.

84. Ibid.

85. Ibid.

86. BAR 200021, Revelstoke Petrograd Mission Diary, 8 February 1917.

87. Ibid.

88. BAR 203986, Memorandum of Conversation at Russian Ministry of Finance, 15 February 1917.

89. BAR 200021, Revelstoke Petrograd Mission Diary, 17 February 1917.

90. "History of the Operations of the Petrograd and Moscow Branches of the National City Bank of New York," 5.

91. BAR 101950, Revelstoke to Abdy, 23 March 1917.

92. BAR 101950, Holdings to Lambert, 12 April 1917.

93. BAR 200021, Memorandum of Meeting of Lord Revelstoke with Mr. de Routkowsky, 18 July 1917.

94. BAR 200021, Revelstoke Petrograd Mission Diary, 3 February 1917.

95. Ibid.

96. Ibid.

97. HSBC/151/2, Bunker to Midland, 31 May 1917.

98. Operating leverage can be defined as the ratio of fixed costs to total costs. Railroads are a classic case of high operating leverage in that revenue growth in the form of rate increases and/or additional carloads is achieved at minimal marginal cost, driving a disproportionate increase in earnings. Conversely, a loss of carloads on a railroad does not achieve a proportionate decrease in costs, creating a disproportionate drop in earnings.

99. RGIA/624/1/5/22–23, Meserve to New York, 12 October 1915.

100. Union Pacific Railroad Company, "Annual Report" (1915).

101. RGIA/624/1/5/24, Meserve to New York, 12 October 1915.

102. "Russian Revolution and Russian War Finance," *Economist*, 17 March 1917.

103. "Russian Budget for 1915," *Economist*, 22 May 1915.

104. "Russian Revolution and Russian War Finance," *Economist*, 17 March 1917.

105. ML ARC 1214 Box 33, E. C. Grenfell to H. Harjes, 24 November 1914.

106. ML ARC 1215 Box 33, Morgan Grenfell to J. P. Morgan & Co., 12 March 1915.

107. Siegel, *For Peace and Money*, 134–36.

108. BAR 203987, J. M. Keynes, "Gold Arrangements with Allies," 19 December 1916.

109. BAR 203986, Speech of Lord Revelstoke at the dinner in honor of the English delegates of the Petrograd Conference, 12 February 1917.

110. Harold van B. Cleveland, Rachel Strauber, Thomas F. Huertas, and Alfred D. Chandler, *Citibank, 1812–1970*, Harvard Studies in Business History 37 (Cambridge, MA: Harvard University Press, 1985), 101.

111. RGIA/624/1/5/23, Meserve to New York, 12 October 1915.

112. Ibid.

113. Samuel McRoberts, "Russia," *No. 8*, February 1917, 3.

114. RGIA/624/1/5/186–187, J. Block to Meserve, 23 September 1916.

115. RGIA/624/1/5/163–164, Meserve to New York, 29 August 1916.

116. RGIA/624/1/5/161, Meserve to New York, 17 August 1916.

117. RGIA/624/1/5/114, Meserve to New York, 21 March 1916.

118. Cleveland et al., *Citibank*, 76–79.

119. RGIA/624/1/5/112, Meserve to New York, 13 February 1916.

120. RGIA/624/1/5/112–113a, Meserve to New York, 13 February 1916.

121. RGIA/624/1/5/113a, Meserve to New York, 13 February 1916.

122. Even after the US entry into the war, American Jewish investment banks like Kuhn, Loeb were notably absent from the Russian markets due to the sharp rise in anti-Semitic violence under Nicholas II. During the Russo-Japanese War, they vigorously sought to block Tsarist Russia from accessing the New York capital markets and actively supported Japanese war

finance. See Chapter 2 and, for example, Jeffry A. Frieden, *Banking on the World: The Politics of American International Finance* (New York: Harper & Row, 1987), 23.

123. RGIA/624/1/5/76, Meserve to New York, 23 November 1916.

124. Ibid.

125. RGIA/624/1/5/113a, Meserve to New York, 13 February 1916.

126. RGIA/624/1/5/103, Meserve to New York, 31 December 1915.

127. RGIA/624/1/5/158, Meserve to New York, 11 August 1916.

128. RGIA/624/1/5/118, Meserve to New York, 21 March 1916.

129. RGIA/624/1/5/68, Meserve to New York, 16 November 1915.

130. Ibid.

131. RGIA/624/1/5/125, Meserve to New York, 19 April 1916.

132. RGIA/624/1/5/126, Meserve to New York, 19 April 1916.

133. RGIA/624/1/5/129, Meserve to New York, 19 April 1916.

134. RGIA/624/1/5/118, Meserve to New York, 21 March 1916.

135. RGIA/624/1/5/78, Meserve to New York, 24 November 1915.

136. RGIA/624/1/5/62, Meserve to New York, 6 November 1915.

137. RGIA/624/1/5/58a, Meserve to New York, 3 November 1915.

138. RGIA/624/1/5/169, Meserve to New York, 12 September 1916.

139. HSBC/151/1, Bunker to Holden, 11 April 1917.

140. Ibid.

141. HSBC/151/2, Bunker to Holden, 29 June 1917.

142. Ibid.

143. HSBC/151/2, Bunker to Holden, 31 May 1917.

144. HSBC/151/2, Bunker to Holden, 29 June 1917.

145. HSBC/151/2, Bunker to Holden, 4 October 1917.

146. HSBC/151/2 Bunker to Holden, 18 September 1917.

147. HSBC/151/2 Bunker to Holden, 4 October 1917.

148. HSBC/151/2, Bunker to Kaye, 1 November 1917.

149. HSBC/151/2, Overseas Manager to Bunker, 17 November 1917.

150. HSBC/151/2, Bunker to Midland, 2 February 1918.

151. HSBC/151/2, Bunker to Midland, 7 June 1917.

152. HSBC/151/2, William Higgs & Co. Moscow to Midland, 15 September 1917.

153. HSBC/151/2, Bunker to Kaye, 1 November 1917.

154. RGIA/624/1/5/125, Meserve to New York, 19 April 1916.

155. Ibid.

156. Cleveland et al., *Citibank*, 89–92.

157. Ibid., 92.

158. Ibid., 93–94. Citi RG5 D&E Speech by C. A. Stone, 21 November 1918.

159. Charles Jenkinson, "The National City Bank of New York in Petrograd," *No. 8*, February 1917, 32.

160. Citi RG5 D&E, Speech by C. A. Stone, 21 November 1918.

161. Cleveland et al., *Citibank*, 100; Priscilla Roberts, "Frank A. Vanderlip and the National City Bank during the First World War," *Essays in Economic & Business History* 20 (2002): 151, http://www.ebhsoc.org/journal/index.php/journal/article/view/120.

162. BAR/200175/83–84, Vanderlip to Revelstoke, 14 September 1916.

163. BAR/200175/84, Memorandum on visit of Holbrook to Barings, 5 October 1916.

164. Citi RG2 NCBNY Frank Vanderlip Memo on the Creation of the American International Company, 27 November 1915.

165. BAR/200175/87, Memorandum on Holbrook and Russia, 10 October 1916.

166. HSBC/151/2, Bunker to Midland, 7 June 1917.

167. RGIA/624/1/5/122, Meserve to New York, 19 April 1916.

168. RGIA/624/1/5/122–123, Meserve to New York, 19 April 1916.

169. RGIA/624/1/5/86, Meserve to New York, 1 December 1915.

170. RGIA/624/1/5/86, Meserve to New York, 1 December 1915.

171. "The Proposed Prohibition of Intoxicants," *Economist*, 3 April 1915.

172. "Letters to the Editor: Prohibition of Vodka in Russia and Its Salutary Effects," *Economist*, 10 April 1915.

173. Ibid.

174. Ibid.

175. North and Weingast, "Constitutions and Commitment." See the introduction for a detailed discussion of this and other theories.

176. See the introduction for a detailed review of this literature.

177. Mauro, Sussman, and Yafeh, *Emerging Markets and Financial Globalization*. See the introduction for a fuller discussion of this and related literature.

178. Ibid., 162–63.

179. "Russian Revolution and Russian War Finance," *Economist*, 17 March 1917.

180. "France—Resignation of the Cabinet—Estimates for Second Quarter of 1917—Public Accounts—Cost of Living in France—Mutual Guarantee Societies—the Bourse," *Economist*, 24 March 1917.

181. Ibid.

182. HSBC/151/2, Bunker to Holden, 28 April 1917.

183. BA/200175/142, Smith to Whishaw, 7 May 1917.

184. BA/200175/143, Smith to Whishaw, 7 May 1917.

185. BA/200175/144, Smith to Whishaw, 7 May 1917.

186. BA/200175/145, Smith to Whishaw, 7 May 1917.

187. "Stock Exchange News," *Economist*, 2 June 1917.

188. "After Three Years," *Economist*, 4 August 1917.

189. "Kerensky Quits?," *Wall Street Journal*, 3 November 1917.

190. Ibid.

191. "An Awakening Giant," *Wall Street Journal*, 10 November 1917.

192. "Holland's Letter," *Wall Street Journal*, 17 November 1917.

193. RGIA/624/1/5/225, Meserve to New York, 15 September 1917.

194. "An Awakening Giant," *Wall Street Journal*, 10 November 1917.

195. A notable recent addition to scholarship in this vein is Siegel, *For Peace and Money*. However, this account is principally focused on diplomatic dimensions to Allied lending to Russia and focuses less on the activity of National City in the years before the revolution.

196. MAE/2e/Personnel/1538 (Verstraete), Concours d'Admission, 10 January 1888; Préfet du Nord to Foreign Minister, 7 January 1888.

197. MAE/2e/Personnel/1538 (Verstraete), Concours d'Admission, 10 January 1888; Préfet du Nord to Foreign Minister, 7 January 1888.

198. R. K. I. Quested, *The Russo-Chinese Bank: A Multinational Financial Base of Tsarism in China*, vol. 2, Birmingham Slavonic Monographs no. 2 (Birmingham: Department of Russian Language and Literature, University of Birmingham, 1977), 6.

199. MAE/2e/Personnel/1538 (Verstraete), Verstraete to Delcassé, 1 October 1901.

200. Valerii Ivanovich Bovykin, *Finansovyi Kapital v Rossii Nakanune Pervoi Mirovoi Voiny* (Moscow: ROSSPEN, 2001), 186, 191.

201. Maurice Verstraete, *Mes Cahiers Russes: L'Ancien Régime, Le Gouvernement Provisoire, Le Pouvoir Des Soviets* (Paris: G. Crès, 1920), 127–28.

202. Ibid., 137.

203. Ibid., 178, 184.

204. Ibid., 203.

205. Ibid., 103.

206. Ibid., 108, 115.

207. Ibid., 116.

208. Ibid., 129–30.

209. Ibid., 132–34.

210. Ibid., 135.

211. Ibid., 137.

212. Ibid., 140–41.

213. Ibid., 147.

214. Ibid., 153.

215. Ibid., 156.

216. Ibid., 156.

217. Ibid., 156.

218. Ibid., 225.

219. Sergei Lebedev, "Russian Banks during the First World War and the Revolution," in Green, Lampe, and Štiblar, *Crisis and Renewal in Twentieth Century Banking*, 24.

220. Ibid., 24–25.

221. For a detailed comparison of the data, see Chapter 5.

222. Reinhart and Rogoff, *This Time Is Different*, 12. French debts were not settled until even later, in November 1996.

Chapter 5: Revolutionary Default

1. SGA/BUP/14802, Saint-Sauveur to Paris, 31 December 1917.

2. Sokol'nikov, *Finansovaia Politika Revoliutsii*, 1:5.

3. Verstraete, *Mes Cahiers Russes*, 237.

4. Ibid., 236–37.

5. Macdonald, *Free Nation*, 430. Macdonald dates the repudiation as taking place in 1917; in fact it occurred in 1918 but was backdated to apply to payments of December 1917.

6. See the appendix.

7. Tomz, *Reputation and International Cooperation*, 17–18.

8. Peter H. Lindert and Peter J. Morton, "How Sovereign Debt Has Worked," in *Developing Country Debt and Economic Performance, Volume 1: The International Financial System*, ed. Jeffrey D. Sachs (Chicago: University of Chicago Press, 1989), 78.

9. Tomz, *Reputation and International Cooperation*, 22.

10. Vladimir Il'ich Lenin, "An Open Letter to Boris Souvarine (December 1916)," in *V. I. Lenin: Collected Works*, 23:197.

11. Vladimir Il'ich Lenin, "The Tasks of the Russian Social-Democratic Labour Party in the Russian Revolution: Report of a Lecture," in *V. I. Lenin: Collected Works*, 23:355.

12. Ibid., 23:355–56.

13. Ibid., 23:406–7.

14. Vladimir Il'ich Lenin, "Fourth Letter from Afar: How to Achieve Peace (25 March 1917)," in *V. I. Lenin: Collected Works*, 23:337–38.

15. Ibid., 23:338–39.

16. Ibid., 23:338.

17. Lenin, "Tasks of the Russian Social-Democratic Labour Party," 361.

18. Vladimir Il'ich Lenin, "How They Tied Themselves to the Capitalists (3 May, 1917)," in *V. I. Lenin: Collected Works*, 24:176–77.

19. Vladimir Il'ich Lenin, "Mandate to Deputies of the Soviet Elected at Factories and Regiments (before 20 May 1917)," in *V. I. Lenin: Collected Works*, 24:354.

20. Ibid., 24:356.

21. Vladimir Il'ich Lenin, *V. I. Lenin: Collected Works*, 24:588.

22. Vladimir Il'ich Lenin, "Draft Resolution on the War," in *V. I. Lenin: Collected Works*, 24:161–62.

23. Ibid., 24:162.

24. Vladimir Il'ich Lenin, "Report on the Current Situation April 24 (May 7)," in *V. I. Lenin: Collected Works*, 24:233.

25. Michelson, Apostol, and Bernatzky, *Russian Public Finance during the War*, 274.

26. Ibid., vii.

27. Ibid., 274.

28. Ibid., 275.

29. Vladimir Il'ich Lenin, "How the Capitalists Conceal Their Profits: Concerning the Issue of Control," in *V. I. Lenin: Collected Works*, 25:140–41.

30. Ibid., 25:140.

31. Vladimir Il'ich Lenin, "The Impending Catastrophe and How to Combat It (23–27 September 1917)," in *V. I. Lenin: Collected Works*, 25:334.

32. Ibid., 25:336.

33. Vladimir Il'ich Lenin, "Revision of the Party Programme (October 1917)," in *V. I. Lenin: Collected Works*, 26:177–78.

34. Vladimir Il'ich Lenin, "How and Why the Peasants Were Deceived (14 July 1917)," in *V. I. Lenin: Collected Works*, 25:149.

35. Vladimir Il'ich Lenin, "From a Publicists' Diary (11 September 1917)," in *V. I. Lenin: Collected Works*, 25:279–80.

36. Ibid., 25:280.

37. Vladimir Il'ich Lenin, "Speech on the Agrarian Question—Newspaper Report (27 November 1917)," in *V. I. Lenin: Collected Works*, 26:325.

38. McMeekin, *History's Greatest Heist*, xx–xxi.

39. Ibid., xxi.

40. Ibid., xxi–xxii.

41. Ibid., xxii.

42. Ibid.

43. Ibid.

44. Ibid., 23.

45. Ibid., 23–24.

46. Ibid., 25.

47. Ibid.

48. Derived from figures in ibid.

49. Peter Gatrell, *Russia's First World War: A Social and Economic History* (Harlow, England: Pearson/Longman, 2005), 249–50.

50. Markevich and Harrison, "Great War, Civil War, and Recovery," 682.

51. Ibid., 684.

52. Harold Glenn Moulton and Leo Pasvolsky, *Russian Debts and Russian Reconstruction: A Study of the Relation of Russia's Foreign Debts to Her Economic Recovery* (New York: McGraw-Hill, 1924), 60.

53. HSBC/151/2, Bunker to Holden, 15 December 1917.

54. See in particular John Maynard Keynes, *A Tract on Monetary Reform* (London: Macmillan, 1924), which was inspired in part by the monetary chaos of revolutionary Russia.

55. Michelson, Apostol, and Bernatzky, *Russian Public Finance during the War*, 372.

56. Ibid., 379.

57. Ibid.

58. Ibid., 380.

59. Ibid.

60. Ibid.

61. Ibid.

62. Keynes, *Tract on Monetary Reform*, 48.

63. Ibid., 50.

64. Diane Koenker and William G. Rosenberg, *Strikes and Revolution in Russia, 1917* (Princeton: Princeton University Press, 1989), 273–74.

65. McMeekin, *History's Greatest Heist*, xxii.

66. Michelson, Apostol, and Bernatzky, *Russian Public Finance during the War*, 121.

67. Ibid.

68. Ibid., 211.

69. Ibid., 126.

70. Ibid., 169.

71. Ibid., 123.

72. Quoted in ibid., 145.

73. Ibid., 164.

74. Ibid., 176.

75. Ibid., 172, 177.

76. Ibid., 172.

77. Ibid., 196.

78. Ibid., 159.

79. Ibid., 197.

80. Ibid., 194.

81. Ibid., 207–8.

82. Ibid., 213.

83. Ibid., 189–90.

84. Ibid., 190.

85. Ibid., 220.

86. Calculated from ibid.

87. Calculated from ibid.

88. Hew Strachan, *Financing the First World War* (Oxford: Oxford University Press, 2004), 181.

89. McMeekin, *History's Greatest Heist*, xxii.

90. Ibid., 234; Strachan, *Financing the First World War*, 133–34.

91. Calculated from Michelson, Apostol, and Bernatzky, *Russian Public Finance during the War*, 254.

92. Ibid., 255.

93. Ibid., 253.

94. Calculated from data in ibid., 252.

95. Ibid., 269.

96. Ibid.

97. Ibid., 269.

98. Ibid., 268.

99. Stone, *Eastern Front*, 290–91.

100. Michelson, Apostol, and Bernatzky, *Russian Public Finance during the War*, 280–81.

101. Ibid., 284.

102. Ibid.

103. Ibid., 283.

104. Ibid.

105. Ibid., 285.

106. Gatrell, *Russia's First World War*, 133, 135.

107. Calculated from Michelson, Apostol, and Bernatzky, *Russian Public Finance during the War*, 220.

108. In finance, policymakers are constrained by what has been called the "trilemma" of monetary policy, whereby they can at best achieve two of three things: fixed exchange rates, free capital flows, and an independent monetary policy. Much to the irritation of the British and French, the Russian government made only halfhearted moves to enact exchange controls. Even then it was not able to enforce them, leading to a flood of rubles in foreign markets that depressed the ruble exchange rate, which Allied governments were propping up. The outflow also incidentally helped the German war effort by allowing German agents in neutral countries to buy up currency at cheap rates that the German military then used in the territories of the Russian Empire that it occupied. See Niall Ferguson, *The Cash Nexus: Money and Power in the Modern World, 1700–2000* (New York: Basic Books, 2001), 334; Michelson, Apostol, and Bernatzky, *Russian Public Finance during the War*, 420–21; Strachan, *Financing the First World War*, 182–83.

109. Strachan, *Financing the First World War*, 181.

110. Irving Fisher, "How the Public Should Pay for the War," *Annals of the American Academy of Political and Social Science* 78 (1918): 115.

111. Even Bernatzky, who was an outspoken critic of the failure of both the Imperial and Provisional governments to implement exchange controls, for example, ultimately conceded that their ability to do so was constrained and that such policies would have had little marginal impact in the long run. Michelson, Apostol, and Bernatzky, *Russian Public Finance during the War*, 437.

112. Figes, *People's Tragedy*, 483.

113. McMeekin, *History's Greatest Heist*, 11–12.

114. Ibid., 18.

115. Carr, *Bolshevik Revolution*, 2:138–39.

116. Pipes, *Russian Revolution*, 672, 601–2.

117. Ibid., 601.

118. Ibid.

119. Ibid.

120. State Archive of the Russian Federation (GARF), GARF/R130/1/36/5, Tezisy tt. Vladimira Mikhailovicha Smirnova i Valeriana Valerianovicha Obolenskogo [AKA Osinski], 10 November 1917.

121. Ibid.

122. Ibid.

123. GARF/R130/1/36/5–6, Tezisy tt. Vladimira Mikhailovicha Smirnova i Valeriana Valerianovicha Obolenskogo, 10 November 1917.

124. GARF/R130/1/36/6, Tezisy tt. Vladimira Mikhailovicha Smirnova i Valeriana Valerianovicha Obolenskogo, 10 November 1917.

125. GARF/R130/1/36/7, Tezisy tt. Vladimira Mikhailovicha Smirnova i Valeriana Valerianovicha Obolenskogo, 10 November 1917.

126. Service, *Lenin*, 324.

127. Ibid., 351.

128. Ibid., 351–52.

129. GARF/R130/1/20/48, O Russko-Belgiiskom Metallurgicheskom Obshchestve, 28 December 1917.

130. Ibid.

131. GARF/R130/1/2/1, Sovnarkom Protocol, 28 November 1917.

132. GARF/R130/1/2/3, Sovnarkom Protocol, 29 November 1917.

133. Ibid.

134. Harold Williams, "Lenin Tells Peasants Government Is Theirs; Petrograd, Without Rulers, Goes Aimlessly On," *New York Times*, 22 November 1917.

135. McMeekin, *History's Greatest Heist*, 12–13.

136. Williams, "Lenin Tells Peasants."

137. Ibid.

138. Ibid.

139. Ibid.

140. GARF/R130/1/2/3–36, Sovnarkom Protocol, 29 November 1917.

141. GARF/R130/1/2/7–8, Sovnarkom Protocol, 2 December 1917.

142. GARF/R130/1/2/11, Sovnarkom Protocol, 4 December 1917.

143. GARF/R130/1/2/53, Sovnarkom Protocol, 5 January 1918.

144. GARF/R130/1/2/17, Sovnarkom Protocol, 8 December 1917, and Efim Moiseevich Epshtein, *Rossiiskie Kommercheskie Banki: Rol' v Ekonomicheskom Razvitii Rossii i ikh Natsionalizatsiia*, trans. Mikhail Arkad'evich Elistratov (1925; Moscow: ROSSPEN, 2011), 99–100.

145. GARF/R130/1/2/53, Sovnarkom Protocol, 5 January 1918.

146. GARF/R130/2/1/1, Sovnarkom Protocol, 14 January 1918.

147. GARF/R130/2/673/1–4, Shenkman to Sovnarkom, 2 January 1918.

148. GARF/R130/2/5/7, "O vypuske obligatsii b. 'Zaima Svobody' v kachestve denezhnykh znakov," 14 February 1918.

149. US Congress, Senate Committee on the Judiciary, "Bolshevik Propaganda: Hearings Before a Subcommittee Pursuant to S. Res. 439 & 469, February 11 to March 10, 1919" (Washington, DC: Government Printing Office, 1919), 763.

150. Ibid.

151. Ibid., 763–64.

152. Ibid., 830.

153. Alex Lichtenstein, "In the Shade of the Lenin Oak: 'Colonel' Raymond Robins, Senator Claude Pepper, and the Cold War," *American Communist History* 3, no. 2 (2004): 188–91.

154. Judiciary, "Bolshevik Propaganda," 812.

155. Ibid., 813.

156. Ibid., 813.

157. Ibid.

158. John L. H. Keep, ed., *The Debate on Soviet Power: Minutes of the All-Russian Central Executive Committee of Soviets, Second Convocation, October 1917–January 1918* (Oxford: Oxford University Press, 1979), 138; VTsIK Protocol, 28 November 1917.

159. Ibid.

160. Pipes, *Russian Revolution*, 601.

161. Keep, *Debate on Soviet Power*, 138; VTsIK Protocol, 28 November 1917.

162. Keep, *Debate on Soviet Power*, 245–46, 250; VTsIK Protocol, 4 January 1918.

163. Keep, *Debate on Soviet Power*, 250; VTsIK Protocol, 28 November 1917.

164. Keep, *Debate on Soviet Power*, 406.

165. Ibid., 258; VTsIK Protocol, 16 January 1918. There is substantial disagreement and confusion on the timing of the Bolshevik repudiation. For more details, see the appendix.

166. Keep, *Debate on Soviet Power*, 258–59; VTsIK Protocol, 16 January 1918.

167. Pipes, *Russian Revolution*, 601.

168. Lenin, "How They Tied Themselves," 176–77.

169. Ibid., 177.

170. Ibid., 177.

171. Ibid., 177.

172. Ibid., 177.

173. Ibid., 177.

174. "United States—Advances to Allies—Financial Position," *Economist*, 5 January 1918.

175. Ibid.

176. Claude Béaud, "Investissements et Profits du Groupe Multinational Schneider," *Histoire, Économie et Société* 7, no. 1 (1988): 135, doi:10.3406/hes.1988.1507.

177. Ibid.

178. Ibid., 137.

179. SGA/BUP/14802, Saint-Sauveur to Paris, 2 January 1918.

180. Ibid.

181. SGA/BUP/14802, Saint-Sauveur to Paris, 31 December 1917.

182. Ibid.

183. SGA/BUP/14802, Saint-Sauveur to Paris, 5 January 1918.

184. SGA/BUP/14802, Saint-Sauveur to Paris, 13 January 1918.

185. Ibid.

186. CAEF/B/0067198/1, Clipping from *Frankfurter Zeitung*, 11 January 1918.

187. CAEF/B/0063626/2, "Payment of Interest on Russian Government Credit," 12 January 1918.

188. SGA/BUP/14802, Saint-Sauveur to Schneider in Paris, 14 January 1918.

189. Moulton and Pasvolsky, *Russian Debts and Russian Reconstruction*, 197.

190. "France—Russian Funds—Railway Legislation—Tobacco Shortage—The Bourse," *Economist*, 26 January 1918. The historical basis for this claim, of course, was dubious even at the time. In *Lending to the Borrower from Hell*, 173–210, for example, Drelichman and Voth show how lenders could be incentivized to extend credit to serial defaulters. Of course the difference in the Russian case was that the country had a much better track record of repayment than Philip II's Spain—until the 1918 default.

191. "France—Russian Funds."

192. SGA/BUP/14802, *La Revue de la Bourse & de la Banque* to Paribas, 22 January 1918.

193. "France—Russian Funds."

194. "France—The 1918 Budget—Russian Securities in France—Bread Crisis—Lighting Restrictions—Appointment of a Flax Committee—Science and Industry—The Bourse," *Economist*, 2 February 1918.

195. Arthur Raffalovich, "Russia's Economic Position," *Economist*, 19 January 1918.

196. "Russian Bills," *Economist*, 19 January 1918. In finance, treasury "notes" and "bills" are shorter-maturity debt instruments of a government, while "bonds" are instruments with longer maturities.

197. Ibid.

198. Ibid.

199. Ibid.

200. Ibid.

201. ML ARC 1214 Box 33, E. C. Grenfell to J. P. Morgan, Jr., 17 January 1918.

202. Ibid.

203. Ibid.

204. "Russian Bills," *Economist*, 19 January 1918.

205. ML ARC 1214 Box 33, E. C. Grenfell to J. P. Morgan, Jr., 17 January 1918.

206. "France—Russian Funds."

207. Ibid.

208. "France and the Russian Debt," *Economist*, 26 January 1918.

209. Ibid.

210. Raffalovich, "Russia's Economic Position." Although technically true, such statements downplayed the history of inflationary policies in which the Tsarist government frequently engaged in the eighteenth and nineteenth centuries.

211. "The Russian Kaleidoscope," *Economist*, 22 December 1917.

212. Citi RG 12, "History of the Operations of the Petrograd and Moscow Branches of the National City Bank of New York," 1922, 9.

213. Ibid.

214. Ibid.

215. Citi RG 12, Remarks or Exceptions of Mr. H. A. Koelsch, Jr., Accountant or Pro-Manager of the Moscow Branch of the National City Bank of New York, 15–16.

216. Ibid., 16.

217. Ibid., 19.

218. Citi RG 12, "History of the Operations of the Petrograd and Moscow Branches of the National City Bank of New York," 24.

219. Ibid., 26.

220. Ibid., 29.

221. ML ARC 1214 Box 18, Thomas Lamont to J. P. Morgan & Co., 4 March 1919.

222. SGA/BUP/144761, Verstraete and Lombardo in Saint Petersburg to Villars in Paris, 16 January 1908.

223. McMeekin, *History's Greatest Heist*, 168–69.

224. Oosterlinck and Landon-Lane, "Hope Springs Eternal."

225. Keynes, *Tract on Monetary Reform*, 52.

226. Quoted in G. Ia. Sokol'nikov, Elena Varneck, Lincoln Hutchinson, and Carl C. Plehn, *Soviet Policy in Public Finance, 1917–1928* (Stanford: Stanford University Press, 1931), 111.

227. Nikolai Ivanovich Bukharin and Evgenii Alekseevich Preobrazhensky, *The ABC of Communism: A Popular Explanation of the Program of the Communist Party of Russia* (London: Communist Party of Great Britain, 1922), 333.

228. Sokol'nikov, *Finansovaia Politika Revoliutsii*, 1:73.

229. M. V. Glenny, "The Anglo-Soviet Trade Agreement, March 1921," *Journal of Contemporary History* 5, no. 2 (1970): 66.

230. Vladimir Il'ich Lenin, *The Unknown Lenin: From the Secret Archive*, Annals of Communism, edited by Richard Pipes, David Brandenberger, and Catherine A. Fitzpatrick (New Haven: Yale University Press, 1996), 196–97; Chicherin to Lenin, 30 January 1922.

231. Moulton and Pasvolsky, *Russian Debts and Russian Reconstruction*, 210–11; Russian reply to the Genoa Memorandum.

232. Ibid., 211, 215.

233. ML ARC 1214 Box 15 Morgan Grenfell to J. P. Morgan & Co., 2 July 1918.

234. Moulton and Pasvolsky, *Russian Debts and Russian Reconstruction*, 218–19.

235. ML ARC 1216 (062) Box 118, J. P. Morgan, Jr. to Jacob Schiff, 3 February 1915.

236. Verstraete, *Mes Cahiers Russes*, 236.

Notes to Conclusion

1. NA/FO800/72/0/2, Grey to Spring Rice, 22 December 1905 "British Foreign Office," n.d. FO800/72/0/2.

2. Abraham Ascher, *The Revolution of 1905: A Short History* (Stanford: Stanford University Press, 2004), xii.

3. Brinton, *Anatomy of Revolution*, 69.

4. Michelson, Apostol, and Bernatzky, *Russian Public Finance during the War*, 387–88.

5. The default has of course led to many studies by French authors, but largely from the standpoint of journalistic or sociological perspectives. See, for example, Joël Freymond, *Les Emprunts Russes: Histoire de La plus Grande Spoliation Du Siècle* (Paris: Journal des finances, 1995); Jean-Claude Ducros, *L'Emprunt de l'Etat* (Paris: Editions L'Harmattan, 2008); Jean-Claude Ducros, *Sociologie Financière*, Thémis. Droit (Paris: Presses Universitaires de France, 1982).

6. See, for example, "La Voix Des Emprunts Russes," http://empruntsrusses.winnerbb .com/.

7. Holmes and Green, *Midland*, 140.

8. Ibid.

9. Ibid., 164.

10. BAR 200021, Memorandum of Conversation with Sir Arthur Davidson at Marlborough House, 30 March 1919.

11. BAR 200021, Memorandum of Conversation with Count Etienne Tyszkiewcz, 22 December 1921.

12. Ziegler, *Sixth Great Power*, 357.

13. Craig Forman, "Soviets, British Reach Accord on Czarist Debt," *Wall Street Journal*, 16 July 1986. The Bolsheviks had tried to claim the funds in 1918 through their British solicitors, but the British Treasury froze the sum of approximately £3.5 million. See Ziegler, *Sixth Great Power*, 331–32.

14. Citi RG 12, "Remarks or Exceptions of Mr. H. A. Koelsch, Jr., Accountant or Pro-Manager of the Moscow Branch of the National City Bank of New York," 12 May 1922, 16.

15. Citi RG 12, "History of the Operations of the Petrograd and Moscow Branches of the National City Bank of New York," 1922, 9.

16. Ibid., 15.

17. Ibid., 26.

18. Ibid., 29.

19. Ibid.

20. William Rhodes, *Banker to the World: Leadership Lessons from the Front Lines of Global Finance* (New York: McGraw-Hill, 2011), 154.

21. Ibid., 155. The author is grateful to Allan Hirst for this anecdote.

22. Thomas F. Huertas, "The Rise of the Modern Business Enterprise: The Case of Citibank," *Business and Economic History* 14 (1985): 152.

23. Citi RG 12, "History of the Operations of the Petrograd and Moscow Branches of the National City Bank of New York," 1922, 33.

24. Ibid., 35.

25. Citi RG 12, "Expression of Opinion by George B. Link, Ex-Sub-Manager, and William W. Welsh, Ex-Accountant, of the Petrograd Branch of The National City Bank of New York," October 1921, 56.

26. Huertas, "Rise of the Modern Business Enterprise," 152.

27. "Mrs. H. F. Meserve Dies in Paris," *New York Times*, 29 April 1919.

28. "Miss Meserve to Wed Abroad," *New York Times*, 20 October 1919.

29. BOE G/17/3, Bark to Norman, 13 February 1924, "Bank of England," n.d.

30. "Sir Peter Bark, 68, Financier, Is Dead," *The New York Times*, 18 January 1937.

31. BOE G/17/3, Bark to Norman, 13 February 1924.

32. BOE G/17/3, Note to the Governor, 27 July 1935.

33. Verstraete, *Mes Cahiers Russes*, 241–42.

Notes to Appendix

1. ISDA, "2003 ISDA Credit Derivatives Definitions" (2003), 30, http://cbs.db.com/new/docs/2003_ISDA_Credit_Derivatives_Definitions.pdf.

2. ISDA, "EMEA Determinations Committee Decision" (9 March 2012), http://www.isda.org/dc/docs/EMEA_Determinations_Committee_Decision_09032012.pdf.

3. "It's Official: ISDA Triggers Greek Credit Event in Unanimous Decision," *Business Insider*, 9 March 2012, http://www.businessinsider.com/its-official-isda-triggers-greek-cds-2012-3; Daniel Bases, "ISDA Declares Greek Credit Event, CDS Payments Triggered," *Reuters*, 9 March 2012, http://www.reuters.com/article/2012/03/09/us-greece-cds-isda-trigger-idUSBRE82817B20120309.

4. Katie Linsell and Alastair Marsh, "Default Seen Averted in Swaps by Greek Failure to Pay IMF," *Bloomberg*, 30 June 2015, http://www.bloomberg.com/news/articles/2015-06-30/no-default-seen-in-credit-swaps-by-greece-s-failure-to-pay-imf. The IMF itself backtracked from statements suggesting a default, ultimately declaring that Greece was "in arrears."

5. Reinhart and Rogoff, *This Time Is Different*, 11.

6. Arturo C. Porzecanski, "From Rogue Creditors to Rogue Debtors: Implications of Argentina's Default," *Chicago Journal of International Law* 6 (2005): 317.

7. For more on LGD, see Til Schuermann, "What Do We Know about Loss Given Default?" (Wharton Financial Institutions Center Working Paper 04-01, 2004).

8. Reinhart and Rogoff, *This Time Is Different*, 10, 12.

9. *Bloomberg*, "Argentina to Repay IMF Debt Four Years after Default (Fourth Update)," http://www.bloomberg.com/apps/news?pid=newsarchive&sid=asY3HZQLSfEw; Sophie Arie and Andrew Cave, "Argentina Makes Biggest Debt Default in History," *Telegraph*, 24 December 2001, http://www.telegraph.co.uk/news/worldnews/southamerica/argentina/1366218/Argentina-makes-biggest-debt-default-in-history.html.

10. Porzecanski, "From Rogue Creditors to Rogue Debtors," 317.

11. J. F. Hornbeck, "Argentina's Defaulted Sovereign Debt: Dealing with the 'Holdouts'" (Congressional Research Service, 6 February 2013), 5, http://www.fas.org/sgp/crs/row/R41029.pdf.

12. Reinhart and Rogoff, *This Time Is Different*, 12.

13. ISDA, "ISDA Americas Credit Derivatives Determinations Committee: Argentine Republic Failure to Pay Credit Event" (New York, 1 August 2014), https://www.isda.org/2014/08/01/isda-americas-credit-derivatives-determinations-committee-argentine-republic-failure-to-pay-credit-event/.

14. Camila Russo and Katia Porzecanski, "Argentina Declared in Default by S&P as Talks Fail," *Bloomberg News*, 31 July 2014.

15. Michael Tomz and Mark L. J. Wright, "Empirical Research on Sovereign Debt and Default," *Annual Review of Economics* 5 (2013): 256, doi:10.1146/annurev-economics-061109-080443.

16. "Greece's Default: The Wait Is Over," *Economist*, 17 March 2012, http://www.economist.com/node/21550271.

17. Hellenic Republic of Greece, "Hellenic Republic Ministry of Finance Press Release" (9 March 2012), http://av.r.ftdata.co.uk/files/2012/03/9-MARCH-2012.pdf; European Commission, "Financial Assistance to Greece," http://ec.europa.eu/economy_finance/assistance_eu_ms/greek_loan_facility/.

18. Reinhart and Rogoff, *This Time Is Different*, 9.

19. Ibid.

20. Ibid., 9.

21. Hellenic Republic of Greece, "Hellenic Republic Ministry of Finance Press Release."

22. European Commission, "Financial Assistance to Greece."

23. Macdonald, *Free Nation*, 430.

24. Oosterlinck and Landon-Lane, "Hope Springs Eternal," 507.

25. Pipes, *Russian Revolution*, 578.

26. Moulton and Pasvolsky, *Russian Debts and Russian Reconstruction*, 197.

27. Francis in Petrograd to State Department, 8 February 1918, in US Department of State, *Papers Relating to the Foreign Relations of the United States: Russia, 1918*, vol. 3 (Washington, DC: Government Printing Office, 1932), 31.

28. "Text of the Soviet Decree on the Annulment of Foreign Debts," in Moulton and Pasvolsky, *Russian Debts and Russian Reconstruction*, 197.

29. Ibid., 197–98.

30. Ibid., 197.

31. Ibid.

32. Ibid.

33. Ibid., 197–98.

34. Noel Maurer and Aldo Musacchio, "The Barber of Buenos Aires: Argentina's Debt Renegotiation" (Harvard Business School case no. 9-706-034, 4 December 2006), 4.

35. Marcos Chamon, Alejo Costa, and Luca Ricci, "Is There a Novelty Premium on New Financial Instruments? The Argentine Experience with GDP-Indexed Warrants" (IMF Working Paper 08/109, 2008), 7.

36. In finance, a haircut refers to the reduction in the face value of a loan a creditor must suffer in a restructuring.

37. Michelson, Apostol, and Bernatzky, *Russian Public Finance during the War*, 242.

38. Ibid.

39. A bearer bond is a bond with physical coupons on the bond certificate. The holder, or "bearer" of the bond, presents individual coupons for payment at designated banks, which pay interest in exchange for the coupons. The physical coupon obviates the need to maintain a central registry of bondholders, which facilitated trading of the bonds in the secondary market in an era before computerized recordkeeping. Today, bearer bonds are less common, partly because of electronic recordkeeping, and partly because major governments keen to prevent tax fraud and money laundering actively discourage the use of this instrument that allows for cash-like anonymity.

40. Vladimir Il'ich Lenin, "Inevitable Catastrophe and Extravagant Promises (29–30 May 1917)," in *V. I. Lenin: Collected Works*, 24:424–30; Vladimir Il'ich Lenin, "The Capitalists Must Be Exposed (9 June 1917)," in *V. I. Lenin: Collected Works*, 24:424–30.

41. McMeekin, *History's Greatest Heist*, 17.

42. Lindert and Morton, "How Sovereign Debt Has Worked," 39–106; Miller, *Economic Development of Russia*.

43. Data provided by the authors via email on 23 December 2012.

44. Moulton and Pasvolsky, *Russian Debts and Russian Reconstruction*, vii.

45. Brookings Institution, "Brookings Institution History," http://www.brookings.edu /about/history.

46. Data provided directly by the authors on 23 December 2012.

47. Michelson, Apostol, and Bernatzky, *Russian Public Finance during the War*, 252.

48. Ibid.

49. Pavel Vasil'evich Volobuev, *Ekonomicheskaia Politika Vremennogo Pravitel'stva* (Moscow: USSR Academy of Sciences, 1962), 379.

50. I. F. Gindin, "O Velichenii i Kharaktere Gosudarstvennogo Dolga Rossii v Kontse 1917 Goda," *Istoriia SSSR* 1957, nos. 4–5 (1957): 167.

51. Ibid., 169. The decision to treat short-term debt as currency was declared in Clause 4 of the repudiation decree.

52. Email from Mark Wright, 5 December 2012.

53. Lawrence Officer and Samuel Williamson, "Better Measurements of Worth," *Challenge* 49, no. 4 (July 1, 2006): 104, doi:10.2753/CHA0577-5132490407. The authors also maintain the measuringworth.com website used in the comparative debt figures developed in this appendix.

54. McMeekin, *History's Greatest Heist*, xiii.

55. Barry J. Eichengreen, *Golden Fetters: The Gold Standard and the Great Depression, 1919–1939* (New York: Oxford University Press, 1996), 67.

56. Global Financial Data database (2012), http://globalfinancialdata.com.

57. McMeekin, *History's Greatest Heist*, xii.

58. Eichengreen, *Golden Fetters*, 49–50.

59. "A Market View—Germans Buying Russian Bonds," *Wall Street Journal*, 9 February 1918.

BIBLIOGRAPHY

Archives

Archives Diplomatiques du Ministère des Affaires Étrangères, Paris
Bank of England, London
Baring Archive, London
BNP Paribas Archive, Paris
Centre des Archives Économiques et Financières, Savigny-le-Temple
Citi Center for Heritage, New York
Crédit Lyonnais-Crédit Agricole Archive, Paris
HSBC Group Archives, London
Morgan Library, New York
National Archives, London
Rothschild Archive, London
Russian State Historical Archive, Saint Petersburg
Société Générale Archive, Paris
State Archive of the Russian Federation, Moscow

Financial Databases

Bloomberg
Global Financial Data

Periodicals

Daily Telegraph
Economist
Financial Times
Investors' Monthly Manual
New York Times
New York Tribune
No. 8
Times (London)
Wall Street Journal
Washington Post

Primary Sources

Barron, Clarence W., Arthur Pound, and Samuel Taylor Moore. *They Told Barron: Conversations and Revelations of an American Pepys in Wall Street.* New York: Harper & Brothers, 1930.

Browder, Robert Paul, and Aleksandr Fyodorovich Kerensky, eds. *The Russian Provisional Government, 1917: Documents.* Stanford: Stanford University Press, 1961.

Bukharin, Nikolai Ivanovich, and Evgenii Alekseevich Preobrazhensky. *The ABC of Communism: A Popular Explanation of the Program of the Communist Party of Russia.* London: Communist Party of Great Britain, 1922.

Cyon, Élie de. "M. Witte et les Finances Russes d'Après des Documents Officiels et Inédits." Paris: Chamerot et Renouard, 1895.

———. *M. Witte et ses Projects de Faillite: Devant le Conseil de l'Empire.* Translated by Victor Derély. Paris: Haar & Steinert, A. Eichler, 1897.

———. "Où la Dictature de M. Witte Conduit la Russie." Paris: Haar et Steinert, Eichler Successeur, 1897.

Epshtein, Efim Moiseevich. *Rossiiskie Kommercheskie Banki: Rol' v Ekonomicheskom Razvitii Rossii i ikh Natsionalizatsiia.* Translated by Mikhail Arkad'evich Elistratov. 1925. Moscow: ROSSPEN, 2011.

First National City Bank of New York. "Annual Report." 4 March 1919.

Fisher, Irving. "How the Public Should Pay for the War." *Annals of the American Academy of Political and Social Science* 78 (1918): 112–17.

Gorkii, Maxim. *Prekrasnaia Frantsiia.* Stuttgart: J.H.W. Dietz Nachfolger, 1906.

Keep, John L. H., ed. *The Debate on Soviet Power: Minutes of the All-Russian Central Executive Committee of Soviets, Second Convocation, October 1917–January 1918.* Oxford: Oxford University Press, 1979.

Keynes, John Maynard. *A Tract on Monetary Reform.* London: Macmillan, 1924.

Kokovtsov, Vladimir Nikolaevich. *Out of My Past: The Memoirs of Count Kokovtsov, Russian Minister of Finance, 1904–1914, Chairman of the Council of Ministers, 1911–1914.* Translated by Harold H. Fisher and Laura Matveev. Stanford: Stanford University Press, 1935.

Lenin, Vladimir Il'ich. *V. I. Lenin: Collected Works.* 45 vols. Moscow: Progress, 1960–77.

———. *The Unknown Lenin: From the Secret Archive.* Annals of Communism. Edited by Richard Pipes. New Haven: Yale University Press, 1996.

Michelson, Aleksandr Mikhailovich, P. N. Apostol, and M. V. Bernatzky. *Russian Public Finance during the War.* New Haven: Yale University Press, 1928.

Moulton, Harold Glenn, and Leo Pasvolsky. *Russian Debts and Russian Reconstruction: A Study of the Relation of Russia's Foreign Debts to Her Economic Recovery.* New York: McGraw-Hill, 1924.

Nabokov, Vladimir. *Speak, Memory: An Autobiography Revisited.* New York: Vintage, 1989.

Proust, Marcel. *Remembrance of Things Past, Vol. 2: Within a Budding Grove.* Translated by C. K. Scott Moncrieff. New York: Albert & Charles Boni, 1930.

Sidorov, A. L. *Finansovoe Polozhenie Rossii v Gody Pervoi Mirovoi Voiny.* Moscow: Nauka, 1960.

———, ed. "Finansovoe Polozhenie Tsarskogo Samoderzhaviia v Period Russko-Iaponskoi Voiny i Pervoi Russkoi Revoliutsii." *Istoricheskii Arkhiv* 1955, no. 2 (January–February): 121–49.

Sokol'nikov, G. Ia. *Finansovaia Politika Revoliutsii*. 2 vols. 1928. Moscow: Obshchestvo Kuptsov i Promyshlennikov Rossii, 2006.

Sokol'nikov, G. Ia., Elena Varneck, Lincoln Hutchinson, and Carl C. Plehn. *Soviet Policy in Public Finance, 1917–1928*. Stanford: Stanford University Press, 1931.

Trotsky, Leon. *My Life*. New York: Charles Scribner's Sons, 1930.

Union Pacific Railroad Company. "Annual Report." 1915.

US Congress, Senate Committee on the Judiciary. "Bolshevik Propaganda: Hearings Before a Subcommittee Pursuant to S. Res. 439 & 469, February 11 to March 10, 1919." Washington, DC: Government Printing Office, 1919.

US Department of State. *Papers Relating to the Foreign Relations of the United States: Russia, 1918*. Vol. 3. Washington, DC: Government Printing Office, 1932.

Verstraete, Maurice. *Mes Cahiers Russes: l'Ancien Régime, le Gouvernement Provisoire, le Pouvoir Des Soviets*. Paris: G. Crès, 1920.

Witte, Sergei. *S. Iu. Vitte: Sobranie Sochinenii i Dokumental'nykh Materialov*. 4 vols. Moscow: Nauka, 2003.

———. *The Memoirs of Count Witte*. Translated and edited by Sidney Harcave. New York: Routledge, 2015.

———. *The Memoirs of Count Witte*. Translated and edited by Abraham Yarmolinsky. Garden City, NY: Doubleday, 1921.

———. *Vospominaniia: Tsarstvovanie Nikolaia II*. 2 vols. Berlin: Slovo, 1922.

Secondary Sources

Anan'ich, B. V. *Bankirskie Doma v Rossii, 1860–1914 gg.: Ocherki Istorii Chastnogo Predprinimatel'stva*. 2nd ed. Moscow: ROSSPEN, 2006.

Anan'ich, B. V., and Valerii I. Bovykin. "Foreign Banks and Foreign Investment in Russia." In Cameron, Bovykin, and Anan'ich, *International Banking*.

Anan'ich, B. V., and R. Sh. Ganelin. *Sergei Iul'evich Vitte I Ego Vremia*. Saint Petersburg: Russian Academy of Sciences, 1999.

Ascher, Abraham. *P.A. Stolypin: The Search for Stability in Late Imperial Russia*. Stanford: Stanford University Press, 2001.

———. *The Revolution of 1905: Authority Restored*. Stanford: Stanford University Press, 1992.

———. *The Revolution of 1905: Russia in Disarray*. Stanford: Stanford University Press, 1988.

———. *The Revolution of 1905: A Short History*. Stanford: Stanford University Press, 2004.

Balmuth, Daniel. "Novoe Vremia's War Against the Jews." *East European Jewish Affairs* 35, no. 1 (2005): 33–54. doi:10.1080/13501670500191645.

Béaud, Claude. "Investissements et Profits du Groupe Multinational Schneider." *Histoire, Économie et Société* 7, no. 1 (1988): 127–38. doi:10.3406/hes.1988.1507.

Berger, Suzanne. "Puzzles from the First Globalization." In *Politics in the New Hard Times*, edited by Miles Kahler and David Lake. Ithaca, NY: Cornell University Press, 2013. http://dspace.mit.edu/handle/1721.1/71702.

Bignon, Vincent, and Marc Flandreau. "The Economics of Badmouthing: Libel Law and the Underworld of the Financial Press in France Before World War I." *Journal of Economic History* 71, no. 3 (2011): 616–53. doi:10.1017/S0022050711001860.

Bloomberg. "Argentina to Repay IMF Debt Four Years after Default (Fourth Update)."
http://www.bloomberg.com/apps/news?pid=newsarchive&sid=asY3HZQLSfEw.

Bordo, Michael D., and Hugh Rockoff. "The Gold Standard as a 'Good Housekeeping Seal of
Approval.'" *Journal of Economic History* 56, no. 2 (June 1996): 389–428. doi:10.2307/2123971.

Bovykin, Valerii Ivanovich. *Finansovyi Kapital v Rossii Nakanune Pervoi Mirovoi Voiny.* Moscow:
ROSSPEN, 2001.

Brinton, Crane. *The Anatomy of Revolution.* 2nd ed. New York: Vintage, 1965.

Brumfield, William Craft, Boris V. Anan'ich, and Yuri A. Petrov, eds. *Commerce in Russian Urban
Culture, 1861–1914.* Washington, DC: Baltimore: Johns Hopkins University Press, 2002.

Bruner, Robert F., and Sean D. Carr. *The Panic of 1907: Lessons Learned from the Market's Perfect
Storm.* Hoboken, NJ: John Wiley, 2007.

Budnitskii, Oleg V. *Den'gi Russkoi Emigratsii: Kolchakovskoe Zoloto, 1918–1957.* Moscow: Novoe
Literaturnoe Obozrenie, 2008.

Cameron, Rondo E., Valerii I. Bovykin, and Boris V. Anan'ich, eds. *International Banking, 1870–
1914.* New York: Oxford University Press, 1991.

Carr, Edward Hallett. *The Bolshevik Revolution 1917–1923.* 3 vols. New York: Macmillan, 1952.

Carter, William C. *Marcel Proust: A Life.* New Haven: Yale University Press, 2000.

Cassis, Youssef. *Capitals of Capital: A History of International Financial Centres, 1780–2005.* Translated by Jacqueline Collier. Cambridge: Cambridge University Press, 2006.

Chamon, Marcos, Alejo Costa, and Luca Ricci. "Is There a Novelty Premium on New Financial
Instruments? The Argentine Experience with GDP-Indexed Warrants." IMF Working Paper
08/109, 2008.

Clark, Gregory. "The Price History of English Agriculture, 1209–1914." *Research in Economic
History* 22 (2004): 41–123.

Cleveland, Harold van B., Rachel Strauber, Thomas F. Huertas, and Alfred D. Chandler. *Citibank,
1812–1970.* Harvard Studies in Business History 37. Cambridge, MA: Harvard University
Press, 1985.

Crisp, Olga. "Russian Financial Policy and the Gold Standard at the End of the Nineteenth
Century." *Economic History Review,* n.s., 6, no. 2 (January 1953): 156–72. doi:10.2307/2590949.

———. "The Russian Liberals and the 1906 Anglo-French Loan to Russia." *Slavonic and East
European Review* 39, no. 93 (June 1961): 497–511.

———. *Studies in the Russian Economy before 1914.* London: Macmillan, 1976.

Dempster, G. M. "The Fiscal Background of the Russian Revolution." *European Review of Economic History* 10, no. 1 (2006): 35–50.

Drelichman, Mauricio, and Hans-Joachim Voth. *Lending to the Borrower from Hell: Debt, Taxes,
and Default in the Age of Philip II.* Princeton: Princeton University Press, 2014.

Dronin, N. M., and E. G. Bellinger. *Climate Dependence and Food Problems in Russia, 1900–1990:
The Interaction of Climate and Agricultural Policy and Their Effect on Food Problems.* Budapest:
Central European University Press, 2005.

Ducros, Jean-Claude. *L'Emprunt de l'Etat.* Paris: Editions L'Harmattan, 2008.

———. *Sociologie Financière.* Thémis. Droit. Paris: Presses Universitaires de France, 1982.

Eichengreen, Barry J. *Golden Fetters: The Gold Standard and the Great Depression, 1919–1939.* New
York: Oxford University Press, 1996.

European Commission. "Financial Assistance to Greece." http://ec.europa.eu/economy
_finance/assistance_eu_ms/greek_loan_facility/.

Ferguson, Niall. *The Cash Nexus: Money and Power in the Modern World, 1700–2000.* New York: Basic Books, 2001.

———. *The House of Rothschild: The World's Banker, 1849–1999.* Vol. 2. New York: Penguin, 1998.

———. *The Pity of War.* New York: Basic Books, 1999.

———. "Political Risk and the International Bond Market between the 1848 Revolution and the Outbreak of the First World War." *Economic History Review* 59, no. 1 (1 February 2006): 70–112. doi:10.2307/3806003.

Ferguson, Niall, and Moritz Schularick. "The Empire Effect: The Determinants of Country Risk in the First Age of Globalization, 1880–1913." *Journal of Economic History* 66, no. 2 (June 2006): 283–312.

———. "The 'Thin Film of Gold': Monetary Rules and Policy Credibility." *European Review of Economic History* 16 (2012): 384–407. doi:10.1093/ereh/hes006.

Figes, Orlando. *A People's Tragedy: The Russian Revolution, 1891–1924.* New York: Penguin, 1998.

Fisher, Irving. "How the Public Should Pay for the War." *Annals of the American Academy of Political and Social Science* 78 (1918): 112–17.

Fitzpatrick, Sheila. *The Russian Revolution.* 2nd ed. Oxford: Oxford University Press, 2001.

Flandreau, Marc, and Juan H. Flores. "The Peaceful Conspiracy: Bond Markets and International Relations During the Pax Britannica." *International Organization* 66, no. 2 (2012): 211–41.

Flandreau, Marc, Juan H. Flores, Norbert Gaillard, and Sebastián Nieto-Parra. "The End of Gatekeeping: Underwriters and the Quality of Sovereign Bond Markets, 1815–2007." *NBER International Seminar on Macroeconomics* 6, no. 1 (2009): 53–92.

Flandreau, Marc, and Frédéric Zumer. *The Making of Global Finance, 1880–1913.* Paris: Organisation for Economic Co-operation and Development, 2004.

Freymond, Joël. *Les Emprunts Russes: Histoire de la Plus Grande Spoliation Du Siècle.* Paris: Journal des finances, 1995.

Frieden, Jeffry A. *Banking on the World: The Politics of American International Finance.* New York: Harper & Row, 1987.

Galai, Shmuel. "The Impact of the Vyborg Manifesto on the Fortunes of the Kadet Party." *Revolutionary Russia* 20, no. 2 (2007): 197–224. doi:10.1080/09546540701633486.

Garvy, George. "The Financial Manifesto of the St. Petersburg Soviet, 1905." *International Review of Social History* 20, no. 1 (1975): 16–32. doi:10.1017/S0020859000004818.

Gatrell, Peter. *Government, Industry, and Rearmament in Russia, 1900–1914: The Last Argument of Tsarism.* Cambridge: Cambridge University Press, 1994.

———. *Russia's First World War: A Social and Economic History.* Harlow, England: Pearson/Longman, 2005.

———. *The Tsarist Economy 1850–1917.* London: Batsford, 1986.

———. *A Whole Empire Walking: Refugees in Russia during World War I.* Bloomington: Indiana University Press, 2005.

Gatrell, Peter, and Mark Harrison. "The Russian and Soviet Economies in Two World Wars: A Comparative View." *Economic History Review* 46, no. 3 (August 1993): 425–52. doi:10.2307/2598362.

Gerschenkron, Alexander. "The Rate of Industrial Growth in Russia since 1885." *Journal of Economic History* 7 (January 1947): 144–74. doi:10.2307/2113273.

Gindin, I. F. "O Velichenii i Kharaktere Gosudarstvennogo Dolga Rossii v Kontse 1917 Goda." *Istoriia SSSR* 1957, nos. 4–5 (1957): 166–72.

Girault, René. *Emprunts Russes et Investissements Français En Russie, 1887–1914*. 1973. Paris: Comité pour l'Histoire Economique et Financière de la France, 1999.

Glenny, M. V. "The Anglo-Soviet Trade Agreement, March 1921." *Journal of Contemporary History* 5, no. 2 (1970): 63–82.

Goldman, Marshall I. *The Enigma of Soviet Petroleum: Half-Full or Half-Empty?* Boston: Allen & Unwin, 1980.

Green, Edwin, John Lampe, and Franjo Štiblar, eds. *Crisis and Renewal in Twentieth Century Banking: Exploring the History and Archives of Banking at Times of Political and Social Stress*. Aldershot, England: Ashgate, 2004.

Gregory, Paul R. "The Russian Balance of Payments, the Gold Standard, and Monetary Policy: A Historical Example of Foreign Capital Movements." *Journal of Economic History* 39, no. 2 (June 1979): 379–400. doi:10.2307/2118944.

———. *Russian National Income, 1885–1913*. Cambridge: Cambridge University Press, 1982.

Haimson, Leopold. "'The Problem of Political and Social Stability in Urban Russia on the Eve of War and Revolution' Revisited." *Slavic Review* 59, no. 4 (December 2000): 848–75. doi:10.2307/2697422.

———. "The Problem of Social Stability in Urban Russia, 1905–1917 (Part One)." *Slavic Review* 23, no. 4 (December 1964): 619–42. doi:10.2307/2492201.

———. "The Problem of Social Stability in Urban Russia, 1905–1917 (Part Two)." *Slavic Review* 24, no. 1 (March 1965): 1–22. doi:10.2307/2492986.

———. "Reply." *Slavic Review* 24, no. 1 (March 1965): 47–56. doi:10.2307/2492989.

Harcave, Sidney. *Count Sergei Witte and the Twilight of Imperial Russia: A Biography*. Armonk, NY: M.E. Sharpe, 2004.

Hellenic Republic of Greece. "Hellenic Republic Ministry of Finance Press Release," 9 March 2012. http://av.r.ftdata.co.uk/files/2012/03/9-MARCH-2012.pdf.

Holmes, A. R., and Edwin Green. *Midland: 150 Years of Banking Business*. London: B.T. Batsford, 1986.

Hornbeck, J. F. "Argentina's Defaulted Sovereign Debt: Dealing with the 'Holdouts.'" Congressional Research Service, 6 February 2013. http://www.fas.org/sgp/crs/row/R41029.pdf.

Huertas, Thomas F. "The Rise of the Modern Business Enterprise: The Case of Citibank." *Business and Economic History* 14 (1985): 143–57.

Jayachandran, Seema, and Michael Kremer. "Odious Debt." *American Economic Review* 96, no. 1 (March 2006): 82–92. doi:10.2307/30034355.

Kahan, Arcadius. *Russian Economic History: The Nineteenth Century*. Edited by Roger Weiss. Chicago: University of Chicago Press, 1989.

Kennan, George F. "The Curious Monsieur Cyon." *American Scholar* 55, no. 4 (September 1986): 449–75.

Khromov, P. A. *Ekonomicheskoe Razvitie Rossii v XIX–XX Vekakh, 1800–1917*. Moscow: Gosudarstvennoe Izdatel'stvo Politicheskoi Literatury, 1950.

Koenker, Diane, and William G. Rosenberg. *Strikes and Revolution in Russia, 1917*. Princeton: Princeton University Press, 1989.

La Fontaine, Jean de. *Once Again, La Fontaine: Sixty More Fables*. Translated by Norman Shapiro. Hanover, NH: Wesleyan University Press, 2000.

"La Voix Des Emprunts Russes." http://empruntsrusses.winnerbb.com/.

Lebedev, S. K. "Biudzhet i Gosudarstvennyi Dolg Rossii pri S.Iu. Vitte." In *Sobranie Sochinenii i Dokumental'nykh Materialov S. Iu. Vitte*, vol. 2, bk. 2. Moscow: Nauka, 2002.

———. "Russian Banks during the First World War and the Revolution." In Green, Lampe, and Štiblar, *Crisis and Renewal in Twentieth Century Banking*, 16–33.

Lebedev, V. V. *Russko-Amerikanskie Ekonomicheskie Otnosheniia: 1900–1917 gg.* Moscow: Mezhdunarodnye Otnosheniia, 1964.

Lichtenstein, Alex. "In the Shade of the Lenin Oak: 'Colonel' Raymond Robins, Senator Claude Pepper, and the Cold War." *American Communist History* 3, no. 2 (2004): 185–214.

Lieven, Dominic. *The End of Tsarist Russia: The March to World War I and Revolution*. New York: Viking, 2015.

Lindert, Peter H., and Peter J. Morton. "How Sovereign Debt Has Worked." In *Developing Country Debt and Economic Performance, Volume 1: The International Financial System*, edited by Jeffrey D. Sachs, 39–106. Chicago: University of Chicago Press, 1989.

Long, James W. "Franco-Russian Relations during the Russo-Japanese War." *Slavonic and East European Review* 52, no. 127 (April 1974): 213–33. doi:10.2307/4206868.

———. "French Attempts at Constitutional Reform in Russia." *Jahrbücher Für Geschichte Osteuropas* 23, no. 4 (January 1975): 496–503. doi:10.2307/41045104.

———. "Organized Protest Against the 1906 Russian Loan." *Cahiers Du Monde Russe et Soviétique* 13, no. 1 (January 1972): 24–39.

———. "Russian Manipulation of the French Press, 1904–1906." *Slavic Review* 31, no. 2 (June 1972): 343–54. doi:10.2307/2494338.

Lucas, Robert E. "Why Doesn't Capital Flow from Rich to Poor Countries?" *American Economic Review* 80, no. 2 (May 1990): 92–96. doi:10.2307/2006549.

Macdonald, James. *A Free Nation Deep in Debt: The Financial Roots of Democracy*. Princeton: Princeton University Press, 2006.

Markevich, Andrei, and Mark Harrison. "Great War, Civil War, and Recovery: Russia's National Income, 1913 to 1928." *Journal of Economic History* 71, no. 3 (2011): 672–703. https://doi.org/10.1017/S0022050711001884.

Mau, Vladimir A., and Irina Starodubrovskaya. *The Challenge of Revolution: Contemporary Russia in Historical Perspective*. New York: Oxford University Press, 2001.

Maurer, Noel, and Aldo Musacchio. "The Barber of Buenos Aires: Argentina's Debt Renegotiation." Harvard Business School case no. 9-706-034, 4 December 2006.

Mauro, Paolo, Nathan Sussman, and Yishay Yafeh. *Emerging Markets and Financial Globalization: Sovereign Bond Spreads in 1870–1913 and Today*. Oxford: Oxford University Press, 2006.

McMeekin, Sean. *History's Greatest Heist: The Looting of Russia by the Bolsheviks*. New Haven: Yale University Press, 2009.

———. *The Red Millionaire: A Political Biography of Willy Münzenberg, Moscow's Secret Propaganda Tsar in the West, 1917–1940*. New Haven: Yale University Press, 2004.

Mendel, Arthur P. "Peasant and Worker on the Eve of the First World War." *Slavic Review* 24, no. 1 (March 1965): 23–33. doi:10.2307/2492987.

Miller, Margaret Stevenson. *The Economic Development of Russia, 1905–1914: With Special Reference to Trade, Industry, and Finance*. London: P. S. King & Son, 1926. 2nd ed., 1967.

North, Douglass C., and Barry R. Weingast. "Constitutions and Commitment: The Evolution of Institutions Governing Public Choice in Seventeenth-Century England." *Journal of Economic History* 49, no. 4 (December 1989): 803–32. doi:10.2307/2122739.

Obstfeld, Maurice, and Alan M. Taylor. "Sovereign Risk, Credibility and the Gold Standard: 1870–1913 versus 1925–31." *Economic Journal* 113, no. 487 (April 2003): 241–75.

Officer, Lawrence, and Samuel Williamson. "Better Measurements of Worth." *Challenge* 49, no. 4 (July 2006): 86–110. doi:10.2753/CHA0577-5132490407.

O'Neill, Jim. "Building Better Global Economic BRICs." Goldman Sachs Global Economic Papers, 30 November 2001. http://www.goldmansachs.com/our-thinking/archive/archive-pdfs/build-better-brics.pdf.

Oosterlinck, Kim, and John S. Landon-Lane. "Hope Springs Eternal—French Bondholders and the Soviet Repudiation (1915–1919)." *Review of Finance* 10, no. 4 (2006): 507–35.

Oppenheim, Samuel A. "Between Right and Left: G. Ia. Sokolnikov and the Development of the Soviet State, 1921–1929." *Slavic Review* 48, no. 4 (December 1989): 592–613. doi:10.2307/2499785.

Pipes, Richard. *The Russian Revolution*. New York: Knopf, 1990.

Porzecanski, Arturo C. "From Rogue Creditors to Rogue Debtors: Implications of Argentina's Default." *Chicago Journal of International Law* 6 (2005): 311–32.

Potier, Catherine. "Witnesses to Revolution: The Archives of Foreign Banks in Russia." In Green, Lampe, and Štiblar, *Crisis and Renewal in Twentieth Century Banking*, 34–52.

Pravilova, Ekaterina A. *Finansy Imperii: Den'gi i Vlast' v Politike Rossii na Natsional'nykh Okrainakh, 1801–1917*. Moscow: Novoe Izdatel'stvo, 2006.

Quested, R. K. I. *The Russo-Chinese Bank: A Multinational Financial Base of Tsarism in China*. Vol. 2. Birmingham Slavonic Monographs no. 2. Birmingham: Department of Russian Language and Literature, University of Birmingham, 1977.

Reinhart, Carmen M., and Kenneth S. Rogoff. *This Time Is Different: Eight Centuries of Financial Folly*. Reprint ed. Princeton: Princeton University Press, 2009.

Rhodes, William. *Banker to the World: Leadership Lessons from the Front Lines of Global Finance*. New York: McGraw-Hill, 2011.

Riha, Thomas. "'Riech': A Portrait of a Russian Newspaper." *Slavic Review* 22, no. 4 (December 1963): 663–82. doi:10.2307/2492564.

Roberts, Priscilla. "Frank A. Vanderlip and the National City Bank during the First World War." *Essays in Economic & Business History* 20 (2002). http://www.ebhsoc.org/journal/index.php/journal/article/view/120.

Robertson, Charles, Yvonne Mhango, and Michael Moran. *The Fastest Billion: The Story Behind Africa's Economic Revolution*. London: Renaissance Capital, 2012.

Roosa, Ruth Amende. "Banking and Financial Relations between Russia and the United States." In Cameron, Bovykin, and Anan'ich, *International Banking*.

Schuermann, Til. "What Do We Know about Loss Given Default?" Wharton Financial Institutions Center Working Paper 04-01, 2004.

Schularick, Moritz. "A Tale of Two 'Globalizations': Capital Flows from Rich to Poor in Two Eras of Global Finance." *International Journal of Finance and Economics* 11 (2006): 339–54. doi:100.1002/ijfe.302.

Service, Robert. *Lenin: A Biography*. Cambridge, MA: Harvard University Press, 2000.

Siegel, Jennifer. *Endgame: Britain, Russia, and the Final Struggle for Central Asia*. New York: I.B. Tauris, 2002.

———. *For Peace and Money: French and British Finance in the Service of Tsars and Commissars*. Oxford: Oxford University Press, 2014.

Skocpol, Theda. *States and Social Revolutions: A Comparative Analysis of France, Russia, and China*. Cambridge: Cambridge University Press, 1979.

Sorokin, D. E. "Vvodnoe Slovo: S. Iu. Vitte i Finansy Rossii." In *S. Iu. Vitte: Sobranie Sochinenii i Dokumental'nykh Materialov*, vol. 2, bk. 1, 5–15. Moscow: Nauka, 2003.

Soros, George. *The Alchemy of Finance*. Hoboken, NJ: John Wiley, 2003.

Stepanov, V. L. "Laying the Groundwork for Sergei Witte's Monetary Reform: The Policy of Finance Minister I.A. Vyshnegradskii (1887–1892)." *Russian Studies in History* 47, no. 3 (December 2008): 38–70. doi:10.2753/RSH1061-1983470302.

Stone, Norman. *Eastern Front 1914–1917*. 2nd ed. New York: Penguin, 2004.

Strachan, Hew. *Financing the First World War*. Oxford: Oxford University Press, 2004.

Suny, Ronald Grigor. "Revision and Retreat in the Historiography of 1917: Social History and Its Critics." *Russian Review* 53, no. 2 (April 1994): 165–82. doi:10.2307/130821.

Tadié, Jean-Yves. *Marcel Proust*. New York: Viking, 2000.

Taleb, Nassim Nicholas. *Antifragile*. New York: Random House, 2012.

Tomz, Michael. *Reputation and International Cooperation: Sovereign Debt across Three Centuries*. Princeton: Princeton University Press, 2007.

Tomz, Michael, and Mark L. J. Wright. "Empirical Research on Sovereign Debt and Default." *Annual Review of Economics* 5 (2013): 247–72. doi:10.1146/annurev-economics-061109-080443.

Ukhov, Andrey. "Financial Innovation and Russian Government Debt Before 1918." Yale ICF Working Paper 03-20, May 2003.

Volobuev, Pavel Vasil'evich. *Ekonomicheskaia Politika Vremennogo Pravitel'stva*. Moscow: USSR Academy of Sciences, 1962.

Von Laue, Theodore H. "The Chances for Liberal Constitutionalism." *Slavic Review* 24, no. 1 (March 1965): 34–46. doi:10.2307/2492988.

———. *Sergei Witte and the Industrialization of Russia*. New York: Columbia University Press, 1963.

Wcislo, Francis William. "Sergei Witte and His Times: A Historiographical Note." *Kritika: Explorations in Russian and Eurasian History* 5, no. 4 (2004): 749–58. doi:10.1353/kri.2004.0064.

———. *Tales of Imperial Russia: The Life and Times of Sergei Witte, 1849–1915*. New York: Oxford University Press, 2011.

Yergin, Daniel. *The Prize: The Epic Quest for Oil, Money, & Power*. New York: Free Press, 1993.

Ziegler, Philip. *The Sixth Great Power: Barings 1762–1929*. London: Collins, 1988.

INDEX

Abaza, A. A., 25

agriculture: borrowing boom and strains in, 120–21; perceptions of a revival in, 90–95

Alexander III (Tsar of Russia), 19, 37

Altchevskii, A. K., 100

American financial sector: Anglo-American deal, 1899 attempt to revive, 42–51; Russo-American ties in the Witte period, question of, 40–42. *See also* First National City Bank of New York; J. P. Morgan & Co.; Morgan, J. P.; Morgan, J. P. "Jack," Jr.

American International Corporation (AIC), 150–51

Anan'ich, B. V.: on bureaucratic and managerial skills of Witte, 35–36; retail shareholders of Moscow International, estimate of, 102; Russo-American financial relations, 41; Witte's 1898–1899 attempt to penetrate New York and London markets, 52–53

Angell, Norman, 98

Anglo-Russian Convention of 1907, 96, 127

Antonovich, A. Ia., 35–36

Apostol, Paul N.: Bolshevik responsibility for difficulties in obtaining loans, 166–67; bookkeeping discontinued after the Bolshevik Revolution, 176; expansion of the monetary base, domestic bond sales and, 180; investment of private capital in Treasury bills, overstatement of success of, 184; kinds of debt issued by the central government, shift in, 117–18; savings banks opened during the war, number

of, 181; size of the default, estimates of, 224–25, 227–28; wartime expenses and financing, 178–79

Argentina: as Barings territory, 16; borrowing by, 10; default by, 186, 217, 219–20, 222–23, 231; gold standard, as less credible adherent to, 11; yields on debt of, 198

Ascher, Abraham, 70, 75, 90, 208, 250n9

Baker, G. F., 78

Bank of Siberia, 104

banks and bankers: capital flows, role in facilitating, 15; competition between, 145–46; competitive dynamics within, the Russia market and, 106–10; French and Russian bankers, 1907 meetings between, 89; joint-stock banks, international finance and, 104; Lenin's view of, 2–5. *See also* names of individual banks and bankers

Banque de Commerce de l'Azoff Don, 134

Banque de Commerce de Sibérie, 143

Banque de Commerce Privée of St. Petersburg, 44

Banque de l'Union Parisienne (BUP): Banque du Nord as joint venture including, 85; cooperation on defense work of Schneider firm and, 196; Lombardo's recommendation to advance funds against wheat, 91; repudiation decree, preparation of confirmed, 197; Union Bank, investment in, 103, 122

Banque de Paris et des Pays-Bas (Paribas): cartel arrangement in Russia, discussion

Banque de Paris et des Pays-Bas (*continued*) of, 99; French reaction to the default and, 198; the 1906 loan, 65; the Russo-Chinese Bank, investment in, 104. *See also* Noetzlin, Edouard

Banque du Nord: building housing the, 85; creation of, 100; the Poliakov banks and, 102; popular resentment in Russia, incident illustrating, 115; Russo-Chinese Bank, merger with, 103–4, 158; Verstraete on the board of, 157

Baring, Cecil, 214

Baring, Magoun & Co., 42–44, 46–47

Baring, Thomas, 47–48

Baring Brothers & Co.: as active lender to the Russian government in the nineteenth century, 242n162; Anglo-American deal, 1899 attempt to revive, 42–53; Argentina as the territory of, 16; geopolitical motivations to invest in wartime Russia, 150–51; investor perceptions, shaping of, 15; the 1906 loan, 62, 65, 82; release of frozen Imperial Russian Government funds, 214; the revolution, Smith's report on, 156; Russian émigrés' attempts to borrow from, 214; Russian government's loyalty to, 105; third-party brokers, use of, 44; Witte and Russian affairs, dealing with, 42. *See also* Revelstoke, 2nd Baron, John Baring

Bark, P. L.: hard times after leaving Russia, 215–16; loan from National City in 1914, 129; Meserve, interview with, 146; original loan request from, 257n2; Russian industry hungry for capital, report of, 89; uncertainty over future policies of, 123; wartime revenue, urgency of increasing, 177

Benckendorff, Count Alexander, 151

Bernatzky, M. V., 173, 225, 267n111

Bert, Paul, 23

Bethenod, Émile, 109

Betzold, W., 44, 46

Bignon, Vincent, 16, 38

Bismarck, Otto von, 35

Bloch, Ivan Stanislavovich, 98

Block, J., 144

Bogolepov, Dmitri Petrovich, 190

Bolsheviks, the: default and the repudiation of debts, 186–94 (*see also* revolutionary default, the); the financial fight after default, 204–6; international finance, conception of, 2–3; Verstraete's view of, 158–60. *See also* Lenin, Vladimir

Bonar Law, Andrew, 201

bonds: bearer, 273n39; callable, 248n144; current yield and spreads on, 238n69; face value and discounted value of, 238n66; maturities and embedded options in, 239n70; parameters of deals in, 43–44; treasury notes and bills distinguished from, 269n196

Bordo, Michael D., 11–12, 33

borrowing cost for a country, 28–30

Boutry, M., 197

Bovykin, Valerii I., 41, 52–53

Brinton, Crane, 5–7, 208

British financial sector: Anglo-American deal, 1899 attempt to revive, 42–53; competition in the Russian market, French insecurity and, 108–10; the default, reaction to, 199, 201–2; diplomatic relations with Russia and, 96–97; in the interrevolutionary investment boom, 210; Koch-Morgan episode, 39–42; London as the center of global finance, 39; securities traded on the London Stock Exchange, increase in, 39. *See also* Baring Brothers & Co.; Bunker, John Frederick; London City and Midland Bank; Revelstoke, 2nd Baron, John Baring

Bronshtein, Lev. *See* Trotsky, Leon

Bruner, Robert F., 81

Budnitskii, Oleg, 4–5

Bukharin, Nikolai, 205

Bunge, Nikolai: Antonovich, Witte's appointment of, 36; monetary policy under, 35; policies of, 21; replacement as finance minister, 19; Witte's grudging recognition of, 37

Bunker, John Frederick: escape from Russia and post-Russia career of, 214; Midland office in Saint Petersburg, in charge of, 134; National City, dubious view of, 147–48; perspective of reports from, 135, 141; reports from Russia, 138–39, 149–50; the revolution, optimism regarding, 155–57; wartime income tax, impact on personal income of, 171

BUP. *See* Banque de l'Union Parisienne

Burdett, Sir Henry, 104–5

Caillaux, Joseph, 100

capital flows: competition as a driver of foreign investment, 106–10; conversion loan of 1909, 95–96; financial globalization and Russia, 8–10; foreign investment during Witte's tenure as finance minister, 27–34 (*see also* Witte, Sergei); foreign investors in Russia, explaining the behavior of, 212–13; geopolitics, influence of, 96–98; during the interrevolutionary rally, 86–87; investment boom in wartime Russia (*see* wartime Russia); macroeconomic and political fundamentals, literature on, 12–16; monetary architecture and the gold standard, literature on, 11–12; 5 percent Russian State Loan of 1906 (*see* 5 percent Russian State Loan of 1906); portfolio investment and foreign direct investment, distinction between, 238n65; during Witte's tenure as finance minister, 27–34

Caprivi, Georg Leo Graf von, 52

Carr, E. H., 187, 247n127

Carr, Sean D., 81

Cassel, Sir Ernest, 133

Chicherin, Georgy, 206

China, People's Republic of, 234n32

Citibank/Citigroup, 43, 136, 214. *See also* First National City Bank of New York

Clark, Gregory, 94

Cochery, Georges, 108–9

Comptoir d'Escompte, 104

Congressional Budget Office, U.S., 219

conversion loan of 1909, 95–96

Crane, G. F., 46–47

Crédit Lyonnais: distribution of loans by, 44; global bond market, as prominent financial institution in, 13; Kokovtsov's relations with, 107–8; popular resentment in Russia, incident illustrating, 115; research department of, 102; Russo-Chinese bank, contribution to seed money for, 104; Saint Petersburg municipal bond, compromise regarding, 111–12

Crisp, Olga, 28–29, 59–61

Cunliffe, Walter, 1st Baron Cunliffe, 201

Curzon, George Nathaniel, 1st Marquess Curzon of Kedleston, 204

Cyon, Élie de, 23, 25–26, 237n32

Davison, Henry, 156–57

Davydov, L., 105–7, 109

Davydov, Victor, 91–92, 108

defaults: Argentinean, 219–20, 222–23, 231; Bolshevik in Russia (*see* revolutionary default, the); defining default, 217–19; Greek, 217–18, 220–22, 272n4; in Latin America, 86; measuring the size of, 219; ranking, 217, 219–21; ranking, contextualizing the Bolshevik repudiation and, 221–31

Dillon, Joseph, 79

discount rate, 239n89, 248n140

Doumergue, Gaston, 122

Dreher, Harold J., 138, 203, 214

Drelichman, Mauricio, 249n183, 269n190

Duma, the: closure of the Second, 88; conflict with the court, 113; dissolution of First, 87; Kokovtsov and, 113–15; Third, expectations regarding, 91

Dzerszhinskii, Feliks, 160

economics of the revolutionary default: conditions of the real economy, 171–76;

economics of the revolutionary default (*continued*)

    domestic bonds for war financing, 180–82; economic collapse, responsibility for, 169–70; financing the war, 176–86; foreign debt for war financing, 178–80; printing money for war financing, 184–86; the Provisional Government as catalyst, 186; taxation for war financing, 177–78; Treasury bills for war financing, 182–84

Economist, the: British reaction to the default, 201–202; cautious optimism about Russia in, 88, 92–93; complacency of the U.S. government regarding the possibility of default, 196; French reaction to the default, 197–98; Greek default, size of, 220; initial positive coverage of the revolution, 155–56; pre-Bolshevik wartime Russia, optimistic view of, 134; Russian budget in 1915, bleak picture of, 142; temperance campaign in Russia, support for, 152–53

Egyptian Revolution of 2010–2011, 5

Eichengreen, Barry J., 229

Elliott Management, 219

Ferguson, Niall, 12–13, 22, 51, 52

Figes, Orlando, 3–5, 59, 114, 131–32

financial globalization: Russia and, 8–10. *See also* capital flows

Financial Manifesto, 66–71, 73, 75, 83, 164, 166, 247n127

First Moroccan Crisis, 75–76

First National City Bank of New York: Anglo-American deal, 1899 attempt to revive, 46–47; Barings-led effort in 1899, involvement with, 42–44; Bunker's criticisms of, 147–48; competitive pressures and risk management/appetite, 144–47; documents left behind in Russia, story of, 214–15; geopolitical motivations to invest in wartime Russia, 150–51; investment in wartime Russia, difficulty of explaining, 212; moral hazard in the approach to pre-Bolshevik wartime Russia, 143–44; Moscow branch, opening of, 203; operations after the Revolution, 214; pre-Bolshevik wartime Russia, optimistic view of/plans for, 133–39, 141; risk appetite regarding pre-Bolshevik wartime Russia, 141–42; Roosa's inattentiveness to the role of, 41; Russia, office opened in, 129; Saint Petersburg International Commercial Bank, negotiations with, 42; Vladivostock branch, opening of, 204, 214; Witte and Russian affairs, dealing with, 42. *See also* Citibank/Citigroup; Meserve, H. Fessenden

Fischel, Arthur: Anglo-American deal, 1899 attempt to revive, 48; heart attack during negotiations for the 1906 loan, 63; negotiations for the 1906 loan, 62; Revelstoke and Kokovtsov, meeting with, 97

Fisher, Irving, 185–86

Fitzpatrick, Sheila, 20, 59

Five percent Russian State Loan of 1906: domestic opposition to, the Financial Manifesto and, 66–75; historical narrative/literature on, 58–61; internationalization of Russian finance as a goal of, 78–80; international opposition to, 75–82; market crisis and, 80–82; negotiations begin, 62–66; Noetzlin's secret trip to negotiate, 55–56, 58; policymaking assessment of, 82–84, 209; political/historical background to, 56–58; signing of the contract, issuing the bonds, 80–81; as "the loan that saved Russia," 56, 59, 82–83, 209, 244n26

Flandreau, Marc, 13, 15–16, 38, 99, 235n51

Flores, Juan, 15, 99

Francis, David R., 151

Franco-Russian alliance, 97–98

French financial sector: competition for the Russian market, response to, 108–10; the default, impact of, 213; the default, reaction to, 197–98, 202; investment in

Russia, increase in, 27–28; Kokovtsov's pre-1906 activities in, 58; Russian activities in compared to London and New York, 49–50; Witte's overcommitment to, 52, 54. *See also* Banque de l'Union Parisienne; Banque de Paris et des Pays Bas; Banque du Nord; Crédit Lyonnais; Noetzlin, Edouard; Paris Bourse

Gaillard, Norbert, 15, 99
Galai, Shmuel, 74
Gambetta, Léon, 23
Ganelin, R. Sh., 35–36
Garvy, George, 70
gatekeepers and gatekeeper finance: conception of, 15–16, 99; foreign investors in Russia, explaining capital flows and, 212–13; geopolitics and, 96–98; individuals as, the aftermath of default and, 213–16; the Russian Revolution and, 16–17
Gatrell, Peter: annual fluctuations in grain production, problem of, 122; defense spending in the late Tsarist period, role of, 124–25; economic crisis and military losses in wartime Russia, 131–32; "free balance of the Treasury" quickly exhausted by war financing, 184–85; manufacturing output during wartime years, drop in, 171, 173; size of the default, estimates of, 225; syndicate system, comfort level of investors and, 101
General Electric (GE), 144–45
Genoa Memorandum, 206
geopolitics: capital flows and, 96–98; investment in wartime Russia and, 150–51
Germain, Henri, 49
German financial sector: the 1906 loan and, 76–77; Witte's activities in the Berlin financial market, 38–39. *See also* Mendelssohn & Co.
Gerschenkron, Alexander, 90
Gindin, I. F., 225–28
Girault, René: French foreign direct investment in Russia, estimates of, 28, 32,

99; on the 1906 loan, 60, 77; "loan that saved Russia," incorrect attribution of the phrase, 244n26; Russian securities traded in the Paris market, estimates of, 27; Witte's achievements deploying government funds and rationalizing the railroad, 21
globalization: Russia and financial, 9–10; the two ages of, 8–9
gold standard: Financial Manifesto, as target in, 67, 69; as foundational element of the Witte System, 34; inflation metric, use as a, 229; introduction in Russia, 23–25; investors and the adoption of, 33–34; monetary architecture and, 11–12; state gold reserves, depletion of and capital outflow, 71–72
Gorkii, Maxim, 95
Greece: default by, 186, 217–18, 220–22, 272n4; as Eurozone member, 230; yields on debt of, 198
Gregory, Paul, 28, 30–34, 57, 90
Greig, Samuil, 25
Grenfell, E. C., 201
Grenfell, Morgan, 133, 206
Grey, Sir Edward, 79, 208
Guaranty Trust, 145

Haimson, Leopold, 126–27
haircut (in finance), 273n36
Hardinge, Charles, 62
Harrison, Mark, 131–33, 171–72
Hilferding, Rudolf, 2
Hitchcock, E. A., 42
Hobson, J. A., 2
Holbrook, F., 151
Holden, Norman, 105, 107
Holden, Sir Edward, 105, 111, 134, 214
Hong Kong, 234n32
Hope & Co.: attempted Russian loan of 1899, involvement in, 44–45, 49–50, 53; bond issue of 1769, 34–35; Russian loans in tandem with Barings in the nineteenth century, 242n162

Imperialism, the Highest Stage of Capitalism (Lenin), 2–3, 5
international finance: Bolshevik conception of, 2–3; personal dimension of, 213–16; the Russian Revolution and, limitations of literature on, 3–5. *See also* capital flows
International Swaps and Derivatives Association (ISDA), 218–20
interrevolutionary rally, the, 85–87, 127–28, 209–10; competition as a driver of foreign investment, 106–10; the defense stimulus, 123–25; distressed investment opportunities, 101–6; economic drivers of, 87–90; economic drivers of: agriculture, 90–95; economic drivers of: bond market, 95–96; fragility underlying (*see* pre-First World War Russia, fragility of); gatekeepers and, 99; influence of geopolitics on capital flows and, 96–98; market coordination, protecting investors through, 99–101; municipal finance during, 110–12
ISDA. *See* International Swaps and Derivatives Association
Ivens, William M., 42

J. P. Morgan & Co.: Anglo-American deal, 1899 attempt to revive, 42–43, 46–49; the 1906 loan, limited involvement in, 80; repudiation, balancing investors and other claimants in the face of, 206; Witte and Russian affairs, dealing with, 42. *See also* Morgan, J. P.; Morgan, J. P. "Jack," Jr.
J. S. Morgan, 46–47
Jewish financial houses: absence of American from the Russian market, 260n122; opposition to the 1906 loan, 79–82; Tsarist anti-Semitism, concerns regarding, 51, 61, 82. *See also* Rothschilds, the

Kankrin, G. F., 35
Katkov, Mikhail, 23, 35
Kennan, George F., 23
Kerensky, Alexander, 156, 158, 191

Keynes, John Maynard, 143, 148, 174, 205
Kharkov Land Bank, 100
Koch, Alexander, 39–40, 42
Koelsch, H. A., Jr., 203–4, 214
Kokovtsov, Vladimir: agricultural reform, opposition to, 91; budget proposal of 1909, 93; conversion loan of 1909, 95–96; de Verneuil, negotiations with, 98; French loans in 1904, securing, 58; interrevolutionary foreign investment, actions regarding, 106–8, 110; introduction to the Michelson, Bernatzky, and Apostol volume, author of, 225; Lion, meeting with, 89; the 1906 loan, 59, 61, 63, 65, 80–81, 83; loan for railroad construction in 1914, attempt to arrange, 124; "loan that saved Russia" phrase attributed to, 244n26; memoirs penned in exile, 215; "merciless taxation," call for, 177; mistaking Russia for Turkey, warning against, 204; the Poliakov banks, resolution of, 103; the political opposition, dismissal of, 113–16, 166–67; pre-Bolshevik wartime Russia, optimistic view of, 139–40; Revelstoke and Fischel, meeting with, 97; second-tier bonds, Revelstoke's concerns regarding, 111
Kolchak, Alexander, 4
Kollontai, Alexandra, 165
Krasin, Leonid, 204, 215
Kuhn, Loeb, 260n122
Kulomzin, A. N., 35

Lafargue, Paul, 192
Lamont, Thomas, 156–57, 204
Land Bank of the Nobility, 117, 181, 190, 223
Landon-Lane, John, 221
Larin, Iurii, 187
Law, John, 26
Lebedev, S. K., 52
Lenin, Vladimir: banks and bankers, view of, 2–5, 16; on default, 191–93; on the Financial Manifesto, 70; financial policy, critique of the government's, 115, 164–68,

194; Genoa diplomatic settlement, firm
line regarding, 206; growing more conservative, perceived as, 204; *Imperialism,
the Highest Stage of Capitalism,* 2–3, 5;
Liberty Loan, opposition to, 195–96;
money famine, struggle with, 205; at the
National Hotel, 203; 1905 Revolution
as "a dress rehearsal" for 1917, 208; Paris
Commune, measuring the revolution
against the standard of, 5; practical incentive for default, appeal to the peasantry
as, 168–69; on the 1905 Revolution, 57;
the Smirnov-Osinski report, nationalizations and, 189; striking workers as a
headache for, 190; Verstraete's commercial ideas pitched to, 160; on Witte, 20
Liberty Loan, 166–67, 180, 183, 195
Lindert, Peter H., 163
Lion, L., 88–89
List, Friedrich, 21, 37
Lombardo, Théophile, 85, 91–92, 94, 102
London City and Midland Bank: boom in
Russia business in the 1920s, 214; Bunker's
reports from Russia, 134–35, 138–39,
147–50; buying assets at distressed prices,
interest in, 112; competition between
banks in the Russian market, 108; the
Higgs group's appeal to, 149; initial forays
into the Russian market, 102–6; in the
interrevolutionary investment boom, 210;
investment in wartime Russia, difficulty of
explaining, 212; municipal deals, interest
in, 111; pre-Bolshevik wartime Russia,
optimistic perspective on, 134
Long, James William, 60–61, 75, 247n127
Louis, Georges, 111
Lozovsky, Solomon, 192, 206
Lucas, Robert, 8
Lucas paradox, 8
Luden, John, 48

Macdonald, James, 221, 263n5
Maklakov, Vasilii, 60
Maria (Dowager Empress of Russia), 214

Markevich, Andrei, 131–33, 171–72
Martens, F. F., 76
Mau, Vladimir, 6–7
Mauro, Paulo, 14, 155
McMeekin, Sean: on the Bolshevik's
responsibility for economic crisis,
169–70; counterfactual analysis of, 176;
default, narrative explaining the, 186–87;
economic conditions, the Provisional
Government's responsibility for, 186;
finance as a consideration in the work
of, 4–5; inflation metrics applicable to
the Russian debt, 229; overstatement of
Russian borrowing during the war by,
180; Tsarist Russia's gold reserves spent
by the Bolsheviks, 132
McRoberts, Samuel, 136–37
Mendel, Arthur, 126
Mendelssohn & Co.: Anglo-American deal,
1899 attempt to revive, 46, 48–49, 52; the
loan of 1906, 62; rollover of existing debt
in 1905, 74; Witte and Russian affairs,
dealing with, 42. *See also* Fischel, Arthur
Mering, M. F., 36
Mering, Sonia, 36
Meserve, H. Fessenden: Bunker and, differences in perspective and recommendations of, 147–50; departure from Russia,
214; doubling of salary of, 147; Moscow
branch of National City, opening of, 203;
as National City's agent in Russia, 129;
optimistic reports on wartime Russia
from, 134–39; optimistic stance on
Russia, maintenance of, 157; post-Russia
career of, 215; Revelstoke, meeting with,
141; risk appetite, moral hazard, and
bank competition evident in the reports
of, 141–46; social factors influencing his
thinking on Russia, 152–54
Michelson, Aleksandr Mikhailovich, 225
Midland Bank. *See* London City and Midland Bank
Miliukov, Paul, 75, 113–14
Miller, D. A., 105, 108, 110–11

Miller, Margaret Stevenson, 224

Moiseyev, Boris, 192

monetary architecture, the gold standard and, 11–12

monetary policy: of the Bolsheviks, 204–5, 258n19; gold standard, from a silver standard to a, 23–25 (*see also* gold standard); printing money for war financing, 184–86; trilemma of, 266n108; the wartime economic crisis and, 132; under Witte, 34–35

Montebello, Gustave Lannes de, 20

Morgan, J. P.: Anglo-American deal, 1899 attempt to revive, 46–47, 49–51; Koch-Morgan episode, 39–42; the loan of 1906, 62–65, 77–78, 83; Saint Petersburg International Commercial Bank, negotiations with, 42. *See also* J. P. Morgan & Co.

Morgan, J. P. "Jack," Jr.: Anglo-American loan, 1899 attempt to revive, 48–50; the British reaction to the default, 201; invitation to join the board of the American-Russian Chamber of Commerce, decline of, 138; the loan of 1906, 62–66, 77–78; political and financial considerations, separation of, 207; Russia, perspective on, 135; Spring Rice, conversations with, 248n135

Morton, Peter J., 163

Moscow International Bank, 101–2

Moscow Union Bank. *See* Union Bank

Moulton, Harold G., 224–26, 228

multinational corporations, 144–45

municipal finance, 110–12

Muranyi, H., 44–45, 50–51

Murray, Samuel B., 105–7

N. M. Rothschild, 43

Nabokov, Vladmir Dmitrievitch, 75

National City. *See* First National City Bank of New York

nationalizations: of banks, 191; Bolshevik implementation of, 189

New York Life Insurance Company, 40–41

New York markets. *See* American financial sector

Nicholas II (Tsar of Russia): anti-Semitism under, 260n122; Cyon's view of, 26; Hague Peace Conference initiative, 98; incompetence of, 21; murder of, 214; public opinion, attitude towards, 59

Nieto-Parra, Sebastián, 15, 99

Nikolaevich, Grand Duke Nicholas, 88

Noetzlin, Edouard: conversion loan of 1909, 95–96; crisis management of the 1906 loan, 80–81; interrevolutionary rally, actions during, 106–7; negotiations for the 1906 loan, 62–63; Raffalovich, constant contact with, 49; second-tier bonds, Revelstoke's concerns regarding, 111; secret trip to negotiate the 1906 loan, 55–56, 58, 76–77

Norman, Montagu, 215

North, Douglass, 12–13, 154

Nosar, Georgii Stepanovich, 66

Obstfeld, Maurice, 11–12

October Manifesto, 65

O'Neill, Jim, 9

Oosterlinck, Kim, 221

operational leverage/operating leverage, 118–20, 260n98

Orel Commercial Bank, 101–2

Osinski, Nicholas, 187–90

Paléologue, Maurice, 122–23, 135

Panafieu, H. A. de, 109–10

Panic of 2007, 56, 81, 84, 86, 91, 97, 122

Paribas. *See* Banque de Paris et des Pays-Bas

Paris Bourse: dual market operated by, 89; Raffalovich's activities in, 37–38

Pasvolsky, Leo, 171, 224–26, 228

Peasants' Land Bank, 117, 168, 181, 190, 223

Perkins, G. W., 62–65, 78

Philip II (king of Spain), 249n183

Pichon, Stephen, 95, 98, 108–9

Pipes, Richard: default, date of, 221–22; default, narrative explaining the, 187,

192–93; finance as secondary in the narrative of, 3–5; on the 1906 loan, 59; on Witte, 20

Pobedonostsev, Konstantin, 35

Poliakov, Lazar Solomonovich, 101–3

Poliakov, Solomon Lazarevich, 101

Poliakov affair, the, 101–6

Pravilova, Ekaterina, 4

pre-First World War Russia, fragility of, 112, 125; agriculture, 120–21; defense spending, impact of, 123–25, 128; financial system: debt profile, 116–18; financial system: operational leverage, 118–22; industrial slump, 121–22; the Russian Revolution and, 125–27; signs of trouble, 122–23; social and political fissures, financial policy and, 113–16

Preobrazhensky, Yevgeni, 205

Prodamet (Society for the Sale of the Output of Russian Metallurgical Factories), 100–101, 188

Prodparovoz, 101

Produgol, 101, 188

Prodvagon, 101

Proust, Marcel, 1, 213

Putilov, Aleksei Ivanovich, 107, 196–97

Raffalovich, Arthur: Apostol as assistant to, 225; connections to the French financial community, 49–50; English Rothschilds, meeting with, 79; promoting the Russian market even after the default, 198; Russian position in Paris, as advocate of, 36; as tutor to Witte, 35; underutilizing of, 51; Witte's use of, 37–38

Rapallo Accords, 206

redemption payments, 246n99

Reed, John, 203

Reinhart, Carmen, 160, 217–21, 224–25, 228

Reutern, Mikhail von, 21, 24–25, 35

Revelstoke, 2nd Baron, John Baring: Anglo-American deal, 1899 attempt to revive, 44–50, 53; British financial support for pre-Bolshevik wartime Russia, 143; crisis

management of the 1906 loan, 80–81; dairy entries from early 1917 trip to Russia, 135; end of the career of, 214; Holbrook, national interests and the meeting with, 151; interrevolutionary rally, actions during, 106–7; Kokovtsov and Fischel, meeting with, 97; Kokovtsov's claims about the Duma, warning about, 115; Mendelssohn partner's pessimism about the chances for a Russian deal, 242n172; negotiations for the 1906 loan, 63, 65; pre-Bolshevik wartime Russia, optimistic view of, 133–34, 139–41; second-tier bonds, concerns regarding, 111; wartime revenue, urgency of increasing, 177

revolution, the sociology of, 5–7

revolutionary default, the, 162–63, 207, 211; Bolshevik Revolution, intertwined with, 211–12; contextualizing, comparative default rankings and, 221–31; continuing the financial fight, 1918–1922, 204–6; the decision to default, 186–94; the economics of (see economics of the revolutionary default); ideological drivers of, 164–68; impact of, 1–2; investors' dismissal of the possibility of, 194–97; investors' reactions to, 197–204; Lenin's early support for, 165, 167–68; mistaken predictions regarding, 140; the politics of, 163–69; practical political reasons for, 168–69; the repudiation decree, issuance of, 197, 222; size and duration of, 160, 217, 220, 223, 228–31, 233n2

Rhodes, Bill, 214

Richelieu, 5th Duc de, Armand Emmanuel de Vignerot du Plessis, 49

Robins, Raymond, 191–92

Rockoff, Hugh, 11–12, 33

Rodzianko, Mikhail, 168

Rogoff, Kenneth, 160, 217–21, 224–25, 228

Roosa, Ruth Amende, 40–42

Rothschild, Lionel Walter, 2nd Baron of, 82

Rothschilds, the: Brazil as the domain of, 16; competition for municipal loan

Rothschilds, the (*continued*)
business, comments on, 111; investor
perceptions, shaping of, 15; the 1906
loan and, 79–82; Raffalovich and, 51;
third-party brokers, use of, 44; Tsarist
anti-Semitism as a factor for, 51; Witte's
appointment and, 22
Rothstein, Adolph, 39, 48–49, 51
Russian Empire: the first age of financial
globalization and, 8, 10, 53–54; foreign investment in, 1913–1914, 8; fragility of pre-
First World War (*see* pre-First World War
Russia, fragility of); interrevolutionary
economic rally in (*see* interrevolutionary
rally); the 5 percent Russian State Loan
of 1906 (*see* 5 percent Russian State Loan
of 1906); wartime (*see* wartime Russia);
during Witte's tenure as finance minister
(*see* Witte, Sergei)
Russian Federation, 9–10
Russian Revolution: dates of, Julian/
Gregorian calendar differences and,
233n6; extant literature on, 3–5, 7; financial fragility and the outbreak of war, role
of, 125–27; gatekeeper finance and, 16–17;
the revolutionary default (*see* revolutionary default, the)
Russo-Asiatic Bank, 85, 145, 157–58
Russo-Belgian Metallurgical Company, 189
Russo-Chinese Bank, 85, 103–4, 157
Russo-Japanese War, 57–58, 67
Rutkovskii, M. V., 36, 41–42, 50, 82

Saint Petersburg International Commercial
Bank, 41–42, 51
Saint-Sauveur, A., 196–97
Saunders & Co., 48–49
Schiff, Jacob, 82, 207
Schneider industrial firm, 196–97
Schröders, 41
Schularick, Moritz, 8, 12–13, 234n32
Seattle National Bank, 137
Service, Robert, 188–89
Shenkman, Iakov, 191

Shingarev, Andrei Ivanovich, 114, 207, 216
Shipov, I. P., 35, 56, 73, 190
short positions/"shorting," 240n112
Sidorov, A. L., 132
Siegel, Jennifer, 4–5, 262n195
Skocpol, Theda, 6
Smirnov, Vladimir, 187
Smith, Rowland, 156
Sobchak, Anatoly, 214
Société Générale: the Banque du Nord,
creation of, 85, 100; the Banque du Nord,
hesitance to increase investment in, 102;
bargaining power of, 108; cooperation on
defense work of Schneider firm and, 196;
popular resentment in Russia, incident
illustrating, 115; repudiation decree,
preparation of confirmed, 197
Société Russo-Belge, 197
Sokol'nikov, Grigorii, 132, 162, 205, 258n19
Soros, George, 252n68
South-Russian Industrial Bank, 101–2
Sovnarkom (Council of People's Commis-
sars), 189–93, 197, 222
Speyer, 46
Spring Rice, Cecil: Grey's communication
regarding the Revolution, 208; Jewish
opposition to the loan, perspective on,
82; Morgans, maintenance of active dia-
logue with, 248n135; the revolutionaries
in 1906, report on, 66, 75; Witte's desire
for a British loan, conversations with
Dillon regarding, 79
Stalin, Joseph, 5, 21, 26, 203
Standard and Poor's, 220
Starodubrovskaya, Irina, 6–7
Stepanov, V. L., 37
Stevens, R. R., 129
Stillman, James, 43, 46–48, 150, 215
Stolypin, Pyotr: agrarian reforms promoted
by, opposition to, 90–91; assassination
of, 86, 113; counterfactual implicit in
famous statement by, 126; Poliakov affair,
pressure to resolve, 103
Stone, Norman, 132, 169, 171, 186

Strachan, Hew, 179–80

Strong, Benjamin, 143

sunk cost perspective, 119–20

Sussman, Nathan, 14, 155

Suvorin, Aleksei, 74

Taleb, Nassim, 250n8

Tatishchev, S. S., 35–36, 45, 50, 105

Taylor, Alan, 11–12

temperance campaign, 152–53

Théry, Edmond, 198

Thompson, William Boyce, 130

Times of London: calm on the eve of the
Second Duma, report of, 88; complaints
about, 81–82; coverage of Russia after
the 1906 bonds were issued, 81; Financial
Manifesto, impact of, 73–74; Judeophobic newspaper read by the Tsar,
247n106

Tomz, Michael: Bolsheviks, debtor reputation model applied to, 163–64; debtor
reputation model, 13–14, 16; default
rankings by, 217, 219–20, 224–25, 228;
sovereign debt payments contingent on
two variables, 170

Treasury bills, 182–84, 269n196

Trotsky, Leon: annulment of debts, conversation with Robins regarding, 191; Financial Manifesto and the takeover of the
Saint Petersburg Soviet, 66, 70; radical
line of, 204; on the Russian Revolution, 5

Trutovsky, V. E., 192–93

Tsion, Ilya Fadeyevich, 23. See also Cyon,
Élie de

Ukhov, Andrey, 34

Union Bank, 103–6, 122

Vanderlip, Frank A.: American International Corporation, leadership of, 150–51;
letter to Meserve, 137; Meserve's letters
to, 135; ousted in boardroom coup, 215;
Russian default, denial of the possibility
of, 143

Verneuil, Maurice de, 89, 98, 106

Verstraete, Maurice, 157–60, 162, 197, 207

Vidal, Emmanuel, 197–98

Villars, R., 88, 102

Viola, Lynne, 3

Volga-Kama Bank, 89

Volobuev, Pavel Vasil'evich, 225–28

Von Laue, Theodore, 21, 126

Voth, Hans-Joachim, 249n183, 269n190

Vyborg Manifesto, 74–75, 84, 164, 166,
247n127

Vyshnegradskii, A. I., 41–42, 50

Vyshnegradskii, Ivan: Cyon's criticism of,
23, 25–26; grain exports maintained by,
32; industrial policy of, 37; monetary
policy under, 35; personal profits from
Russian government loans by, 237n34;
Raffalovich, appointment of, 36; reorientation of borrowing from Germany
to France, overseeing of, 35; resignation
of, 19; at the Southwestern Railroad,
98; Witte's break from the approach of,
20–21; Witte's grudging recognition of, 37

wartime Russia: the default (see revolutionary default, the); the economic
crisis, 130–33; exchange controls, lack of,
266n108, 267n111; the foreign financial
community's optimism about, 133–41;
the French perspective on, 157–60; geopolitics as motivation to invest, 150–51;
investing in the revolution, improving
Russia by, 152–54; investment boom in,
129–30, 160–61, 210–11; moral hazard in
decision making by the foreign financial
community, 142–44, 149; the revolution's
lack of impact on foreign investors,
154–57; risk appetite in decision making
by the foreign financial community,
141–42, 144–50

Weingast, Barry, 12–13, 154

Wilhelm II (kaiser of Germany), 75, 80

William Higgs & Co., 149, 151

Wishaw, James, 140

Witte, Matilda Ivanova, 22
Witte, Sergei: appointment as minister of finance, 19–20; appointments by, 35–36; capital markets, performance in, 37–39; continuity in policymaking under, 54; currency, limit on issuing, 173; death of, 215; domestic opposition to the 1906 loan, reaction to, 70–71, 73; early career of, 98, 124; evolution of the Witte System, 34–37; foreign cartels, changing position on, 99–101; ignoring of London and New York financial markets, 40, 42, 49–52, 54, 79, 82, 209; industrial policy of, 36–37; the 1906 loan, narrative on, 58–59, 61; the 1906 loan, negotiations for, 62–66, 76–80, 83; "loan that saved Russia" incorrectly attributed to, 244n26; monetary policy of, 34–35; negative views of, 22–27; Noetzlin, secret meeting with, 55–56, 58; Poliakov banks, concerns regarding, 102; positive views of, 20–22; the Russo-Chinese Bank, creation of, 103–4; tactical failure of, 50–52, 54, 82, 84, 110, 209
Wright, Mark, 217, 219–20, 224–25, 228

Yafeh, Yishay, 14, 155
Yergin, Daniel, 21

Zinoviev, Grigory, 192
Zumer, Frédéric, 13, 15–16, 235n51

A NOTE ON THE TYPE

This book has been composed in Arno, an Old-style serif typeface in the
classic Venetian tradition, designed by Robert Slimbach at Adobe.